INSIGHT GUIDES

US NATIONAL PARKS WEST

APA PUBLICATIONS
Part of the Langenscheidt Publishing Group

※ INSIGHT GUIDE

US NATIONAL PARKS WEST

Editorial

Project Editor
Paula Soper
Art Director
Steven Lawrence
Picture Manager
Tom Smyth
Series Manager
Rachel Fox

Distribution

UK & Ireland
GeoCenter International Ltd
Meridian House, Churchill Way West
Basingstoke, Hampshire RG21 6YR
sales@geocenter.co.uk

United States
Ingram Publisher Services
One Ingram Boulevard
PO Box 3006
La Vergne, TN 37086-1986
customerservice@
ingrampublisherservices.com

Australia
Universal Publishers
1 Waterloo Road
Macquarie Park, NSW 2113
sales@universalpublishers.com.au

New Zealand
Hema Maps New Zealand Ltd (HNZ)
Unit 2, 10 Cryers Road
East Tamaki, Auckland 2013
sales.hema@clear.net.nz

Worldwide
**Apa Publications GmbH & Co.
Verlag KG (Singapore branch)**
7030 Ang Mo Kio Ave 5
08-65 Northstar @ AMK
Singapore 569880
apasin@singnet.com.sg

Printing

CTPS-China

©2011 Apa Publications GmbH & Co.
Verlag KG (Singapore branch)
All Rights Reserved

First Edition 1995
Fourth Edition 2011

CONTACTING THE EDITORS

We would appreciate it if readers
would alert us to errors or out-
dated information by writing to:
**Insight Guides, PO Box 7910,
London SE1 1WE, England.
insight@apaguide.co.uk**
NO part of this book may be reproduced,
stored in a retrieval system or transmitted
in any form or means electronic, mech-
anical, photocopying, recording or otherwise, without prior written permission of
Apa Publications. Brief text quotations
with use of photographs are exempted
for book review purposes only. Information has been obtained from sources
believed to be reliable, but its accuracy
and completeness, and the opinions
based thereon, are not guaranteed.

www.insightguides.com

ABOUT THIS BOOK

The first Insight Guide pioneered the use of creative full-color photography in travel guides in 1970. Since then, we have expanded our range to cater for our readers' need, not only for reliable and practical information about their chosen destination but also for a real understanding of the culture and workings of that destination. Now, when the internet can supply us with inexhaustible (but not always reliable) facts, our books marry text and pictures to provide those much more elusive qualities: knowledge and discernment. To achieve this, they rely heavily on the authority of locally based writers and photographers.

How to use this book

"The USA's national parks," wrote John B. Oakes of the *New York Times*, "are as sacred to most Americans as the flag, motherhood, and apple pie." And nowhere is this more true than in the West, where the parks protect some of the world's most sublime landscapes and wildlife.

This book is carefully structured to convey an understanding of these parks and to guide readers through their wild diversity:

◆ The **Best Of** section at the front of the guide helps you to prioritize what you want to do.

◆ The **Features** section, with a yellow color bar, covers the history of the parks, their flora, fauna, and geology, and opportunities for sport and recreation.

◆ The **Places** section, with a blue bar, provides full details of all the parks in the West, plus many national monuments and other sites within the park system. The chief places of interest are coordinated by number with specially drawn maps.

LEFT: Joshua Tree National Park, California

flora and fauna and many other subjects in the first edition, which was produced by **John Gattuso** and **Martha Ellen Zenfell**.

Other contributors include **John Gattuso** (the Dakotas and history of the National Park System), **Jeremy Schmidt** (Grand Canyon, Yellowstone, and Grand Teton); **Todd Wilkinson** (the Pacific Northwest); **Stewart Aitchison** (geology, wildlife, and the Californian Desert); **Rose Houk** (Great Basin and prehistoric Indian sites); **George Wuerthner** (Big Bend); **Eugene Rose** (Sequoia and Kings Canyon); **John Levine** (Lassen and Redwood); **Steven Medley** (Yosemite); **Thomas Schmidt** (Glacier); **Rita Ariyoshi** (Hawaii); **Bill Sherwonit** (Alaska), and **George Hardeen** (outdoor recreations).

Sandra Scott contributed the photo features on the Hidden Grand Canyon, Rockies wildlife, desert plants, and Native American art.

Mick Meikleham edited the text, which was proofread by **Janet McCann** and indexed by **Isobel McLean**.

Map Legend

—··—	International Boundary
—— —	State Boundary
—·—	National Park/Reserve
— — —	Ferry Route
✈ ✈	Airport: International/Regional
❶	Tourist Information
⌂	Ranger Station
■	Building
Ⱥ	Campground
✷	Viewpoint
⊼	Picnic Area
★	Place of Interest

The main places of interest in the Places section are coordinated by number with a full-color map (eg ❶), and a symbol at the top of every right-hand page tells you where to find the map.

◆ The **Travel Tips** listings section, with an orange bar, has practical information on getting to the parks, opening times, weather, accommodations, and recommended activities. Information may be located quickly using the index printed on the back cover flap, which also serves as a handy bookmark.

The contributors

This comprehensively updated edition was managed by Insight Guide editor **Paula Soper**, building on earlier contributions by photojournalist **Jeffery Pike**. The guide was expertly overhauled by **Nicky Leach**, an award-winning, Santa Fe-based writer and editor specializing in US national parks.

Nicky enjoyed revisiting this guide, for which she wrote the chapters on the parks of Southern Utah and Southern Arizona, plus features on

Contents

LEFT: Park Boulevard,
Joshua Tree National Park,
California.

Travel Tips

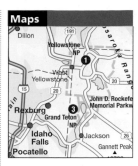

Maps

THE BEST OF US NATIONAL PARKS WEST: TOP SIGHTS

From the heat of spectacularly eroded desert river canyons and fiery volcanoes to the icy strongholds of glaciers, snowy peaks, and decorated caves, and a panoply of natural and cultural history, from saguaros and sequoias to pithouses and pueblos, here are some of the most awe-inspiring national parks in the West.

△ The Colorado River and relentless erosion carved the colorful buttes, mesas, and 2 billion-year-old rock formations in **Grand Canyon National Park**. *See Page 157*

▷ **Denali National Park** (above left) is in a class of its own and home to vast numbers of wildlife including Alaska's grizzly bear, Dall sheep, moose and caribou. *See Page 343*

◁ Walk among towering old-growth trees and lush ferns in one of the world's few temperate rain forests at **Olympic National Park**. *See Page 315*

▷ The fantastically decorated limestone caves at **Carlsbad Caverns National Park** are also a haven for 400,000 Brazilian free-tailed bats. *See Page 220*

▷ Famous for a sea of craggy peaks over 12,000ft (3,660 meters), **Rocky Mountain National Park** gives new meaning to the term "breathtaking." *See Page 299*

▽ The Ancestral Pueblo culture reaches its apotheosis in the 13th-century cliff dwellings of **Mesa Verde National Park** in Colorado's San Juan Mountains. *See Page 237*

△ Wade the famous Zion Narrows, and backpack across miles of silent high-country peaks and plateaus at **Zion National Park**, a nature sanctuary in the heart of southern Utah's pioneer Mormon Country. *See Page 149*

△ Watch lava flowing and new land being created at **Hawaii Volcanoes National Park** on the volcanically active Big Island of Hawaii. *See Page 125*

▽ **Yosemite National Park**, with its glaciated granite domes, lush river valley and Sierra Nevada high country, deserves its reputation as California's most beloved national park. *See Page 71*

△ Spewing geysers, sizzling hot springs, and other geothermal features are scattered amid the scenic Rocky Mountains in Wyoming's **Yellowstone National Park**. *See Page 255*

THE BEST OF US NATIONAL PARKS WEST: EDITOR'S CHOICE

Immense glaciers and soaring redwood forests, stunning mountain peaks and otherworldly rock formations... the western national parks have it all.

BEST SCENERY

● **Canyonlands National Park**
Breathtaking views of the Colorado River canyons characterize this mesmerizing wilderness park near Moab. *See page 185.*

● **Crater Lake National Park**
A spectacular seasonal rim drive and fascinating boat tour around America's deepest lake awaits visitors to

Oregon's only national park. *See page 335.*

● **Arches National Park**
An easy drive and trails lead to some of the 2,000 sandstone arches clustered in this family-friendly park. *See page 195.*

● **Grand Canyon National Park**
Explore rustic architecture at Grand Canyon's South or North rims. *See page 157.*

BEST WILDLIFE WATCHING

● **Katmai National Park**
In late summer, large numbers of the park's 2,000 resident brown bears visit Brooks Camp on the Katmai Peninsula to fish for salmon. *See page 349.*

● **Glacier Bay National Park and Preserve**
Whale watching is a popular summer activity in this land of glaciers and fjords, where humpbacks and grays bulk up on herring before heading south. *See page 350.*

● **Yellowstone National Park**
The chance to see thriving wolf and bison

populations in the wild is just one of the reasons to visit Yellowstone, an intact ecosystem. *See page 255.*

● **Channel Islands National Park**
These southern California islands offer sanctuary to six species of seals and sea lions, sea otters, whales, and marine birds. *See page 117.*

● **Zion National Park**
Water in the desert attracts large numbers of animals to this canyon refuge, including wild turkeys, canyon tree frogs, peregrine falcons, mule deer, and cougars. *See page 149.*

ABOVE: Crater Lake National Park.
LEFT: Glacier Bay National Park.

BEST SCENIC DRIVES

● **Glacier National Park**
Going-to-the-Sun Road traverses some of the most dramatic Rocky Mountain scenery in the West, even as the park's glaciers melt. *See page 275.*

● **Badlands National Park**
A starkly beautiful landscape of rolling grasslands and twisted canyons stretches across the windswept plains of the South Dakota, Lakota Sioux homeland. *See page 290.*

● **North Cascades National Park**
Linking the fertile Puget Sound with the dry Methow Valley east of the Cascades, State Route 20 is a favorite Northwest drive. *See page 321.*

● **Bryce Canyon National Park**
Thirteen spectacular overlooks offer views of Bryce's rainbow-colored hoodoos (spires) eroded into the Paunsaugunt Plateau on the 18-mile (29km) scenic drive. *See page 176.*

ABOVE: Mount Rushmore National Memorial.

BEST HISTORIC SITES

● **Chaco Culture National Historical Park**
Chaco's enigmatic great houses, built AD 900–1100, now lie in ruins surrounded by the Navajo reservation. *See page 239.*

● **Mesa Verde National Park**
Mesa Verde populations exploded in the 1200s, when newcomers built Cliff Palace and other villages in the cliffs. *See page 237.*

● **Canyon de Chelly National Monument**
Two lush canyons on the Navajo reservation protect 13th-century

Ancestral Pueblo cliff dwellings. *See page 239.*

● **Pipe Spring National Monument**
This fortified Mormon ranch on the Kaibab Paiute Indian Reservation in the Arizona Strip interprets early Mormon polygamy and Paiute culture. *See page 155.*

● **Mount Rushmore National Memorial**
Sculptor Gutzon Borglum's patriotic portraits blasted out of the Black Hills include busts of presidents Washington, Jefferson, Lincoln and Roosevelt. *See page 289.*

BEST FOR OUTDOOR ADVENTURE

● **Mount Rainier National Park**
Climbing routes and the 93-mile (150km) Wonderland Trail and other trails explore varied Mount Rainier habitats, from alpine to temperate rainforest. *See page 329.*

● **Grand Staircase-Escalante National Monument**
Sandwiched between Capitol Reef and Lake Powell, this undeveloped park invites explorations of Indian rock art and scenic slot canyons. *See page 176.*

● **Big Bend National Park**
Raft Rio Grande canyons, hike the Chisos Mountains, and explore old mining roads in this spectacular Texas park on the US-Mexico border. *See page 227.*

● **Dinosaur National Monument**
Famous for its dinosaur quarry and magnificent scenic canyons, Dinosaur is popular with river runners floating the conjoining Green and Yampa rivers. *See page 304.*

ABOVE: a bull elk. **RIGHT:** rafting Rio Grande canyon.

THE SPIRIT OF THE PARKS

The modern citizen has a profound need for wilderness. The US National Park System embodies that need and strives to preserve the wild places

The national parks of the United States are a promise that Americans have made to themselves. As a people, they have resolved to protect a small portion of their precious wildlands from the ravages of "progress," to leave room for the bears and butterflies, wildflowers and ancient forests, to preserve as a "vignette of primitive America" the crown jewels of America's natural and cultural heritage.

But the parks are more than islands of nature. They are sanctuaries of the human heart. More than just pretty places where one can snap a few pictures, they are an acknowledgment of the human need for wilderness. These are places where there's room for lone hikers to lose, or find, themselves, for mountaineers to test their mettle against the elements; for scientists to study the natural world in a nearly pristine environment; for ordinary visitors to gape at something greater than themselves and let their dreams run wild.

Land of dreams

The wilderness of the American West has always attracted dreamers. Hope seems to rise where the sun sets – over the next mountain, across the plains, beyond the horizon. And perhaps dreams are the best way to understand the riveting, almost surreal, landscapes of the West. After all, what clear-thinking person could imagine the improbable eroded stone arches of the Colorado Plateau, the unearthly tablelands of South Dakota's Badlands, or the inconceivable span of the Grand Canyon?

To Native American Indians, these improbable landscapes are still sacred ground. Landmarks like the Black Hills and the Grand Canyon are part of a spiritual topography, an identification between land and people that comes with ancient tenure. Different tribes can point to mountains, forests, rivers, and canyons and declare, "This

PRECEDING PAGES: Mesquite Dunes near Stovepipe Wells, Death Valley; sunset at Joshua Tree National Park, California; Mt Whitney from Alabama Hills, Lone Pine, California. **LEFT:** Glen Canyon Dam. **ABOVE LEFT:** General Grant Sequoia, Kings Canyon National Park. **ABOVE RIGHT:** climbing at Joshua Tree National Park.

is where our people came from." They can point to the ruins of ancient villages and say, "These are the footprints of our ancestors."

But to the young nation of immigrants whose spiritual attachments lay elsewhere, the West was terra incognita, an open book to be colored by foreign dreams and ideologies. And these dreams – or were they delusions? – took a toll on the land. The intruding settlers chopped and plowed and burned and hunted, wresting land from the native people and changing the face of the earth with little regard for the long-term effects. Rivers were dammed, forests cleared, streams fouled, wildlife was exterminated, the earth torn open, and the soil exhausted and left to blow away.

Through it all, the land remained, altered but enduring, reminding us of both its power and fragility and of the great need for stewardship. For if the parks are indeed a promise, they are equally a responsibility. Americans have an obligation to keep them whole and healthy for future generations.

The National Park Service Organic Act, which created the National Park Service (NPS) in 1916, defined in verbose constitutional terms this national obligation: "The Service thus established shall promote and regulate the use of the Federal areas known as national parks, monuments, and reservations... by such means and measures as conform to the fundamental purpose of the said parks, monuments, and reservations, which purpose is to conserve the scenery and the natural and historic objects and the wild life therein and to provide for the enjoyment of the same in such manner and by such means as will leave them unimpaired for the enjoyment of future generations."

The NPS still strives to meet those original goals, while filling many other roles as well: guardian of the nation's diverse cultural and recreational resources, environmental advocate, world leader in the parks and preservation community, and pioneer in the drive to protect America's open space.

The job isn't getting any easier. It's not that visitors don't care about the parks. In fact, if attendance is any indication, they may love them too much. Of the many problems that beset the parks, popularity – the sheer number of people – may prove to be the most serious.

Leave no tracks

You may remember visiting a national park as a child and thrilling at the sight of a bison wallowing in the dust, or a black bear sauntering across a road, trying to get a peek at the tourists who were trying to get a peek at him.

It's a feeling people don't forget, that keeps them coming back with friends and family and especially children. Because the parks are a gift, too. They're a gift that Americans give to themselves and to the world, and to generations of children who will experience the parks as they were meant to be experienced: wide-eyed and filled with wonder. ❏

TOP: early tourists take to the open road. **ABOVE RIGHT:** smoking a calumet (peace pipe) in Glacier Park. **RIGHT:** Half Dome from Cook's Meadow, Yosemite National Park, California.

DECISIVE DATES

Army soldiers patrol the remote park, under the aegis of the War Department.

1889
While searching for lost cattle in southwest Colorado, the Wetherill brothers become the first white men to view the Ancestral Pueblo ruin of Cliff Palace at what will become Mesa Verde National Park. Richard Wetherill parlays the find into a career as a cowboy-archeologist and helps excavate this and other Pueblo ruins in the Southwest. He is the first to describe the former inhabitants as "Anasazi," a Navajo word meaning "enemy ancestors," and coins the term "basketmakers" for the early pithouse phase of the culture.

1832
Artist George Catlin paints a record of disappearing Indian tribes and suggests their preservation through "some great protecting policy of government.... A nation's park, containing man and beast, in all the wild and freshness of their nature's beauty!"

1851
Members of the Mariposa Battalion become the first white men to see Yosemite.

1864
President Abraham Lincoln signs the Yosemite Land Grant, ceding Yosemite Valley and the Mariposa Grove of Sequoias to the state of California for protection "upon the express conditions that the premises shall be held for public use, resort, and recreation; shall be inalienable for all time." This act forms the basis for the later national and state park systems.

1871
Following eyewitness accounts from early explorers, the Hayden Expedition, led by US Geological Survey director Ferdinand Hayden and including photographers and artists, visits Yellowstone to evaluate the resources on behalf of the federal government.

1872
Yellowstone is designated the first US national park by President Ulysses S. Grant. US

1890
Yosemite becomes a national park. Yosemite Valley and the Mariposa Grove will be transferred to the park in 1905, but to the dismay of conservationist John Muir, Hetch Hetchy Lake will be left out and dammed to provide drinking water to San Francisco.

1891
The Forest Reserve Act is signed into law by US President Benjamin Harrison, empowering presidents to set aside federal lands as national forests.

1898
Gifford Pinchot is appointed the first chief forester of the newly formed Division of Forestry. It is later renamed the US Forest Service, a division of the Department of Agriculture.

1899
Mount Rainier becomes the first national park created from a national forest.

1903
President Theodore Roosevelt visits Yellowstone in April, followed by Yosemite in May. In Yosemite, he camps out for three nights with John Muir and catches the conservation bug. During his presidency, Roosevelt designates five national parks, 18 national monuments, 51 bird reserves, four game preserves, and 150 national forests.

1906
President Theodore Roosevelt signs the Antiquities Act, empowering presidents to set aside places of scientific and cultural significance without congressional approval. Devils Tower becomes the first US national monument, followed by Petrified Forest, El Morro, and Montezuma Castle. Mesa Verde becomes a national park on June 29.

1907
Chaco Canyon, Tonto, Lassen Peak, and Gila Cliff Dwellings become national monuments. Chaco is expanded and redesignated Chaco Culture National Historical Park in 1980.

1908
Grand Canyon is designated a national monument. It will receive national park status in 1919.

FAR LEFT TOP: George Catlin with Mah-to-toh-pah, the second chief of the Mandans, *c.* 1830. LEFT: President Abraham Lincoln. RIGHT TOP: Theodore Roosevelt. RIGHT: Two Digger Indians of the Yosemite Valley, 1866.

1909
Mount Olympus becomes a national monument and is incorporated into Olympic National Park in 1938. Other national monuments this year include Navajo, Oregon Caves, Mukuntuweap (later incorporated into Zion National Park), and Gran Quivira (incorporated into Salinas Pueblo Missions in 1980).

1910
Glacier becomes a national park. Rainbow Bridge and Sitka are designated national monuments.

1911
Colorado National Monument, near Grand Junction, Colorado, and Devil's Postpile National Monument in California are set aside.

1913
Cabrillo National Monument in San Diego, California, is designated.

1915
Dinosaur and Walnut Canyon become national monuments. Rocky Mountain National Park is set aside.

1916
At the invitation of the Secretary of the Interior, businessman Stephen Mather moves to Washington

and forms the National Park Service. He becomes its first director, assisted by lawyer Horace Albright, managing 35 designated parks. The agency's mission, as stated in The National Park Service Organic Act, is to "conserve the scenery and the natural and historic objects and the wildlife therein and to provide for the enjoyment of the same in such manner and by such means as will leave them unimpaired for the enjoyment of future generations." A tough agenda, then and now.

1917
Mount McKinley (Denali) becomes a national park.

1919
Congress creates Zion National Park, incorporating Mukuntuweap National Monument (1909) and Zion National Monument (1918).

1920
National park visitors exceed 1 million a year.

1923
Aztec Ruin, Hovenweep, Pipe Spring, Bryce Canyon, and Carlsbad Cave become

national monuments. Bryce is redesignated a national park in 1928, Carlsbad is redesignated Carlsbad Caverns National Park in 1930.

1925
Glacier Bay becomes a national monument. It receives national park status in 1980. Mount Rushmore becomes a national memorial.

1929
Grand Teton is designated a national park. Arches National Monument is set aside (redesignated a national park in 1978). Lawyer Horace

Albright, Stephen Mather's second in command, becomes the second director of the National Park Service.

1933
The National Park Service, within the Department of the Interior, consolidates management of national parks and monuments previously under the jurisdiction of the War Department and the US Forest Service. President Franklin D. Roosevelt creates the Civilian Conservation Corps (CCC), as part of the government's New Deal, in response to the economic Great Depression. More than 120,000 CCC personnel work in national parks as part of Roosevelt's "Tree Army," building features such as trails, lodges, and tourist facilities.

1943
President Franklin D. Roosevelt designates Jackson Hole as a national monument. It, and lands gifted by John D. Rockefeller, Jr., will later be incorporated into Grand Teton National Park.

1955
National Park Service Director Conrad Wirth announces the Mission 66 initiative to mark the NPS's first half-century in 1966. Many visitor centers and other park buildings are built.

1961
Arizona native Stewart Udall is named Secretary of the Interior by President John F. Kennedy and serves under Kennedy and Lyndon B. Johnson. Four national parks, six national monuments, and dozens of wildlife refuges, his-

toric sites, and recreation areas are created during his watch.

1964
The Wilderness Act and Land and Conservation Fund Act are signed by President Johnson. Canyonlands becomes a national park.

1968
President Johnson signs the Wild and Scenic Rivers Act, creating eight wild rivers. By 2010, the number of US rivers receiving this designation had expanded to more than 250.

1973
President Nixon signs the powerful Endangered Species Act, designed to prevent the extinction of listed flora and fauna and restore populations through habitat conservation and other measures administered by the US Fish and Wildlife Service and National Marine Fisheries Service.

1980
The Alaska Lands Act, signed by President Clinton, confirms and expands the protection of 17 Alaska national monuments created by President Carter, including designation of Kenai Fjords as a national park. During his eight years in office, President Clinton designates a record 19 national monuments, the most of any US president.

FAR LEFT TOP: Native American Rights Association meet with representative Harry Shepard. LEFT: having a clean up at Mount Rushmore, South Dakota. RIGHT TOP: President Barack Obama visits Yellowstone National Park, Wyoming with his family. RIGHT: Bill Clinton at an outdoor press conference, Grand Teton National Park, 1995.

1990
Native American Graves and Repatriation Act (NAGPRA) is signed into law, requiring agencies and institutions that receive federal funding to return Native American cultural items and remains to their respective peoples.

2000
The National Landscape Conservation System is established to protect, conserve, and restore 26 million acres (10.5 million hectares) of Bureau of Land Management lands in the West of exceptional merit. The system's 800 units include 18 national monuments, 13 national conservation areas, 38 wild and scenic rivers, 183 wilderness areas, more than 5,100 miles (8,200km) of national scenic and historic trails, and 604 wilderness study areas.

2009
On October 28, President Obama sets aside Port Chicago Naval Magazine National Memorial, bringing the number of units in the National Park System to 392, of which 58 are national parks. National park visitation exceeds 285 million people a year.

2010
Global warming impacts are being clearly documented in America's national parks. In 2010, researchers announce that Glacier National Park contains only 25 remaining glaciers, a dramatic decline from the 150 glaciers that led to the park being set aside in 1910.

PIONEERS AND PROTECTORS

Most 19th-century Americans were more concerned with conquering nature than preserving it – but a few visionaries saw the need to safeguard the land

The national parks may be the best idea America has ever had. Some people have suggested as much. But the urge to protect nature, to preserve vast stretches of wilderness for future generations, hasn't come easy. If you told an American in the early 19th century that the day would come when his country would lack for wild places, he would probably think you were joking. Perched on the edge of a vast and untamed continent, Americans had more wilderness than they knew what to do with.

"The happiness of my country arises from the great plenty of land," declared Albert Gallatin, the Secretary of the Treasury. His superior, President Thomas Jefferson, thought that the Western

The pioneer Americans who set out in wagons across the Great Plains to carve new lives out of an unknown wilderness, regarded themselves as conquerors rather than protectors of nature.

lands contained "room enough for our descendants to the thousandth and ten thousandth generation." Indeed, many Americans saw the land as an inexhaustible source of wealth in animal furs, timber, rocks, mineral, and tillable soil.

And yet, there was deep ambivalence about nature, a sense of foreboding that went back at least as far as the Pilgrims. Peering into the New England woods, William Bradford, governor of Plymouth Colony, saw a "hideous and desolate wilderness of wild beasts and wild men." There was a moral imperative behind these words, an

injunction to subjugate nature, to conquer wildness, and cast the devil out of Eden.

Nearly 200 years later, as settlers struck out across the Great Plains, the urge to subdue nature was a duty. Many saw it as America's "manifest destiny" to occupy the continent from ocean to ocean and to bring the land and its native people under the dominion of the civilized world. According to President James Monroe, the vast wilderness occupied by Indians "requires a greater extent of territory… than is compatible with the progress and just claims of civilized life… and must yield to it."

The French historian Alexis de Tocqueville visited the young United States and observed

---

LEFT: Abraham Lincoln under construction at Mount Rushmore. **RIGHT:** early visitors at Yellowstone.

in 1832 that Americans "may be said not to perceive the mighty forests that surround them till they fall beneath the hatchet. Their eyes are fixed upon another sight: the American people march across these wilds, draining swamps, turning the course of rivers, peopling solitudes, and subduing nature."

A nation's park

In the same year, George Catlin, the American painter who visually chronicled the tribes of the West, realized that the wild country beyond the Mississippi River would soon be "tamed" by civilization. With great foresight, he proposed

parks be set aside in every town so that residents would never be far from the healing power of living things. "In wildness is the preservation of the world," he wrote, suggesting that experiencing nature is a deep human need.

In the West, the cause of wilderness was championed with greatest passion by Scottish-born John Muir, co-founder of the Sierra Club and an inspired naturalist, writer, wanderer, and organizer. Traipsing around the great mountain ranges of the West, particularly his beloved Sierra Nevada, Muir developed a vision of wilderness as an ecological and spiritual necessity. By the time he first strode into

that the Great Plains be set aside in a "magnificent park." He wrote: "What a beautiful and thrilling specimen for America to preserve and hold up to the view of her refined citizens and the world, in future ages! A *nation's park*, containing man and beast, in all the wild[ness] and freshness of their nature's beauty."

Busy building a nation, most Americans weren't ready to hear what Catlin had to say. There were exceptions – those who, like Catlin, found a deeper value in nature. On the East Coast, Transcendentalist writer/philosophers Ralph Waldo Emerson and Henry David Thoreau and poet Walt Whitman looked to the natural world for spiritual renewal, for a sense of the divine. Thoreau suggested that small

COMMUNING WITH NATURE

John Muir sought union with the natural world by immersing himself in it, climbing to the top of a 100ft (30-meter) fir tree to experience firsthand the rage of a windstorm, riding an avalanche above Yosemite Valley and calling it "the most spiritual and exhilarating of all the modes of motion" and hiking the Sierra for weeks with little more than bread and tea to sustain him. "Climb the mountains and get their good tidings," he advised his fellow Sierrans. "Nature's peace will flow into you as sunshine flows into trees. The winds will blow their own freshness into you and the storms their energy, while cares will drop off like autumn leaves."

Yosemite Valley, the idea for a national park had already begun to germinate. In 1864, four years before his arrival, the valley and nearby Mariposa Big Tree Grove had been granted to the state of California by the Congress of the United States to be "held for public use, resort, and recreation… inalienable for all time." Several years later, as reports by surveyors and explorers about the beauty and endowments of the Yellowstone region began fascinating the rest of the nation, a campaign was mounted to preserve Yellowstone for public use. Because the territories of Montana and Wyoming were not yet states, Yellowstone was placed under the supervision of the federal government, which, in 1872, was empowered to "provide for the preservation, from injury or spoliation, of all timber, mineral deposits, natural curiosities, or wonders within said park, and their retention in their natural condition."

Saving scenic resources

In California, John Muir was fighting to protect the Sierra. He campaigned against the spoliation of the forest by unrestrained logging and overgrazing sheep – which he called "hoofed locusts." Finally, in 1890, thanks in large part to his efforts, legislation creating Sequoia, General Grant (later incorporated into Kings Canyon), and Yosemite national parks was signed by President Benjamin Harrison.

In 1892, Muir and others formed the Sierra Club and, in 1906, after a ten-year battle with legislators and public opinion, the Yosemite Valley itself was surrendered by the state of California and incorporated into Yosemite National Park.

Meanwhile, several more areas of exceptional natural features were being designated national parks, including Mount Rainier, Crater Lake, and Wind Cave. A new, conservation-minded chief executive, Theodore Roosevelt, pushed his administration to create the 1906 Antiquities Act, allowing the president to set aside national monuments without congressional approval in areas of historic or scientific interest such as Petrified Forest, Mesa Verde, Devils Tower, and Chaco Canyon, many of which have since been designated national parks.

FAR LEFT: George Catlin by William Fisk, 1849. **LEFT:** John Muir, naturalist. **RIGHT:** Theodore Roosevelt and John Muir during a visit to Yosemite in 1903.

The rape of Hetch Hetchy

But Muir's struggle to save Yosemite and, in a larger sense, to safeguard all national parks wasn't over yet. In 1901, the city of San Francisco filed a request to dam the Tuolumne River in Yosemite National Park and drown the Hetch Hetchy Valley.

Muir considered Hetch Hetchy among the most sublime locations in the Sierra, and he crusaded angrily against the proposal: "These temple destroyers, devotees of ravaging commercialism, seem to have a perfect contempt for Nature, and, instead of lifting their eyes to the God of the Mountains, lift them to the

Almighty Dollar. Dam Hetch Hetchy! As well dam for watertanks the people's cathedrals and churches, for no holier temple has ever been consecrated by the heart of man."

Hetch Hetchy was a divisive issue that is with us even today. Essentially, it boiled down to a struggle between two pivotal figures. One was Muir, who felt a moral imperative to protect wilderness for its own sake and on its own terms. The other was a charismatic and committed conservationist, Gifford Pinchot, who, as President Roosevelt's chief forester, took a utilitarian view of wilderness – protection, yes, but protection for the sake of use.

Pinchot regarded conservation as a deeply democratic movement, a way of reclaiming the wealth of federal lands from the lumber barons and land grabbers and distributing it more equitably. "People have not only the right but the duty to control the use of the natural resources, which are the great sources of prosperity," he declared.

Conservation programs

It was Pinchot, in fact, who engineered some of the federal government's most important conservation programs and legislation in the first years of the century. Under Pinchot's guidance, Theodore Roosevelt set aside 130 million acres (52.6 million hectares) of national forest

and 18 national monuments and launched a system of wildlife refuges. Roosevelt, too, was a champion of wilderness. An avid outdoorsman, he had learned the lessons of conservation firsthand during a brief career as a rancher in North Dakota, and he was dedicated to protecting America's remaining wild places. "Leave it as it is," he said of the Grand Canyon, which he saved from developers by designating it as a national monument in 1908. "You cannot improve on it. Keep it for your children, your children's children, and for all who come after you as the one great sight which every American should see."

But for both Roosevelt and Pinchot, conservation meant balancing economic use with

preservation. Despite Muir's campaign, Roosevelt and Pinchot ultimately agreed to the dam, and Congress approved the flooding of Hetch Hetchy in 1913. Exhausted and disheartened, Muir died the following year.

The so-called rape of Hetch Hetchy, however, fired up many national park supporters. One of them, Stephen T. Mather, an influential Chicago entrepreneur, industrialist, and conservationist, was invited to Washington in 1916 to take overall charge of park policy.

Although the Interior Department was responsible for 35 national parks and monuments, it had to rely on the United States

> The largest site in today's National Park System is Wrangell-St Elias National Park, Alaska, at 20,587 sq miles (53,297 sq km) – bigger than some states of the US.

Army troops to patrol them. Mather advocated a centralized park administration, leading, in August of that year, to the creation of the National Park Service (NPS).

The system expands

Mather was appointed director and, together with his young assistant Horace M. Albright, began to push for expansion of national parks, especially historic sites.

By the 1930s, a dozen natural areas and more than 40 historic parks were added to the National Park System. Today, the NPS manages 392 sites covering more than 132,000 sq miles (340,000 sq km). The number of visitors has exploded. In 1916, there were about 350,000 recorded visits to the existing parks. By 1940, the number of visits had risen to nearly 17 million. In 2009, the number was a phenomenal 285 million.

John Muir's poetic observation of more than 90 years ago rings truer than ever today: "Thousands of tired, nerve-shaken, over-civilized people are beginning to find out that going to the mountains is going home; that wilderness is a necessity; and that mountain parks and reservations are useful not only as fountains of timber and irrigating rivers, but as fountains of life." ❏

LEFT: Stephen T. Mather riding sidecar.

National Treasures

Different titles are assigned to America's natural assets, including 'national recreation areas' and 'national monuments'

The great diversity of parks in the National Park System is reflected in the titles that are applied to the different units of the system. In addition to national parks, you'll come across areas designated as national preserves, national monuments, national memorials, national historic sites, national historical parks, national seashores, and national battlefields. Some names are self-explanatory; others are umbrella terms. The 74 national monuments, for example, include natural reservations, historic military fortifications, prehistoric ruins, fossil sites, landscape parks that are units of the National Land Conservation System managed by the Bureau of Land Management (BLM) – and the Statue of Liberty.

Congress and the NPS have attempted to simplify the nomenclature and basic criteria associated with the official titles. Generally, **national parks** contain diverse natural resources – areas of scenic or scientific importance, for instance, or habitats of rare or abundant wildlife or flora, or distinctive physical attributes such as forest, tundra, desert, river systems, thermal springs, caverns, and so on.

National monuments are intended to preserve at least one nationally significant resource. They are often smaller than national parks and do not contain the same diversity of attractions or visitor facilities.

In 1974, Big Cypress in Florida and Big Thicket in Texas were designated the first **national preserves**. This category was established primarily to protect certain resources, although activities such as hunting, fishing, and the extraction of minerals and fuels may be permitted, if they don't jeopardize the natural values. **National reserves** are similar to preserves: the first reserve, City of Rocks in Idaho, was established in 1988.

National lakeshores and **national seashores** were established to preserve shoreline areas and offshore islands, while at the same time providing water-based recreation. All four of the existing national lakeshores are to be found on the Great Lakes, while there are national seashores on the Atlantic, Gulf, and Pacific coasts.

The first **national recreation areas** were regions around reservoirs created by dams built by other federal agencies, but managed by the NPS under cooperative agreements. The concept of recreational areas has grown to encompass other lands and waters set aside for recreational use by acts of Congress, and now includes major areas in urban centers. **National rivers** and **wild and scenic riverways** preserve ribbons of land bordering free-flowing streams that have not been dammed, channelized, or otherwise altered.

Although the National Park System is best known for its scenic parks, more than half the areas preserve places and commemorate people and events important in the nation's history. These include archeological sites, places associated with notable Americans, fortified outposts, and scenes of battles. **National historic site** is the most common title for these areas, but there are also **national historical parks**, **national military parks**, and so on.

The title **national memorial** is most often used for areas that are primarily commemorative, such as Mount Rushmore in South Dakota.

In this book, while we concentrate on the national parks of the Western US, we also mention many of the national monuments, reserves, and recreation areas. *See Travel Tips pages 370–404.* ❏

RIGHT: the preserved cliff dwellings of Montezuma Castle National Monument.

GEOLOGY

The national parks of the American West speak eloquently to a geologist. And the story told by the rocks is nothing less than the creation of the earth

Surveying the Western landscape, travelers are often gripped by a sense of timelessness. The "standing rocks" of the Colorado Plateau or the frozen peaks of Alaska seem unchanging, unmoving, eternal. And yet, compared to the age of the earth, these formations are little more than a blink of the geologic eye, lasting only a few millennia at most.

Elsewhere, geologic events occur so quickly and with such force that one can't comprehend their magnitude of change – the devastation wrought by the eruption of Mount Saint Helens in 1980, the ongoing lava flows of Hawaii's Kilauea, debris-laden flash floods in the desert Southwest and, to a lesser extent, the erosion of South Dakota's Badlands. These events remind us that, no matter how stable the West's landscapes appear, they are only temporary features on the surface of a restless planet.

In the beginning

Some 4.6 billion years ago, the earth was a ball of cosmic gases and flowing, bubbling magma. Volcanic activity ruled this young world as the crust slowly congealed, producing gases such as hydrogen, methane, ammonia, and water vapor, which was released back onto the surface in the form of rain. For perhaps a billion years, endless torrents of rain cooled the earth's outer shell, filling low-lying areas with seas, lakes, and rivers. Beneath the surface, the earth continued to churn, heaving and folding the newly formed crust. Great mountain ranges rose from the surface of what would become North America, only to be broken down by wind, ice, and rain and

LEFT: Bryce Canyon National Park, Utah.
RIGHT: Theodore Roosevelt National Park, North Dakota.

replaced with yet other towering masses of rock. Debris gathered in the lower elevations and, in time, became the first sedimentary rocks.

Later, as the continental plate drifted and the climate changed, a succession of rivers, deserts, swamps, and seas deposited thousands of vertical feet of sediment: sand, mud, volcanic ash, seashells, skeletons, and other organic matter destined to become sandstone, shale, tuff, limestone, and other sedimentary rocks.

All the while, the North American plate continued to drift, constantly changing its position relative to the equator and neighboring continents. At least 140 million years ago, one of the oceanic plates began to crash into the western margin of the continent. In Alaska, land masses (their exact origin is still unknown and geologists therefore call them "suspect terrain") came rafting along on the oceanic plate and smashed into what is now the central part of the state. Sections of oceanic crust were ground into the geologic melange. Tremendous pressure and heat metamorphosed much of the rock as it was heaved into a series of complex mountain ranges such as the Alaska Range in Denali and Lake Clark national parks, the Baird Mountains in Kobuk Valley National Park and the Endicott Mountains of Gates of the Arctic National Park. As a result, Alaska's geology is a scrambled jigsaw puzzle, with pieces from different puzzles thrown into the mix.

Suspect terrain was also crashing into the West Coast, forcing sections of the ocean bed under the continental plate in a process called subduction. The friction of plate rubbing against plate melted subterranean rocks, turning them into great wads of molten magma. The magma rose in massive bubbles, cooled underground, and, in some cases, small portions were eroded and exposed millions of years later as giant granite domes such as those in Yosemite National Park. Farther north, magma exploded onto the surface in great rivers of lava

HOT SPOT HAWAII

Hawaii is a center of thermal upwelling. Most volcanic activity takes place along plate boundaries, but scattered across the globe are permanent upwellings of molten rock (Yellowstone National Park is another example), called "hot spots." In Hawaii Volcanoes National Park, Kilauea and Mauna Loa continue to pump hot glowing lava down their slopes. Offshore, magma bubbles out of underwater vents. When the deposits rise above sea level, a new island will be formed, and as the Pacific plate moves, it will be rafted away. Why these hot spots stay put while the plate moves across them is a question that geologists continue to ponder.

and showers of hot cinders that, over millennia, built up the Cascade Range in Washington, Oregon, and Northern California. Mount Rainier, Crater Lake, Olympic, and North Cascades national parks contain volcanoes, craters, and lava flows that are a result of subduction.

Mountain building

While all this activity was going on along the coast, the Rocky Mountains were being pushed up. The major mountain ranges of the world usually form along a plate boundary. The Rockies, however, march down the interior of a presumably stable continent. Some geologists believe that the rise of the Rockies is somehow related to the oceanic plate colliding with the West Coast, but the exact mechanism is still being debated. What is known is that, by 70 million years ago, thrusts and uplifts were folding huge areas of ancient sediments and even older granite and metamorphic rock into the Rockies.

Glaciers finished the job. The great sheets of ice plowed through the Rockies as well as the Cascades and Sierra Nevada. They widened valleys, gouged out bowl-like cirques, chiseled pinnacles, and deposited huge mounds of debris before retreating between 6,000 and 8,000 years ago. Glacier, Grand Teton, and Rocky Mountain national parks contain prime features of the mountain-building period.

Cascades – the continent was being stretched. The spreading of the land created long parallel faults in the crust. Between the faults, massive blocks of rock rotated slightly along their longest axis, forming mountain ranges with a typical profile: steep on one side, gradual on the other. Most of these ranges are separated by long, nar-

> *The Great Salt Lake – the West's only major lake – is but a small remnant of one of the huge inland seas that once covered the land between the mountain ranges.*

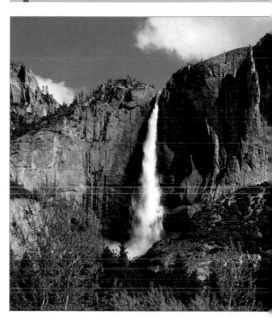

The Great Plains were being lifted, too, although much more gently. An eastern outpost of the Rockies now known as the Black Hills was pushed toward the sky – an island of granite peaks in a sea of prairie. Streams gathered into rivers and flowed from the mountains onto the plains. They cut into soft layers of rock and eroded the landscape into a complex network of gullies, ravines, canyons, and tables such as those at Badlands national park.

Between the Rockies and the great mountain ranges of the West Coast – the Sierra Nevada and

row valleys with no outlet to the ocean. During wetter periods, the basins were filled with immense inland lakes.

Amid all of this geologic chaos was a huge 130,000-sq-mile (337,000-sq-km) block of colorful, sedimentary real estate – the Colorado Plateau – which was uplifted, on average, a mile above sea level. Again, pressure from plate movements is thought to have caused the elevation. Although little folding occurred, the Colorado River and its tributaries carved the plateau into a labyrinth of awesome canyons, mesas, and majestic buttes. Many parks and monuments, including Grand Canyon, Bryce Canyon, Zion, and Canyonlands, preserve remarkable pieces of the Colorado Plateau. ❏

FAR LEFT: Mobius Arch, Alabama hills. **LEFT:** Zabriskie Point, Death Valley. **ABOVE LEFT:** Delicate Arch, Utah. **ABOVE RIGHT:** Upper Yosemite Falls.

FLORA OF THE WEST

The parks display an amazing variety of vegetation, from the mighty trees of the mountain forests to the hardy specialists of the desert

The enormous diversity of landscapes in the American West is one of its enduring attractions. Geology and climate continu ally shape the land into a jigsaw of distinct interlocking environments and micro-environments. Legions of highly adapted flowers, trees, and shrubs clothe the vast and varied contours of this changing panorama, with some species endemic to certain locations while others manage to gain a foothold almost everywhere. Nowhere in the United States are there more flowering plant species than in the West.

The country from the Pacific to the Rockies can be broadly divided into four regions: coast, deserts, mountains, and wetlands. Alaska, far to the north, has the short summers and endless winters associated with the Arctic tundra. By contrast, the isolated Hawaiian Islands, in the middle of the Pacific, are warm year-round, with a generally humid, tropical climate.

Geographic location, climate, sunlight, amount of water, elevation, soil type, exposure, and plant and animal neighbors all affect what will grow within each region and what it will look like, creating habitats where specific plant associations regularly occur as well as "ecotones," or overlapping habitats, within them.

Coast and sand dunes

Most of the West is affected by weather from the Pacific Ocean. Moist Pacific winds buffet the coasts of Washington, Oregon, and California, making this a challenging environment for plants. Many native flowers, such as sand verbena and sea asters, maintain low profiles, deep

LEFT: Cholla Cactus Garden, Joshua Tree National Park. **RIGHT:** wild geranium in the Rocky Mountains.

HAWAII'S HOTHOUSE PLANTS

The climate of Hawaii is dictated by trade winds that create either warm and moist or hot and dry conditions, depending on where you are on each island. The western exposure is frequently dry and relatively unvegetated, while the east may support lush rainforests, filled with orchids, lobelias, and other hothouse rarities that benefit from daily rainfall hitting the world's tallest mountains (that is, when they're measured from the ocean bottom to the summits).

The remote Hawaiian islands are the only place in the world to have so many diverse plant species evolved from so few ancestors.

roots, fleshy leaves, and a matted appearance in order to survive the sand dunes, high winds, salt spray, fog, and inadequate water intake.

On exposed cliffs, cypresses and Monterey, Bishop and Torrey pines look like bonsai plants, their branches blown back by the wind and

Although wildfires are frequently brought under control by nervous humans, many plants need fire in order to regenerate. The glorious rebirth of Yellowstone flora after the great fire of 1988 was ample evidence that nature knows best.

tains and the imposing Sierra Nevada massif. Hundreds of species of wildflowers enjoy these soggy locations each spring.

The mountains

Mountains of varying heights exist throughout the West, even in the hottest deserts, where they rise through the heat haze as what are dubbed "sky islands" amid salt flats and dry oceans of sand. The mountains of the region, with their weathered pinnacles and domes, cooler temperatures and increased moisture, contain the greatest variety of vegetation – although some, like the Inyo and White mountains of the Great

wrapped in wraithlike fog. Along the tinder-dry Southern California coastal foothills, the famed miniature oaks grow alongside manzanita and a variety of shrubs in a dense chaparral mix that scratches passing hikers.

The groves of tall redwood trees are happiest in foggy river valleys near the Northern California and Oregon coasts. Like the giant sequoias along the western Sierra Nevada and the mixed conifer forests of Texas' Guadalupe Mountains, the redwoods were stranded here by the last Ice Age around 10,000 years ago and now grow in only a few locations.

Other Ice Age relics are the glaciated vernal pools found only in California's grassy Great Valley, which sits between the coastal moun-

Basin, are overshadowed by taller mountains that block rainfall.

Washington's Olympic Mountains are the wettest peaks in the contiguous US, home to the Hoh Rain Forest, whose dripping glades foster a climax forest of western hemlock, Sitka spruce, and western red cedar and provide cover for deciduous underlings and shade-loving plants like leafy trillium and rhododendrons.

In the cool north, one often reaches the tree line at 4,000ft (1,200 meters) – far lower than in the south. This means that giants like Alaska's Mount Denali and Washington's Mount Rainier remain snowcapped and dotted with glaciers all year round. The exposed location, thin soils, and cold temperatures ensure that only the hardiest of mosses, lichens, and ground-hugging perennials can survive the harsh elements. Below these boulder-strewn summits, in the alpine and subalpine zones, spruce, fir, and various pines, such as lodgepole, limber, and occasionally bristlecone, endure admirably by using water conservatively and retaining their waxy needles year-round.

These conifers are gradually joined at lower elevations by silvery-barked aspens, ruddy maples, toothy oaks, and other deciduous trees that leaf out in spring and die so colorfully in the fall. In one of nature's ironies, aspens are often the first to colonize the subalpine zone between 8,000ft (2,400 meters) and 10,500ft

where, alongside Gambel oak, it forms a transition zone between high desert and mountain. As elevation drops and water is more scarce, the ponderosa habitat disappears, making way for pygmy juniper and pinyon trees, dryland grasses, yuccas, sagebrush, prickly poppies, sunflowers, globemallows, and other flora that must be content with the thin, rocky soils of the high desert. The mesas, high plains, and gullies of the Southwest, around the 6,000ft (1,800-meter) mark, are prime habitat for pinyon-juniper forests, as much a hallmark of the mile-high Colorado Plateau as California's redwoods or Joshua trees in the Mojave Desert.

(3,200 meters), but these pioneers are soon overshadowed by incoming conifers and forced to seek sunlight in clearings. An eye-popping array of bluebells, columbines, shooting stars, gentians, primroses, monkeyflowers, sunflowers, and other dazzlers bloom in waves from warm, damp May to August, splashing forests and meadows across the West with color.

Around the 7,000–8,000ft (2,100–2,400-meter) mark, swaying forests of ponderosa pine make an appearance. Ponderosa reaches its greatest density south of the Grand Canyon

FAR LEFT: prickly pear cactus in bloom.
LEFT: wild iris growing in Redwood National Park.
RIGHT: Joshua trees, symbol of the Mojave.

The deserts

The four great Western deserts – the Mojave, Great Basin, Sonoran, and Chihuahuan – owe their existence to the barrier of California's Sierra Nevada, which throws an enormous rain shadow across land to the east. No prevailing ocean influences moderate the conditions in these low-lying regions, making the Western deserts frighteningly hot in summer, frigid in winter, and subject to flash flooding during storms that saturate easily eroded sandy soils.

For any vegetation to make it here, it must tough out long droughts (deserts average only 10ins/25cm of rainfall a year, much of it coming in a short rainy season); it must compete effectively for water; and it must have mutually beneficial relationships with birds, insects, and other animals to reproduce.

Tough-barked mesquite, sagebrush, creosote bush, blackbrush, and bitterbrush manage quite well, and some bushes, like saltbush, have made a specialty of salt flats where nothing else grows. But cacti are perhaps the best adapted to desert conditions. Although the giant, many-limbed saguaro of the Sonoran Desert is the most famous, more than 100 cacti find their home in the Western desert, among them teddybear cholla, prickly pear, pincushion, and hedgehog.

Cacti have expandable, gelatinous tissues into which they suck up rainfall through shallow

roots – a strategy that allows them to go up to a year without water. A waxy coating keeps the water in, and spines keep away thirsty neighbors. The cactus uses its broad trunk or paddles to photosynthesize sunlight, water, and minerals into food. In spring, many species sprout a crown of large, creamy blooms attractive to nocturnal migratory bats and moths, which pollinate each cactus as they search for nectar. By late summer, bright, globular fruits appear – a delicacy for animals and humans alike. Some larger cacti also provide nesting sites for birds.

Agaves, or yuccas, are another common sight, their tall, thick spikes rising like giant asparagus from a rosette of fleshy, sword-like "leaves." Yuccas have been particularly useful to desert dwell-

ers, who use the roots for shampoo, the fibers for clothing, and the fall fruits as a starchy food. The shaggy Joshua tree (*Yucca brevifolia*), the symbol of the Mojave Desert, is a well-known member of the Agave family.

The desert's low elevation allows wildflowers to begin blooming early. From February or March, brilliant carpets of wildflowers enliven the subtle tones of the land, bringing admirers from near and far. No two years are the same, with different species awaiting just the right amount of rain to awaken. Some of the most beautiful flowers are spring annuals, such as poppies and owl's clover, which burst on the scene early during years of abundant rainfall. The Sonoran Desert is particularly noted for its floral displays.

Wetlands

Wetlands, or riparian areas, are found throughout the West, wherever springs, pools, streams, rivers, and seeps are located. Recognizable from miles away by the ribbon of green that announces the presence of cottonwoods, willows, box elders, and sedges, these shady groves provide water, shelter, and food for many plants, animals, and people. Monkeyflowers, columbines, ferns, and mosses form hanging gardens deep in the desert beneath dripping sandstone cliffs and along riverbanks.

But water is now a precious commodity throughout much of the West, as native flora compete with ranching, agriculture, industry, and recreation for access to this essential resource. Approximately 90 percent of riparian environments in California and Arizona have been lost through overdevelopment, and nearly all the West's major rivers have been tapped.

Damming, too, has its consequences. In the Grand Canyon, beach erosion along the banks of the Colorado River during dam operation has altered habitat for native plants. In recent years, new partnerships among the dam operators, the NPS, and environmental organizations have led to experimental efforts to restore the Grand Canyon below the dam and balance human needs with those of nature. Introduced tamarisk is monopolizing many southwestern waterways, crowding out other plants along washes and rivers that cannot tolerate the salty conditions this attractive but exotic intruder generates.   ❏

LEFT: the rose-purple flower of the beavertail cactus.
RIGHT: Giant Redwoods in Stout Grove, Redwood National Park.

WILDLIFE

From the torrid flats of the Sonoran Desert to the glacier-capped summit of Mount McKinley, the national parks represent the full range of animal habitats

Wildlife is one of the great treasures of the national parks. Few things evoke the spirit of wildness like the sight of bald eagles snatching salmon from the frigid waters of the Katmai coast, bighorn rams butting heads in the Rockies, a cloud of Brazilian free-tailed bats spiraling out of caves in Carlsbad Caverns, thousands of caribou migrating across the vast tundra of Gates of the Arctic, or the howl of gray wolves echoing across Yellowstone after a 70-year silence.

In the contiguous Western states alone, there are some 700 species of birds, 340 species of mammals, 250 species of reptiles and amphibians, and 300 species of fish. And the national parks shelter almost all of them. Some species, such as the resourceful coyote, mule deer, and raven, flourish in a wide range of environments. Others, such as the Grand Canyon's Kaibab squirrel, Olympic marmot, and rare Hawaiian honeycreepers, are limited to specific areas.

Coniferous forest and woodland

The cool, moist boreal (northern) forest extends from southern Alaska to the Rocky Mountains, where it overlaps with the drier montane forest. Rodents such as shrews, chipmunks, lemmings, and voles are characteristic of the northern range and make tasty little morsels for a variety of predators such as fishers, lynx, and bears. Moose inhabit this community, as do woodland caribou, known for massive seasonal migrations.

Two endangered birds, the spotted owl and the northern goshawk, have become celebrities. The spotted owl, in particular, is at the center of

LEFT: bison on the move. **RIGHT:** a mountain lion roams through the Rocky Mountains.

a much publicized controversy between environmentalists and the timber industry over the fate of the Northwest's old-growth forest.

The relatively warmer and drier montane forest is found throughout the Rocky Mountains, the Sierra Nevada, and parts of the Cascades, as well as in large swaths of the Intermountain West. Mule deer and elk are the most frequently seen large mammals here. Consider yourself lucky if you spy a black bear, a mountain lion, or a bobcat, which usually stay hidden.

There tend to be fewer birds in the montane forest, but there's plenty of variety. Listen for the loud "shook-shook-shook" of large, blue Steller's jays, the "tsick-a-zee-zee-zee" of diminutive mountain chickadees, and the "kit-kit" of pygmy nuthatches, which are often seen gleaning insects from tree trunks and branches. Flycatchers snatch insects in midair and quickly return to their perch. Warblers let melodies drift down from the canopy. And male western tanagers, evening grosbeaks, and red-capped Cassin's finch bring flashes of color to the understory. At night, you'll hear the mellow "hoot" of the flammulated owl or the single, whistle-like "hoo" of the northern pygmy owl.

Scattered woodlands of pinyon pine, pygmy juniper, and evergreen oak are common throughout the West. Mule deer browse in the woodlands in winter, and mountain lions and coyotes come to hunt. Bobcats pass through, too, and, before overhunting, grizzly bears were not uncommon. The most distinctive rodent is the pinyon mouse, the most arboreal of the deer mice, which makes its den in hollow branches.

A bounty of seeds, nuts, and berries attracts a variety of birdlife. You may hear the nasal buzz of blue-gray gnatcatchers, the rapid-fire tapping of woodpeckers, and, in the considerably drier chaparral, the catlike call of the rufous-sided towhee. The ash-throated flycatcher and western bluebird dart into the air hunting insects, the plain titmouse and bushtit spend hours

TROPICAL INVADERS

In terms of biodiversity, the tropics are the richest habitat on the planet – but the Hawaiian islands are a poor example. There, since the arrival of humans, introduced species have proliferated at the expense of native creatures. An endemic bird family, Hawaiian honeycreepers, is perhaps the world's best example of "adaptive radiation" – a process by which one species evolves into many in order to take advantage of different ecological niches. Tragically, more than a third of honeycreeper species are now extinct. Introduced species have been so successful that, in most lowland areas, all the mammals and birds are non-natives.

gleaning bugs from the foliage, and both the pinyon and scrub jay cache pine nuts against the long winter months. There's no lack of color here, either. Among the most flamboyant is the handsome male Scott's oriole, which sports a black head and back, and a yellow breast.

Grasslands

As the song says, grasslands are where "the buffalo roam and the antelope play," although any biologist will tell you that American buffalo are properly called bison and antelope are pronghorn. The massive bison herds that once roamed the Great Plains – amounting to more than 60 million animals – were systematically exterminated in the late 19th century. Had it not been for the efforts of conservationists at Yellowstone National Park and elsewhere, the shaggy beasts might have been lost forever. Today, remnant herds remain at Yellowstone, Wind Cave, Badlands, and several other parks and reserves.

Swift-running pronghorns didn't fare much better. Vast numbers of them died when the rangeland was fenced in the late 19th century. Fortunately, herds at Wind Cave, Grand Teton, and other parks have increased thanks to transplantation and better management.

Highly social prairie dogs were targeted for eradication, too, and large-scale poisoning nearly

> *Some desert rodents, such as kangaroo rats and pocket mice, never have to drink water; they produce it metabolically from high-carbohydrate seeds.*

led to the extinction of their main predator, the black-footed ferret. You'll find prairie-dog "towns" at several parks, including Bryce Canyon; efforts to restore ferrets are under way.

Grassland birds are primarily ground-nesters, although a few, like the ferruginous hawk, find an occasional tree for nesting. The lovely, flute-like song of the western meadowlark can be heard most summer mornings. And, if you're lucky, you may hear the "booming" of prairie chickens during courtship. The male's elaborate displays include inflated throat sacs and erect, horn-like neck feathers. The sharp-tailed grouse also has inflatable throat sacs but makes a single, low "coo-coo" accompanied by quill-rattling and foot-shuffling.

The long-billed curlew and upland sandpiper are shorebirds that summer in the grasslands. The curlew uses its long, sickle-shaped bill to probe the soil for invertebrates. You may see a short-eared owl coursing back and forth close to the ground looking for prey, or a burrowing owl "still-hunting" – waiting motionless until a rodent or large insect happens by. Although they don't actually nest in grasslands, golden eagles, turkey vultures, and various hawks can be seen patrolling the skies.

FAR LEFT: a bull elk displays his antlers. **LEFT:** Alaskan wolf. **RIGHT:** a rock squirrel searching for food at Cedar Ridge, Grand Canyon.

The desert

Survival in the searing heat and bone-dry conditions of the Mojave, Sonoran, and Chihuahuan deserts requires special adaptations. Don't expect to see much animal life during the day. Most mammals are nocturnal, although a few, such as the antelope ground squirrel, can tolerate soaring daytime temperatures. In the cooler deserts of the Great Basin and Colorado Plateau, you find Nuttall's cottontails, pygmy rabbits, kangaroo mice, and sagebrush voles feeding almost exclusively on sagebrush.

There is a conspicuous lack of large mammals here. Mountain lions and bobcats tend to be

nocturnal and secretive, coyotes are usually shy, and desert bighorn sheep remain extremely rare despite efforts to reintroduce them into several parks. At the first hint of a spring dawn, however, bird calls pierce the clear desert air. From a hidden pool, or *tinaja*, comes the hollow "coah, coo, coo, coo" of a mourning dove, followed by the harsh "who cooks for you?" of a white-winged dove. In canyons, listen for graceful notes tripping down the scale – a canyon wren in love. Along dry washes, the brown-crested flycatcher utters a sharp "whit," curve-billed thrashers and Abert's towhees scratch the dirt looking for a meal, and black-tailed gnatcatchers flit about.

Keep your eyes and ears open for a black phainopeplas eating mistletoe berries, or a tiny

Lucy's warbler singing from the top of a mesquite tree. You may see a family of plump, grayish Gambel's quail scurry between the bushes, or hear the drumming of a woodpecker in a grove of tall saguaros. Suddenly, a greater roadrunner races by, chasing a lizard.

High on the cliffs, lone peregrine falcons survey their domain. Nearly wiped out by pesticides in the contiguous United States, they have made a comeback in remote desert regions. As the day heats up, vultures catch a thermal and spiral upward, their keen sense of smell alert for carrion. A red-tailed hawk cruises by looking for an unsuspecting rabbit. Ravens cartwheel and

DESERT CREEPY CRAWLIES

Rattlesnakes can't tolerate high ground temperatures and usually spend the day under a ledge or shady bush. The large hairy tarantulas sometimes seen in the fall are usually males looking for a mate. They almost never bite humans, even when molested. Scorpions, too, have little interest in people, although their sting packs a wallop. Consider yourself lucky if you happen upon a Gila monster, North America's only venomous lizard. They do not have fangs but have to chew on their victims – mostly small rodents and lizards – in order to work in the venom. Keep your distance from these creatures and it's unlikely you'll be bitten or stung.

tumble in the cloudless sky. And, after nightfall, great horned owls and tiny elf owls come out to hunt, while lesser nighthawks glide through the air, scooping insects into their large mouths.

Tundra

Alaska's tundra is the richest in North America. Here, the most abundant mammal is the mouse-like lemming. Every three to four years, the lemming population peaks, providing a bountiful food supply for arctic foxes, gray wolves, and also grizzly bears. No, lemmings do not rush headlong into the sea, but high populations do cause frenzied dispersals and animals may drown while crossing rivers or lakes. Other mammals include arctic shrew, arctic ground squirrel, tundra vole, polar bear, weasel, and wolverine.

In the lower 48 states, alpine tundra covers a relatively small area atop mountain peaks, and there are only a few characteristic species. Collared pika, hoary marmots, singing voles, mountain goats, and bighorn sheep are found in the tundra of the Rockies, Cascades, and Sierra Nevada. Pikas, relatives of the rabbit, pile grasses into little haystacks that sustain them with food through the harsh winter. Marmots, on the other hand, build up a thick layer of fat for their long hibernation. Other mammals, such as bears, weasels, badgers, elk, and mule deer, sometimes range through the alpine tundra in summer.

Arctic birds generally rely on ponds and lakes for food and nest sites. Few sounds are more haunting then the falsetto wail and yodel of loons. A variety of shorebirds, such as plovers and sandpipers, populates the Alaskan coast. Flocks of red-necked phalaropes feed on the water, sometimes spinning like tops to stir up insect larvae and crustaceans. Herring gulls dive for fish, glaucous gulls prey on young birds and lemmings, and jaegers – dark, hawk-like seabirds – harass gulls and terns. The arctic tern makes the longest migration in the animal kingdom; it nests in the Arctic and spends its winters in the Antarctic.

One of the first birds of prey to arrive on the tundra in the spring is the rough-legged hawk. Other raptors include gyrfalcons, North America's largest, which tend to fly low in their hunt for large birds, and bald eagles, which gorge on spawning salmon. ❏

LEFT: the arctic fox's white coat provides warmth and camouflage. **RIGHT:** a bald eagle gets ready to swoop.

RADICAL RECREATION

Enjoying the parks can be a passive and absorbing experience – or it can involve pitting your body and mind against the power of wind, water, and rock

During the week, Bob Kerry is a mild-mannered, middle-aged lawyer. But, on weekends, he's a rock jock – a member of the growing cadre of athletes who get a kick out of scaling sheer rock walls. You may see them clinging to the side of a canyon, looking like tiny specks against the massive stone face. The most radical are "free climbers," those who use no safety ropes. And, at bedtime during an overnight climb, they simply attach a hammock to the rock and dangle in the breeze.

Rock climbers are part of a new breed of high-octane athletes that includes river runners, hang-gliders, cavers, mountain bikers, and others who approach the outdoors with daring spirits and an eagerness to test their limits. More than ever, people want a firsthand experience of wilderness. Athletes are out for a good time, to be sure. But they are looking for something more, too – adventure, achievement, excitement, and, to quote John Muir, a way of "getting in touch with the nerves of Mother Nature."

Rock jocks

"Everybody does it for different reasons," says Bob Kerry, who has been rock climbing for 20 years. He calls himself a "lifelong adrenalin junkie," but says that other rock climbers do it for the exercise, a sense of accomplishment, and a feeling that both their minds and bodies are in top condition.

During a recent climb in the Grand Canyon, for example, Kerry made a tricky ascent of an 80ft (24-meter) crack known as a chimney. "It's

PRECEDING PAGES: grizzly bears fish for salmon in Brook Falls, Katmai National Park. **LEFT:** climbing El Capitan, Yosemite. **RIGHT:** essential equipment.

an awfully scary feeling because you're not standing on any footholds," he says. "If you relax your body even for a moment, you just drop straight down. You don't have any handholds or footholds to keep you up. All you have is the tension on either side of your body."

Controlling fear in these situations, he explains, is what separates novices from experienced climbers. "There's something inside you that puts a chill in your brain. All you can see are the little edges in the rock, and you just continue to go up." Climbing is good therapy, too. It teaches you how to eliminate distractions and focus completely on what you're doing. Clinging to a rock several hundred feet above the ground has a way of putting life's mundane problems in their proper perspective. As Kerry says, "You're going to die if you fall even 50 feet... The rest is immaterial, really."

If climbing doesn't get you high enough, consider flying. Once the domain of steely-nerved

> Hang-gliding instructor Bill Holmes reckons that today's "flexwing" is one of the safest forms of aviation. "We joke about the good old days when sex was safe and hang-gliding was dangerous."

and awareness that is hard to find anywhere else. "It's so intimate up there that the hawks share the thermals with you," he says. He especially enjoys flying in the evening, when smooth air currents, or "wonder wind," let hang-gliders float around for two or three hours while the sun sets, catching "marshmallowy thermals" and soaring above snowy mountaintops.

Reading the river

The West is braided with some of the most powerful and scenic waterways in North America. Larry Rice, a wildlife biologist and avid outdoorsman, finds that traveling by water is among the

20-year-olds, the sport of hang-gliding has come of age. According to instructor Bill Holmes, the age of many first-time flyers is now well over 30. The change is due in part to innovations in design and technique. After a few lessons in "ground school," Holmes wastes no time getting his students airborne. "My philosophy is to get students as high as we can as quickly as we can, and give them enough altitude to make three mistakes." After a dozen lessons, he says, his students can be soaring at an altitude of 15,000ft (4,600 meters) for an hour or more.

He does make it sound appealing. The sensation, he says, "is purely sexual." The constant buzz of surface life gives way to the sound of wind rippling across the wings and a sense of peace

quickest and easiest ways of getting into the backcountry. "Canoeing and kayaking let you enter a wilderness area almost effortlessly, without the restraints or encumbrances of a heavy backpack. It's a more contemplative form of travel and permits a quicker change of scenery than hiking. It tends to free the mind without the numbing sensation of heavy equipment on your back."

He's quick to point out that traveling by water doesn't preclude hiking. In fact, combining the two can make the experience more rewarding. "Letting the power of the river, rather than your

LEFT: hang-gliding in the Grand Canyon.
RIGHT: cycling the coastal path near Enderts Beach, Redwood National Park.

legs, carry you into the backcountry frees up a lot of energy to make camp and take day hikes. You can really experience the best of both worlds in one trip."

He also finds it's easier to get close to wildlife in a small watercraft. Animals tend to be "less frightened and more curious" when they're approached in a kayak or canoe. He recalls drifting near a perplexed grizzly bear on the Upper Missouri River in Montana, paddling past seals among the ice floes of Alaska's Glacier Bay, and, in a truly magical episode that he describes as a "wildlife nugget," encountering gray whales off the coast of Baja California.

"Four adult whales were spyhopping [poking their heads vertically out of the water] around my kayak, doing a kind of ballet with me at the center of the circle… I remember looking into their dark black eyes; it was one of those transcendental moments. I was looking at them, they were looking at me, and for a moment there was almost a spanning of the species."

It's at times like these, Rice says, that he feels "really privileged to be in that kind of environment, a real wilderness beyond sight and sound of civilization, where you either sink or swim on your own skills and experience."

For some people, like Colorado River guide Jenny Gold, river running is a lifelong passion. Gold works as a river guide around the world at least 10 months a year. She says there's a hard-to-define romance and freedom in river life. Most trips last a week or two or longer, so there's plenty of time to get close to the elements, to experience rock, sky, and wildlife and, most importantly, to learn how to "read the river."

"Water has a way of teaching you things," she explains. "There's a lot of finesse involved in allowing the river to take you where you want to go without fighting it."

Gold says a good river guide knows instinctively how to clear the mind and how to assess a potentially dangerous situation: the speed and direction of the boat, the waves bouncing off boulders, rocks hidden beneath the surface, and the condition of the water downstream. Above all, she says, a river runner needs to stay humble. "You find out fast that no matter who you are or what you do, you'll never be more powerful than the river."

HIKING ON TWO WHEELS

Mountain biking was once described by *Newsweek* magazine as a "mode of transportation that combines the strenuousness of push-ups with the comfort of falling down a flight of steps in a shopping cart."

"The self-powered thing is cool," says Lou Warner, who runs a bike touring company in Moab, Utah, considered by freewheelers to be the capital of the world when it comes to mountain biking. The red rock country of southeastern Utah is crosshatched with thousands of miles of dirt roads left behind by miners and ranchers, giving bikers plenty of spare room to spin their wheels.

"The riding is excellent because the scenery is excellent. You can go from an elevation of 4,000ft (1,200 meters) at the Colorado River to almost 14,000ft (4,300 meters) on the snowcapped peaks of the La Sal Mountains." For Lou, mountain biking combines the best aspects of hiking and skiing – access to the hills and downhill speed – and leaves behind the worst one – slow travel.

In national parks, biking is allowed only on paved or dirt roads and a few designated trails; however, surrounding BLM and US Forest Service lands allow mountain biking on designated hiking trails. It's a great way to see the country without fouling up the atmosphere and to reach remote locations that you might miss on foot. And who says it has to be fast and bumpy? Biking at a nice slow pace lets the landscape unfold in glorious detail.

Descending order

Much the same can be said about caving – spelunking, as it used to be known. Caves have a way of surprising even the best-prepared and best-trained cavers. Serious cavers are particular about what they do and how it's done. Generally speaking, they take pains to distance themselves from weekend thrill-seekers. They particularly despise being portrayed as subterranean daredevils engaged in some sort of Indiana Jones adventurism. They emphasize that caving is not for everyone and definitely not something you want to jump into without proper instruction.

"Caving is safe if practiced with the proper

equipment and the proper training," says Jay Jansen, a spokesman for the National Speleological Society. "It can be dangerous if people don't know what they're doing. That's the bottom line." And he should know. Every year, society members are called upon to pull out of caves people who went in with a cotton clothesline, inspired by something they saw on television.

Cavers tend to be secretive about the locations of their caves, and for good reason. As elsewhere, vandalism and accidental damage taking a toll on the underworld. Even experienced cavers may damage underground formations that have taken thousands of years to form. "Caves are nonrenewable resources and can be damaged easily even by people who think they

know what they're doing," Jansen says.

The society has 200 caving clubs around the country and urges attendance at one of their meetings. Or, to learn about caving, visit any one of several national parks. At Wind Cave and Carlsbad Caverns, for example, you can sign up for a ranger-led "exploration tour". You may be surprised at just how fascinating caving can be. There's something alluring about being in a dark place far removed from the outside world. And, as a ranger explained, it gives people an entirely new way of "experiencing the earth. People are so disconnected from the planet, and this is one way of bringing that connection back."

Take a hike

Finally, if you're just trying to get away from it all and don't have a lot of time or resources, consider hiking. The Western parks are wrinkled with intriguing canyons and mountains and scattershot with lakes, rivers, meadows, and forests. There are easy trails, difficult trails, and, in some areas, no trails at all. All it takes to get started are a few common-sense essentials like a sturdy pair of shoes, the proper clothing, food, water, and a decent map.

Hiking can be done by just about anyone at any pace. And, like the more radical sports, it's as much mental as physical. The sound of the trail crunching underfoot slows the mind, and clears away distractions so you can focus on the world around you.

"The tendency nowadays to wander in wilderness is delightful to see," wrote John Muir, who was not only a great naturalist and writer but a great hiker as well. He'd take to the Sierra Nevada for days with little more than a few biscuits and a blanket. Hiking took him to the place where his inspiration was born. "There is peace to be found," he wrote, in "sauntering in rosiny pinewoods or in gentian meadows… jumping from rock to rock, feeling the life of them, learning the songs of them, panting in whole-souled exercise, and rejoicing in deep, long-drawn breaths of pure wildness."

Since those words were written, millions have come to the national parks to find their own inspiration and, as Muir envisioned, to renew themselves with the power of nature. ❏

LEFT: the entrance to Carlsbad Caverns in the Guadalupe Mountains. **RIGHT:** hikers make their way up Fern Canyon in Redwood National Park.

PARK RANGERS

The 20,000 national park rangers have a proud tradition of
service and, despite the formidable challenges they face,
a deep personal commitment to the parks

For 84 years, national park rangers have been identified with a single article of clothing and a challenging mission. Like Canadian Mounties, a distinctive *chapeau* sets them apart. The Smokey Bear hat is a holdover from the 19th century when the US Cavalry patrolled Yellowstone and the California parks and the lifestyle of park rangers was modeled after the military.

Rangers then were almost always men who lived in crude barracks, ate communal meals, were frequently transferred from post to post, and kept long working days that began before the crack of dawn and ended after sundown. "Rangers loved their jobs and put their commitment to the resource – whether it was natural or cultural – before everything else," says Rick Gale, a retired 46-year veteran of the agency. "You weren't in it for the money. If you worked for the National Park Service (NPS) you understood that you were no longer your own master and accepted it. You gave your life to the park and in return you always had a piece of it with you in your heart."

Gale is a product of the esprit de corps that makes the NPS one of the most distinguished branches of public service. He was born near Virginia's Colonial National Historical Park in 1936 to a father who spent his career as a park ranger. By the time he graduated from high school, young Rick had already lived in Wyoming's Grand Teton, Arizona's Petrified Forest, and New Mexico's Carlsbad Caverns. And the legacy continues. Gale's three daughters and two sons-in-law all work for the NPS.

LEFT: a ranger at Roaring River Falls, Kings Canyon.
RIGHT: Jim White, the discoverer and explorer of Carlsbad Caverns, with a tame bobcat.

The ranger romance

Western park rangers in particular cut a romantic figure in the public eye. Clad in their wide-brimmed hats, gray service shirts, and forest-green pants, the park ranger is an icon of the wilderness. "My favorite ranger story involves a legendary veteran ranger who was called on the radio by one of his subordinates," writes author Paul Schullery. "The younger ranger thought he needed advice on some sticky law enforcement situation he was embroiled in. The senior ranger's advice was simple and complete: just remember who you are, and what you stand for."

Schullery says the ranger mystique continues to this day. "When you arrive at a [park entrance] gate," he notes, "you have every right to expect you will be greeted by one of these singular figures, and usually you are. If he or she is doing good work, the greeting will be friendly, and the information will be accurate. If he or she is a really good ranger, the information will be given with pride."

Some of the more famous park rangers over the years include a former president, Gerald R. Ford, and the late environmental writer Edward Abbey, who spent several summers at a fire lookout tower. In 1916, the inaugural year of the NPS, agency director Stephen Mather summarized the varied demands on a ranger: "They

A FAMILY TRADITION

Allan O'Neill and his late identical twin brother Brian typify the deep family bonds in the park service. Passionate about the outdoors, affable, and entrepreneurial, their can-do spirit and diplomatic skills have been vital to the success of new urban parks bordering cities with large populations. Raised in Washington DC, the O'Neill brothers were inseparable, both majoring in geography at the same college and starting work for the NPS. Each rose to superintendent – Allan at Lake Mead National Recreation Area, near Las Vegas, and Brian at Golden Gate National Recreation Area, bordering San Francisco. It was always fun trying to tell the two apart. Both O'Neill sons also work for the NPS.

are a fine, earnest, intelligent, and public-spirited body of men, the rangers," he said. "Though small in number, their influence is large. Many and long are the duties heaped upon their shoulders. If a trail is to be blazed, it is 'send a ranger.' If an animal is floundering in the snow, a ranger is sent to pull him out; if a bear is in the hotel, if a fire threatens a forest, if someone is to be saved, it is 'send a ranger.'"

Over the past few decades, however, the NPS has undergone a period of modernization – in its responsibilities, demography, infrastructure, and, to some extent, its values. The world is infinitely more complex than in the halcyon days when park rangers patrolled the backcountry on horseback looking for poachers. Most wildland parks are no longer remote sanctuaries and urban areas have encroached upon the doorsteps of many parks. Despite manpower shortages and budget cuts, today's rangers are called on to confront drug dealers, thieves, and well-armed

> The Park Service's longest-serving ranger was Dr Carl Sharsmith, a botanist who spent over 60 years as a seasonal ranger-interpreter at Yosemite.

poachers; they carry out search-and-rescue missions, direct traffic, fight fires, manage wildlife, conduct research, and cope with the needs of more than 290 million annual visitors.

A profound change in the NPS since the early days is the inclusion of women and minorities. The first woman to be a permanent ranger was Herma Baggley, who came to Yellowstone in 1927 – 55 years after the park's creation. Today, about one-third of the NPS's employees are women, one-tenth African-American and one-twentieth Hispanic. Robert Stanton became the first African-American director of the park service in 1997. He was followed by Fran Mainella, the agency's first woman director in 2001.

The internal landscape

There's no way to describe the typical ranger. Each one is different, bound only by a passion for the job. The best way to become acquainted with a ranger is to approach one and chat either at a park visitor center or at one of the enormously popular campfire talks or ranger walks delivered daily at most parks.

"Ranger walks can set you on the high road to adventure as well as give you new insights into the world of animals," writes Art Miller, who went on ranger walks throughout Glacier National Park and later chronicled his experiences in *The Park Ranger Guide to Wildlife*.

"Our ranger-guide was Mike Wacker, a sturdily built outdoorsman and a member of the Blackfeet Indian tribe. Mike was working as a ranger for the summer, and then planned to return to the University of Wisconsin to complete his bachelor's degree in geology." In fact, most park rangers have at least an undergraduate degree, and about a third have a master's degree or PhD.

The agency has also tried to ensure that rangers reflect the ethnic ties of an area. At Badlands National Park, Navajo National Monument, and Little Bighorn Battlefield National Monument, for example, American Indian rangers are employed to interpret the history of the area from their perspective; at the Booker T. Washington National Monument, black rangers man the information desks and develop exhibits on Washington's role in African-American culture. At Coronado National Memorial near the Mexican border, interpreters explain the history of the trail to Spanish-speaking visitors. Much has been accomplished, but officials admit that more needs to be done to achieve complete equality.

Modern challenges

In 1983, sociologist Darryll Johnson and three colleagues conducted an in-depth survey in order to gain insight into the modern ranger. While an overwhelming majority of rangers professed dedication to the goals and principles of the NPS, they cited formidable challenges such as low wages, poor housing conditions, and an antiquated system of relocation. Generally speaking, they are less willing to accept the rigid military type of lifestyle that was standard during the agency's early years. For example, only about half said they approved of a policy that causes most rangers to be transferred several times over the course of their careers.

"Younger people coming into the service have different values than the dinosaurs now at the tail end of our careers," says Rick Gale. "I'm not sure the agency or anybody else has

kept up with them. I think some of the changes are manifested in the unwillingness to sacrifice family for the job. We are also seeing some changes in morale. There's a general dissatisfaction in the way things are going because each year we are having to do more with less. It stems from the frustration of knowing that you need to do more to protect the resource, yet you don't have the money or manpower to get the job done. And yet, you won't find a prouder group of people in government. They will try to get the job done in any way they can."

In the end, what distinguishes park rangers is a personal commitment to the parks themselves.

It's something that former rangers Kim and Melanie Heacox (who met as rangers at Glacier Bay Park and married in 1986) describe as an "internal landscape – a love of the land that runs so deep it's almost Thoreauvian." There are problems, Kim says, but there are also benefits, such as a sense of community among staff members.

"The park service becomes your second family," he explains. "You're in an environment where everybody shares the same values." In the best cases, it becomes a place where people "develop a special bond with each other."

There's a special bond with the land, too, that grows stronger "every time you put on a backpack, get away from it all, and remind yourself why you're there." ❑

LEFT: a ranger gives a tour of Yosemite National Park.
RIGHT: a popular ranger with a big following.

PLACES

A detailed guide to the parks of the West,
with principal sites clearly cross-referenced
by number to the maps

There are 392 units in the National Park System, welcoming 285 million visitors annually. It's a long-standing American tradition to load the kids and camping gear into the car and visit the national parks, but people from every continent are drawn to the splendor of the US parklands. Whether it's Yosemite Valley or the Statue of Liberty, the Alaskan wilderness or a Civil War battlefield, the National Park Service (NPS) is dedicated to preserving America's natural and cultural heritage and making it accessible to everyone.

The park system is dominated by large wilderness areas. The landscapes are of mythic proportions – the Rocky Mountains, the Badlands, the Grand Canyon, Yellowstone, Yosemite, Death Valley – places of such power and resonance that they have become icons of the American West.

For travelers who want a first-hand look at the parks' natural wonders or a genuine wilderness experience, there are numerous options. In addition to scheduled campfire talks and ranger-led tours, nearly every park has easy, interpretive trails near the visitor center that acquaint visitors with elements of the park's natural and cultural history.

More adventurous visitors can strike out on a network of well-maintained trails for day hikes of various length and difficulty. Backpackers can explore parks for days, even weeks, taking advantage of designated backcountry campgrounds.

This section of the book supplies all the information and insight you need to experience the parks at whatever level you choose. We have divided the area into regions – California and the Pacific Islands, the Southwest, the Rocky Mountains, the Pacific Northwest, and Alaska. With typical Insight thoroughness, the maps and text deliver full details of the roads, the trails, the campgrounds, the museums and visitor centers, and, above all, the spectacular variety of natural wonders that make the parks an American treasure. ❏

PRECEDING PAGES: Monument Valley Navajo Tribal Park; Half Dome, Glacier Point, Yosemite; Battery Point lighthouse at Crescent City with Redwood National Park coast in the background. **LEFT:** beach at Crescent City. **ABOVE LEFT:** a bull elk. **ABOVE RIGHT:** hiking through the Grand Canyon.

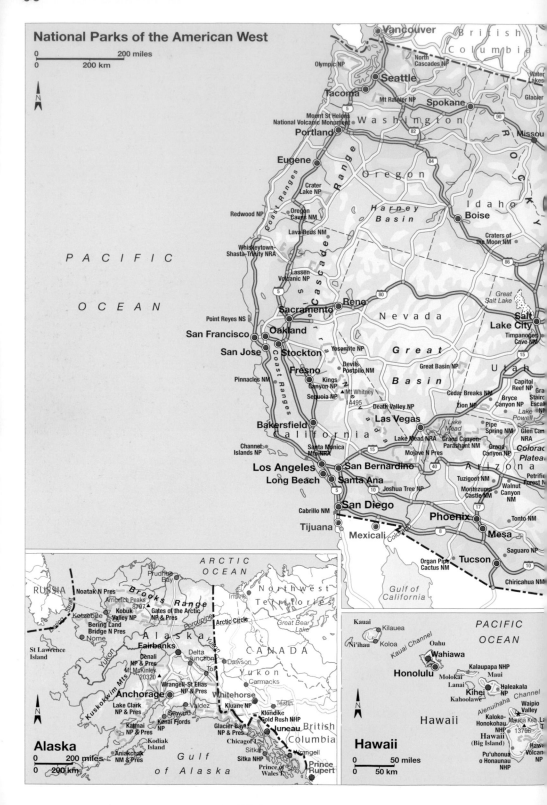

National Parks of the American West

0 ____ 200 miles
0 ____ 200 km

N

PACIFIC OCEAN

Vancouver
British Columbia
Olympic NP
North Cascades NP
Water Lakes
Seattle
Tacoma
Mt Rainier NP
Spokane
Glacier
Mount St Helens National Volcanic Monument
Missou
Portland
Washington
82
Eugene
84
Oregon
Crater Lake NP
Range
Idaho
Redwood NP
Oregon Caves NM
Harney Basin
Boise
Lava Beds NM
Craters of the Moon NM
Whiskeytown-Shasta-Trinity NRA
Lassen Volcanic NP
86
Great Salt Lake
Sacramento
Reno
80
Salt Lake City
Point Reyes NS
Nevada
Timpanogos Cave NM
San Francisco
Oakland
15
Great
Utah
San Jose
Stockton
Yosemite NP
Basin
Fresno
Devils Postpile NM
Great Basin NP
Capitol Reef NP
Gra
Pinnacles NM
Kings Canyon NP
Cedar Breaks NM
Bryce Canyon NP
Stairc Escal
Sequoia NP
Mt Whitney 14495
Zion NP
Death Valley NP
Lake Powell
Bakersfield
California
Las Vegas
Lake Mead
Pipe Spring NM
Glen Canyon NRA
Channel Islands NP
Santa Monica Mts NRA
Lake Mead NRA
Grand Canyon-Parashant NM
Mojave N Pres
Grand Canyon NP
Colorad Platea
Los Angeles
San Bernardino
Arizona
Long Beach
Santa Ana
Joshua Tree NP
Tuzigoot NM
Petrifie Forest N
10
Montezuma Castle NM
Walnut Canyon NM
San Diego
Cabrillo NM
5
Phoenix
17
Tonto NM
Tijuana
Mexicali
8
Mesa
Saguaro NP
Organ Pipe Cactus NM
Tucson
10
Gulf of California
Chiricahua NM

Alaska

0 ____ 200 miles
0 ____ 200 km

N

ARCTIC OCEAN
Prudhoe Bay
RUSSIA
Noatak N Pres
Brooks Range
Northwest Territories
Arrigetch Peaks 8707
Gates of the Arctic NP & Pres
Inuvik
Kotzebue
Kobuk Valley NP
Bering Strait
Bering Land Bridge N Pres
Nome
Alaska
Porcupine
Arctic Circle
Great Bear Lake
St Lawrence Island
Yukon
Fairbanks
CANADA
Denali NP & Pres
Delta Junction
Dawson
Mt McKinley 20320
Yukon
Carmacks
Anchorage
Wrangell-St Elias NP & Pres
Whitehorse
Teslin
Lake Clark NP & Pres
Valdez
Kluane NP
Seward
Kenai Fjords NP
Klondike Gold Rush NHP
British Columbia
Katmai NP & Pres
Glacier Bay NP & Pres
Juneau
Kodiak Island
Sitka
Aniakchak NM & Pres
Chicago
Sitka NHP
Gulf of Alaska
Prince of Wales I.
Wrangell
Prince Rupert

Hawaii

0 ____ 50 miles
0 ____ 50 km

N

PACIFIC OCEAN
Kauai
Kilauea
Ni'ihau
Koloa
Oahu
Kauai Channel
Wahiawa
Honolulu
Molokai
Kalaupapa NHP
Maui
Lanai
Haleakala NP
Kahoolawe
Kihei
Alenuihaha Channel
Waipio Valley
Kaloko-Honokohau NHP
Hawaii
Mauna Kea La 13796
Pu'uhonua o Honaunau NHP
Hawaii (Big Island)
Hawi
Volcan NP

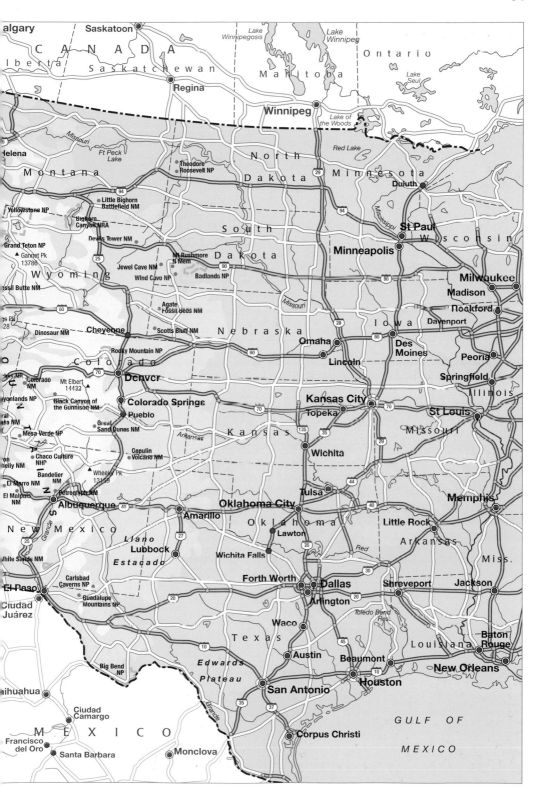

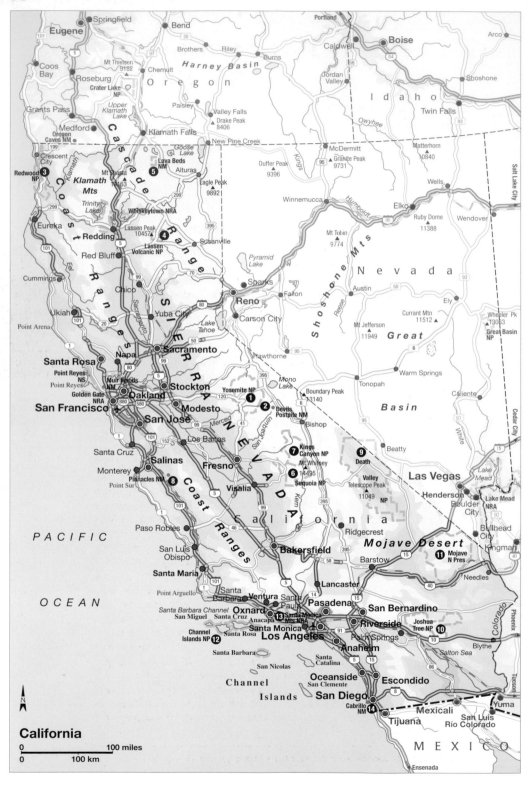

Springfield
Eugene
Bend
Portland
Caldwell
Boise
Arco

Coos Bay
Roseburg
Brothers
Riley
Burns
Jordan Valley
Shoshone

Grants Pass
Harney Basin
Oregon
Idaho

Medford
Oregon Caves NM
Crater Lake NP
Paisley
Valley Falls
Drake Peak 8406
McDermitt
Twin Falls

Crescent City
Redwood NP
Upper Klamath Lake
Klamath Falls
New Pine Creek
Goose Lake
Duffer Peak 9396
Granite Peak 9731
Matterhorn 10840

Eureka
Mt Shasta 14163
Lava Beds NM
Alturas
Eagle Peak 9892
Winnemucca
Elko
Ruby Dome 11388
Wells
Wendover
Salt Lake City

Klamath Mts
Trinity Lake
Whiskeytown NRA
Humboldt
Nevada

Redding
Lassen Peak 10457
Lassen Volcanic NP
Susanville
Mt Tobin 9774

Red Bluff
Pyramid Lake
Austin
Mt Jefferson 11949
Currant Mtn 11512
Ely
Wheeler Pk 13063
Great Basin NP

Cummings
Chico
Sparks
Reno
Fallon
Great Basin

Ukiah
Point Arena
Yuba City
Carson City
Lake Tahoe
Hawthorne
Warm Springs
Tonopah
Caliente

Napa
Santa Rosa
Sacramento
Mono Lake
Boundary Peak 13140

Point Reyes NS
Point Reyes
Muir Woods NM
Stockton
Yosemite NP
Devils Postpile NM
Bishop

Golden Gate NRA
Oakland
San Francisco
Modesto
Merced

San José
Santa Cruz
Los Banos
Kings Canyon NP
Mt Whitney
Death Valley
Las Vegas
Lake Mead

Monterey
Point Sur
Salinas
Pinacles NM
Fresno
Visalia
Sequoia NP
Telescope Peak 11049
Henderson
Boulder City
Lake Mead NRA

PACIFIC
Paso Robles
Coast Ranges
California
Ridgecrest
Mojave Desert
Bullhead City
Kingman

San Luis Obispo
Bakersfield
Barstow
Needles

OCEAN
Santa Maria
Point Arguello
Lancaster
Mojave N Pres

Santa Barbara
Ventura
Santa Paula
Pasadena
San Bernardino
Joshua Tree NP
Blythe
Phoenix

San Miguel
Santa Cruz
Anacapa
Oxnard
Santa Monica Mts NRA
Riverside
Palm Springs
Salton Sea
Tucson

Channel Islands NP
Santa Rosa
Santa Monica
Los Angeles
Anaheim

Santa Barbara
San Nicolas
Santa Catalina
Oceanside
San Clemente
Escondido

Channel Islands
San Diego
Cabrillo NM
Mexicali
Yuma

Tijuana
San Luis Río Colorado

MEXICO
Ensenada

California

0 ——— 100 miles

0 ——— 100 km

CALIFORNIA AND THE PACIFIC

The state that was a major inspiration for the first national park is home to deserts and volcanoes, and the world's largest trees

California is graced with snowcapped mountains and torrid deserts, with ancient forests and tranquil islands, and with the highest and lowest points in the contiguous USA. The crown jewel is Yosemite National Park, a magical tableau of granite domes, leaping water, wildflower meadows, and old-growth forests that attracts some 3.8 million visitors a year. You'll find a less-traveled pocket of the Sierra among the sheer canyons of Sequoia and Kings Canyon national parks, where backpackers can explore 800 miles (1,300km) of trails in a rugged wilderness frequented by black bears and mule deer. All three parks protect the mighty sequoia tree, the largest living thing on the planet.

A mountain refuge awaits at Lassen Volcanic National Park. Above slopes of Douglas fir and lodgepole pine, Lassen Peak is surrounded by bubbling mudpots and steaming fumaroles – evidence of its explosive past.

The giant sequoia's cousin, the coast redwood, dominates Redwood National Park, hugging the surf-pounded shore, where one can spot seals, sea lions, sea otters, and migrating gray whales. In the San Francisco area, as if to demonstrate the variety of the parks today, Golden Gate National Recreation Area includes urban parklands, ocean beaches, redwood forest, marshes, cultural centers, and Alcatraz Island.

Far to the south, the Channel Islands are a marine life sanctuary, too. Only 7 miles (11km) from the mainland, the tiny, wind tossed archipelago, once visited by Chumash Indians, is a vital outpost for sea mammals and seabirds.

Inland, Death Valley and Joshua Tree national parks, along with Mojave National Preserve, protect the fragile plant and animal communities of the Californian desert, a land of unrelenting heat and aridity that sustains a surprising variety of life. To round off this section, there's a chapter on the parks in America's Pacific islands. In far-off Hawaii, rare native plants and animals are protected at Haleakala and at Hawaii Volcanoes. American Samoa is a world of turquoise lagoons, volcanic ridges, lush rainforests, and pristine coral reefs. ❑

ABOVE LEFT: ancient redwood forest. **ABOVE RIGHT:** a brown bear sniffs the air.

YOSEMITE

The first natural area to be federally protected, Yosemite is today one of the most visited parks in the US, thanks largely to its remarkable and startlingly beautiful scenery

The essence of **Yosemite National Park ❶** is rock. Everywhere, granite creates a rough gray canvas upon which are painted brilliant jade forests, sparkling silver lakes and streams, and multihued flowers, leaves, and grasses. Rock dominates. Towering cliffs, solitary spires, subtle domes, jumbled piles of boulders, and thin, undulating ridges make up a landscape sculpted over the ages by ice, water, and wind. Together, ubiquitous granite with various metamorphic and volcanic rocks form what geologist King Huber calls "Yosemite's foundation."

Water runs on this rock. Two major rivers, the Merced and the Tuolumne, take life in Yosemite, then course resolutely across its breadth. Along their route, they create rapids, pools, and several of the free-leaping waterfalls for which the park is famed. Glaciers gouged out hundreds of high country lakes, and, in spring, scores of minor tributaries collect melting snow and send it downhill in tendrils of icy water, producing seasonal cascades and ephemeral falls.

This remarkable terrain is vitalized by an abundance of living creatures, from the world's largest trees to diminutive pocket gophers to microscopic fungi to several endangered birds, mammals, and plants. An original commissioner for the park, Frederick Law

Olmsted, writing in 1865, was among the first to recognize in Yosemite "the value of the district… as a museum of natural science and the danger, indeed the certainty, that without care many of the species of plants now flourishing upon it will be lost and many interesting objects be defaced or obscured if not destroyed." Olmsted was prescient. Yosemite serves as an environmental test station, gauging the health of the natural world. And what the gauge has been showing lately is that the park is vulnerable to a number of external

Main attractions

YOSEMITE VALLEY
EL CAPITAN
BRIDALVEIL FALLS
YOSEMITE FALLS
HALF DOME
GLACIER POINT
AHWAHNEE HOTEL
WAWONA
MARIPOSA GROVE OF BIG TREES
TIOGA PASS
TUOLUMNE MEADOWS

LEFT: El Capitan and its reflection.
RIGHT: the Merced River.

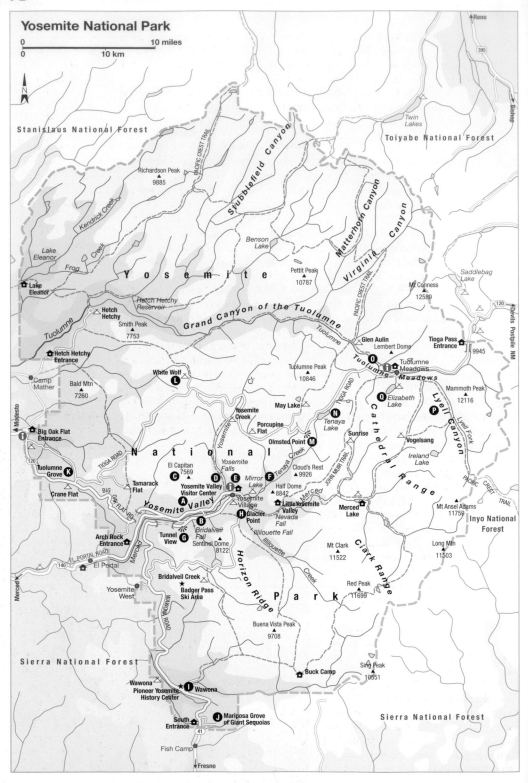

Yosemite National Park

0 — 10 miles
0 — 10 km

N

Stanislaus National Forest

Richardson Peak
9885

Kendrick Creek

Lake
Eleanor

Frog Creek

Lake
Eleanor

Benson
Lake

Pettit Peak
10787

Stubblefield Canyon

Virginia Canyon

Matterhorn Canyon

Toiyabe National Forest

Twin
Lakes

Reno

395

Bishop

Saddlebag
Lake

Mt Conness
12589

PACIFIC CREST TRAIL

Y o s e m i t e

Hetch Hetchy
Reservoir

Hetch
Hetchy

Smith Peak
7753

Grand Canyon of the Tuolumne

Tuolumne

Glen Aulin

Lembert Dome

Tioga Pass
Entrance
9945

120

Devils Postpile NM

Hetch Hetchy
Entrance

Camp
Mather

Bald Mtn
7260

White Wolf
L

Tuolumne Peak
10846

Cr.

Tioga Road

Tuolumne
Meadows
O

Tuolumne
Meadows

Mammoth Peak
12116

Big Oak Flat
Entrance

120

Modesto

Tuolumne
Grove
K

Tamarack
Flat

Crane Flat

BIG OAK FLAT RD

TIOGA ROAD

National

El Capitan
7569
C

Yosemite
Falls

Yosemite Creek

Porcupine
Flat

May Lake

Olmsted Point
M

Tenaya
Lake
N

Tenaya Creek

Cloud's Rest
9926

Sunrise

Elizabeth
Lake
Q

Vogelsang

Ireland
Lake

Cathedral Range

Lyell Canyon

Lyell Fork

P

PACIFIC CREST TRAIL

Yosemite
Falls

Mirror
Lake

D E
F

Yosemite Valley
Visitor Center
A

Yosemite
Village
I

Half Dome
8842

Merced

Nevada
Fall

Little Yosemite
Valley

JOHN MUIR TRAIL

Merced
Lake

Mt Ansel Adams
11759

**Inyo National
Forest**

Arch Rock
Entrance

El Portal Road

Merced

140

El Portal

Yosemite
West

Tunnel View
G

Bridalveil
Fall

Sentinel Dome
8122

B

Glacier
Point
H

Illilouette Fall

Illilouette Creek

Horizon Ridge

Mt Clark
11522

Clark Range

Long Mtn
11503

Bridalveil Creek

Badger Pass
Ski Area

WAWONA ROAD

Red Peak
11699

P a r k

Buena Vista Peak
9708

Creek

Sing Peak
10551

Sierra National Forest

Wawona
Pioneer Yosemite
History Center

I Wawona

South
Entrance

J Mariposa Grove
of Giant Sequoias

Buck Camp

41

Fish Camp

Fresno

Sierra National Forest

threats, including air pollution, acid rain, and development at its doorstep.

Despite its wealth of scenic and natural wonders, it is now the human presence that overshadows all else in Yosemite. Euro-Americans did not begin visiting the park in meaningful numbers until late in the 19th century; in 1899, only 4,500 "tourists" were counted in Yosemite. Now, more than 3.8 million visit the park each year. This onslaught has at times resulted in congestion, resource damage, and crowding, and has brought into urgent focus the conflict between the use and protection of this spectacular national treasure.

The simple years

This crush of humans is, indeed, new to Yosemite. For hundreds of years, it supported a modest population of Southern Miwok people who enjoyed a simple hunter-gatherer lifestyle. Anthropologists believe that the Southern Miwok first occupied the region about 3,500 years ago. They followed a way of life that changed little during the 600 years before Europeans arrived. Most of the Yosemite Miwoks, or Ahwahneechees, occupied brush-shelter villages in Yosemite Valley during the warmer months and migrated to the western foothills in winter.

The 1849 Gold Rush shattered the Ahwahneechees' world. Miners flooded into the foothills. The Ahwahneechees raided a few mining camps but didn't have much of a chance against the well-armed intruders. In 1851, a group of volunteers known as the Mariposa Battalion was formed to subdue the Indian "marauders." While pursuing the Indians into their mountain stronghold, they became the first white men to set foot in Yosemite Valley.

Lafayette Bunnell, a member of the battalion, wrote glowingly of his first glimpse of the place. "None but those who have visited this most wonderful valley can even imagine the feelings with which I looked upon the view that was there presented… a peculiar exalted sensation seemed to fill my whole being, and I found my eyes in tears with emotion." Those who followed in his footsteps had similarly passionate reactions, and, before long, the wonders of Yosemite were being proclaimed throughout the world.

The first park

Newcomers quickly recognized that Yosemite's attractions had enormous commercial potential. Acting to safeguard Yosemite, early settlers convinced Congress to establish the Yosemite Grant in 1864. Although not designating a national park as such, the act created a reserve (administered by the state of California) that was the first federally protected natural area in the world. In the ensuing years, Yosemite's fame grew, along with a public awareness that the greater region surrounding the valley was likewise an invaluable scenic and natural resource that deserved to have governmental protection. Thanks largely to the efforts of conservationist John Muir and his colleagues, Yosemite National Park was created in 1890. In 1906, the larger national park and the

The first residents, the Ahwahneechees, visited Yosemite's rugged high country only in the summer, to trade with neighboring tribes. They exchanged arrows, baskets, manzanita berries, and acorns for salt, obsidian, pinyon pine nuts, and insect larvae – a favorite delicacy.

BELOW: Yosemite Chapel.

An acorn woodpecker.

BELOW: the awesome Yosemite Falls.

state grant were combined to form the park that we know today.

Yosemite, an inspiring, liberating, almost irresistible natural place, has come a long way from its early, peaceful days. Its popularity has spawned both special problems and a devoted constituency. The park is a mecca for rock climbers, photographers, hanggliders, fishermen, artists, backpackers, recreational vehicle owners, mountain bikers, shoppers, birders, horseback riders, rafters, and others. And every visitor has a different expectation about how Yosemite should be used and managed.

The park is also popular because it provides security and comfort. Yosemite is the most revisited park in the United States, probably because, in our world of constant flux and tension, it is a fixed point of unchanging, rock-solid beauty. "The massive shapes that time, weather, and ice have carved out of the walls are so grandly simple, the broad flat forested meadow-breasted river-veined valley is so gentle, that we are invited in, not shut out," wrote Wallace Stegner.

Heart of the Sierra

Yosemite National Park is mostly wilderness, accessible only on foot. The portion of the park that can be visited by automobiles can be divided into three sections: Yosemite Valley; the area south of Yosemite Valley, which includes Wawona and the Mariposa Grove of Big Trees; and the area north of Yosemite Valley, which encompasses Tioga Road and Tuolumne Meadows.

Yosemite Valley Ⓐ, only 7 sq miles (18 sq km) long and a tiny fraction of the park's whole, offers more startlingly beautiful scenery than perhaps anywhere else in the world. Breathtaking waterfalls, sheer granite cliffs, imposing rock formations, and the sinuous Merced River come together in sheer perfection. For some 80 percent of visitors, the valley is the main attraction of the park.

There are three year-round routes into the valley: from the west, take Highway 140 through Mariposa; from the northwest, take Highway 120 through Groveland; and, from the south, take Highway 41 through Fish Camp. (A fourth route, from the east on Highway 120 through Lee Vining, enters the park by the Tioga Pass entrance. But this is closed from the first major snowfall in November until early June, due to snow.)

All traffic is routed onto a 12-mile (19km) one-way loop that circles Yosemite Valley. Increasingly, however, visitors are encouraged to park their vehicles and climb aboard one of the free shuttle buses that service the valley. As tourist and pollution figures mount, this need becomes more and more pressing.

As you enter the valley, a panorama of unparalleled beauty unfolds. To the south, lacy **Bridalveil Fall** Ⓑ drops 620ft (190 meters) from a "hanging valley." Bridalveil's gentle charm is almost overpowered by the granite bulk of **El Capitan** Ⓒ at the valley's opposite side. "El Cap," one of the world's largest rock monoliths, is so steep that its only denizens are

feathered (peregrine falcons, swifts, and other avians) or fearless (rugged climbers who often spend seven days or more scaling the stone face). In spring, watch for wispy **Horsetail Fall** on El Capitan's eastern shoulder. Past Bridalveil, the almost architectural formations of **Cathedral Rocks** and **Spires** grace the south wall.

Beyond El Capitan rises a trio of triangular rock shapes, each one atop the next, known as the **Three Brothers**. The tallest of the group, Eagle Peak, offers one of the best views from the valley's north rim. Across the valley, **Sentinel Rock**, a four-sided granite column, stands guard over this mountain paradise. When the road finally permits a clear view to the north, you'll marvel at inimitable **Yosemite Falls** as its white water plunges nearly half a mile (1km) in three sections. The falls are most spectacular during the spring runoff but are often little more than a trickle by late summer. As the road progresses eastward, picnicking is available at **Cathedral Beach** and **Sentinel Beach**, both under the trees on the sandy banks of the Merced River, and at other locations along the way. There are also plenty of pullout points for serious sightseeing, wandering along the base of dizzying cliffs, or just sitting on a rock to soak in the wonderful scene.

Yosemite Valley's developed area, where campgrounds, lodges, restaurants, and stores are to be found, is located at its eastern end. The **Yosemite Valley Visitor Center** offers a slide show, information services, exhibits, a bookstore, and more. Most ranger-led interpretive programs originate here, and next door there's the Yosemite Museum, Ansel Adams Gallery, and Indian Village.

To explore further in Yosemite Valley's eastern end, you are urged to use the free **Yosemite Valley Shuttle Bus**. The buses operate all year round 7am to 10pm. The 21 stops include many locations that are off-limits to private automobiles. The shuttle bus can be boarded in front of the visitor center, or at campgrounds, hotels, and other convenient spots. On the bus route, the **Nature Center at Happy Isles** (stop number 16) offers something

BELOW: camping in view of Merced Lake.

African-American Rangers

Shelton Johnson has worked in several western parks as an interpretive park ranger. Of African-American descent, he specializes in the role of African-American Buffalo Soldiers – so-named by the Cherokee and Plains Indians who likened their dark skin and curly black hair to that of buffalo – who joined the US Army and worked alongside their white counterparts to patrol parks and keep them safe from Indian incursions and resource damage. Some 500 Buffalo Soldiers worked in Yosemite, their duties ranging from evicting poachers to extinguishing forest fires. Johnson's eloquent on-camera comments on the role of people of color in the parks were featured in Ken Burns's 2009 documentary miniseries *The National Parks*. Johnson was awarded the Freeman Tilden Award For Excellence in Interpretation in 2009.

for the whole family. Located near the banks of the **Merced River**, the nature center is designed for kids and offers many exhibits and programs for them, including a Junior Ranger program. Happy Isles is also the trailhead for the hike to Vernal and Nevada falls. In spring, the walk up the **Mist Trail** is a drenching experience; mist blown from Vernal Fall rains down on the daring hikers who attempt the trip. It's only 2 miles (3km) to the top of Vernal and about twice that distance to the overlook of Nevada Fall.

Among other notable locations on the shuttle bus route are Mirror Lake, the Ahwahnee hotel and Lower Yosemite Fall. From shuttle stop 17, a mile-long walk leads to **Mirror Lake ❻** (once a bona fide lake, now a wide spot in the stream), the still surface of which reflects the imposing face of **Half Dome**, which sits in silent repose high above. There's more hiking up **Tenaya Canyon** (a 3-mile/5km loop up one side of Tenaya Creek and down the other) and shallow pools in the creek – useful for cooling off.

The shuttle also stops at the classic

1927 **Ahwahnee hotel**. The handsome stone-and-timber structure is built in the rustic architectural style and provides luxurious accommodations in this remote mountain setting. The grand lounge, with a walk-in double fireplace and decorated overall in an American Indian motif, is well worth a visit.

No one should pass up the walk to **Lower Yosemite Fall**. Get off the shuttle at stop number 6 and stroll to the bridge at the base of the lower fall. It's particularly impressive in spring when the volume of water is at its greatest. When there's a full moon, a nighttime excursion to this vantage point is utterly enchanting. It's one of the few places in the world where you can experience a prismatic phenomenon known as a "moon-bow," which appears in the watery spray.

The park concessionaire offers a two-hour bus tour of the valley year-round. Open-air trams leave from Yosemite Lodge throughout the day May to October; motor coaches operate late October to the end of April. Tickets are available at the transportation desk in **Yosemite Village**. The more athletically inclined may want to consider exploring the valley's paved loop by bicycle. Rentals are available at **Curry Village** or **Yosemite Lodge**.

South of the valley

The Wawona area, with its famed giant sequoias, is a logical next stop. From Yosemite Valley, take a once-daily free morning shuttle to Wawona (it returns mid-afternoon), or drive. The 36-mile (58km) route heads south over **Wawona Road** (Highway 41), providing access to two key attractions along the way. About 2 miles (3km) out of the valley, you'll reach **Tunnel View ❼**, a glorious panorama of granite cliffs, thundering waterfalls, and rock monoliths. It is spectacular – and easily the most photographed view in the park.

Farther south, the road detours to **Glacier Point ❽**, a lookout on the

BELOW: the Ahwahnee Hotel.

rim of Yosemite Valley affording a remarkable perspective on the valley floor, the north wall, Tenaya Canyon, Half Dome, and the High Sierra stretching to the north and east. The trip is about 30 miles (48km) off the main route but well worth it. Besides the view, there are geologic exhibits, ranger talks, a snack bar, and a gift shop. The moderate 1-mile (1.5km) hike from Glacier Point to nearby Sentinel Rock leads to the famous 360° view from the roof of the south rim. The wildflowers can be dazzling in spring and summer, and the top of the dome offers a great vantage point for watching the sun rise or set.

The meadow known as **Wawona** ❶ is historically rich and filled with recreational opportunities. Originally a stagecoach stop on the route to Yosemite Valley, Wawona is home to one of the oldest resort-hotels in California. The 1879 **Wawona Hotel** comprises several rambling whitewashed buildings that have undergone a thorough restoration. Today its rooms are nicely appointed, comfortable, and modern. Amenities include an inviting dining room, old-time piano music in the lounge, a swimming tank, and a nine-hole golf course (complete with mule deer grazing).

The park's past is also the theme of Wawona's **Pioneer Yosemite History Center.** The center is a collection of significant old buildings that were moved from various locations in Yosemite. In summer, park rangers dressed in period costumes engage in "living history" demonstrations. When funding allows, there are stagecoach rides, a working blacksmith, a bookshop, and other activities. A gas station, post office, grocery store, and gift shop are near the center.

The biggest draw of Yosemite's south end is the world-famous **Mariposa Grove of Giant Sequoias** ❶. About 7 miles (11km) from Wawona, the Mariposa Grove contains 500 big trees, some more than 2,000 years old. The **Grizzly Giant** is renowned for its huge girth and gnarled grandeur. The famous **Wawona Tunnel Tree** stood here until it toppled under a heavy snowfall in 1969.

The trees in the Mariposa Grove can be reached by foot (a 2½-mile/4km hike to the upper grove) or via the free shuttle between Wawona and Mariposa Grove that runs between spring and fall. A 1¼-hour concessionaire-run scenic tram tour between May and September. Recommended walks include the moderate 1-mile (1.5km) trail to the promontory at **Wawona Point** and the easy 2-mile (3km) return from the museum to the parking lot.

North of the valley

The opposite end of the park contains Yosemite's fabled high country – a rugged landscape bisected by the Tioga Road, which is usually open from Memorial Day to the start of November. From Yosemite Valley, follow the **Big Oak Flat Road** 13 miles (21km) to **Crane Flat**, where you can pick up the Tioga Road for the stunning 39-mile (63km) drive to Tuolumne Meadows.

From Crane Flat, it's about a

BELOW:
Mariposa Grove.

A pine at Olmsted Point.

BELOW: climbing above Tenaya Lake.

20-minute walk down to **Tuolumne Grove Ⓚ**, the park's second-largest stand of sequoias. If you don't have time to see the Mariposa Grove, this is a good place for an introduction to the colossal trees. Listen for the hoot of the great horned owl or the drumming of the blue grouse. Farther up the Tioga Road, about 14 miles (23km) from Crane Flat, **White Wolf Ⓛ** offers camping and overnight lodging amid lodgepole pines and a lovely spray of shooting stars, paintbrush, and owl's clover.

The road winds ever higher, crossing Yosemite Creek and climbing to the glacier-scoured highlands near the head of Tenaya Canyon, where you'll find **Olmsted Point Ⓜ**, a large turnout overlooking an enormous expanse of granite, including Cloud's Rest and the back side of Half Dome. To the east, the view of **Tenaya Lake Ⓝ** and the peaks ringing Tuolumne Meadows is superb. This is a likely spot to come face to face with a fat, furry, yellow-bellied marmot. A rock-loving mammal, the marmot prefers higher elevations and has developed a taste for tourist

handouts – but do them a favor and let them find their own food.

The road passes Tenaya Lake (there's good picnicking and swimming at its northeast end) before finally dropping into **Tuolumne Meadows Ⓞ** proper. This "meadow in the sky" sits at 8,600ft (2,621 meters) in one of the most picturesque alpine regions in the world. At the height of the season, the huge meadow complex is vibrant with the blooms of wildflowers like mountain pride, elephant's heads, Lemmon's paintbrush, and columbine.

The hiking is tremendous, with abundant day-hike and backpacking opportunities in every direction, including a pleasant 8-mile (12.8km) round-trip hike along the Tuolumne River in **Lyell Canyon Ⓟ**, a moderate 4.8-mile (7.7km) round-trip to **Elizabeth Lake Ⓠ**, or a 2.8-mile (4.5km) scramble to the top of Lembert Dome. Other popular activities include fishing, camping, and swimming. In summer, Tuolumne becomes the center of rock-climbing activities in the park. To the east, the road exits the park through **Tioga Pass**, at 9,945ft (3,031 meters) the highest paved road in the Sierra Nevada.

Devils Postpile

Those departing Yosemite through its eastern gate should consider visiting **Devils Postpile National Monument ❷**, about 40 miles (64km) to the southeast. It is home to a remarkable geological formation made up of 40–60ft (12–18-meter) -high basaltic columns formed about 100,000 years ago. There are trails to the postpile, to soda springs, and to the imposing Rainbow Falls. Devils Postpile is usually closed by heavy snowfall between November and June.

There are several National Park Service units in the Bay Area surrounding San Francisco. See the Travel Tips section for information on Golden Gate National Recreation Area, Muir Woods National Monument, and Point Reyes National Seashore. ❏

Early Visitors

Three eminent men – John Muir, Ralph Waldo Emerson, and Theodore Roosevelt – all came to Yosemite and fell in love with it

Among Yosemite Valley's first residents was renowned Scots-born naturalist and conservationist John Muir, who was hired to run a sawmill owned by an early settler. Muir hosted two especially famous visitors during his many years in Yosemite Valley. The first, in May 1871, was Ralph Waldo Emerson, the placid philosopher of transcendentalism who ranks among the most renowned Americans of the 19th century.

The other visitor, three decades later, was Theodore Roosevelt, the dynamic young president of a new century who touted the virtues of "the strenuous life" and shared Muir's enthusiasm for the great outdoors.

Emerson arrived only two years after Muir first encountered, and had been smitten by, the Sierra Nevada. During their brief stay in the California valley, Emerson's 12-member party put up at Leidig's Hotel. The tall, lanky, bearded Muir screwed up his courage, visited the hotel (38 and unknown, he was taken for a "local menial"), and delivered a note inviting Emerson to join him in the wild.

Surprisingly, Emerson took up the offer. He rode out the next day to Muir's "hang-nest," a ramshackle cabin in the woods, and together the young western naturalist and the 68-year-old sage of Concord, Massachusetts, spent the day communing with the wonders of Creation. Muir was delighted by Emerson's receptivity for such phenomena as the venerable sequoias, and he invited his guest – who had so famously extolled "Nature" in his written works – to abandon the dubious comforts of hotel accommodations and to camp out.

Emerson consented, but, alas, his traveling companions, male and female, vetoed his decision, fearing that he might be too frail to withstand life in the raw. And so, on May 11, Emerson's party took their leave at Mariposa Grove, riding slowly away on horseback, the philosopher trailing behind somewhat wistfully, waving to the naturalist. We're told that the prophetic Emerson said of Muir: "There is a young man from whom we shall hear."

It was a different story with Theodore Roosevelt (TR). By 1903, Muir was a nationally prominent champion of the wilderness. The US president had, in fact, proposed the visit to him, and TR was, at 44, a robust type who liked nothing more than to venture into untamed country. Muir wrote afterward that he "fairly fell in love with him."

Muir's rapport with the surrounding habitat impressed Theodore Roosevelt and fueled the president's enthusiasm for conservation measures. On their last morning together, the pair awoke under a dusting of snow – the "grandest day of my life," Roosevelt proclaimed.

Ralph Waldo Emerson and John Muir corresponded but never actually met again. In 1893, the naturalist visited Concord and laid flowers at the graves of both Emerson and Henry David Thoreau, whom we now regard, like Muir, as an American patron saint of conservation.

Upon Muir's own death, on Christmas Eve in 1914, Roosevelt paid public tribute to his "dauntless soul" and said of him that he was "brimming over with friendliness and kindliness." Coincidentally, it was a teenaged Teddy Roosevelt who, many years before, had rowed Emerson to shore during a chance encounter on a sailing trip along the Nile in Egypt.

In such a way did the lives of three famous Americans intersect. ❏

RIGHT: John Muir with his dog.

REDWOOD

As its name implies, Redwood National Park
is famed for its trees. Enormous, ancient
redwoods characterize the park, which also
has a fascinating coastline

The landscape architect Frederick Law Olmsted once wrote: "This generation has received, as a free inheritance from past ages, a hoard of forest wealth. But if any of the future generations for thousands of years to come are to have the opportunity of enjoying the spiritual values obtainable from such primeval forests, this generation must exercise the economic self-restraint necessary for passing on some portion of his inheritance, instead of 'cashing in' on it all."

Olmsted could well have been talking about **Redwood National Park** ❸, which was established in 1968 to protect Northern California's redwood forest from logging. Here, one of the few remaining groves of coastal redwood, *Sequoia sempervirens*, grows just a few minutes' walk from the relentlessly pounding surf of the Pacific Ocean. The giants rise prodigiously, some to a height of more than 300ft (91 meters). Roosevelt elk graze in nearby prairies, seals and sea lions splash in the waves, salmon and trout swim in streams and rivers, and a wide range of birdlife inhabits the shore and forest.

Fifty miles (80km) long from north to south and totaling nearly 132,000 acres (53,418 hectares), Redwood National Park and State Parks includes the national park and three California state parks – Prairie Creek Redwoods,

Del Norte Coast Redwoods, and Jedediah Smith Redwoods – all four jointly managed by the National Park Service and the California Department of Parks and Recreation.

From forest to sea

Approaching the parks from the south along US Highway 101 (by way of Eureka), stop first at **Thomas H. Kuchel Visitor Center** Ⓐ to discuss your visit with a ranger, view exhibits, and pick up the park brochure and a map of trails in the national and state

Main attractions

PRAIRIE CREEK STATE PARK
LADY BIRD JOHNSON NATURE TRAIL
TALL TREES GROVE
KLAMATH
DEL NORTE COAST REDWOODS
   STATE PARK
KLAMATH RIVER OVERLOOK
COASTAL TRAIL
JEDEDIAH SMITH REDWOODS STATE
   PARK
STOUT MEMORIAL GROVE

Thomas H. Kuc
Visitor Cent

Redwood National & State

LEFT: Redwood Grove in the mist.
RIGHT: Redwood Vistor Center.

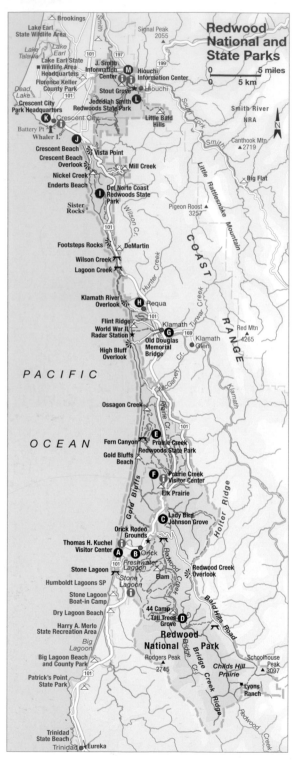

Redwood National and State Parks

parks. During the winter season, there is a telescope set up at the center for viewing gray whales as they migrate along the coastline.

Continuing north along Highway 101, you'll catch your first glimpse of the "wilds" of Redwood. Impressive Roosevelt elk – many weighing more than 1,000lbs (454kg) – graze on the prairies, often right beside the highway. Native to the area, the animals once roamed from the central California valley to the north's Mount Shasta. Like other indigenous wildlife, their numbers have diminished over the years. If you stop to watch them, they may look up momentarily, but most will simply ignore you as long as you keep your distance. The male elk's giant rack of antlers is there for good reason and the elk will charge if they feel threatened.

The tiny logging town of **Orick** Ⓑ is the first sign of civilization north of the national park visitor center. Dominated by a strip of redwood souvenir stands, the town has a grocery store and a few motels and restaurants.

For a good introduction to the natural features of the area, enjoy a walk along the **Lady Bird Johnson Grove** Ⓒ Nature Loop Trail. The trail begins 2 miles (3km) up Bald Hills Road, just north of Orick. (Note: The road is extremely steep and may be difficult for motor homes and trailers.) The easy self-guided nature trail is a mile (1.5km) long. A free interpretive booklet is available at the trailhead.

If time allows, consider visiting the **Tall Trees Grove** Ⓓ in the southern end of the park. During the summer, a shuttle bus transports visitors down the rugged 7-mile (11km) road to the Tall Trees trailhead.

Fifty daily private-vehicle permits are distributed on a first-come, first-served basis. The access road travels through an extensively logged area where reforesting is a work-in-progress. Expect to spend several hours exploring the area. Hike down the steep 3-mile (5km) trail, spend time in the Tall Trees Grove where the tallest known tree

(367ft/112 meters) stands, and allow plenty of time to hike back out. In summer, park rangers lead tours and discussions on logging damage and reforestation methods. At other times, an interpretive brochure is available for self-guided tours of the grove.

Generally speaking, the trails of Redwood National Park are wider and shorter than those of the adjacent state parks, which tend to run longer and venture deeper into the forested wilderness. From the south, **Prairie Creek** Ⓔ (14,000 acres/5,700 hectares) is the first state park you'll encounter. The trailheads for many of this area's nature trails are located next to **Prairie Creek Visitor Center** Ⓕ along the Newton B. Drury Scenic Parkway. Stop at the visitor center for information about the trails, or just put one foot in front of the other and start hiking.

For an interesting day-long hike, take the James Irvine Trail, Miner's Ridge Trail, or Prairie Creek Trail through the lush redwood forest. Keep your eyes open as you pass the creek: salmon and steelhead may be visible. Beneath the towering redwood and fir trees, plant life along these trails includes various ferns – which flourish in the moist, shaded environment of the forest – and redwood sorrel, with its clover-like leaves green on top and red on the underside. Many trails interconnect; you can extend your hike or cut it short depending on time and energy.

A unique feature of Prairie Creek is its 0.3-mile (0.5km) **Revelation Trail**. Designed for the visually impaired, the trailhead is located just south of the visitor center and offers many "sights" that can be experienced through the other senses. Wooden and rope handrails run the length of the trail and a Braille guide describes attractions along the way. Short hikes along Little Creek Trail, Ten Taypo Trail, and Hope Creek Trail take from 10 minutes to an hour and offer quick surveys of old-growth redwood forests for hikers interested in the "woodsy" experience.

Besides the forest, Redwood's other spectacular attribute, the Pacific Coast, is accessible to hikers via the Coastal Trail, which runs the length of the national park. In Prairie Creek State Park, the trail can be reached from Davison

Lady Bird Grove was the site of the 1969 dedication of the park, attended by Lady Bird Johnson, her husband, President Lyndon B. Johnson, Richard M. Nixon, and the then governor of California, Ronald Reagan.

BELOW:
Roosevelt elks

Saving Marbled Murrelets

Endangered marbled murrelets find a welcome sanctuary in Redwood National Park, which contains most of the last remaining population of the birds in California. These robin-sized birds live at sea but travel two miles (3.2km) inland to nest in the branches of the redwoods, where their camouflage helps them blend with their surroundings. At dawn and dusk, they visit the ocean to hunt for anchovies and smelts and return to the nest, covering the distance rapidly, flying 60 to 80mph (96 to 128kph). Murrelet chicks in the nest are at risk of being hunted by corvids such as Steller's jays, ravens, and crows, which are on the rise in the park. To deter opportunistic corvids and keep them away from murrelets, visitors are asked to keep a clean campground and not feed the birds.

The majestic bald eagle.

BELOW: the Klamath River.

Road, Gold Bluffs Beach Campground, Ossagon Trail, and Carruthers Cove Trail (at low tide only). Be sure to make a mental note of where you entered the beach. Once you're on the sand, it's difficult to distinguish entry points.

The Coastal Trail is an excellent place for picnicking, tide pool exploration, birding, and whale-watching. In the north part of the national park, the coast can be reached via the Flint Ridge Trail, Hidden Beach Trail, DeMartin Campground, Damnation Creek Trail, and Crescent Beach Trail.

Leaving Prairie Creek State Park, heading north on 101, your next stop should be the **Klamath G** area. This was once a precious fishing and hunting region for the Yurok Indians, but their numbers were severely reduced by miners who ruined the fisheries and burned Yurok villages. Today, Klamath and the neighboring community of Klamath Glen provide access to the Klamath River, a favorite among salmon and steelhead fishermen. The annual summer Salmon Festival has a salmon barbecue and displays of traditional Yurok arts and crafts.

Into the ancient forest

Also in the Klamath area are the **Trees of Mystery**, a popular tourist spot containing huge likenesses of the mythical Paul Bunyan and his Blue Ox, Babe, and chainsaw-sculpted trees. Nearby is **Sky Trail**, a 1,570ft (480-meter) -long lift that offers treetop views of the redwoods. Farther north along the Klamath River is the tiny town of **Requa H**, another important historic Yurok settlement. You will find a variety of restaurants and lodging in both Klamath and Requa.

Moving north, the next state park you'll visit is **Del Norte Coast Redwoods State Park I**. Its 6,400 acres (2,600 hectares) make it the smallest of the three state parks. It boasts a variety of foliage, from old-growth redwoods to wild rhododendrons (growing much taller than their suburban counterparts). Several trails lead from the forest to the sea, allowing you to sample diverse habitats. Along the relatively challenging **Damnation Creek Trail**, which begins near Highway 101 north of False Klamath Cove, you'll hike through old-growth spruce, redwood and Oregon grape and end up at a hidden sea cove replete with offshore sea stacks and tide pools. You can also reach a stretch of the Coastal Trail by way of Enderts Beach Road southeast of Crescent City.

For excellent birding and views of second-growth redwood forest, take the nearly 4-mile (6km) **Hobbs Wall Trail**, named for the Hobbs Wall Company, a primary enterprise of the Del Norte timber industry back in the 1860s. The trail is accessible from Highway 101. For a shorter hike in Del Norte, the **Nature Loop Trail** begins across from Mill Creek Campground and makes a 1-mile (1.5km) loop through stunning redwood forest. Notable along the trail is the madrone tree, recognizable by its red bark.

Information on Del Norte Coast Redwoods is available about 2 miles (3km) past **Crescent Beach J** in **Crescent City K** where you'll find

an information center near park head-quarters at 2nd and K streets. Crescent City offers plenty of good places to eat and sleep as well as markets, museums, and historic sights.

Towering redwoods

Proceed north on Highway 101 until you come to the junction of Highway 199, gateway to **Jedediah Smith Redwoods State Park ❶**. This 10,000-acre (4,050-hectare) park is ideal for hiking, camping, picnicking, fishing, or swimming in the Smith River, California's only undammed river system. An alternative approach to the park is via **Howland Hill Road**, an unpaved artery offering a scenic route through the lush redwood forest and access to **Stout Memorial Grove**, site of the park's largest measured redwood tree, 340ft (104 meters) tall and 16ft (5 meters) in diameter. This state park was named for mountain explorer Jedediah Smith, who led a party of 20 men across the area in 1828 in a grueling effort to reach the Pacific Coast.

There are a number of excellent hiking trails within Jedediah Smith.

For more information, stop and talk to rangers at the **Jedediah Smith Visitor Center ⓜ** on Highway 101 at Hiouchi, which is open from May 20 to September 30.

For an easy 2-mile (3km) hike, try the **Simpson-Reed Trail** on Highway 199. Several species of fern and skunk cabbage nestle beneath spectacular old-growth redwoods that frequently have large burls. Another short sampler hike is the 2.6-mile (4.2km) **Leiffer-Ellsworth Loop Trail**. The trailhead is 0.4 mile (1km) north of the junction of Highway 101/199, along Walker Road. The trails contain some steep grades along a moss-laden path through big leaf maple and old-growth redwood forest.

For a longer hike, try the 2.8-mile (4.5km) **Boy Scout Tree Trail** along Howland Hill Road, which can be covered in about 4 hours round-trip. The trail forks about 3 miles (4.8km) in. The right fork leads to the Boy Scout Tree, the left to **Fern Falls**. Excellent for birdwatching, the hike is sure to reveal winter wrens, Steller's jays, and Allen's hummingbirds. ❑

During the 1800s, Chinese gold mines operated along the route that is now the Boy Scout Tree Trail.

BELOW LEFT: magical Fern Canyon.
RIGHT: Avenue of the Giants.

LASSEN

This volcanic national park is not just beautiful and remote: it is also a geological hotspot, where mudpots bubble, hot springs steam, and a volcano last erupted less than a century ago

ew places testify to the awesome power of nature like **Lassen Volcanic National Park** ❹. Tucked away in a remote corner of the southern Cascade Range, this 106,372-acre (43,000-hectare) park is still very much in the throes of creation – a place where the earth bubbles and sputters and where the explosive power of volcanism has left behind a trail of destruction.

One of the least-visited national parks in the continental US, Lassen is also a place of precious solitude. Even during the summer months, Lassen offers opportunities to escape into the wilderness, where your only company is likely to be mule deer, chipmunks, and an occasional black bear. And with an elevation range of 5,000–10,000ft (1,500–3,000 meters), you can explore a variety of life zones in a short period of time, from crystal-clear lakes, wildflower meadows, and dense coniferous forests at the lower elevations to the treeless snowfields atop 10,457ft (3,187-meter) Lassen Peak.

Lassen Peak ❹ owes its existence to an ancient volcano, Mount Tehama (11,500ft/3,500 meters), which stood in the southwest corner of the park before collapsing 350,000 years ago. Little of Tehama remains today; its crater was scraped away by successive waves of glaciers, leaving behind only a few jagged peaks. But lava continued to flow, creating the younger peaks to the north. Of these, Lassen Peak is the highest and the last to erupt. The cataclysm began with a blast of steam and ash in May 1915 and reached its climax with devastating waves of debris and lava that wiped out a patch of forest 3 miles (5km) long. Although it has been dormant since 1921, Lassen remains a geologic hotspot where bubbling mudpots and hot-water springs are getting hotter – a sign that more activity may be on the way.

Main attractions
MAIN PARK ROAD SCENIC DRIVE
SULPHUR WORKS
BUMPASS HELL TRAIL
LASSEN PEAK TRAIL
SUMMIT LAKE
CINDER CONE NATURE TRAIL

PRECEDING PAGES: the coast near Westport.
LEFT: Lassen Peak. **RIGHT:** the steaming springs of Bumpass Hell.

A golden-mantled ground squirrel.

To hell and back

The western half of the park can be surveyed by automobile via the **Main Park Road**. This, the park's one paved road, can be covered in an hour or two. It loops around three sides of Lassen Peak and offers access to trails, lakes, and geothermal features. There are numbered markers along the route, indicating some 67 points of interest. Most of the road is closed between November and May, when it's used as a cross-country skiing trail.

Enter the park at its Southwest entrance on Highway 89 and stop at the new-year round **Kohm Yah-mah-nee Visitor Center** to view a film and exhibits, get information, and enjoy ranger programs. The park's first attraction is the **Sulphur Works** Ⓑ, where you can stroll along a well-signed boardwalk past sulfurous mudpots and fumaroles. This was the heart of ancient Mount Tehama, and it still brims with awesome geothermal power. The parking area also serves as a starting point for the gradually ascending trail to **Ridge Lakes**.

Back along the park road, proceed 4½ miles (7km) to the **Bumpass Hell Trail**, catching your first view of Lassen Peak, due north. The trail, a 3-mile (5km) round-trip with an easy 300ft (91-meter) descent, was named for mountain man Kendall Vanhook Bumpass, who discovered the hydrothermal area in 1865 and lost a leg from burns when he stepped into a boiling mudpot. Bumpass later described the mishap as his "easy descent into hell."

This is one of the park's most popular trails, with views of deep-blue **Lake Helen** Ⓒ, impressive glacier-carved rock formations, hemlock trees, and pinemat manzanita, as well as the hotspot itself at the end of the trail. Remarkably, a few species of bacteria and algae manage to grow in the hot, acidic water – it's between 125°F (52°C) and 196°F (91°C).

The next notable stop along the park road is Lassen Peak itself. The huge parking lot at the foot of the mountain is testimony to the popularity of the **Lassen Peak Trail**. The hike to the summit and back is almost 5 miles (8km) and ascends from 8,450 to 10,457ft (2,576 to 3,187 meters). The air is relatively thin here, so go slowly.

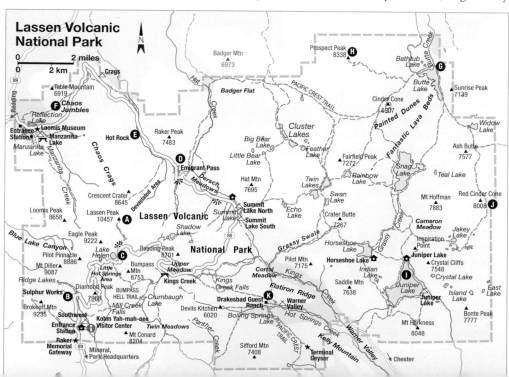

In season, you'll see plenty of wildflowers (including violets, irises, lupines, and monkeyflowers) and, before reaching the summit, you'll probably trudge through patches of snow. Once on top, if the weather is clear, you'll be treated to views of **Mount Shasta** to the north and **Sutter Butte** to the south.

The mountain was named for Danish guide Peter Lassen, an explorer of questionable skill. General John Bidwell, a friend, confided that Lassen "was a singular man, very industrious, very ingenious, and very fond of pioneering – in fact, of the latter, very stubbornly so. He had great confidence in his own power as a woodsman, but strangely enough, he always got lost." As the story goes, he once mistook Lassen Peak for Shasta Peak and inadvertently led a party of murderously angry pioneers 200 miles (322km) out of their way.

Back in the car, the road winds along the eastern side of Lassen Peak past red fir, lodgepole, and western white pine to **Summit Lake**, the starting point for a number of good day hikes to Echo and Twin lakes, Horseshoe Lake and Cluster Lakes. The next stop is **Emi-grant Pass ⓓ**, a 19th-century pioneer trail and the best place to view the **Devastated Area**, a section of forest that was virtually destroyed when Lassen Peak blew its stack in 1915. The eruptions sent lava spilling down the mountainside, blew down a 3-mile (5km) patch of trees, and smothered the entire area in mud and ash.

Proceeding northwest, you'll come to **Hot Rock ⓔ**, a 300-ton (270-tonne) remnant of the mudflow of May 19, 1915. This boulder, one of the many that were transported from Lassen's summit more than 4 miles (6km) away, is one of the larger rocks that descended the mountain.

As you near the park's North Entrance, you'll see **Chaos Jumbles ⓕ** north of Chaos Crags, a group of plug dome mountains. Chaos Jumbles was formed about 300 years ago after a series of avalanches was triggered by a steam explosion on the northwest face of Chaos Crags. Just before reaching the North Entrance Station, the road is flanked by lovely Reflection and Manzanita lakes, created in the wake of Chaos Jumbles.

TIP

As snow covers much of the park from October through mid-June, the best time for hiking and car touring is August–September. The best time for cross-country skiing and snowshoeing is January–March.

BELOW: trekking in the snow.

Winter Wonderland

Heavy snow closes the Main Park Road in winter, usually from November to April. During the quiet winter season, the park remains open for winter sports, and appreciation of the scenery and geothermal features. Some 15 beginner-intermediate snowshoeing trails can be found near the park's Loomis Ranger Station near the North Entrance; intermediate-advanced cross-country skiers will enjoy the more challenging terrain along the Main Park Road accessed from the park's Southwest Entrance. The 1-mile (1.6km) stretch between the entrance station and the Kohm Yah-mah-nee Visitor Center is plowed for snow play, including sledding, and tubing on the hills. Wilderness snow camping is allowed with a free permit. For information, enquire at the visitor center or self-register at the Loomis Ranger Station.

Into the wilderness

For adventure beyond the park road, try exploring the hiking trails in the eastern half of the park. The Butte Lake, Juniper Lake and Warner Valley regions are excellent starting points for day hikes. For longer stays, campgrounds are located near major trailheads. To reach the **Butte Lake** Ⓖ area, follow Highway 44 for 11 miles (18km) east after it splits with Highway 89 and take the unpaved road south to the Butte Lake ranger station. There are four trailheads at the Butte Lake parking lot. A short hike to **Bathtub Lake** can be broken up by a refreshing summer swim. Another hike, a bit longer and more strenuous, leads to **Prospect Peak** Ⓗ along part of the Cinder Cone Nature Trail.

The **Cinder Cone Nature Trail** offers a variety of routes. Cinder Cone was a volcano that shot lava, or tephra, straight up. The lava shattered in mid-air and piled up around the vent. Hiking the nearly symmetrical Cinder Cone takes 3 to 4 hours, is quite strenuous and features black lava formations, devastated tree stumps, and multicolored ash fields along an 800ft (244-meter) ascent. Alter-

native routes along the same trail go as far as Snag Lake to the south.

To reach the **Juniper Lake** Ⓘ area by car, head northwest along Feather River Drive just off Highway 36. Go about a half-mile (1km) to a fork in the road and angle right all the way to the Juniper Lake ranger station. Most trails from this area can be hiked in a single day, although some are more strenuous.

Hikes to 8,048ft (2,453-meter) Mount Harkness, Inspiration Point, Horseshoe Lake, Crystal Lake, Indian Lake, Swan Lake, and Snag Lake offer a whole variety of scenery and physical workouts. The trail east to Jakey Lake and **Red Cinder Cone** Ⓙ (another volcano) takes you into some of Lassen's least explored backcountry.

There are hundreds of other hiking options at Lassen, including the **Pacific Crest Trail**, which intersects trails from Butte and Juniper lakes. You can devise other variations by consulting a park map or, if you are proficient with compass and topographic map, you can head cross-country. There are nine campgrounds in the park. A wilderness permit is needed for backcountry camping: apply in advance to park headquarters.

Remember to bring water, food, and warm clothing. Temperatures can be extreme and the weather can change quickly. Signs warning campers to keep food away from bears should be taken seriously; they have been known to help themselves to a midnight snack.

Lodging in the park is limited to the secluded **Drakesbad Guest Ranch** Ⓚ – the only working dude ranch within a national park – just west of **Warner Valley** campgrounds. The inn opened in the mid-19th century as a hot-springs spa and now offers a lodge, cabins, and bungalows (most with no electricity). The park's campgrounds are open June through September on a first-come basis. **Lava Beds National Monument** ❺ is another rugged volcanic park north of Lassen, and Whiskeytown-Shasta-Trinity National Recreation Area, to the west, an ideal for water sports of all kinds. ❑

BELOW: the Oregon sunshine wildflower.
RIGHT: Mirror Lake.

SEQUOIA AND KINGS CANYON

John Muir described the canyon of the Kings River as "a rival to Yosemite." The scenery is spectacular, but these twin parks are even better known for their trees – the largest in the world

Sequoia National Park **6** and Kings Canyon National Park **7** are the twin jewels of California's towering Sierra Nevada. Here, under the gaze of the Golden State's highest peaks, a tiara of snowcapped mountains stands guard over alpine lakes. Sparkling streams flow through canyons rimmed with dense forests. Foothills and meadows sustain wildflowers and wildlife. And, of course, visitors can touch the famed sequoia trees, the largest living things on the face of the earth – some more than 3,000 years old.

Located along the western flank of the southern Sierra Nevada, the 1,350-sq-mile (3,495-sq-km) parks rise out of the highest and most rugged section of California. Surveying the Sierra from the summits of Mount Brewer and Mount Tyndall, a member of the 1864 Brewer Expedition described a land of "thin ridges topped with pinnacles sharp as needles, successions of great amphitheaters with crowning precipices. Over-sweeping snow fields and frozen lakes, everywhere naked and shattered granite…"

Creating the park

This rugged mountain terrain was once the homeland of the Monache Indians, who made summer camps in the high country to gather acorns, hunt deer and small game and occasionally cross the crest of the Sierra Nevada to trade with Paiute Indians in the Owens Valley. The Gold Rush of 1849 put a swift end to all that. Miners swarmed into the Sierra by the thousands, ruthlessly uprooting native people wherever they went. Loggers and stockmen quickly followed, indiscriminately felling trees, overgrazing mountain meadows and scattering game.

In the 1870s, John Muir, then a voice in the wilderness, began speaking out against the destruction, and, soon

Main attractions
GENERALS HIGHWAY
CRYSTAL CAVE
GENERAL SHERMAN TREE
TOKOPAH FALLS TRAIL
MINERAL KING
REDWOOD MOUNTAIN GROVE
GENERAL GRANT TREE
ROARING RIVER FALLS
MIST FALLS TRAIL

LEFT: General Grant Sequoia, Kings Canyon.
RIGHT: re-enacting John Muir's life.

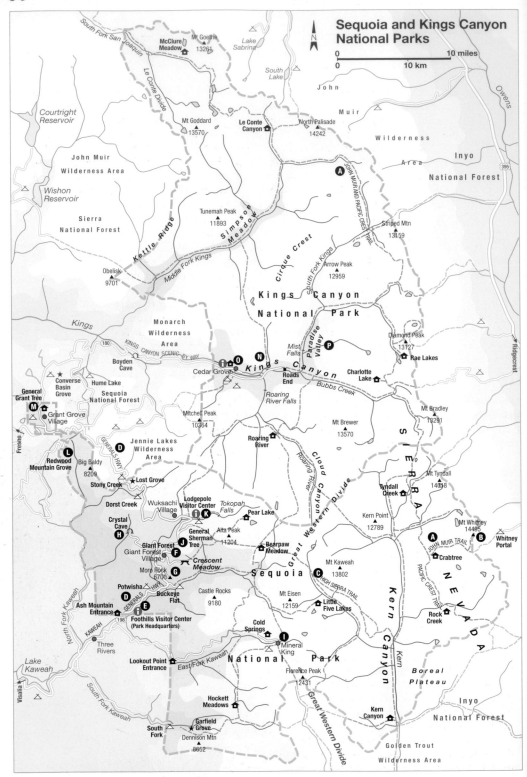

Sequoia and Kings Canyon National Parks

afterward, a newspaperman, George Stewart, took up the cause and began sounding the alarm to conservationists throughout California. The word finally reached Washington, and, in 1890, Sequoia and General Grant (now in the western unit of Kings Canyon) national parks were created. Damage was still being done outside the parks, however, and it wasn't until 1940 that the Kings River country was protected within Kings Canyon National Park. Today, Sequoia and Kings Canyon are among the most pristine units in the National Park System.

Sequoia and Kings Canyon are mainly backcountry parks. Ninety percent of the land is accessible by trail only, and none of its 2,600 lakes and ponds can be reached by motor vehicle. And yet, less than 5 percent of visitors are backcountry users. Bill Tweed, a Park Service veteran, describes the parks as "wilderness islands in a sea of urban California."

"These are parks that you have to hike to really enjoy," he says, and, with 800 miles (1,290km) of trails, there's plenty of opportunity to venture into the wilderness. Among the most famous is the **John Muir Trail** **A**, which stretches 219 miles (352km) along the crest of the Sierra Nevada from Yosemite Valley to **Mount Whitney** **B**, the highest peak in the contiguous United States, which rises at the parks' borders. The Muir Trail is generally regarded as the most spectacular segment of the longer Pacific Crest Trail, which runs between the Mexican and Canadian borders.

Another major trail, the **High Sierra** **C**, runs 71 miles (114km) from Crescent Meadow to Mount Whitney's 14,495ft (4,418-meter) summit. There is also a maze of secondary trails that fan out across the mountains and canyons, providing a variety of rewarding, high-mountain experiences for hikers at just about any level of skill and fitness. Motorists, too, can enjoy the wonders of Sequoia and Kings Canyon. Two major roads link the parks together,

affording spectacular views of the big trees, deep canyons, and other scenic wonders. Most visitors start at the Ash Mountain entrance, where Highway 198 from Visalia becomes the **Generals Highway** **D**, a 47-mile (76km) scenic road that winds through some of the parks' most stunning landscapes. Your first stop should be the **Foothills Visitor Center** **E**, about a mile (1.5km) from the park border, where you can consult with rangers about special tours and events and check weather conditions – extremely important during fall and winter when sudden snowfalls can make roads impassable.

From Ash Mountain, elevation 1,500ft (457 meters), the Generals Highway climbs steeply out of the foothills, passing several vista points along the way. About 15 miles (24km) from the visitor center, the **Four Guardsmen** – a quartet of stately sequoias – introduce visitors to the "big trees." The **Giant Forest** **F**, centerpiece of Sequoia National Park, is a mile (1.6km) beyond. Here, standing at an elevation of 6,500ft (1,981 meters), are the largest organisms in the world,

Sequoia National Park has a "drive-through" tree – a 275ft (84-meter) sequoia that fell across the Crescent Meadow Road in 1937. It still lies there, with a tunnel cut through it for cars to pass through.

BELOW:
follow the Mount Whitney Trail.

Hiker on the way to Bearpaw High Sierra Camp.

BELOW: the Giant Forest Museum.

Sequoiadendron giganteum, the giant sequoia. Hundreds of the huge trees dominate the landscape, their massive, rust-colored trunks rising in solemn majesty. This is a relict species. Its ancestors once grew throughout western North America before climatic and geologic changes left them stranded in the southern Sierra. The oldest have been standing here for at least 2,500 years. The ancient trees are so magnificent, so utterly huge, they must be experienced to be believed.

Housed in a historic market building in the old **Giant Forest Village**, **Giant Forest Museum** offers an in-depth look at the surrounding sequoias and conservation efforts. Open year-round, the museum provides books, maps, restrooms, and phones. Nearby, Moro Rock-Crescent Meadow Road leads through the sequoias to Crescent Meadow, one of the gems of the Giant Forest area. The trees are truly spectacular. Crescent Meadow is an idyllic spot for those who want to get off the beaten path.

In summer, park interpreters guide visitors around wildflower meadows and to the log cabin of Hale Tharp, the first white pioneer to settle in the Giant Forest.

A turn-off in the same road leads to **Moro Rock G**, a 6,700ft (2,042-meter) granite monolith with glorious views of Alta Peak, the Great Western Divide, and the Kaweah River basin. A long, steep stairway climbs to the summit. Several easy foot trails radiate out of Giant Forest Village, making loops of various lengths through the lush meadows and sequoia groves. Here, visitors can take a few hours or an entire day to experience the big trees close up, occasionally spotting a black bear or mule deer browsing in the brush.

Off the beaten path

Visitors with enough time and a sense of adventure should consider wandering off the main roads and journeying into the parks' wilderness areas, if only for a day or two. An easy introduction might be a half-day excursion to **Crystal Cave H** (summer only), at the end of a narrow mountain road just north of Giant Forest Village. The beautiful cave was carved by water out of subterranean marble. In places, stalagmites and stalactites, formed drop by drop over thousands of years, are joined into single columns. The cave remains at a constant 48°F (9°C) year-round.

A steep, partially paved road off Highway 198 near the Ash Mountain entrance leads to **Mineral King I** (summer only), a stunning region of high valleys, sheer mountain sides, and isolated alpine lakes. It takes about 90 minutes to drive to the ranger station near the end of the road; campgrounds are available but fill rapidly on weekends. Trails start at an elevation of 7,500ft (2,300 meters) and climb steeply in a long series of switchbacks. Along the trails are dazzling displays of lupine, Indian paintbrush, orchid and shooting star, turquoise lakes in glacier-carved basins, excellent wildlife-watching, sweeping views at every turn, and a seemingly endless supply of solitude. Congress transferred Mineral

King to Sequoia National Park in 1978, ending 20 years of controversy over a proposed ski resort development.

The gigantic General

Beyond Giant Forest Village, the Generals Highway winds a short way through a forest of pines, firs, and sequoias to the famed **General Sherman Tree ❶**, the world's largest living thing. This monarch has a diameter of 30ft (9 meters) and rises 274ft (84 meters) into the Sierra sky. It contains approximately 52,500 cubic ft (1,487 cubic meters) of lumber – enough for about 85 average-sized homes. One of its upper branches is about 6ft (2 meters) in diameter and 80ft (24 meters) long – bigger than many trees. **Congress Trail** starts at the Sherman Tree and makes a pleasant 2-mile (3km) loop through the sequoia grove where, in summer, you're likely to see or hear Steller's jays, Clark's nutcrackers, juncoes, white-headed woodpeckers, and chickadees, among a variety of other native birds.

Back on the road, the Generals Highway winds toward a rugged mountain canyon known as **Tokopah Valley**, where you'll find the **Lodgepole Visitor Center ❿**, several stores, and a large campground on the Marble Fork of the Kaweah River. An easy 2-mile (3km) trail runs along the canyon to **Tokopah Falls**, a spectacular 1,200ft (366-meter) cascade that thunders down a rocky chute.

West of Lodgepole, the highway passes **Wuksachi Village**, where the Park Service has replaced aging visitor facilities once scattered in Giant Forest. The road exits the park at Lost Grove and winds through Sequoia National Forest for about 11 miles (18km) before entering the western unit of Kings Canyon National Park.

The trees of Kings Canyon

Just past the park boundary, near Quail Flat, a rough, 2-mile (3km)-long road (closed in winter) runs out to **Redwood Mountain Grove ❶**, the largest stand of *Sequoiadendron giganteum* in the whole of America. Redwood Mountain is a park unto itself, containing thousands of sequoias of varying size. Unlike the more popular

Maps:
Area 68
Park 96

> **TIP**
>
> Crystal Cave can only be visited as part of a guided tour (mid-June–September). Tickets must be bought in advance at Foothills or Lodgepole visitor centers.

BELOW: the General Sherman sequoia is the world's largest living 'thing'.

A Landmark Court Battle

In 1978, 12,600 acres (5,100 hectares) of the stunning glaciated valley known as Mineral King were transferred to Sequoia National Park from the US Forest Service by an Act of Congress. The action ended a 20-year legal battle between California's Sierra Club and the Disney Corporation, which had been granted permission to build a ski resort in the valley. The Sierra Club v Morton case went as far as the US Supreme Court, which ruled against the Sierra Club "having standing" in its corporate capacity but recognized its right to bring suit on behalf of any individual members who could show that their use of the lands in question were affected. An important legal precedent in environmental circles, the legal decision is examined in detail in Christopher Stone's book *Should Trees Have Standing?*

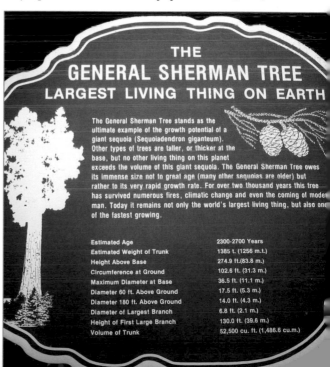

THE
GENERAL SHERMAN TREE
LARGEST LIVING THING ON EARTH

The General Sherman Tree stands as the ultimate example of the growth potential of a giant sequoia (Sequoiadendron giganteum). Other types of trees are taller, or thicker at the base, but no other living thing on this planet exceeds the volume of this giant sequoia. The General Sherman Tree owes its immense size not to great age (many other sequoias are older) but rather to its very rapid growth rate. For over two thousand years this tree has survived numerous fires, climatic change and even the coming of modern man. Today it remains not only the world's largest living thing, but also one of the fastest growing.

Estimated Age	2300-2700 Years
Estimated Weight of Trunk	1385 t. (1256 m.t.)
Height Above Base	274.9 ft.(83.8 m.)
Circumference at Ground	102.6 ft. (31.3 m.)
Maximum Diameter at Base	36.5 ft. (11.1 m.)
Diameter 60 ft. Above Ground	17.5 ft. (5.3 m.)
Diameter 180 ft. Above Ground	14.0 ft. (4.3 m.)
Diameter of Largest Branch	6.8 ft. (2.1 m.)
Height of First Large Branch	130.0 ft. (39.6 m.)
Volume of Trunk	52,500 cu. ft. (1,486.6 cu.m.)

In 1926, President Calvin Coolidge designated the General Grant as the Nation's Christmas Tree. Hundreds of people gather here every December for a brief Christmas service.

BELOW: trout fishing at Roaring River Falls.
RIGHT: General's Highway.

groves, there are no protective railings standing around the trunks – it's a tree hugger's paradise.

Continue west on the Generals Highway, bypassing the intersection of Highway 180. Drive on to **Grant Grove**, where you'll find a visitor center; half a mile (1km) beyond, a left turn takes you down a hillside to the famed **General Grant Tree** . Over 267ft (81 meters) tall and 107ft (33 meters) around, it's the third largest in the world. For more adventurous drivers, a steep, narrow road leads 2½ miles (4km) to **Panoramic Point**. A quarter-mile trail leads to the overlook with sweeping vistas of the surrounding peaks.

The 30 miles (48km) between Grant Grove and Cedar Grove (across Sequoia National Forest) are officially designated a National Scenic Byway and constitute one of the most spectacular drives in the West. The road plummets nearly 4,500ft (1,370 meters) to the depths of the majestic **Kings Canyon** . In the upper elevations, you'll pass stumps of sequoias felled by loggers a century ago – a reminder

of the destructive practices that led to the founding of the parks. Beyond, the highway provides sweeping views of the country's deepest canyons.

The road re-enters Kings Canyon National Park and leads to **Cedar Grove** in the dramatic, glacially-shaped Kings Canyon where you'll find a ranger station, a general store, a restaurant, campgrounds, and lodging (summer only). The east end of the canyon offers a wide range of hiking trails from easy to extreme.

A stop at **Roaring River Falls** is at the top of most visitors' lists. A pleasant quarter-mile stroll, the falls are worth at least a 30-minute visit and numerous photographs. A mile (1.6km) up the road, the self-guiding **Cedar Grove Motor Nature Trail** runs down the north side of the river, offering a less strenuous way to enjoy Kings Canyon.

Roads End lies another 3 miles (5km) up the canyon. At **Zumwalt Meadow**, a self-guiding trail leads to the opposite bank of the Kings River over a suspension bridge. For the meek mountaineer, the popular **Mist Falls Trail** is an 8-mile (13km) round-trip along a fork of the majestic Kings River; the trail climbs 800 vertical feet (244 meters) in 4 miles (6km). **Paradise Valley** , about another half-mile up the trail, is a lovely spot for a picnic or an afternoon stroll.

Both Sequoia and Kings Canyon national parks offer a variety of winter activities, and travelers who are willing to brave the snow and chilly temperatures will be able to appreciate the parks in an entirely different light. Skiing or snowshoeing among the big trees, for example, is magical, especially after a fresh snowfall, when sounds are muffled by a trackless white blanket.

There's more rugged mountain terrain at **Pinnacles National Monument** , another Californian treasure, where spire-like rock formations up to 1,200ft (366 meters) high rise dramatically above the smooth contours of the surrounding countryside. ❑

THE CALIFORNIAN DESERT

Spectacular and varied scenery, rare and curious wildlife, complex geology, undisturbed wilderness, sites of cultural and historic interest... the desert is not dull

The California desert is actually the meeting place of three individual deserts: the Mojave, the Sonoran, and the Great Basin. Sprawling across 39,000 sq miles (101,000 sq km) under the rain shadow of the Sierra Nevada and San Bernardino Mountains, it is the hottest, driest place in North America, with summer temperatures exceeding 115°F (46°C).

In October 1994, the California Desert Protection Act created three federal parks here: **Death Valley National Park ❾**, **Joshua Tree National Park ❿**, and **Mojave National Preserve ⓫**. Although harsh and unrelenting, this is nonetheless a land of subtle – almost surreal – beauty and a surprising variety of life.

Because of extreme heat and aridity, desert wildlife is largely nocturnal. At dusk, when temperatures drop, the acute silence of day is broken by the distant yapping of a coyote, the hooting of a great horned owl, or the croaking of tree frogs hidden in secret springs.

Many animals avoid the hottest part of the day by burrowing underground or seeking shade under rocks and plants. Some estivate (become dormant) for the entire summer or during droughts. Others, like the kangaroo rat, produce water metabolically from high-carbohydrate seeds. A few

species, such as mourning doves and California quail, can tolerate extraordinary levels of dehydration.

Other animals that have adapted to the harsh desert environment include roadrunners, peregrine falcons, and kit foxes. Bobcats, bighorn sheep, and desert tortoises, a protected species, are more rarely seen.

Ocotillo, creosote bush, and other desert plants slow evaporation by reducing the size of their leaves or dropping them entirely during the driest part of the year. Many desert

Main attractions

DEATH VALLEY NATIONAL PARK
ZABRISKIE POINT
DANTES VIEW
DEVILS GOLF COURSE
ARTISTS DRIVE
BADWATER
SCOTTY'S CASTLE
THE RACETRACK
UBEHEBE CRATER
JOSHUA TREE NATIONAL PARK
WONDERLAND OF ROCKS
KEYS VIEW
MOJAVE NATIONAL PRESERVE
MITCHELL CAVERNS
DESERT STUDIES CENTER
MOJAVE CINDER CONES NATIONAL
  NATURAL LANDMARK
KELSO DUNES

PRECEDING PAGES: Route 66, Amboy.
LEFT: Dante's View. **RIGHT:** Zabriskie Point, Death Valley.

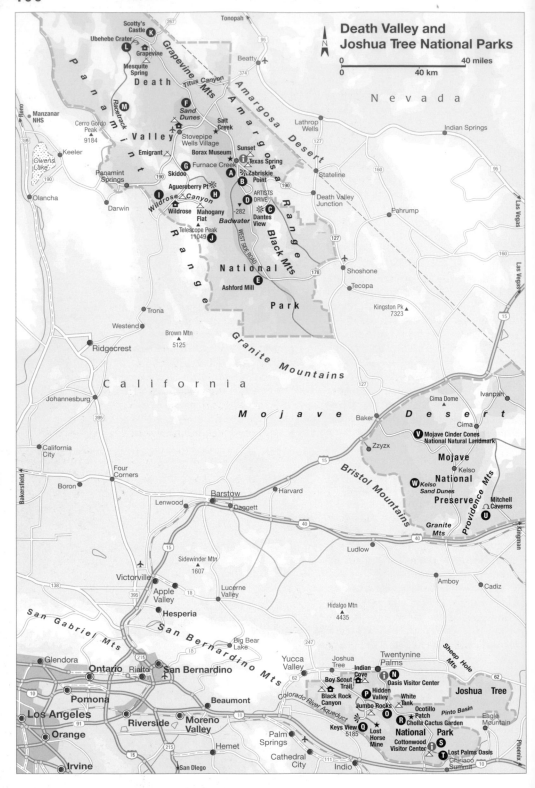

Death Valley and Joshua Tree National Parks

N

| 0 | | 40 miles |
| 0 | | 40 km |

Nevada

Tonopah

Beatty

Scotty's Castle **K**
Ubehebe Crater **L**
Grapevine
Mesquite Spring

Death

Sand Dunes **F**
Salt Creek
Stovepipe Wells Village
Borax Museum
Emigrant
Furnace Creek **A**
Skidoo **G**
Aguereberry Pt **H**
Wildrose **I**
Mahogany Flat
Telescope Peak 11049 **J**

Sunset
Texas Spring
Zabriskie Point **B**
ARTISTS DRIVE
Dantes View **C**
Badwater **D**
-282

Valley

Manzanar NHS
Cerro Gordo Peak 9184
Reno
Racetrack **M**
Keeler
Owens Lake
190
395
Olancha
Panamint Springs
Darwin
Wildrose Canyon

Panamint

Range

Ashford Mill **E**

National

Park

Lathrop Wells
Indian Springs
Stateline
Death Valley Junction
Pahrump
Shoshone
Tecopa
Kingston Pk 7323

Amargosa Desert

Amargosa Range

Black Mts

Las Vegas

Trona
Westend
Brown Mtn 5125
Ridgecrest
Johannesburg
California City
Four Corners
Boron
Bakersfield

Granite Mountains

California

Mojave **Desert**

Baker
Zzyzx
Cima Dome
Cima
Ivanpah

V Mojave Cinder Cones National Natural Landmark

Mojave

Kelso

National

W Kelso Sand Dunes

Preserve

Granite Mts
Mitchell Caverns **U**
Providence Mts
Kingman

Lenwood
Barstow
Harvard
Daggett
Ludlow
Amboy
Cadiz

Bristol Mountains

Sidewinder Mtn 1607
Victorville
Apple Valley
Lucerne Valley
Hesperia

Hidalgo Mtn 4435

San Gabriel Mts

San Bernardino Mts

Big Bear Lake
Glendora
Ontario
Rialto
San Bernardino
Pomona
Beaumont
Los Angeles
Riverside
Moreno Valley
Orange
Hemet
Irvine
San Diego
Palm Springs
Cathedral City
Indio

Yucca Valley
Joshua Tree
Twentynine Palms
Indian Cove
Boy Scout Trail
Black Rock Canyon
Hidden Valley **P**
Jumbo Rocks
Keys View **Q** 5185
Lost Horse Mine
Cottonwood Visitor Center
Oasis Visitor Center **O**
White Tank
Ocotillo Patch
Cholla Cactus Garden **R**
Pinto Basin
Eagle Mountain

Joshua Tree

National

Park

Colorado River Aqueduct

Sheep Hole Mts

Lost Palms Oasis **T**
Chiriaco Summit

Phoenix

plants, such as Joshua trees, have thick, waxy leaves to impede water loss. The sponge-like tissues of cactus soak up moisture during brief downpours.

Most desert wildflowers – such as locoweed, purple lupine, and desert primrose – bide their time during dry spells and then explode into bloom after a good soaking, sometimes lasting only a few days before drying out. Juniper, pinyon, and bristlecone pines stand in the higher elevations; palm trees, cottonwoods, and mesquite crowd the few oases – prime places for viewing wildlife.

Death Valley National Park

A portion of the Mojave Desert, Death Valley is a 140-mile (225km) trough set between steep mountain walls of virtually naked rock. The shallow Pleistocene lake that once filled the valley slowly evaporated, leaving behind salt-pans, cracked mudflats and undulating dunes. To the west, the deeply eroded walls of the Panamint Range tower to an elevation of 11,000ft (3,350 meters), while, to the east, the Amargosa Range reaches 8,000ft (2,440 meters).

Furnace Creek Ⓐ is the best place to start a tour. Furnace Creek Visitor Center and the nearby **Borax Museum** (daily, 8am–5pm) supply background information on the area's human and natural history, and rangers can advise you on camping, hiking, and scheduled tours. If you plan to stay for a few days, the Mediterranean-style **Furnace Creek Inn** (reservations required well in advance) is an oasis of creature comforts with fine dining, shopping, swimming, golfing, and more.

You can get your first good overview of Death Valley about 3 miles (5km) southeast on Highway 190 at **Zabriskie Point** Ⓑ, which overlooks a multihued panorama of sun-baked peaks and ridges. About a mile (1.6km) farther south, an unpaved road loops through the wrinkled landscape and subtle colors of **Twenty Mule Team Canyon**, named after the wagon teams that once hauled ore through moun-

tain passes. Continue on Highway 190 to the 13-mile (21km) spur road to **Dantes View** Ⓒ, a 5,475ft (1,669-meter) perch overlooking the salt flats at Badwater, which, at 282ft (86 meters) below sea level, is the lowest spot in the United States.

Double back toward Furnace Creek and then head south on Highway 178, stopping for an easy mile-long walk through colorful layered formations along the **Golden Canyon Trail**. Pick up the one-way **Artists Drive** Ⓓ loop about 7 miles (11km) farther south; the short, winding drive takes you through a rainbow region of colored rocks eroded from the lake-bed over thousands of years. Continuing south on Highway 178, you'll pass a short dirt road to **Devils Golf Course**, a vast expanse of knobby salt formations rising from the earth.

Just beyond, a spur road on the left leads to the **Natural Bridge Canyon Trail**, a mile long (1.5km) walk to a 50ft (15-meter) -high stone bridge carved by water gushing over the dry falls at the end of the trail.

The highway continues south

To the west of Death Valley National Park, on Highway 395, is Manzanar National Historic Site, which commemorates the internment of Japanese-Americans in World War II.

BELOW:
Furnace Creek.

through Badwater and eventually swings west into the **Black Mountains** at **Ashford Mill** ⓔ, where the ruins of an old gold-processing operation are scattered across the stark landscape. There are hundreds of abandoned mining sites all over the park; many have not yet been made safe for visitors. Never enter mine shafts or abandoned buildings without conferring with park rangers.

Return to Furnace Creek Visitor Center and head north on Highway 190 to the **Harmony Borax Works Interpretive Trail**, where you can explore the remains of a cleanser-processing plant dating to the 1880s. About 10 miles (16km) farther north, the short and easy **Salt Creek Interpretive Trail** explains the life history of the endangered pupfish, a tiny relict species found in only a few locations in the West. It is about another 5 miles (8km) on Highway 190 to the shifting patterns of the **Sand Dunes** ⓕ, where giant piles of wind-scoured quartz grains, some as high as 80ft (24 meters), are continually sculpted by the wind.

You can stop for gas, food, and lodg-ing at **Stovepipe Wells Village** and then make a long, winding side trip through Emigrant Canyon, which, like most roads in the park, was once used by miners to haul ore and equipment. Dirt spur roads (four-wheel drive recommended) lead to **Skidoo** ⓖ ghost town and to 6,433ft (1,961-meter) **Aguereberry Point** ⓗ. The main road finally winds through **Wildrose Canyon** ⓘ, where a row of 30ft (9-meter) beehive-shaped kilns was once used to make charcoal for silver smelters across the Panamint Valley. You can start two long, strenuous hikes from this area. The 9-mile (14km), round-trip Wildrose Peak Trail climbs through pinyon and juniper forest to spectacular views at the 9,064ft (2,763-meter) summit.

Starting at Mahogany Flat Campground, **Telescope Peak Trail** (you can expect snow from October to April) makes a rough 3,000ft (910-meter) climb over 7 miles (11km) before reaching the ancient bristlecone pines at the summit. At 11,049ft (3,368 meters), **Telescope Peak** ⓙ is the highest point in the park and simultaneously offers magnificent views of

both Badwater, the lowest point in the country, and 14,495ft (4,418-meter) **Mount Whitney**, the highest peak in the contiguous United States.

Scotty's Castle

Finally, you'll find Death Valley's most popular attraction, **Scotty's Castle** Ⓚ, in the far north of the park, about 45 miles (72km) from Stovepipe Wells Village. Scotty's Castle is a magnificent, 25-room, Spanish-style villa that was started as a retreat in 1922 by Albert M. Johnson, a Chicago millionaire. It was looked after and later occupied by Johnson's unlikely friend, a former prospector, cowboy, mule driver, tale-spinner, and self-promoter extraordinaire by the name of Walter Scott – otherwise known as Death Valley Scotty. The interior, still decorated with fine art and furnishings, is a virtual chronicle of pre-Depression opulence. Tours are given hourly in season. About 8 miles (13km) away, the gaping maw of **Ubehebe Crater** Ⓛ – about a half-mile (1km) across and 500ft (150 meters) deep – was blasted out of the earth's crust several thousand years ago by a volcanic eruption. From Ubehebe Crater, it's a 25-mile (40km) drive on a rough dirt road (four-wheel drive recommended) to the **Racetrack** Ⓜ, where rocks seem to move across the *playa* on their own power. (Geologists think the rocks are actually blown by high winds across a fine layer of ice or slippery clay.)

Because of the high temperatures, hiking in lowlands during summer can be extremely dangerous. Remember to bring at least a gallon (4 liters) of water per person per day – more if possible – and watch for flash floods while hiking in canyon bottoms.

Joshua Tree National Park

Explorer John C. Frémont happened upon a Joshua tree in 1844 and called it "the most repulsive tree in the vegetable kingdom." But, to a colony of California Mormons journeying to Utah, the tree's outstretched branches resembled arms beckoning them across the desert to the promised land. The tufts of shaggy leaves reminded them of the beard of an Old Testament patriarch; they named the tree – a member of the yucca family – after Joshua, who led the Israelites into the land of Canaan.

Established as a national monument in 1936, and a Biosphere Reserve in 1984, it became a national park, along with Death Valley, in 1994. It not only preserves a portion of the Mojave Desert's Joshua tree forest but several long fingers of the Sonoran Desert that penetrate the lower valleys. More than 90 percent of the park is classified as wilderness, but two paved roads and several dirt roads provide access to some of the most scenic areas.

In more verdant times, one of the Southwest's earliest inhabitants, Pinto Man, lived here, hunting and gathering along a slow-moving river that ran through the now dry Pinto Basin. Later Indians traveled through this area in tune with harvests of pinyon nuts, acorns, and cactus fruit, leaving behind rock paintings and pottery ollas as reminders of their passing.

TIP

There are costumed living history tours of Scotty's Castle daily 9am–5pm. Tickets are sold at the Castle on the day of the tour on a first-come, first-served basis (maximum 19 people per tour).

The Keys Ranch

The California desert has always attracted rugged individualists. Between 1867 and 1977, hard-working families moved here, determined to carve out a life for themselves on lands offered for free to homesteaders (until 1936 in the future Joshua Tree National Park) in return for improvements.

William Keys and his wife Frances came to the area to try their hand at mining, cattle ranching, and farming. The couple homesteaded a rocky canyon in a remote area of Joshua Tree and over 60 years raised five children and built up their ranch. Now part of the park, the ranch house, school house, store, and workshop still stand; the orchard has been replanted; and the grounds are full of the cars, trucks, mining equipment, and spare parts that are a part of the ranch history. Guided tours of the property lasting 90 minutes are led by rangers in forties costumes daily, between October and May. Group size is restricted to 25. Be sure to call and reserve ahead of your visit.

To find the ranch, pass the entrance to Hidden Valley Campground, turn left at the Y-intersection, then follow the road for approximately 2 miles (3.5km) to the locked gate. Your guide will meet you there. Please arrive 15 minutes before the tour starts. For information and reservations, call (760) 367-5555.

The mysterious moving rocks at Racetrack, Death Valley.

BELOW: the distinctive shape of the Joshua tree.

In the late 1800s, explorers, cattlemen, and miners came to the desert. They built dams to create water tanks and dug up and tunneled the earth in search of gold. They are gone now, and left behind are their remnants, the Lost Horse and Desert Queen mines and the Desert Queen Ranch. In the 1930s, homesteaders came seeking free land and the chance to start new lives. Today, many people visit the park's 790,000 acres (320,000 hectares) seeking clear skies and clean air, and the tranquility and beauty that only deserts offer.

Two large desert ecosystems, their characteristics determined largely by elevation, come together at Joshua Tree. Below about 3,000ft (900 meters), the Colorado Desert (a subdivision of the Sonoran) encompasses the eastern part of the park and contains natural gardens of creosote bush, ocotillo, and cholla cactus. The higher, moister, and slightly cooler Mojave Desert is the signature habitat of the Joshua tree. The western part of the park contains dense stands of Joshua trees, and also some of the most interesting geological displays in California's deserts. In addition, five oases of fan palms dot the park, indicating those few areas where water occurs naturally and where wildlife abounds.

Geologists' heaven

Entering from the north, stop first at **Oasis Visitor Center N** in Twentynine Palms, which has exhibits explaining the natural and cultural history of the region and books and maps available for sale. From the visitor center, follow the park road about 8 miles (13km) to a fork in the road and bear right. The road swings through Queen Valley and Lost Horse Valley, passing the fantastic granite formations of **Jumbo Rocks O**, **Hidden Valley P** (a legendary cattle rustler's hideout), and **Wonderland of Rocks** – favorite areas for rock climbers, who can often be seen scaling boulders.

For a couple of interesting side trips, take a left on the **Geology Tour Road** about a half-mile (1km) past the Jumbo Rocks Campground. The self-guiding tour is 18 miles (29km) long on a rough dirt road into some of the park's most fascinating terrain (four-

wheel drive is recommended). A right turn off the main road into Queen Valley leads to dirt roads that lace through boulders and Joshua trees. A second left off the main road just past the Ryan Campground takes you to 5,185ft (1,580-meter) **Keys View Q** in the **Little San Bernardino Mountains** where, on a clear day, you can see the Salton Sea and Coachella Valley.

Short nature trails at Hidden Valley, Barker Dam, Cap Rock, Skull Rock, and elsewhere introduce visitors to the fragile desert ecology and traces of early human habitation. Longer trips include the 3-mile (5km) round-trip to the top of 4,324ft (1,318-meter) **Ryan Mountain**, the 4-mile (6km) round trip to the ruins of **Lost Horse Mine**, and the 16 mile (26km) round-trip **Boy Scout Trail** through the stunning Wonderland of Rocks.

Return to the fork in the road and head south. As the road descends, you enter the hotter, drier **Colorado Desert**, scattered with a sparse growth of teddy-bear cholla, spidery ocotillo, creosote bush, and smoke trees. You can take a short walk through some of the area's characteristic vegetation at the **Cholla Cactus Garden R** and, about 2 miles (3km) farther along, the Ocotillo Patch. About 15 miles (24km) farther down, you'll reach another small oasis – Cottonwood Spring – and the **Cottonwood Visitor Center S**.

A fairly taxing trail (7½ miles/12km round-trip) leads from the nearby campground to **Lost Palms Oasis T**, the largest in the park and a great place for spotting seldom-seen wildlife like bighorn sheep. You can make a 3-mile (5km) round-trip to **Mastodon Peak** from the campground, too. The views up here are superb – an excellent way to end the day.

Canyons, caverns, and cinder cones

Established in 1994, the 1.6-million-acre (650,000-hectare) **Mojave National Preserve** encompasses one of the most diverse desert environments in the world, dominated by varied crags of limestone, dolomite, rhyolite, and granite, glistening salt flats, coal-black lava flows, tawny dunes, and big, blue sky.

TIP

When exploring the desert, watch where you put your hands and feet, especially in summer when snakes are active.

BELOW: hiking the Boy Scout Trail.
RIGHT: Skull Rock.

Several paved and unpaved roads crisscross the preserve. On the eastern side, Ivanpah-Lanfair Road is one of the best places to see the threatened desert tortoise, especially in the spring. The road (mostly unpaved) passes abandoned mines in the **New York Mountains**, named for their skyscraper turrets, home to desert bighorn sheep.

Farther west, Essex-Black Canyon Road leads from Interstate 40 to the Providence Mountains, which contain **Mitchell Caverns ⓤ**, an intricate network of some 40,000 limestone caves. Ranger-led tours of the caverns are conducted daily from mid-September to mid-June. The self-guiding, half-mile Mary Beal Nature Trail begins near the visitor center. Black Canyon Road runs north through the weird, volcanic landscapes of Hole-in-the-Wall and Wild Horse Mesa and then into the pinyon-juniper woodlands of Mid Hills. At dusk, watch for the black-tailed jackrabbit.

Any place with a name like **Zzyzx** (pronounced *zizz-ex*) deserves a visit. Take I-15 about 60 miles (97km) east of Barstow and then drive south 4

miles (6km) along the shore of **Soda Lake** (usually dry) to the **Desert Studies Center**. During the 1940s and 1950s, this old cavalry outpost site was a health club run by Dr Curtis Springer. Rather eccentric, the good doctor apparently wanted the last word on everything – hence Zzyzx. In 1976, the resort was turned into a university research station. A spring-fed pond and nearby marshes shelter the rare Saratoga Spring pupfish and Mojave tui chub.

"Singing dunes"

A few miles farther east, Kelbaker Road threads through a desolate area of cinder cones and lava beds now designated as **Mojave Cinder Cones National Natural Landmark ⓥ**. Stop at Kelso, site of the grand, Spanish-style, Union Pacific Railroad depot built in 1924. Farther along, you'll pass the 600ft (183-meter) -high **Kelso Sand Dunes ⓦ**, third-highest dune system in the country and one of the so-called "singing dunes" that hum or boom when in motion. The road then climbs through a boulder-choked pass separating the Granite and Providence mountains and descends toward Interstate 40. Double back to Kelso and turn right onto Kelso-Cima Road, which curves northward past **Cima Dome**, a gently sloping geologic "blister" of granite-like monzonite that covers 75 sq miles (194 sq km). You'll also pass one of the finest Joshua tree forests in California.

Along the way, you'll cross the **Mojave Road**, a 140-mile (225km) Indian trade route that connected the Colorado River with Camp Cady on the lower Mojave River. It was later used by the Spanish priest Francisco Garces, mountain men such as Jedediah Smith, merchants, settlers, and the United States mail. Portions of the trail are still passable by four-wheel drive or on foot. Adventurous travelers can still visit the crumbling ruins of **Fort Piute**, built in 1867 to protect mail wagons. ❑

BELOW: Kelso Sand Dunes.

Shooting Nature

Photography is a great way to connect with the wild beauty of the national parks, but get to know your camera first

The world's first national park, Yellowstone, was set aside in 1872 largely as a result of the breathtaking photographs presented to Congress by the Hayden Survey. Now, millions of tourists tote cameras into the parks to shoot family pictures, landscapes, sunsets, and glimpses of wildlife. No matter what your intentions or level of expertise, photography is a wonderful way of connecting with the beauty and grandeur of America's national parks.

Keep a few basic tips in mind. First, know your camera. Don't borrow or buy a new camera the day before your trip and expect to be proficient with it right away. Experiment with different settings and get familiar with the camera's various functions. Check the batteries before you leave home. Nothing is more disappointing than missing that long-awaited eruption of Old Faithful or a chance encounter with wildlife.

Keep it simple

For most amateur photographers, a lot of complicated equipment isn't necessary. A simple, inexpensive camera is all you need. If you have an adjustable camera, learn a little about depth of field. In short, the smaller apertures (lens openings f8, f11, and f16) give the greatest depth of field. They allow objects in the foreground and background to appear sharp in the picture, even if they don't look sharp through the viewfinder.

If you're thinking about additional equipment, consider a polarizing filter. It helps to darken the sky and makes the clouds look more distinct. It also reduces glare from reflective surfaces such as leaves and water.

A tripod is always a good investment. Blurry pictures are more often caused by camera shake than by poor focus. A telephoto lens will come in handy, too, especially if you want to photograph wildlife. A zoom lens that is 80mm to 200mm or 75mm to 300mm will do the trick in most cases.

RIGHT: you will be spoilt for choice with photographic locations.

Remember, light is a photographer's true medium. You're not taking a picture of an object but the light that reflects off that object. Study the colors of sunset and sunrise. Find out exactly when the sun and moon rise and set, as well as their positions on the horizon.

Scout out locations ahead of time and try to anticipate how the light will fall on your subject. Generally speaking, the "magic hours" of dawn and dusk cast a warm glow on the landscape. Bright sunlight tends to cast dark, well-defined shadows, which often make rather unflattering portraits. Use the even light of overcast skies to shoot close-ups of plants, flowers, and other natural elements.

Eyes wide open

Ask rangers about the best places to photograph wildlife. Be patient. As you learn more about an animal's behavior, you'll be in a better position to anticipate a good shot. And don't try to get too close: crowding most animals will only scare them away. Never try to sneak up on animals or use food to lure them closer.

Experiment with various shutter speeds, lenses, filters, and angles. Use photography as a gateway to the natural world. Keep your eyes open, while still enjoying the parks, and bring home memories to share with others. ❑

FLOWERING AGAINST ALL THE ODDS

The plants that grow in the USA's western deserts are unlike those in more temperate zones. They need to be, to survive in this hostile environment

North America has four major deserts: the Great Basin, the Mojave, the Chihuahuan, and the Sonoran. Each is so distinctive that, if a great whirlwind picked you up, spun you around and sat you down in the middle of any one of them, you could know immediately where you were by the "indicator" plants you saw.

The Great Basin Desert's indicator is big sagebrush; the Mojave's is the Joshua tree; the Chihuahuan features agave *lechuguilla*; and, in the Sonoran, it is the *saguaro*. The Great Basin is cool, the others are warm. But they do have one thing in common: all receive 10ins (25cm) or less of precipitation a year, resulting in air so dry that you may see billowing cumulus clouds trailing dark curtains of rain that evaporates before it reaches the ground.

Because deserts generally lack cloud cover, temperatures during a 24-hour period may vary widely, perhaps from 60°F (16°C) at dawn to 100°F (38°C) at mid-afternoon. During the long, hot summers, most desert animals venture out after things begin to cool down. Many plants, too, open their blossoms in the cool of the evening. These night-blooming plants usually have white or pale blooms, each like a small moon beckoning pollinators.

One such plant is the *datura* which thrives in all four deserts. Its 6in (15cm) flowers are gorgeous, but every part of the plant is poisonous in the extreme.

ABOVE: Cacti, like this hedgehog cactus, have forsaken leaves for spines, which amazingly provide up to 80 percent shade from the sun for the plant's growth tips.

BELOW: Most of the year the ocotillo appears dead and lifeless until a burst of rainfall transforms it into a leafy bush with crimson blooms.

SURVIVAL TACTICS IN THE DESERT

The components of desert plants create a suite of arid-land efficiency, each doing its part to make the best of precious moisture. Root systems are either shallow and wide-spreading to benefit from the briefest rains, or long enough to reach moist deep soil. Hairy leaves reflect away sunlight and heat; leaves with waxy coatings minimize evaporation. Green bark on stems and trunks aids photosynthesis and seals in moisture.

Some desert plants evade harsh circumstances by remaining alive but dormant until moisture signals that it is safe to send up new growth. Seeds of annuals grow rapidly after rain, complete their life cycle quickly and die (or escape), leaving new seeds to carry on.

An agave spends 15 years or more accumulating enough nourishment to bloom. Eventually, it sends up a flower stalk, which can grow roughly 2½in (6cm) per day and reach 5–15ft (1.5–4.6 meters) high.

After flowering, the plant, entirely depleted, will die, but it will have produced thousands of seeds.

ABOVE: The pollen from a Saguaro cactus blossom is heavy and sticky and cannot be borne on the wind. Bats, birds and insects must carry it from one plant to another.

LEFT: The blossom of the spiny prickly pear cactus survives for just one day.

CHANNEL ISLANDS

Although these islands are tantalizingly close to the Southern California coast, their isolation has provided a unique and undeveloped environment

One of America's richest national parks consists of five islands – Santa Barbara, Anacapa, Santa Cruz, Santa Rosa, and San Miguel – off the coast of Southern California. Whales. Dolphins. Sea lions. Twenty-five species of shark. Birds of all kinds that nest in its cliffs. People find it remarkable that a wilderness so remote and ecologically significant as this tiny archipelago should endure so close to the Southern California megalopolis. **Channel Islands National Park ⑫** is such an exceptional place, in fact, it is now an International Biosphere Reserve.

When the mist lifts from the sea, the park's mirage-like profile is a focal point for the people of Santa Barbara, across the channel, who take a proprietary view of the place. The larger islands offer serenity for backpackers who choose to explore them, but unrelenting winds, lack of fresh water, and penetrating spells of heat or cold can make exploration a challenge.

Created in 1980, the park has been spared mammoth crowds largely because you can't get there by car. Transportation from the mainland is via commercial boat or chartered flight in a small plane that passes over Anacapa and Santa Cruz islands and lands at an airfield on Santa Rosa. Visitation is, however, increasing. In 2009, 300,000 people visited the islands.

The upwelling of cold sea currents from the northern Pacific combines here with tropical waters from the south to create ideal conditions for marine life, from microscopic plankton to the endangered blue whale. The Santa Barbara Channel serves as a vital migration corridor for marine animals, ranging from whales to sea lions. Until overharvesting took its toll, the coves of the Channel Islands produced vast quantities of sea anemone, sea urchins, and abalone, which are central to the diet of threatened sea otters.

Main attractions
ELEPHANT SEAL COVE AND SEA LION ROOKERY (SANTA BARBARA ISLAND)
OLD LIGHTHOUSE (EAST ANACAPA ISLAND)
PAINTED CAVE (SANTA CRUZ ISLAND)
SCORPION RANCH VISITOR CENTER (SANTA CRUZ ISLAND)
WATER CANYON BEACH TRAIL (SANTA ROSA ISLAND)
POINT BENNETT TRAIL (SAN MIGUEL ISLAND)
CUYLER'S HARBOR BEACH (SAN MIGUEL ISLAND)

LEFT: Channel Islands. **RIGHT:** the lighthouse on Anacapa Island.

Santa Barbara and Anacapa

To visit the islands, start at park headquarters on Spinnaker Drive at the harbor in **Ventura**. The visitor center will acquaint you with the islands' cultural and natural history. It also stocks several useful books and a detailed trail map. Island Packers Cruises, offering boat and hiking tours of the park, and Channel Islands Aviation, offering plane trips to Santa Rosa Island, are official park concessionaires.

Santa Barbara, situated 52 miles (84km) south of Ventura, is often thought of as the "lost Channel Island" because it drifts apart from the others. Camping is allowed with advance reservations (three-night minimum, Fri–Sun). A network of hiking routes totaling just over 5 miles (8km) leads to scenic vistas, Signal Peak, and views of an elephant seal cove and sea lion rookery.

Santa Barbara provides critical refuge for elephant seals in winter and California sea lions in spring. It also yields excellent birdwatching opportunities, including, among others, American kestrels, Xantus murrelets, horned larks, brown pelicans, and barn owls.

After the winter rains, grasses sprouting from island rock are covered with magnificent yellow coreopsis, a tree with giant daisy-like blossoms, that can climb up to 10ft (3 meters) high.

To the northwest, the land forms of **Anacapa** mark a dramatic entrance to the Channel Islands archipelago. Austere and brooding, Anacapa gets its name from the Chumash Indian word "Eneepah," which means deception or mirage. Appropriately, it's not one island but three, 5 miles (8km) long. The smallest and most visited of the archipelago is **East Anacapa**.

These isles, located 13 miles (21km) from Ventura Harbor, are prime territory for scuba diving and snorkeling among the intertidal pools. The coves are rich with marine life and nourished by forests of kelp that attract sea otters, seals, crustaceans, and sea anemone, as well as whales. The sole campground is on East Anacapa where there's a 1½-mile (2.4km) nature trail. A favorite destination is the **old lighthouse**. Rangers here lead free nature tours. Above **West Anacapa**, which is closed to visitors, endangered brown pelicans ride the air currents and coast into their rookeries with freshly caught fish.

Santa Cruz and Santa Rosa

Long, arid, and mountainous, Santa Cruz Island, the biggest island in the park, is blessed with a variety of sites, many, unfortunately, out of bounds. One of them, **Painted Cave**, is a cavern accessible only by boat and is a popular side trip for kayakers. Snaking in and out of the tide pools, harbor seals and sea otters are frequent visitors. Ashore, there are many lizards and birds.

Around 76 percent of **Santa Cruz** is owned by The Nature Conservancy (TNC), a private conservation organization, which offers day hikes and overnight camping permits to small groups of backpackers and kayakers. To visit TNC lands on Santa Cruz, get permission from the organization in advance, or show up at Santa Barbara Museum of Natural History. The museum and

BELOW: a male Californian quail.

Island Packers will coordinate your itinerary and tell you which hiking trails and campgrounds are open.

The National Park Service oversees the eastern end of the island, an area that now sees 50,000 visitors a year, making it the most visited area in the islands. The new **Scorpion Ranch Visitor Center**, opened in April 2009, orients visitors to the island's rich natural and cultural history. Located in an 1866 ranch house, it offers exhibits on the Chumash Indians and marine life. Next door is a bakery originally used by the island's former French and Italian workers to bake bread, but now home to the endangered Townsend's big-ear bat.

Second largest island in the chain, **Santa Rosa** measures 15 miles (24km) long and 10 miles (16km) wide, enough terrain for a multi-day excursion, even though most visitors spend only an afternoon. Following the winter rainy season, the highlands of Santa Rosa turn luminous with blooming wildflowers. Moisture brings a vernal rejuvenation. This mountainous island is crisscrossed by a series of dirt roads that offer a direct overland connection between the ranger station at **Bechers Bay** and **Johnsons Lee** near an abandoned military base on the other side of the island. Among the eight hiking trails is the easy 2-mile (3.2km) **Water Canyon Beach Trail**, which continues another 6 miles (9.6km) through Water Canyon, and 9-mile (14.5km) **Lobo Canyon**, a strenuous climb through a scenic canyon for fine coastal views.

The island can be an inhospitable outpost in late summer when the dry Santa Ana winds desiccate the landscape, but the island greens up between late March and early July. Although the highest named summit, **Soledad Peak**, climbs only 1,574ft (480 meters), the jutting, rounded slope creates a dramatic silhouette against the sky. An unnamed peak about a mile to the west is the tallest point at 1,589ft (484 meters).

Until the early 19th century, Santa Rosa was home to the Chumash Indians, and remains of several villages are scattered across strategic promontories. Hundreds of abalone shell mounds have a ghostly presence. An impressive collection of Chumash artifacts is on permanent display at Santa Barbara Museum

The gray whales that pass through the Santa Barbara Channel are taking part in the longest migration of any mammal, from feeding areas in the Bering Sea to calving grounds off Mexico's Baja Peninsula – a round-trip of 12,500 miles (20,100km).

BELOW:
enjoying a nature cruise.

There are over 2,000 species of terrestrial plants and animals in the park – 145 of them unique to these islands and found nowhere else in the world.

of Natural History, but, remember, removing artifacts or natural objects from the islands is a federal crime.

For most of the 20th century, the island's endemic species have shared the mountainous *arroyos* with the elk and mule deer that were relocated here by private hunters, as well as cattle. The National Park Service reached an agreement with local ranchers to continue grazing their cattle here. Each year, the animals are brought to and from the mainland in an old wooden vessel, the *Vaquero*, that is the last of its kind. A private hunt of elk and deer takes place on the island between mid-August and mid-December annually. Some areas may be closed to hiking.

San Miguel

Pounded by heavy winds and rough seas, San Miguel Island is both the most difficult island to reach and the most enchanting. There is one campground here, limited to 30 people, so call park headquarters well in advance to reserve a site; a minimum stay of three nights is usually required. The island is widely recognized as a premier spot for view-

BELOW: Channel Islands Ranger Station.
RIGHT monument dedicated to Juan Rodríguez Cabrillo.

ing six species of seals and sea lions at the **Point Bennett** cliffs. To get there, it is necessary to make a 15-mile (24km) round-trip from **Cuyler's Landing** with a ranger. **Cuyler's Harbor** beach, **Cabrillo monument**, and the **Lester Ranch** site, the latter two sites accessible via the **Nidever Canyon Trail**, are the only areas on the island that may be explored on your own.

A strange relic found on both San Miguel and Santa Rosa is the caliche forests, and there is one here, near the **Point Bennett Trail**. The branches of individual trees appear to be made of stone, but actually, the weird protrusions were created by minerals that made a cast around living bushes. When the plants died, the shells remained.

The nearest mainland national park unit to the Channel Islands is **Santa Monica Mountains National Recreation Area ⓭**, a beautiful landscape embracing both mountain and seashore within easy reach of LA. Farther south, on San Diego Bay, **Cabrillo National Monument ⓮** combines tide pools, coastal sage scrub, and historical sites. *See Travel Tips p. 370 for park details.* ❏

Cabrillo Monument

San Miguel is reputed to be the burial place of Juan Rodríguez Cabrillo, the Portuguese explorer who "discovered" California in 1542, after having been commissioned by the Viceroy of New Spain to lead an expedition up the Pacific coast in search of trade opportunities. Experts disagree on his fate. In her book *California's Channel Islands*, Marla Daily writes: "It is known that Cabrillo wintered at San Miguel Island in 1542, during which time he broke either an arm or a leg which later became infected. Knowing he was a dying man, Cabrillo turned his expedition over to his chief pilot Bartolomé Ferrer. On January 3, 1543, Cabrillo died as a result of his injury, and many say he was buried on the island." An honorary tombstone to Cabrillo sits at Cuyler's Harbor.

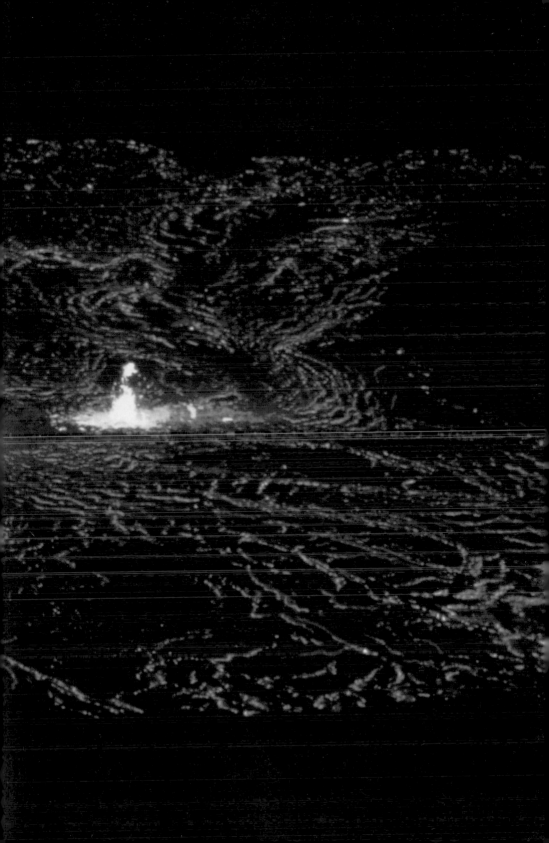

HAWAII AND AMERICAN SAMOA

America's Pacific island national parks contain landscapes that are found nowhere else in the country, from seething active volcanoes to ancient tropical rainforests

Kilauea, one of the world's only drive-up volcanoes, is the red-hot heart of **Hawaii Volcanoes National Park ❶**. Located on the island of Hawaii, or "the Big Island," it also happens to be the world's most active volcano, having erupted continually since January 1983. In its current rampage, Kilauea has added 491 acres (200 hectares) to the largest island in the Hawaiian chain. It has also destroyed more than 187 island structures, including the village of Kalapana, Wahaula Visitor Center, and the famous Black Sand Beach at Kaimu.

Hawaii Volcanoes National Park was founded in 1916 to protect the natural wonders of Kilauea and its fuming neighbor, **Mauna Loa** volcano. The 505-sq-mile (1,307-sq-km) preserve encompasses the summit calderas of both Kilauea and Mauna Loa (currently quiet) and sections of the **Kalapana Coast**, just down slope of Kilauea itself.

The composition of Hawaiian lava is such that eruptions are usually not as explosive as in other parts of the world. Consequently, when a Hawaiian volcano erupts, instead of heading for the nearest escape route, people tend to pack a picnic and head for the park to see the most spectacular fireworks on earth. On a Saturday night, crowds

can number in the thousands when Kilauea is really pumping. Park rangers are heroic in their efforts to help people see the eruption safely, often marking new walking trails several times a day as the lava changes course. A visit is like securing front-row seats at the dawn of creation.

The volcano appears most awesome at night, when the fires rage against the darkened sky. Right after sunset, there is an eerie rosy glow, almost celestial, as Hawaii continues to be born in the flames. The shoreline expands visibly

---

Main attractions

CHAIN OF CRATERS ROAD (HAWAII VOLCANOES)
JAGGAR MUSEUM (HAWAII VOLCANOES)
KILAUEA IKI TRAIL (HAWAII VOLCANOES)
KIPUKA TRAIL (HAWAII VOLCANOES)
MAUNA LOA SUMMIT TRAIL (HAWAII VOLCANOES)
HALEMAU'U TRAIL (HALEAKALA)
SLIDING SANDS TRAIL (HALEAKALA)
PIPIWAI TRAIL (HALEAKALA)
TAU ISLAND (BIRTHPLACE OF SAMOAN CULTURE)
OFU ISLAND CORAL SAND BEACH (SAMOA)
SNORKELING AMONG CORAL REEFS (SAMOA AND GUAM)

PRECEDING PAGES: red-hot Kilauea volcano. **LEFT:** Kilauea erupts. **RIGHT:** lava flows from Kilauea.

Remarkably, the ancient ruined temple of Wahaula Heiau on the Big Island was spared by the lava flow that destroyed the nearby visitor center. The lava went right up to the temple walls, parted and passed around it, leaving a locket of trees and old stone walls on the black bosom of the landscape.

as each wave of lava seethes into the sea. Towering billows of steam rise for miles along the cooking coast. In the most recent phase of Kilauea's eruption, lava has been flowing in blazing cascades down the side of the mountain. Motorists on **Chain of Craters Road** can sometimes see the great falls of fire from their car windows.

River of fire

Every visit to the park should begin at **Kilauea Visitor Center** (daily 7.45am– 4.45pm), inside the park entrance, where daily activities, such as free guided nature walks, are posted, along with the latest eruption information. Anyone planning an overnight back-country hike should register and pick up a free first-come, first-served permit, so rangers know where campers are in the event of an emergency.

Every hour on the hour, a film on the park and the volcanoes' most impressive eruptions is aired in the visitor center's theater. The best orientation, however, is the 11-mile (18km) spin around **Crater Rim Drive**, which skirts the huge steaming craters of

Kilauea Iki, Halemaumau and others.

Chain of Craters Road, which goes toward the coastal section of the park, is now a dead end, closed off by a 1995 lava flow. It is in this area, at Kamoamoa, that the rivers of fire are sometimes so close that people poke them with sticks, which instantly ignite. Unless rangers are present, however, it is best not to approach the active flows; they may also be moving beneath the earth's crust, which can collapse.

At the park's **Jaggar Museum** (daily 8.30am–7.30pm), on the lip of Kilauea's summit caldera, instruments are linked to the next-door **Hawaiian Volcano Observatory**, where scientists monitor Kilauea's every tremble.

At the museum, hands-on exhibits tell the fascinating story of volcanology and how Hawaii's islands were created by molten rock from beneath the earth, starting at least 70 million years ago. The museum overlook is the best place to view the current eruption that began March 11, 2008, in a new crater within Halemaùmaù crater.

Not only is the Big Island still growing, a new island is being formed off

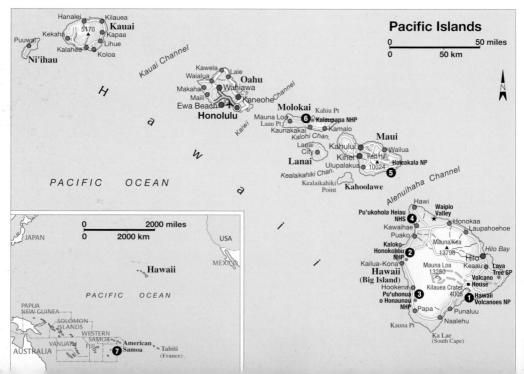

the coast, 15 miles (24km) southeast of the island. From the bowels of the earth, lava is being pumped out upon the ocean bed, where it solidifies, forming pillows and mounds. In about 250,000 years, the submarine volcano will be tall enough to break the surface of the waves and begin its long climb toward the sky – and Hawaii will have a new island: Loihi.

Science, however, has its limits. Exhibits at the Jaggar Museum acknowledge the ancient primal power of Pele, goddess of the volcano. She is considered to be responsible for the volcano's creative energy and its behavior. Many people say she still dwells in Halemaumau Crater, and there is always someone who claims to see her right before a major eruption. She is sometimes perceived as a beautiful lady dressed in red, with flowing hair the color of flames. Other times, she may take the form of an old woman walking a white dog.

Offerings of flowers, rocks, and *ti* leaves are left for her along park trails and at the edge of the crater. Anyone gathering *ohelo* berries, the cranberry-like fruit that grows at Kilauea, throws the first handful into the crater, for the fruit, like the crimson *ohia lehua* blossom, is sacred to Pele. In a modern twist to the Pele tales, it is claimed that the goddess has developed a taste for hooch – gin specifically – so that, too, is tossed into the volcanic stew.

Hope and devastation

Hawaii Volcanoes National Park is more than hellfire and brimstone, however. Even if the volcano were to take a break, the park would still be well worth a visit. "When people come to Kilauea, they want to see red – 'Where's the lava?' they ask," says park ranger Mardie Lane. "It's our job to help visitors understand not only the science of volcanoes but the Hawaiian culture, the native plants and wildlife that don't exist anywhere else on the planet. I'd like everyone who comes here to promise themselves, 'I will park my car and get out and walk.'"

The park offers unusual hiking trails, each revealing different facets of this utterly fascinating terrain. The 4-mile (6.4km) **Kilauea Iki Trail** descends

BELOW LEFT: Kilauea lighthouse. **BELOW:** flower offerings to Pele, the Hawaiian goddess of fire.

400ft (120 meters) through a jungle of tree ferns, then meanders across the floor of Kilauea Iki Crater, warming hikers' toes with heat from the magma that is burning 300ft (90 meters) below the surface. Sulfurous steam escapes through trailside vents.

Devastation Trail is a boardwalk laid out on glistening jet cinders. Skeletons of trees are bleached white by time and sun. Twenty years ago, there was barely a vestige of vegetation beside the boardwalk. Now, the trail is cheered by tawny grasses, clumps of wildflowers, the scarlet *ohia lehua* blossoms, and lavender polyganum.

The ½-mile (0.8km) **Thurston Lava Tube Loop** takes you through a lava tunnel that once surged with magma. The 11-mile (18km) **Crater Rim Trail** circles the summit, beginning at the visitor center. The most interesting section leads from Chain of Craters Road through native forest, across hard black lava flows, and ends at the rim of **Keanakakoi Crater.**

Along the way are eerie tree molds formed when a lava flow rushed through the forest, splashed around trees and hardened in their shape. What's left are phantasmagoric black sculptures, some 10ft (3 meters) high. Nearby, tender new fronds of *amau* fern poke from lava chinks, finding a determined foothold. Native *ohia* trees take root in the impossible terrain. Some are only a foot or two (half-meter) high and already bursting in brilliant red flowers. It's a scene that whispers more than any pop-psychology paperback about encouragement, hope, endurance, triumph over adversity, and beauty from ashes.

The most strenuous trek in the park is the four-day round-trip trek to the top of 13,250ft (4,039-meter) **Mauna Loa** volcano. It is recommended only for those experienced backpackers who are equipped to face snow, wind and high-altitude hiking.

A shorter but equally demanding round-trip trail to the summit begins at the **Mauna Loa Weather Observatory.** Permits are required for both trips. In winter months, the upper slopes of Mauna Loa are usually blanketed with snow. It is said that Poliahu, goddess of the snow and nemesis of

BELOW: the Thurston Lava Tube Loop.

Pele, resides atop Mauna Loa. Through the ages, the two have carried on their feud, using weapons of fire and ice.

Many of the plants at the park are rare and endangered, the last stand for some threatened species. When the Hawaiian islands emerged from the ocean, they were sterile and lifeless. At the rate of one successful new species every 40,000 years, seeds and spores of plants arrived in the jet streams, on the ocean currents, and as gifts of migratory birds. In utter isolation, farther from a landmass than any place else on earth, the plants and birds evolved into a unique biota.

Within the park, in the middle of lava flows, are areas called *kipuka*, which were unmolested by the flows and left as pristine islands of life. Some are quite large and offer refuge to endemic flora and fauna. A hiking trail off **Mauna Loa Road** traverses hilly **Kipuka Puaulu** through stands of *ohia lehua*, with their scarlet blossoms, and *koa* trees, once the king of the Hawaiian forest. The great voyaging canoes that carried early Hawaiians as far as Tahiti were carved from *koa* logs.

Along the **Kipuka Trail** are occasional benches so hikers can pause and listen to a symphony heard nowhere else – the honeyed notes of the apapane, the little red bird with white britches who drinks nectar from the *lehua* blossom; the warbling of the *iiwi*; and the big police whistle of the tiny *omao*. The *nene*, a native goose rescued from the brink of extinction, can once again be spotted waddling among the ferns and trees of the park, often with a line of goslings in tow. Signs warn motorists to brake for one of the world's rarest birds.

Visitors who want to enter this haunting place can stay in **Namakanipaio Cabins** or in the **Volcano House** hotel, the only lodge in the park. The lodge sits at the rim of Kilauea caldera with views of the vast steaming pit. During summit eruptions, it's sometimes possible to sip cocktails while watching the most spectacular dinner show in the world.

Also on the Big Island are **Kaloko-Honokohau National Historical Park ❷**, the site of important Hawaiian settlements before the arrival of

Clouds engulf Mauna Loa volcano.

BELOW LEFT: the Mauna Loa Weather Observatory. **BELOW:** lush vegetation on Mauna Loa.

Europeans; **Pu'uhonua o Honaunau National Historical Park** ❸, a sacred place where native Hawaiians sought sanctuary, and **Pu'ukohola Heiau National Historic Site** ❹, preserving a large offshore temple (*heiau*) dedicated to King Kamehameha the Great.

House of the Sun

Haleakala National Park ❺ on the island of Maui protects parts of the world's largest dormant volcano. At 10,023ft (3,055 meters), Haleakala, which means House of the Sun, rises a mile above any other Maui peak. Its "crater" – actually a high, eroded valley between what was two erupting volcanoes and now filled with small cinder cones – is an awesome sight: 21 miles (34km) in circumference, 3,000ft (900 meters) in depth.

Haleakala last erupted in 1790 and left behind a landscape so unearthly that American astronauts trained here for the first moon landing. The 29,094-acre (11,774-hectare) park encompasses the summit as well as a portion of the Kipahulu Coast. Some areas are virtually unexplored, and new species of

birds and plants are still being found. The park has been designated an International Biosphere Reserve.

There are magnificent views of the wilderness area at **Leleiwi**, **Kalahaku**, and **Puu Ulaula Summit** along the tortuous 11-mile (18km) park road, as well as at the visitor center, which is perched on the rim. But, as always, the best way to experience Haleakala is on foot. The park offers more than 30 miles (48km) of hiking trails, some going right into the "crater" where there are two large wilderness campgrounds and three wilderness cabins (permits and reservations required).

Just beyond the park entrance is the **Hosmer Grove Nature Walk**, an easy half-mile (1km) trail that loops through stands of native and exotic trees planted here about 80 years ago by experimental forester Ralph Hosmer. This is also one of the last refuges of honeycreepers (*iiwi, amakihi, apapane* and *alauahio*), among the rarest birds in the world. About 4 miles (6km) from Hosmer Grove, you'll find the trailhead of **Halemau'u Trail**, which crosses rolling hill

country to the volcano rim. From there, it descends down switchbacks to Holua Cabin on the volcano floor, about a 1,000ft (300-meter) drop. Experienced hikers can continue 6 miles (10km) to **Paliku Cabin**. Here, you can pick up **Kaupo Trail**, a strenuous, rocky descent, which is used as an exit.

The most popular route into the park is the **Sliding Sands Trail**, which begins at the visitor center just below the summit and plunges down a steep 6-mile (10km) incline to **Kapalaoa Cabin** on the valley floor. (Hiking up the loose cinder trail is extremely fatiguing, so consider cutting the hike short or exiting on Halemau'u Trail.)

Along the way are stands of endangered silversword, the rare silver plant that grows only at Haleakala; it blooms only once, then dies. Silversword glows with light and cradles tiny drops of water on its wands. Surprisingly, it is a member of the sunflower family that has adapted to this lunar-like environment and acquired an eerie beauty.

The immense cinder cone **Puu o Maui** dominates the landscape, along with the neighboring cones of **Kamo-**alii and **Puu o Pele** and the multihued crater of **Kalua O Ka O'o**. The colors run from russet, sienna, and umber streaked with yellow, purple, and red to a pale silver and delicate pea green. Nature has painted the landscape with bold strokes of black augite crystals, red cinders, and sparkling green olivine. The shades change with the angle of the sun, and the effect is electrifying.

The shoreline Kipahulu section of the park is a complete contrast to the stark drama of the summit. Ice-cold **Palikea Stream** cascades to the sea through Oheo Gulch in a series of falls with large plunge pools. Popular as swimming spots, the pools are surrounded by rolling grasslands and lush rainforest. They are reached via the 2-mile (3km) **Pipiwai Trail**, which also leads to Waimoku Falls, a tall cascade plunging from the side of the volcano.

In the summit and Kipahulu sections of the park, rangers conduct hikes and guided nature walks. Concessionaires outside the park offer horseback expeditions into the volcano and popular sunrise bike descents from the summit using the park's steep scenic road. On

> *I felt like the last Man, neglected of the judgement and left pinnacled in mid-heaven, a forgotten relic of a vanished world.*
>
> Mark Twain, on gazing down into Haleakala

BELOW LEFT: the silversword plant, endemic to the Haleakala volcanic crater.
BELOW: Black Rock Point, Kaupo.

At 3,000ft (900 meters), the dramatic sea cliffs on the south coast of Tau Island, American Samoa, are the tallest in the world.

the neighboring island of Molokai is **Kalaupapa National Historical Park** ❻, which preserves an early Hawaii leprosy colony renowned for its association with Father Damien, as well as for rare and endangered species.

South Pacific scenery

Located 2,600 miles (4,200km) south-southwest of Hawaii, American Samoa is a United States territory of five volcanic islands and two coral atolls. The **National Park of American Samoa** ❼, established in 1988, is one of America's newest and encompasses nearly 9,000 acres (3,640 hectares) in three units on widely separated islands. The 5,000-acre (2,000-hectare) parcel on **Tau Island** is mostly undisturbed rainforest, containing the sacred site of Saua, considered by many to be the birthplace of the Polynesian people. The beautiful sea cliffs drop from the top of **Lata Mountain**, the highest peak in the territory. The terrain is steep, and the most popular activities include beachwalking, snorkeling among coral reefs, and nature study. The **Tutuila Island** section of the

BELOW AND RIGHT:
Pago Pago,
American Samoa.

park is also mainly rainforest. There is a scenic road from Pago Pago to the north coast with spectacular panoramic views, especially from Afono Pass. **Ofu Island** contains a beach of fine coral sand, considered to be the loveliest in Samoa, and also one of the most exceptional coral reefs in the Pacific.

Within this unique rainforest environment – the only one of its kind in the United States – the park protects a remarkable variety of wildlife including dozens of tropical birds and fish, tortoises, the Pacific boa, and the rare flying fox (actually a large bat).

Due to the communal nature of land tenure in Samoa, most of the parklands are leased from the local villages and largely undeveloped. Entering the park and camping may require special permission, and some areas may be closed to visitors. Although hotels are available on the islands, visitors are encouraged to stay with village families and learn about the Samoan culture. Contact the regional park office in Pago Pago for details well in advance. ❑

A Tsunami Hits Samoa

On September 29, 2009, a magnitude 8.0 earthquake struck the Pacific Ocean near American Samoa. The quake triggered three separate tsunamis (tidal waves), which rose to 5.1ft (1.5 meters) high and washed over the islands. Tsunami warnings were also given for the Hawaiian Islands, but proved uneventful. Several Samoan villages were damaged, and 22 people killed. Visitor facilities in the National Park of American Samoa, including the visitor center in Pago Plaza, were destroyed; temporary visitor facilities have been set up in Ottoville, 8 miles (13km) from Pago Plaza. The rest of the park remains open to visitation and largely unaffected. American Samoa and neighboring Guam have more than 200 coral reefs with 890 species of fish, accounting for the greatest coral biodiversity of any US national park.

THE SOUTHWEST

The parks of the American Southwest preserve some of the world's most beautiful and most extraordinary landscapes

From the red rock country of southern Utah on the north to the torrid flats of the Chihuahuan Desert on the south, the natural beauty of the Southwest is unrivaled. At its heart, the 130,000-sq -mile (33,670-sq-km) rock massif known as the Colorado Plateau rises intact, shaped by water and wind into a dreamscape of canyons, mesas, spires, natural bridges, hoodoos, and arches. Its principal sculptor, the Colorado River, created much of this spectacular topography, most famously at the Grand Canyon, the most popular park in the Southwest.

At heart, though, these are wilderness parks, where back-packers are more likely to see a coyote, mule deer, or rattle-snake than another human being, and little-known corners contain unexpected treasures – prehistoric dwellings and artifacts, rock art and volcanic features in this primarily erosion-built landscape.

The geological heart of the Colorado Plateau is southern Utah's Canyonlands National Park, where the Colorado and Green rivers merge and carve their deepest and most spectacular winding canyons. Neighboring Arches National Park preserves the world's largest known collection of natural arches. To

the west, the lively Fremont River has cut a deep, narrow gorge through the vast sandstone uplift of Capitol Reef, revealing rainbow-colored rock formations. Cliffside erosion created nearby Bryce Canyon's colorful and bizarre pinnacles and spires, while, in Zion, the Virgin River and erosion by water and wind have created remarkable soaring red cliffs alive with the sound of waterfalls and dripping glens.

For millennia, the Colorado Plateau was home to archaic hunter-gatherers, the Fremont culture, and different branches of the Ancestral Pueblo culture whose remarkable rock art and beautifully preserved pueblos are now protected at Mesa Verde, Canyon de Chelly,

PRECEDING PAGES: on the edge at the magnificent Grand Canyon. **LEFT:** the unique Chiricahua National Monument. **TOP:** on the road through Chiricahua National Monument. **ABOVE LEFT:** welcome to Chiricahua . **ABOVE RIGHT:** it's a new day in the Southwest.

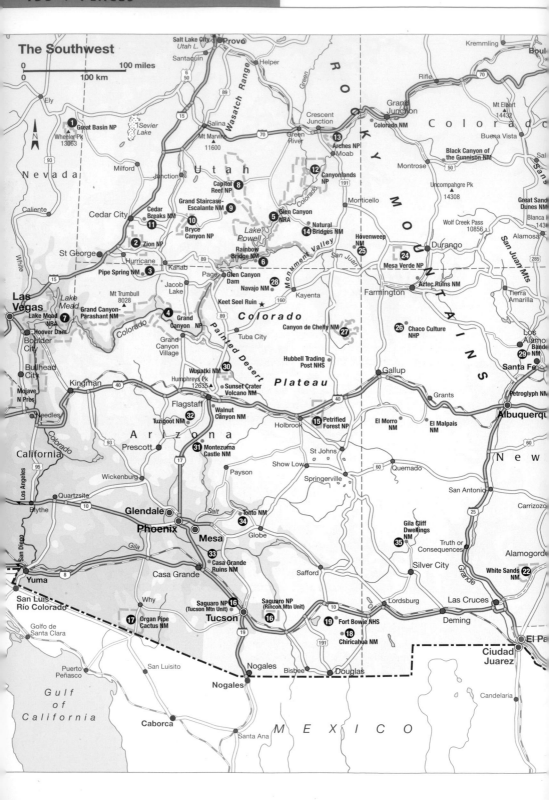

Chaco Canyon, and other Southwest parks. Yet another culture, the Sinagua, lived in Arizona's red rock canyons and high country, where they built pueblos, unusual cliff dwellings, and ballcourts now preserved at Wupatki, Walnut Canyon, Tonto, and Montezuma Castle national monuments. Today, recreation is the main draw on the plateau. People come here to hike, rock climb, mountain bike, run rivers, and otherwise immerse themselves in Canyon Country.

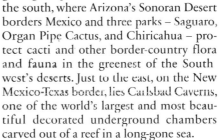

West of the Colorado Plateau, Great Basin National Park is in Nevada's Snake Range, a mountainous pocket of the expansive and searingly hot Great Basin Desert. The Basin and Range geological province continues to the south, where Arizona's Sonoran Desert borders Mexico and three parks – Saguaro, Organ Pipe Cactus, and Chiricahua – protect cacti and other border-country flora and fauna in the greenest of the Southwest's deserts. Just to the east, on the New Mexico-Texas border, lies Carlsbad Caverns, one of the world's largest and most beautiful decorated underground chambers carved out of a reef in a long-gone sea.

In adjoining Texas, the elevated and eroded reef is protected as Guadalupe Mountains National Park, a sanctuary for unusual wildlife. Texas's most spectacular park, 1,250-sq-mile (3,240-sq-km) Big Bend, is due east, tucked into several spectacular gorges carved by the Rio Grande through the Chisos Mountains on the US-Mexico border. The desert appears devoid of life. This is an illusion. Big Bend is among the most biologically diverse sites in the national park system, with more bird species sighted here than in any other park, leading to its designation as an International Biosphere Reserve. ❏

TOP: the futuristic Biosphere 2 Research Center, Oracle, Arizona. **ABOVE:** observe nature in a controlled state at Biosphere 2.

GREAT BASIN

Between the Rocky Mountains and the Sierra Nevada, cool green mountains emerge from an expanse of sagebrush. Here, you can go from desert to alpine tundra in a few miles

In 1843–44, the intrepid Western explorer John Charles Frémont labeled a map of the Great Basin, "contents unknown, but believed to be filled with rivers and lakes which have no connection to the sea." Frémont's pronouncement told the basic hydrologic truth of the Great Basin: its streams and rivers do not flow into the ocean. Instead, water runs off the mountains into the many valleys, sits in salty *playas* and mudflats and eventually evaporates into the air or soaks into the ground.

The Great Basin is the 210,000 sq miles (543,700 sq km) of country between the Wasatch Range in Utah and the Sierra Nevada in California. It is mostly high, cold desert of grassland and sagebrush. Endless valleys stretch to the horizon. Blue mountains float up from the valleys, one after another. Of his overland journey across the Great Basin, the reformer and journalist Horace Greeley wrote in 1859 that the vegetation he was seeing was "the same eternal sage-brush and greasewood, which I am tired of mentioning, but which together or separately, cover two-thirds of all the vast region between the Rocky Mountains and the Sierra Nevada."

Greeley obviously missed what is now **Great Basin National Park ❶**,

an area that is much more than "eternal sage-brush." The park is indeed a classic example of Great Basin landscape, but with the cool, green Snake Range at its heart, it is much more. These terrestrial islands, separated by oceans of sagebrush desert, exhibit striking contrasts, both biological and physical. Some 8,000 feet (2,440 meters) of vertical relief separate the valley floor from the summit of 13,063ft (3,982-meter) **Wheeler Peak ❹**, the second-highest point in Nevada. Here, you can experience several life zones, from hot desert

Main attractions
LEHMAN CAVES
WHEELER PEAK SCENIC DRIVE
WHEELER PEAK GLACIER
BRISTLECONE TRAIL
LEHMAN CREEK TRAIL
LEHMAN ORCHARD

LEFT: Cathedral Gorge, south of Great Basin.
RIGHT: limestone formations inside Lehman Caves.

to alpine tundra, in less than an hour.

Beneath the mountains lies **Lehman Caves B**, actually a single cavern, carved out of the earth by ground water over millions of years and now "decorated" with fascinating limestone formations. Lehman Caves became a national monument in 1922 and, in 1986, was included in newly created Great Basin National Park. Great Basin is located in east-central Nevada, 5 miles (8km) west of Baker, which has the nearest visitor facilities.

Stop at the seasonal Great Basin Visitor Center at Baker, at the junction of Highways 487 and 488, or proceed directly to Lehman Caves Visitor Center to get information, view exhibits and films, buy books and gifts, or get something to eat in the seasonal café. Tickets are available here (or by advance purchase) for frequently scheduled ½-mile (0.75km) ranger-guided cave tours. Inside the cave, you'll marvel at the magical creations made by limestone and water: fanciful stalactites and stalagmites and other unusual features, such as jointed shields. You may also see a bat,

flea, cricket, or pseudoscorpion. Dress warmly, for the temperature inside is a constant cool 50°F (10°C) and the humidity a steady 90 percent – even in the winter months.

Plants of the peak

Interesting though it is, Lehman Caves is one small part of Great Basin National Park. In the extreme elevation change from valley to mountaintop, the park contains seven communities, or zones, of plants and animals. Travelers can glimpse a good portion of this incredible biological diversity by driving or walking part of the 12-mile (19km) **Wheeler Peak Scenic Drive**.

The road starts out amid sagebrush, prickly-pear cactus, and juniper trees, then enters another zone: pinyon pine and curl-leaf mountain mahogany. Though considered a shrub in most places, mountain mahogany here reaches tree size. The edges of the leaves curl under – which helps the plant conserve water during dry times – and the seeds are lovely feathery plumes.

Growing with mountain mahogany at this 6,000–7,000ft (1,800–2,100-

BELOW: bristlecone pine beneath Wheeler Peak.

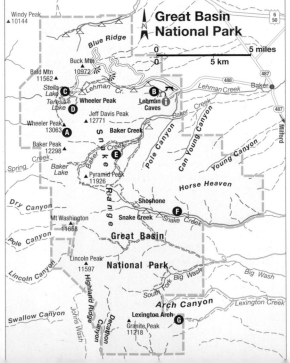

meter) elevation is singleleaf pinyon pine. The tree's cones hold delicious, oily nuts that have served as a staple food of Shoshone inhabitants of the Great Basin for centuries. The nut harvest is still a cherished ritual in early autumn among Shoshone descendants now living in Ely, Nevada. Pinyon nuts are also a staple for pinyon jays, Clark's nutcrackers, rock squirrels, and mice.

As elevation changes, dwarf pinyon woodland cedes to cool aspen forest. Hugging the ground beneath the quaking aspens is a red-stemmed shrub called manzanita. It's a pioneer, one of the first plants to colonize burnt or disturbed land. Among the manzanita grows the sharp-leaved Oregon grape or barberry, sporting yellow flowers that later become edible blue fruits.

Still higher up, stately, loden-hued evergreens – Douglas fir, white fir, and Engelmann spruce – begin to appear along with limber pine and 5,000-year-old bristlecone pine. Together they form a community that one professional botanist calls the "quintessential Great Basin forest."

Wheeler Peak trails

The scenic drive ends at an elevation of 10,000ft (3,000 meters). The air here is crisp and filled with piney fragrance. By now, you've probably dug out a jacket, and maybe a hat and gloves. From a nearby parking area, several trails lead to alpine lakes, a bristlecone grove, the glacier, or the top of Wheeler Peak. These trails are mostly free of snow and passable by early June. (A forewarning: snow can fall all year round on Wheeler Peak, so be ready for any kind of weather.)

In 1885, William Eimbeck, of the US Coast and Geodetic Survey, wrote: "A region more unfavorable for the formation of glaciers could scarcely be found." In fact, there *is* a glacier, and it's on Wheeler Peak.

Ice Age remnants

The glacier is tucked into a cirque on the northeast side of Wheeler Peak. It is a remnant of the Ice Age, when the entire Great Basin was colder and wetter, and the Snake Range was covered with alpine glaciers. Ten to fifteen thousand years ago, the valleys

TIP

Summer months are the best for access to Great Basin's high country. During the winter, most roads and trails are closed by snow, though the road from Baker to the park visitor center is open year-round.

BELOW: the Glacier Trail, Wheeler Peak.

Lehman Orchard

Just below the lower parking lot at the Lehman Caves Visitor Center, is a century-old orchard. It was planted by Absalom (Ab) Lehman, the pioneer rancher who found and helped develop Lehman Caves. Lehman moved here sometime between 1866 and 1869. He built up a 600-acre (240-hectare) ranch that, by 1890, included orchards, a blacksmith's, a carpenter shop, a butcher shop, corrals, a dairy ranch, and a churn run by water power. By the early 1930s, the orchard contained 40 apricot, pear, crabapple, peach, plum, and apple trees and produced the best fruit for miles. Today, only seven apricot trees and one peach tree remain, maintained by the National Park Service. Visitors may pick fruit for personal consumption on the premises; collecting or removing fruit from the park is prohibited.

The crystal clear waters of Teresa Lake.

BELOW: Wheeler Peak's reflection in Stella Lake.

here were filled with lakes comparable in size to the United States' Great Lakes. Big mammals lumbered across the land, occasionally holing up in caves. Although the huge lakes and megafauna are long gone, the isolated mountains of Great Basin National Park still harbor Ice Age holdovers – bristlecone pines, alpine lakes, and tundra plants among them.

The oldest trees on earth

The park has three trails leading to bristlecone groves. The most accessible is the 2.8-mile (4.6km) round-trip **Bristlecone Trail** on Mt. Wheeler, which gains just 400ft (122 meters) in elevation. Take things slowly: the altitude, combined with exercise, may cause headaches or shortness of breath. But the destination is worth the effort. Simply to be among these, the oldest living trees on earth, is a moving experience. Their gnarled, polished bodies evidence their great age and the harsh climate they have endured. Some elders in this grove have lived at least 3,000 years. One, called Prometheus, was a record holder. Ironically, Prometheus

was cut down so the annual growth rings in the wood could be counted to learn its age; the tree turned out to be 4,900 years old.

For a full view of the Wheeler Peak glacier, continue on the trail another mile (1.6km) from the bristlecone grove. Or, as you head back from the grove to the parking lot, you may detour onto a loop to visit **Stella Lake** ● and her nearby sister, **Teresa Lake** ●. These clear lakes are set like sapphires at the feet of the steep mountain peaks. In summer, waves dance across their surfaces and their green grassy shores are dotted with glossy golden buttercups and white phlox.

On another day, you may wish to undertake the rather more demanding hike to the summit of Wheeler Peak: a 3,000ft (900-meter) ascent, 5 miles (8km) up and 5 miles back. Climbing gently at first, the path passes through a forest of limber pines full of squawking Clark's nutcrackers. The wind has pruned the exposed trees and left them stunted. At the tree line, the trail steepens and crosses rockier terrain.

The rubble of pinkish-gray rock

clattering underfoot is quartzite, a nearly pure quartz sandstone changed by great heat and pressure into harder, metamorphic rock.

The quartzite originated as the beaches and continental shelves of extensive oceans that covered this part of the country 600 million years ago. Arriving suddenly on top of Wheeler Peak, you see before you a scene of unearthly beauty.

To the west, there is a vertiginous drop-off. Elegant fans of alluvium – talus, scree, and gravel – sweep down and bury the base of the mountains. Immediately to the east is a 1,500ft (460-meter) vertical wall, the cirque that contains the glacier. Baker, Pyramid, and Washington peaks jut up from the southern end of the Snake Range. And, in all directions, more mountains interrupt the valleys, like battleships plowing through the sea.

You might also want to hike from **Wheeler Peak Campground** down to **Upper Lehman Campground**. This gentle 4-mile (6km) walk along Lehman Creek introduces the diversity of the park in reverse – from aspen forest past those huge mountain mahoganies and back down to sagebrush, following a lovely running stream all the way.

Backcountry sites

Great Basin was made for exploration on unpaved, backcountry roads. Most roads can be negotiated in two-wheel-drive passenger vehicles, but inquire locally to be sure. If you feel fit, you can hike 5 miles (8km) or so up **Baker Creek** ❺ or **Snake Creek** ❻ to alpine lakes, or make a longer loop between the two. Your only company may be a few cows, allowed to graze as part of the agreement that established the park.

Along the way are signs of the mountains' mining history in the form of an old cabin and equipment. A 30-mile (48km) drive south and a mile walk up a creekbed takes you to **Lexington Arch** ❼, the largest limestone arch in the country. Winter, though, offers an entirely different experience. The road up Wheeler Peak is open as far as Upper Lehman Campground. From there, you can explore on snowshoes or skis. ❑

BELOW:
Lehman Creek.

ZION

This spectacular cliff-and-canyon landscape is full of the unexpected, including colorful rocks hewn by erosion into phenomenal shapes, and one of the world's largest natural arches

et in the rocky heart of southern Utah's convoluted canyon country, **Zion National Park ❷** is nature at its most eloquent: a dramatic juxtaposition of towering sandstone monoliths, narrow slot canyons, fast-flowing water, dense greenery, and myriad wildlife. From afar, the park's enormous buttes and domes rise like temples beckoning the faithful. From up close, its sheltering walls seem to offer a protected sanctuary. For the Mormon settlers who came here in the mid-1800s, this seemed to be Zion, "the Heavenly City of God." As a national park since 1919, Zion continues to draw millions of "worshippers" who marvel at the extraordinary geology and natural beauty found in these precipitous canyons.

Dramatically eroded sedimentary rocks are what give Zion its character and have led to its fame. Eight different rock strata may be found in the vicinity, all of which were deposited over a period of 200 million years, as geologic instability and changing climates and topography brought a succession of inland seas, lakes, rivers, streams, volcanic debris, and even a dune-filled desert into the region. It is the latter that was responsible for the park's dominant rocks, the sheer, creamy-pink Navajo Sandstone cliffs, which reach 2,200ft (671 meters) in height in Zion.

PRECEDING PAGES: hiking the Subway, Zion.
LEFT: dramatic formations at Zion National Park. **RIGHT:** a riverbed in the fall.

Reading the rocks

The best way to "read the rocks" is to drive into Zion from the west, via Hurricane, along Highway 9, following the course of the pretty **Virgin River** through spic-and-span villages into the park's South Entrance. From Hurricane, 25 miles (40km) away, you drive over the dramatic **Hurricane Fault** in the Kaibab Limestone cliffs, whose marine sediments make up the rimrock of Grand Canyon, and into the Virgin River Canyon, encountering progressively younger rocks on the journey

Main attractions
ZION CANYON VISITOR CENTER
THE WATCHMAN
ZION CANYON
EMERALD POOLS TRAIL
RIVERSIDE WALK TRAIL
ZION CANYON
WEST RIM TRAIL
KOLOB CANYONS
ZION–MOUNT CARMEL TUNNEL
GHOST TOWN OF GRAFTON
PIPE SPRING NATIONAL MONUMENT

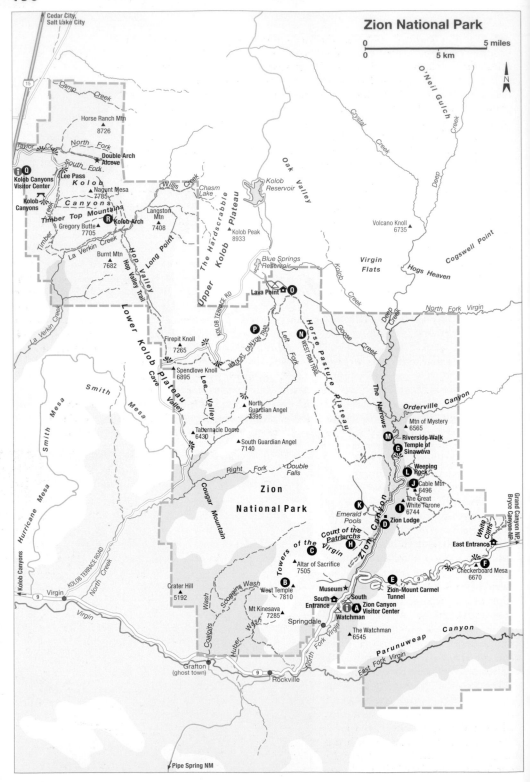

Zion National Park

0 _____ 5 miles
0 _____ 5 km

N

Cedar City,
Salt Lake City

O'Neil Gulch

Horse Ranch Mtn
8726

North Fork

Camp Creek

Taylor Cr.

Crystal Creek

Deep Creek

Oak Valley

Kolob Reservoir

Volcano Knoll
6735

Cogswell Point

Double Arch
Alcove

South Fork

Kolob Canyons Visitor Center Q

Lee Pass

Kolob

Nagunt Mesa
7785

Willis Creek

Chasm Lake

Kolob Canyons

Timber Top Mountains

Gregory Butte
7705

Kolob Arch R

Langston Mtn
7408

Kolob Peak
8933

Blue Springs Reservoir

Virgin Flats

Hogs Heaven

North Fork Virgin

Timber Cr.

La Verkin Creek

Burnt Mtn
7682

Hop Valley

Long Point

Hop Valley Trail

Upper Kolob Plateau

The Hardscrabble

Lava Point O

Kolob Creek

Goose Creek

Deep Creek

La Verkin Creek

Lower Kolob Plateau

Cave Valley

Firepit Knoll
7265

Spendlove Knoll
6895

Lee Valley

North Guardian Angel
7395

Tabernacle Dome
6430

South Guardian Angel
7140

Double Falls

Right Fork

Left Fork

West Rim Trail

P

N

Wildcat Canyon Trail

Kolob Terrace Rd

Horse Pasture Plateau

The Narrows

Orderville Canyon

Mtn of Mystery
6565

Riverside Walk

Temple of Sinawava G

M

Weeping Rock L

Cable Mtn
6496 J

Smith Mesa

Smith Mesa

Zion National Park

Cougar Mountain

Emerald Pools K

Court of the Patriarchs

Towers of the Virgin

Altar of Sacrifice
7505

C

D Zion Lodge

I

The Great White Throne
6744

H

Zion Canyon

White Cliffs

Grand Canyon NP, Bryce Canyon NP

East Entrance

Checkerboard Mesa
6670

F

Hurricane Mesa

Kolob Canyons

Virgin

Kolob Terrace Road

North Creek

Crater Hill
5192

Scoggins Wash

West Temple
7810

B

Mt Kinesava
7285

Museum

South Entrance

South
Zion Canyon Visitor Center A

E Zion–Mount Carmel Tunnel

Watchman

The Watchman
6545

Parunuweap Canyon

Coalpits Wash

Huber Wash

Springdale

North Fork Virgin

Grafton
(ghost town)

Rockville

East Fork Virgin

Pipe Spring NM

east. Near the community of Virgin, the banded Moenkopi Formation is visible. A little farther along, above the colorful gardens of charming little **Rockville**, the multihued Chinle Formation forms crumbling hills scattered with dinosaur-era petrified wood.

At **Springdale**, the compacted red mud shales of the Moenave are visible beneath vermilion-colored Kayenta rocks that sometimes display dinosaur tracks. The sheer cliffs of Navajo Sandstone are now everywhere in sight, topped occasionally by the rounded bald domes, of the Great White Throne and other landmarks. In the farther reaches of the park, younger Carmel Limestone and Dakota Formation appear on only the highest mountains.

The corrosive power of flash flooding rivers, ephemeral waterfalls and seeping water is primarily responsible for the deep canyons, etched rock faces, smooth domes and colorfully streaked rocks found at Zion. Hard though it is to believe, the little **Virgin River** (a tributary of the Colorado River), which rises at 9,000ft (2,740 meters) on the tableland of the Markagunt Plateau just north of Zion, carved **Zion Canyon**.

Beginning some 13 million years ago, the southern Colorado Plateau underwent a period of violent geologic activity that caused it to break and weather along faults, such as the Hurricane, into distinctive plateaus. Seismic activity along this southern spur of the **Wasatch Range** is ongoing. In 1992, a powerful earthquake centered in St George caused a large slide in Springdale. Zion is riddled with fractures in the soft rocks, which, combined with water erosion, account for the unusual U shape of its canyons and the great spalling arches (locally called "bridges") in its sheer walls.

The Virgin River bore down in its course as the land rose, scouring soft rock and bearing away sediments, which ended up in Lake Mead far to the south. The Colorado and its tributaries have removed strata from this portion of the uplifted Colorado Pla-

teau at differing rates, giving the canyon country a colorful, stepped look, referred to as the Grand Staircase. This can best be seen looking north over the Arizona Strip from the Kaibab Plateau, south of Zion. The reds and pinks (and, occasionally, yellows and browns) found in the rocks at Zion generally result from iron within the rock, which has been washed through by percolating ground water. Dark streaking, as on the **Altar of Sacrifice**, occurs when water falling over sheer precipices washes down minerals from vegetation or caprock. Weathering of organic material on rock faces also causes shiny "desert varnish," perhaps the most dramatic of all rock coatings in the Southwest.

Most visitors arrive in Zion via the South Entrance. **Zion Canyon Visitor Center Ⓐ** is just within the park boundary, overlooked by the huge bulk of the **West Temple Ⓑ** and **Towers of the Virgin Ⓒ**. The attractive, new, environmentally built visitor center is the main hub for visitors. It is served by a free shuttle system, linking neighboring Springdale and the main attractions in Zion

Zion's famous Zion-Mt. Carmel Highway was constructed in the 1920s by the Civilian Conservation Corps (CCC), which also built many of the impressive rustic architectural features you see in the park. In 2010, work began on stabilizing and renovating the highway's famous switchbacks. Expect significant delays of up to several hours at certain times of day as you travel through the park while work is taking place.

BELOW: the Altar of Sacrifice.

TIP

Hikers in Zion should
beware of rockfalls and
landslides and stay out
of drainage areas during
thunderstorms, which
can produce flash
floods. Afternoon
storms are common
from mid-July through
mid-September.

Canyon, which is now closed to motorists in summer. Plan your trip with a ranger, view exhibits and films, get a permit for backcountry travel, and browse the gift shop. Large panels on the patio allow after-hours visitors to plan their trip here and through the region.

The park's two campgrounds are near the visitor center and fill quickly. The only other lodging inside the park is the rustic, log-framed **Zion Lodge ⓓ**, which was built in the 1920s by the now-defunct Utah Parks Company to accommodate well-heeled park visitors. With its ice-cream fountain, manicured lawns, and shady trees, it's a good spot to take a breather as you tour Zion Canyon. Just don't expect to spend the night without reservations; bookings must usually be secured a year in advance. There are attractive lodgings and restaurants in Springdale or east of the park along Highway 89, at Mount Carmel or Kanab.

Seeing the park

Many people drive or bicycle through Zion via the **Zion-Mount Carmel Highway** (Highway 9), which heads east following a tributary of the Virgin River. The road zigzags through the canyon until it enters the 1-mile (1.5km) -long **Zion-Mount Carmel Tunnel ⓔ**, built in 1930 to shorten the route between Zion and Bryce Canyon and Grand Canyon national parks. There are size restrictions on vehicles using the tunnel: buses, large RVs, and bicycles require an escort. On the other side of the tunnel, the road passes beneath a huge alcove known as the Great Arch of Zion, then alongside marvelously eroded slickrock formations, which are exactly what they look like: "petrified" sand dunes. The most distinctive of these is the spectacular **Checkerboard Mesa ⓕ**, a huge, creamy giant with crosshatched surfaces caused by horizontal cross-bedding in the dunes and later deepening of vertical fractures by water erosion.

The turn-off for Zion Canyon itself is a short way up from the visitor center. The scenic drive parallels the tree-lined banks of the North Fork of the Virgin River and dead-ends beneath the amphitheater of the **Temple of Sinawava ⓖ**. Within this short

BELOW: glowing
colors in the fall.
BELOW RIGHT: the
narrowing Virgin
River.

drive are the **Court of the Patriarchs ⊕**, the **Great White Throne ⓘ**, and **Cable Mountain ⓙ**, as well as shady hiking trails, where you are surrounded by dripping rocks and colorful hanging plants. From here, you can set out on longer hikes that take you into the high country, or simply dream away the day deep in the canyon paddling in the river shallows.

Three short hiking trails – to **Emerald Pools ⓚ** (2 miles/3km), **Weeping Rock ⓛ** (1½ miles/2km), and **Riverside Walk ⓜ** (2 miles/3km) – meander through sheltered side canyons populated by singleleaf ash, manzanita, cliff rose, and Gambel oak. Here, contact between porous Navajo Sandstone and impervious Kayenta river sandstones and shales below it has created seeping rocks, known as springlines, which are home to delightful "hanging gardens" of soft mosses, ferns, monkeyflowers, and columbines, as well as the park's unique Zion snail. Another leitmotif of the park is sacred datura, or Zion lily, a poisonous, white-trumpeted flower that opens at night along waysides.

Other trails near Zion Lodge lead to famous landmarks, such as the Court of the Patriarchs (100yds/meters), **Angels Landing** (5 miles/8km), and **Hidden Canyon** (2 miles/3km, between Cable Mountain and the Great White Throne). Eight-mile (13km) **Observation Point Trail** skirts the base of Cable Mountain before climbing through woodlands, offering stunning views of the Great White Throne, Cable Mountain, the West Rim, Angels Landing, and Zion Canyon.

Wildlife and white water

Four different life zones are found in the 3,650–8,725ft (1,100–2,660-meter) elevations at Zion, encompassing desert, riparian, woodland, and coniferous forest. In the low, dry areas of the canyons, heavy-fruited prickly-pear cactus is found alongside desert residents such as whip-tailed and desert spiny lizards, slow-moving chuckwallas, and occasionally, western rattlesnakes.

The river is a perfect refuge when temperatures reach 100°F (38°C) in summer. Throngs of Fremont cottonwoods, box elders, willows, and velvet ash crowd its banks, sharing the

Some of Zion's odd names, such as the Temple of Sinawava, Mount Kinesava, and Parunuweap Canyon, are Paiute in origin, although these gentle and peaceful nomads only occasionally entered Zion.

BELOW:
Weeping Rock.

The sharp hair-like barbed spines (glochids) of the beavertail cactus.

location with bank beavers, gnatcatchers, and insects, as well as footsore hikers. The high country supports ponderosa pine, Rocky Mountain juniper, and sagebrush, as well as Douglas fir, and many wildflowers.

At twilight, you may glimpse a coyote, mule deer or bighorn sheep, the latter a recent return resident to Zion after years of persecution. Mountain lions, bobcats, badgers, foxes, and weasels lead very private lives here and are rarely encountered. Your companions throughout much of the park will be sociable little ground squirrels, camp-robbing ringtails, and noisy ravens and pinyon jays, whose chatter usually drowns out the more melodic canyon wren and other songbirds. During the summer rainy season, the full impact of water on rock is evident. Torrents of water pour off vertical rock faces in magnificent waterfalls, and the swollen Virgin River speeds noisily over and around boulders.

In spring, when snowmelt is greatest, or during summer rainstorms, don't even think of wading the 16-mile (26km) **Narrows Trail**, which follows

BELOW: welcome to Zion National Park.

the Virgin River through a slot canyon 2,000ft (600 meters) high and, in places, only 20ft (6 meters) wide. Err on the side of caution during unpredictable weather. Flash floods funnel through the canyon at the speed of a runaway train, destroying everything in their path. Plan to make the trip in dry summer months, and read warning signs before starting out. This is one expedition where you should be prepared to stay wet for hours in a place the sun rarely reaches. Consult with rangers before attempting this hike.

If you have enough time and are reasonably fit, you may want to undertake an overnight backpacking trip along the strenuous, one-way 13-mile (21km) **West Rim Trail** , which links Zion Canyon with **Lava Point** through breathtaking mountainous country. Extend the trip by taking **Wildcat Canyon Trail** into the beautifully carved **Finger Canyons** of the Kolob area. You can also drive to **Kolob Canyons**, proceeding west on Highway 9, then north to Exit 40 on Interstate 15.

Check in at **Kolob Canyons Visitor Center** before taking the 5-mile

Mormons and Methodists

The first white man to see Zion Canyon was probably Nephi Johnson, a Mormon missionary. In 1858, he was guided as far as Oak Creek by a Paiute, who refused to venture farther into the canyon. Shortly thereafter, the canyon became home to the Heaps, Isaac Behunin, and other 19th-century Mormon colonists who farmed the flood plains, raised livestock, and cut timber in the high country.

Joseph Black, who lived in Springdale but frequently explored the upper reaches of Zion Canyon, gave such shining accounts of the place that it was dubbed "Joseph's Glory."

Isaac Behunin apparently named the canyon Zion, a title that caught on with his religious brethren (although after a particularly uncomfortable trip here, the Mormon leader Brigham Young is said to have remarked grumpily that it was definitely "not Zion"). An enterprising young man, David Flanigan, left his mark by building a cable from the mountain summit to the canyon to transport lumber. Cable Mountain commemorates his achievement.

Most of Zion's landmarks owe their fanciful names to an imaginative Methodist minister called Frederick Vining Fisher and his two companions. On a 1916 trip, they gave the Three Patriarchs, the Great White Throne, Angels Landing, and the Organ their evocative monikers.

(8km) scenic drive through the folded and eroded vermilion-colored cliffs. A lot of people miss visiting the Kolob Canyons because of its distance from the main park. There are some fascinating hikes in this section, including a strenuous, 14-mile (23km) round-trip to **Kolob Arch** ®, which, at 310ft (94 meters) wide, is one of the world's longest natural spans.

Pipe Spring

Springdale makes a good base for exploring southern Utah's scenic byways. One unpaved backroad links Rockville and Highway 59 on the Arizona Strip, near the ghost town of **Grafton**, which was inundated by a great flood in 1861–62, then abandoned. Many Rockville residents, descendants of the original settlers, still look after the town and farm adjoining fields.

When you reach Highway 59, drive southeast for about 30 minutes to **Pipe Spring National Monument** ❸, one of those small but fascinating units that abound in the park system but often get overlooked. Ancestral Pueblo people, known as *E'nengweng*

by Kaibab Paiute Indians whose reservation surrounds Pipe Spring, and Mormon settlers were attracted to this spot because of the natural springs that bubble up the Sevier Fault in the **Vermilion Cliffs**.

In 1870, Mormons built a fortified ranch here to accommodate the Church's tithed cattle. The "fort" and its outlying cabins, corrals, pens and ponds remain much as they were in their heyday, when Anson Winsor and his wife constructed the two modest stone houses that were dubbed Winsor Castle (a punning reference to Winsor's British roots).

The Kaibab Band of Paiute Indians co-manages the monument with the National Park Service and helped develop an onsite museum, the only one interpreting Kaibab culture. The tribe also operates a campground next to the park as well as a gas and convenience store near the monument. Costumed rangers guide tours of the fort every 30 minutes all year long; a self-guided trail leads through the old Ancestral Pueblo site, orchards, and other interesting sites. ❏

The ghost town of Grafton was used as the backdrop for a scene in Butch Cassidy and the Sundance Kid.

BELOW LEFT: enjoying the view.
BELOW: Zion Canyon.

GRAND CANYON

The most dramatic example of erosion anywhere in the world, the Grand Canyon is a history book for geologists – and a unique spectacle for millions of visitors

J ohn Hance, a Grand Canyon pioneer and tourist guide, used to tell clients about a fierce snowstorm that howled into northern Arizona with snow so thick you couldn't see from one end of a mule to the other. Even so, Hance had work to do, so he put on snowshoes and headed out. Before long, he was hopelessly lost. Still, he plodded on, and pretty soon the weather began to break. Patches of blue sky appeared above, and then, to his horror, little patches of ground appeared below – way down below.

The storm was so thick, it seems, that Hance had walked out over the canyon edge and was supported only by clouds. And now, as the clouds broke up, he was in danger of falling to his earthly reward. He never ran so hard in his life, he said, and barely made it back to the rim before the last of the clouds evaporated.

A tall tale? John Hance was full of them. It seems that the Grand Canyon encourages these Bunyanesque exaggerations, and he was a master at crafting stories to match its unparalleled landscape. Many of his listeners believed him – the canyon, after all, is a landscape where it seems anything might happen. Who can vouch for reality in a place where solid rock so abruptly meets airy space? A place so deep that, as Hance used to say, it takes

seven days to see all the way to the bottom? Like many of his tales, this one also contains a grain of truth. You can stare all day and still not make sense of the wondrous landscape. You can see, but you cannot quickly comprehend.

It takes at least a week. Only after days of looking and listening and reading will patterns begin to emerge. A sheer cliff face, for example, may seem featureless until your eye suddenly picks out a raven's nest perched on a ledge. Or a small stone building, a prehistoric storage structure, appears

Main attractions
GRAND CANYON HISTORIC DISTRICT, SOUTH RIM
GRAND CANYON RAILWAY
EL TOVAR HOTEL
HOPI HOUSE
YAVAPAI POINT GEOLOGICAL MUSEUM
BRIGHT ANGEL TRAIL
KOLB STUDIO
SOUTH KAIBAB TRAIL
PHANTOM RANCH
HERMIT'S REST
DESERT VIEW WATCHTOWER
NAVAJO BRIDGE
LEES FERRY
LAKE POWELL

LEFT: view down the Colorado river.
RIGHT: Lava Falls Rapid.

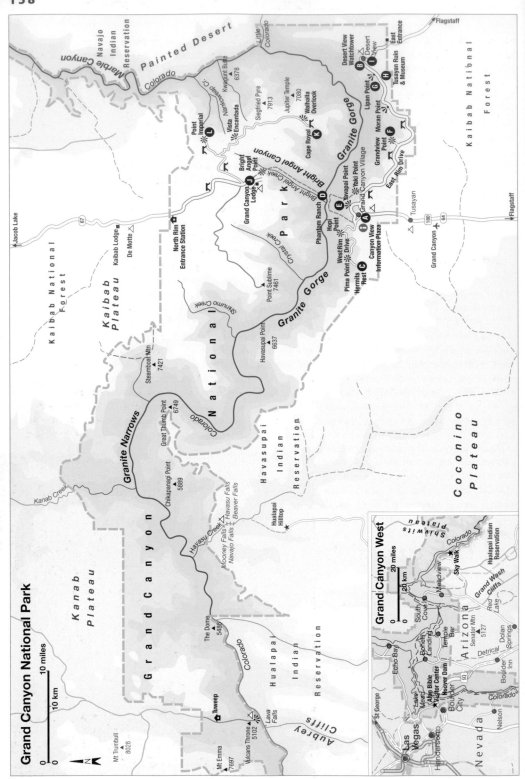

like magic beneath a distant rock over-hang. It was there all along, but to see it required an experienced eye.

In the same way, a sense of scale can be developed. Looking way down to the bottom of the canyon, where the river shows a glimmer of white water, you see a few tiny, bright-colored ovals flash in and out of view. Through binoculars, these reveal themselves to be riverboats, 20ft (6 meters) long, loaded with people crashing through waves that are big enough to swallow them from sight. Suddenly, the canyon acquires a human dimension.

Creating the canyon

How the canyon was carved is no mys-tery: it was eroded. Virtually all the rock that once occupied this space has been carried off by water – primarily the Colorado River. In a geologic sense, it wasn't such a great task; after all, the Mississippi River has carried off a far greater volume of sediment, creating a "canyon" that spreads from the Rockies to the Appalachians. Simple erosion is easy to understand. What challenges geologists even today, however, is that, in doing its work, the river performed a seemingly impossible trick – it cut through the Kaibab Plateau, a 3,000ft (900-meter) -high bulge in the earth's surface. Rivers normally flow around such highlands, not through them. What happened?

Once, it was thought that the plateau rose up beneath the ancient, pre-exist-ing Colorado River; in other words, the river carved the canyon as the land was lifted. This seemed to be a logi-cal explanation until other evidence showed that, only 6 million years ago, the Colorado River as it flows today did not exist, and, therefore, neither could the Grand Canyon. Thus, the Kaibab Plateau reached its current elevation millions of years before the river began its great work.

Nowadays, the most widely accepted idea involves not one but two rivers, going back to when a small river, the ancestral Colorado, wandered across an open landscape, flowing eventually toward the northwest into what is now Nevada. A second river flowed into the Gulf of California. Gradually, the sec-ond river eroded into the highlands at its source, lengthening its reach toward the northeast until finally it broke through a critical divide, tapped into the drainage of the ancestral Colorado and captured that river's water. All this took place some 5½ million years ago. One river was born from two – a new river with a steep gradient, fed by snowmelt from the Rockies – and the carving of the Grand Canyon began in earnest.

For geologists, the rock itself is the canyon's most revealing feature. Lying in largely undisturbed layers, the great mass of exposed stone describes nearly 2 billion years of North American geo-logical history. At the rim, the young-est layer is Kaibab Limestone, loaded with fossil seashells visible to even an untrained eye. At the bottom lies the so-called basement rock of the canyon: the 1.7-billion-year-old Vishnu Schist, a fine-grained, black rock with red marbling that is beautiful even to a layperson's eye.

The Grand Canyon Forest Reserve was designated as early as 1893. It became a national monument in 1908 and the national park was established in 1919.

BELOW: taking in the view from Mather Point on the South Rim.

An immature Californian condor.

BELOW: The Lookout, an observation station in the South Rim Historic District.

Between the Vishnu and the Kaibab lies the rest of the story, as told by nearly 40 layers of mostly sedimentary rocks, including limestone, sandstone and mudstone. Geologists read them like the stacked pages of a vast history book. Just as the rock layers form distinct levels, so do the canyon's life zones. Consider, for example, a trek from the park's highest point on the North Rim down the Kaibab Trail to the river. Your journey will begin at over 9,000ft (2,740 meters) among cool aspen, spruce, and fir. This forest is home to mule deer, coyote, mountain lion, wild turkey, and the unusual white-tailed Kaibab squirrel. As the plateau slopes down toward the rim, conditions become steadily warmer, and the forest cedes to species like pinyon, juniper, and mountain mahogany – plants capable of withstanding the challenges of cold winters and hot, dry summers.

Spilling off the North Rim into the canyon, forest plants mix for some distance. At about 5,000ft (1,500 meters), trees vanish altogether, giving way to a scrubland of blackbrush, yucca, Mormon tea, and various cacti. Animals common to this zone are lizard, jackrabbit, desert bighorn sheep, coyote, and a host of small rodents – notably the kangaroo rat, a mouse-sized creature that never drinks water; it makes all it needs from the seeds it consumes.

The canyon goes deeper still, to elevations between 2,000ft (600 meters) and 3,000ft (900 meters). Here, we find the barrel cacti, ocotillo, and mesquite trees associated with southern Arizona. Temperatures at the canyon bottom can reach 120°F (49°C), and, while thunderstorms drench the forested rim, this zone can remain parched for months at a time. It would be a cruel landscape for humans, were it not for the river and its tributary streams. Water bursts from springs, seeps out of gravel in canyon bottoms and supports lush oases of vegetation, including willows and big, shady cottonwood trees. The streams are home to beavers, dippers, herons, rainbow trout, frogs,v and other undesert-like creatures.

Canyon culture

Grand Canyon National Park ❹ was established in 1919 and enlarged in 1975, but human habitation goes back some 5,000 years, when desert nomads left animal figurines made of split willow twigs in high canyon caves. They were placed carefully, ceremonially, suggesting that they had something to do with hunting rituals. About 2,000 years ago, Ancestral Puebloan farmers began building permanent communities of stone houses here. They were the Kayenta and Virgin branches of the same culture that built, among others, the famous cliff dwellings of Mesa Verde. Here, they built no large structures, but if you look carefully you'll see their granaries tucked into ledges and modest dwellings on mesa tops.

The first Europeans to see the Grand Canyon were Spanish explorers, in 1540 – a scant two generations after Christopher Columbus's epic voyage of discovery to the New World. They were treasure-seekers, members of Coronado's futile expedition in search of the

fabulous Seven Cities of Cibola. One of Coronado's lieutenants, Garcia Lopez de Cardenas, was guided by Indians to the South Rim. Surviving accounts of that first visit are sketchy. The Spanish were duly impressed by the size of the place, but they saw the canyon chiefly as a barrier to further exploration and they left with no recorded regrets.

Some three centuries later, Europeans again encountered the Grand Canyon. They were also explorers and adventurers, dreamers and scoundrels, but this time some of them stayed. A few built reputations here, but others lost everything. The most famous explorer was John Wesley Powell, a geologist who led the first descent down the Colorado River through the canyon. Partly through Powell's influence, the canyon became the focus of American geology and signaled a growing appreciation of the desert landscape.

Touring the park

Today, most visitors arrive at the **South Rim** and spend their time along the roads and trails that skirt the abyss. Visitor services are clustered at **Grand Canyon Village Ⓐ**. Here, you'll find lodging, restaurants, shops, and other facilities. To plan your trip, visit Canyon View Information Plaza, the attractive new South Rim Visitor Center. There is no parking at the plaza itself. Either park in the village and ride a free shuttle to the center, or park in one of the new lots near Mather Point on your way into the park and walk.

Grand Canyon Village Historic District has many buildings of historic importance. Genteel **El Tovar Hotel** was built in 1905, when most tourists arrived by train – which is still possible, thanks to the revival of the historic **Grand Canyon Railway**, which runs from Williams, Arizona, to the South Rim daily. **Bright Angel Lodge** houses a small museum. The lodge was designed by Mary Elizabeth Jane Colter, who also drew plans for other distinctive structures at the canyon, including **Lookout Studio**, a fine

example of how buildings can blend with their surroundings, and Hopi House, a fanciful representation of an Indian pueblo. Colter also designed **Desert View Watchtower Ⓑ**, near the East Entrance, and **Hermits Rest Ⓒ**, a charming little structure at the end of the West Rim Drive.

The two main routes into the canyon – the Bright Angel and South Kaibab trails – lead all the way down to the river. To walk or ride a mule to the bottom and spend a night at rustic **Phantom Ranch Ⓓ** is an unforgettable experience but one that requires planning. Make reservations well in advance.

The South Rim is essentially one grand viewing stand. However, several points provide more expansive panoramas. A good place to begin is **Yavapai Point Ⓔ**, where a geologic museum perched on the canyon's brink explains the canyon's major features. From there, consider touring the **West Rim Drive**. During summer, this road is closed to private vehicles; the park operates free shuttle buses. Although it means leaving your car behind, the system makes it simple to combine walking with riding. Visitors can hop

More than 4 million people visit the Grand Canyon every year. Various forms of crowd control are being explored, as congestion in the summertime and around the South Rim is in danger of damaging the site.

Grand Canyon Facts and Figures

The Grand Canyon is 277 miles (446km) in length, measured along the Colorado River from Lees Ferry to the Grand Wash Cliffs on Lake Mead. If you add tributaries, many of which are great canyons in their own right, the length stretches to thousands of miles.

The Grand Canyon's depth and width vary greatly. Grand Canyon Village, for example, is just under 7,000ft (2,100 meters) elevation. Twelve miles (19km) away on the North Rim, Bright Angel Point stands at 8,145ft (2,483 meters). Between them, at river level, Phantom Ranch breathes the relatively thick air of 2,400ft (730 meters). In its western reaches, where the Hualapai tribe has built the popular Sky Walk on reservation lands, the inner canyon is less deep but narrower.

The climate varies widely, too. Whereas the North Rim gets about 27ins (69cm) of rain a year, the average is only 15ins (38cm) for the South Rim and less than 7ins (18cm) in the canyon bottom. On a typical day in May, temperatures on the South Rim go from 78°F (26°C) down to 36°F (2°C), while, at the river, the high will be 98°F (37°C) with an overnight low of 73°F (23°C). And as much as 200 ins (500cm) of snow falls on the North Rim during winter, while, at the river, a dusting is a rarity.

on and off the bus as they wish.

Going in the other direction is the **East Rim Drive**, which is open all year to private vehicles. Among worthwhile stops are **Grandview Point** , **Moran Point**, and **Lipan Point** , each offering a different perspective. Keep in mind that the eyes become fatigued when confronted by mile after mile of this strange landscape. It's a good idea to take the canyon a bit at a time – better to spend three leisurely hours at one viewpoint than to race from one to the next.

Also along the East Rim Drive, you will find **Tusayan** , which is the remains of a prehistoric pueblo that was home to a small group of perhaps 30 people around 800 years ago. A small archeology museum displays ancient artifacts that are typical of the canyon. Two times a day, park rangers conduct guided tours of the ruin, explaining different aspects of life at the Grand Canyon so many centuries past.

To the North Rim

Near the East Entrance, **Desert View**  provides limited visitor services, including a campground and the Desert View Watchtower. At this point, the Colorado River, having maintained a southerly course for many miles, turns hard to the west and enters the deepest section of the canyon. From here, the North Rim is only a few miles away as the raven flies but over 180 miles (290km) by car. Leaving the park, the highway drops some 3,000ft (900 meters) past the impressive gorge of the **Little Colorado River** on the Navajo reservation, and continues north through the Painted Desert, past the towering **Echo Cliffs**, to the spectacular **Navajo Bridge** spanning **Marble Canyon**. Stop at the delightful green-built interpretive center to see exhibits, buy books, and view the turquoise-hued Colorado River a dizzying 467ft (142 meters) below. From nearby Marble Canyon Trading Post, a road leads north to **Lees Ferry** – historically significant as the only feasible crossing for hundreds of miles in either direction; geologically significant as the official beginning of the Grand Canyon.

From Marble Canyon, Highway 89A

BELOW: floating down river.
BELOW RIGHT: the Desert View Watchtower.

heads west through the Arizona Strip and climbs the **Kaibab Plateau**. The transition from treeless desert to pine forest is dramatic. Squirrels replace lizards, deer bound through the shadows of giant ponderosa pines, and snowbanks last well into June. The word Kaibab comes from two Paiute words, *kaiuw* (mountain) and *a-vwi* (lying down). Indeed, the plateau feels like a "mountain lying down," alpine in character but with no definite summit. It makes for very pleasant driving.

The **North Rim** is the less visited side of the Grand Canyon, partly because the access road is closed by snow for about six months every year, partly because the roads on this side do not parallel the rim for long distances. No one feels disappointed here. The canyon views are, if anything, more spectacular and the uncrowded atmosphere is quite appealing in comparison to the jostling crowds of the South Rim. Most visitors go straight to the **Grand Canyon Lodge** ❶, a superb stone-and-log building surrounded by cabins, some perched right on the canyon brink. A short, paved trail takes

you along a knife-edged ridge to the tip of Bright Angel Point. This path rivals anything anywhere in the National Park System for sheer drama and ends at yet another grand vista.

For many visitors, it comes as a surprise that what they see here is not the Grand Canyon proper but a tributary canyon called **Bright Angel Canyon**. That such an enormous gulf is just an auxiliary branch can be hard to accept. To reach the main canyon, follow Cape Royal Road to its end at **Cape Royal** ❻. Although only 20 miles (32km) in length, this excursion can take at least half a day, stopping at **Point Imperial** ❼ and other viewpoints along the way.

At the heart of the canyon lies the Colorado River – creator and prime mover of this remarkable landscape. It is said that, if you know the river, you know the canyon.

Beginning far upstream in the snowy mountains of Colorado, the river draws strength from tributaries like Wyoming's Green River, pouring cold and clear into Utah's red rock country. Here, it becomes warm in the summer sun and picks up the sediment for which it

Unesco declared the Grand Canyon a World Heritage Site in 1979.

BELOW: Lees Ferry marks the beginning of the Grand Canyon.

The Glen Canyon Dam is the second-largest dam on the Colorado River.

BELOW: Lake Mead National Recreation Area.
RIGHT: Antelope Canyon, a red-orange slot canyon, just outside Glen Canyon National Recreation Area.

was named. *Colorado* is a Spanish word for red. The river once flowed red all the way to the Gulf of California. It built a great delta there, but now a series of dams has diverted the water to booming cities and the Mexican delta is virtually dry.

The most recent obstruction, Glen Canyon Dam, stands just above the Grand Canyon and has created Lake Powell. Emerging from the depths of the lake, the old red river now flows cold and green. Like a string of jade among the red sandstones, it is beautiful, but the dam-controlled river environment is different from what it once was. In permanently cold water, a new assortment of fish and insects has replaced native species. With no new sand flowing downstream, the beaches are disappearing. And, with the disappearance of spring floods, vegetation has grown more dense.

These effects fuel a heated controversy between demands that the natural river environment be maintained and the need for electrical power from the dam. Through the adjustment of flow rates, some of these effects can be

mitigated, but others will bear on the canyon as long as the dam remains.

Meanwhile, Lake Powell is the centerpiece of 1.2-million-acre (485,623-hectare) **Glen Canyon National Recreation Area ❺**, managed by the NPS and beloved by powerboaters and houseboaters and to a lesser extent kayakers and hikers. **Carl Hayden Visitor Center** at the dam is now guarded like Fort Knox, following 9/11, but it's worth the security measures to enter and see the superb scale model of the region or take a tour of the dam.

Those who knew Glen Canyon before it was flooded still regard its inundation as one of the environmental losses of the century. It was a unique place, characterized by soaring walls of sandstone carved in liquid shapes. The Colorado flowed warm and shallow through a child's fantasy of shape and color. Side canyons hundreds of feet deep and only a few yards wide opened into huge amphitheaters beneath the desert surface.

A long-lived drought has, in fact, reduced the lake to historically low levels, revealing lost, once-inundated side canyons and their associated archeological treasures. For now, the lake remains, its serpentine shoreline dotted with coves and beaches, sheer cliffs and domes of smooth, white sandstone. The water is deep blue and warm in summer. Road access is limited to several marinas, the largest of which is **Wahweap**, near the dam. Tour boats ply the lake to various sites, including **Rainbow Bridge National Monument ❻**, where visitors marvel at the graceful and perhaps largest natural bridge on earth.

At the other end of Grand Canyon, near Las Vegas, Nevada, **Lake Mead National Recreation Area ❼** also centers on a reservoir, this one created by the Hoover Dam. Aside from the lake, interest here focuses on the unusual richness of desert flora and fauna. Three distinct desert ecosystems come together here – the Mojave, Sonoran, and Great Basin. The result is rewarding for anyone interested in wildlife. ❑

THE CANYON'S HIDDEN HISTORY

The Grand Canyon impresses all by its sheer magnitude. But hidden in its huge expanse are fascinating details that are easy to overlook

When you stand on the rim, gazing across the Grand Canyon's vast expanses, you have the sense that this is a very still, empty and quiet place. And it is – and it isn't. If you had a great deal of time, and maybe wings like the raven, you could discover many tantalizing stories in its millions of niches and crevices.

The Canyon is a grand example of dry-land erosion, revealing more than 2 billion years of geologic history in the mile-deep stack of rock layers through which the Colorado River and other erosive forces have sliced. Summer's brief but heavy rainstorms send rivulets of red muddy water racing downhill, letting us witness, on a minute scale, continuous canyon-making.

Hidden in the arid landscape, there is water: ephemeral side-canyon streams, gushing springs, peaceful seeps. The wide, tumultuous Colorado River is the canyon's heart line and one of the world's premier white-water rafting courses.

Occasionally, evidence of thousands of years of human occupation shows itself. Archeologists have documented about 2,700 habitation sites in and around the canyon. The pueblo, two *kivas* (ceremonial chambers) and garden plots of the 800-year-old Tusayan Ruin *(illustrated above)* provide us with clues about some of the canyon's prehistoric Puebloan occupants.

ABOVE: Puebloans built this granary at Nankoweap under a rock overhang, sealing it with clay against weather and rodents.

BELOW: Around AD 1100, Puebloan people hid these pots under a ledge, where they were found intact 800 years later.

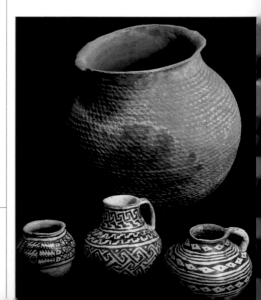

THE EARLIEST INHABITANTS

The earliest evidence of people at Grand Canyon is a projectile point (or arrowhead), broken in the making and discarded about 10,000 years ago. No doubt a constant stream of people passed through on their seasonal rounds of hunting and gathering, but, because they had few possessions and traveled light, they left scant evidence.

The period of most intense population began about 1,250 years ago. Prehistoric Puebloans farmed river deltas and rim fields and hunted and gathered through the whole area, following game and ripening vegetation. They built stone structures partly for shelter, partly for grain storage *(above)*. Among the goods they traded with other groups were vessels, shells, and mineral pigments.

ABOVE: The ancient Desert Archaic culture from 4,000 years ago crafted animal figures, generally a few inches tall, from split willow twigs. Perhaps they were hunting propitiations. Those that were left in dry caves are well preserved.

RIGHT: Ancestral Puebloan larder ruins.

FAR LEFT AND RIGHT: Murals inside the Desert View Watchtower depicting aspects of Hopi mythology and religious ceremonies.

CAPITOL REEF AND BRYCE CANYON

Rainbow-colored cliffs, bizarre eroded hoodoos, mighty natural amphitheaters, curious historical relics, and an abundance of wildlife characterize these southeastern Utah parks

For many people, the desert Southwest seems like a vast dry ocean that stretches endlessly in every direction, its rocky floor occasionally interrupted by broad troughs, tablelands, snowcapped mountains, maze-like twisting canyons, and island communities of wildlife.

But in Utah, the paradox of ocean imagery amid intensely arid land goes one step farther, for here, rolling in long, colorful, petrified breakers across a desert basin, is one of the most dramatic geologic features on the American continent: the Waterpocket Fold, a 100 mile (160km) -long warp on the earth's surface that neatly bisects southeastern Utah, from volcanic Thousand Lake Mountain in the north to man-made Lake Powell in the south. In between, **Capitol Reef National Park** ❽ preserves 75 miles (120km) of the Waterpocket Fold and the plants, animals, and artifacts of Indian and pioneer settlers who have made the area their home.

Capitol Reef is one of the lesser-known parks in the Southwest – a plus for geology fans who are put off by the crowds at Grand Canyon and Zion. It is halfway between Bryce Canyon and Canyonlands national parks and is easily reached from Highway 12 to the south or from Interstate 70 to the

north. Highway 24 cuts across the park, following the winding **Fremont River** beneath tall sandstone cliffs, which open into a series of humpbacks, known to the Paiutes as "the sleeping rainbow," at the eastern exit. Roads on either side of the Waterpocket Fold swing south from Highway 24, providing numerous possibilities for exploring the park by car, by bicycle, or on foot.

Rainbow rocks

Most visitors are intrigued by the Waterpocket Fold. How did it come to be

Main attractions
FRUITA (CAPITOL REEF)
WATERPOCKET FOLD (CAPITOL REEF)
BURR TRAIL ROAD (CAPITOL REEF)
CATHEDRAL VALLEY (CAPITOL REEF)
HIGHWAY 12 SCENIC HIGHWAY
ESCALANTE CANYONS (GRAND STAIRCASE-ESCALANTE NM)
BRYCE CANYON SCENIC DRIVE (BRYCE CANYON)
BRYCE LODGE (BRYCE CANYON)
SUNRISE POINT TRAILS (BRYCE CANYON)
WASATCH RAMPARTS TRAIL (CEDAR BREAKS)

PRECEDING PAGES: historic barn in Capitol Reef. **LEFT:** hiking in Bryce Canyon. **RIGHT:** Spooky Gulch, Capitol Reef.

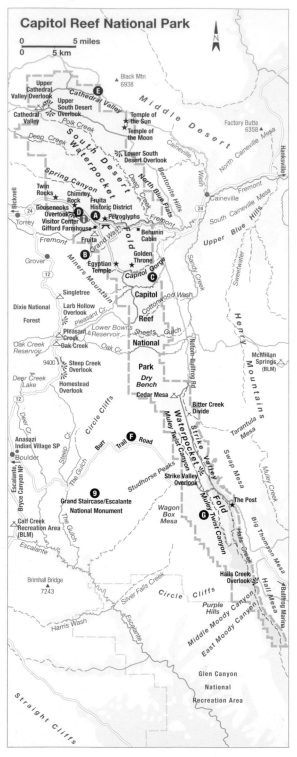

Capitol Reef National Park

0   5 miles
0   5 km

here? Scientists believe that it was created about 65 million years ago, when a period of geologic activity began wrenching the low-lying landscape of western America into its present contorted form. It is generally thought that massive movements along the junction of the Pacific and North American plates around that time forced up the Sierra Nevada in California and continued to reverberate eastward, squeezing the miles of sedimentary rocks that had accumulated across the Southwest.

The monolithic Colorado Plateau rose slowly under this pressure, and a series of steep, north–south-oriented monoclines, or folds, began to form across its surface, of which the Waterpocket Fold is one of the most spectacular examples. The exposed rock surfaces soon became vulnerable to weathering. In this region, wind and water erosion carved the rainbow-colored cliffs, spires, natural bridges, arches, and hogbacks that characterize Capitol Reef today.

Because it follows the Waterpocket Fold, the park is much longer than it is wide and can be divided roughly into three sections: the rugged, remote northern section of **Cathedral Valley** paralleling the northeastern exposure of the Fold; the accessible **Escarpment** section, encompassing park headquarters at **Fruita**, the Fremont River, and a particularly scenic portion of the Fold; and the southernmost section of the park, above Bullfrog Basin in Glen Canyon, where the great rock waves of the Waterpocket Fold reach 1,500ft (460 meters) in height and are cut by a labyrinthine network of deep, impressive canyons.

Mormon settlers

If you haven't been to Capitol Reef before, start your visit at park headquarters in **Fruita Ⓐ**, which sits next to the emerald belt of cottonwoods, tamarisks, and willows along the Fremont River. This old Mormon community (elevation 5,500ft/1,680 meters) grew up in the 1880s, comprising 12 families, some of whom were polygamists

wishing to live quiet, self-supporting lives away from the glare of government disapproval. Names like **Cohab Canyon** linger, commemorating these early settlers.

With a reliable water source at hand, the residents were able to harvest plentiful supplies of apricots, peaches, cherries, and apples, which they used for their own consumption or sold to neighboring towns, transient miners, cowboys, and even outlaws like Butch Cassidy and his Wild Bunch. Cattle ranching also took place at Capitol Reef, evidence of which may still be seen in the park.

These adherents to the Church of Jesus Christ of Latter-day Saints prospered just as nearby communities struggled. They built wagon roads across the nearly impassable ridges and smooth domes of the Waterpocket Fold, which received its name because of the way depressions in the smooth "slickrock" filled with life-giving water when it rained.

The settlers' preoccupation with land and government shows in the very name they gave the area – Capitol Reef. In their eyes, the central section of the Fold welled up like an ocean reef, while one of its larger domes seemed like a dead ringer for the US Capitol. Other unusually eroded rocks sparked equally descriptive names – Chimney Rock, Golden Throne, Egyptian Temple, and the Castle.

These early European settlers were keen to attract visitors to this remote area of Utah, which, in typically grand fashion, they dubbed Wayne Wonderland (Capitol Reef is in Wayne County). It was a combination of their boosterism and continuing political pressure at the state level that directly led to Capitol Reef being designated a national monument in 1937 and a national park in 1971.

Today, all that remains of Fruita are its turn-of-the-20th-century schoolhouse, a barn, a couple of houses, and the orchards. The last of the residents were bought out in the late 1960s.

They have been supplanted by Park Service employees who operate park headquarters, a visitor center, and a lovely grassy campground, which sits among the original orchards (you are welcome to pick fruit for your own consumption, but you must pay for larger quantities).

Desert and river

This is a park that inspires strong emotions. It is remote, overscaled, and desperately hot and dry in the summer (unless you find yourself caught in a summer downpour, when most of the park's scant 7ins/18cm of precipitation falls). To keep cool in summer, either view the park from your car or stick to one of the day hikes off the scenic drive and Highway 24, such as **Grand Wash** **Ⓑ**, **Capitol Gorge Ⓒ**, the **Goosenecks Overlook Ⓓ**, Sunset Point, or Hickman Bridge.

The tree-lined banks of the Fremont River also provide shade on days when the temperature approaches 100°F (38°C). If you hope to explore the park on foot, bring adequate weather protection, water, food, and backpacking

Taking advantage of the apple orchards at Fruita.

BELOW: the Fruita schoolhouse, a remnant of an early Mormon village.

A member of the Backcountry Trail Patrol who are trained to assist all trail users in an emergency.

BELOW: ancient petroglyph.
BELOW RIGHT: two cars pass in Capitol Gorge.

equipment with you – they are not available in the park. There are numerous places where you can hike and camp off-trail. Plan your trip carefully before venturing out by obtaining a free backcountry map from rangers at the visitor center.

The river and the shallow pools at the base of seeping sandstone walls provide an oasis where trees and water-loving plants, such as columbines, monkeyflowers, and ferns, grow. They are also popular haunts for mule deer, warblers, ringtail cats, frogs, and other desert denizens that come to drink and splash during cool desert evenings and mornings. In winter, you can sometimes surprise a mountain lion or bobcat, emboldened by the lack of visitors.

It is a mistake to imagine that the desert is devoid of life. The many creatures, large and small, that live here have adapted to a life beneath rocks, burrowed underground or hidden in narrow canyons, where sunlight and humans rarely interrupt their privacy.

Towering nearly 1,000ft (300 meters) above the river are the vertiginous cliffs of red Wingate Sandstone, narrow ledges of maroon Kayenta, and creamy Navajo slickrock domes that give the Fold its awesome ramparts.

On these slippery surfaces, pinyon and juniper trees struggle with the elements, sending roots into pockets of soil. These dune-deposited rocks were laid down in a vast desert roughly 200 million years ago and, over time, compressed into mineralized rocks several miles thick. A 13-mile (21km) scenic drive from Fruita takes you through the dramatic western exposure of the Waterpocket Fold into **Grand Wash** and **Capitol Gorge**, two water-carved, sheer-walled canyons. Along the drive, older rocks of the Shinarump Conglomerate, Chinle, and Moenkopi formations appear, their ancient origins in sluggish streams and rivers during the time of the dinosaurs.

There are many places where you can stop and hike along trails leading to overlooks, arches, remote canyons, and slickrock wilderness. To the east loom the 11,000ft (3,350-meter), lava-intruded **Henry Mountains**, the last range to be named in the United

States, and, to the west, the great bulk of **Boulder Mountain**. You are never far from evergreen forests of ponderosa, fir, and spruce, or from refreshing mountain streams.

Abundant evidence of geologic activity is on view in the northern section of the park. Here, the enormous drainage area of **Cathedral Valley E** fans southeast from the base of **Thousand Lake Mountain**, where more recent volcanism and glaciation have built and sculpted the high country beyond Capitol Reef. In this extremely arid section of the park, accessible only on foot or by four-wheel drive, thick layers of red Entrada Sandstone have been whittled by erosion into 500ft (150-meter) spires that seem to guard this bleak landscape. The exposed location is home to only the hardiest desert plants.

Burrowing creatures such as kangaroo rats, jackrabbits, and cottontails have found a way to survive here — even though these same animals form the diet of gray foxes, coyotes, mountain lions, golden eagles, ravens, and other desert dwellers.

In this remote spot, there is a single primitive campground close to **Upper Cathedral Valley Overlook**, and another at Elkhorn in Fishlake National Forest, which is outside the park limits.

Desert rats

For "desert rats" used to the rigors of hiking over naked slickrock, the southernmost tip of the Fold is the most alluring. It can be reached via the Notom-Bullfrog dirt road, which runs down the east side of the Fold all the way to Bullfrog Marina at Lake Powell in Glen Canyon National Recreation Area, or by turning off at Boulder along Highway 12 and crossing the famous **Burr Trail Road F**, a prospector's route to the canyons. The best way to explore it is to hike south from where the Burr Trail meets the Notom-Bullfrog Road, through 16-mile (26km) **Muley Twist Canyon G**. This route takes you through steep canyon narrows to an exceptionally wild area of the park around **Lower Halls Creek**, where a ferry took 19th-century pioneers across what used to be the Colorado River.

Muley Twist Canyon was named by early travelers who joked that the canyon zigzagged so sharply that their mules had to twist to get through.

BELOW:
Cathedral Valley in Capitol Reef.

TIP

Bryce Canyon is open year-round and looks spectacular in winter. But, from October through April, the park roads are often temporarily closed while plows clear the effects of snowstorms.

Grand Staircase-Escalante National Monument

Here, at this southern exposure of the Waterpocket Fold, Capitol Reef and Glen Canyon National Recreation Area border largely undeveloped **Grand Staircase-Escalante National Monument 9** which protects the **Escalante River** and canyons on the northeast, the **Kaiparowits Plateau** in its center, and the geological staircase of colorful layered rocks known as the **Grand Staircase** on the southwest. It's a park that welcomes travelers willing to travel a historic landscape of pioneer communities, unpaved backroads, and wild canyons that tempt backpackers for days. Among its many highlights is beautiful rock art created by the prehistoric Fremont and Ancestral Pueblo cultures. Deep in the canyons are panels depicting, among other things, tall, bejeweled, shaman-like anthropomorphs carrying shields and surrounded by bighorn sheep and other game.

Bryce Canyon

A visit to **Bryce Canyon National Park 10** is a highlight for any visitor to southern Utah. A geologic fantasyland of technicolor dreaming spires, natural bridges, gravity-defying arches, precariously balanced rocks, and sky-filled windows, carved deeply into the soft, limestone cliffs of the Paunsaugunt Plateau – this is one national park that lives up to all the hype.

Paiute people, who have lived in the region for centuries, view the remarkable geomorphic forms of Bryce Canyon as part of their creation story, a time when the animal people so displeased powerful Coyote that he punished them by turning them to stone. An apocryphal story holds that Ebenezer Bryce, a Scottish Mormon who homesteaded the **Paria Valley** below the cliffs in 1875–76, was altogether more prosaic about the series of carved amphitheaters towering above him, complaining that it was "a hell of a place to lose a cow!" In fact, Bryce Canyon can be explained by the erosive action of water, snow and ice on the east-facing edge of a lofty plateau. The ending to Bryce's story is always changing, as gravity and erosion continue sculpting this awesome natural masterpiece.

BELOW: a natural bridge in Bryce Canyon.

The Must-See Staircase

The Grand Staircase-Escalante National Monument is comprised of colorful cliffs, mesas, canyons, buttes, and pinnacles and is divided into three distinct sections. Among the park's most popular destinations are the Escalante River, the Pariah movie set, Hole in the Rock Road, and Cottonwood Road. The Grand Staircase itself features tilted terraces and great cliffs of white, gray, pink, and red rock, revealing 200 million years of the earth's history. The park is managed by the Bureau of Land Management (BLM), and all visitor services are situated on the periphery, including campgrounds. Visitor centers at Escalante, Cannonville, and Kanab serve the 1.9-million-acre (768,903-hectare) monument's Escalante Canyons, the high Kaiparowits Plateau, and Grand Staircase sections, respectively.

The **Pink Cliffs** of Bryce Canyon form the sixth and uppermost "step" of the Grand Staircase, which ascends in color-coded formation – oldest to youngest – from the Grand Canyon to the Paunsaugunt Plateau, a distance of more than 100 miles (160km). The rocks, which were pushed up, cracked, and broken into plateaus by movement along faults more than 13 million years ago, originated as sediments laid down over millions of years, when a succession of inland seas, lakes, rivers, streams, and even a dune-filled desert covered the Southwest.

Over time, the sediments hardened into rock, colored by manganese and iron. Today, weathering has oxidized these minerals into the blues, reds, purples, and yellows that bathe the rocks in a wash of pastel hues.

Bryce's Pink Cliffs are the youngest sedimentary rocks in the area, the result of silts, sands, and the limey skeletons of creatures that lived in the ephemeral freshwater lakes that formed here 60 million years ago, when geologic activity elevated the Colorado Plateau. Millions of years later, when southern Utah began to split into its characteristic plateaus, these rocks, known as the **Claron Formation**, were exposed to the action of water speeding down the eastern edge of the Paunsaugunt Plateau. In what is today a semi-arid country, there is an irony in the role water has played in creating the eerie "hoodoos" and other "rock-candy" formations that crowd the amphitheaters of Bryce Canyon.

Exploring the park

You should plan to spend at least a day here to take full advantage of the many interesting summer ranger programs and exhibits at the new visitor center, as well as the different experiences to be had in a park whose elevation ranges from 6,600 to 9,100ft (2,010 to 2,770 meters). Bryce has two pleasant campgrounds as well as the rustic **Bryce Canyon Lodge** (closed in winter), built in the 1920s by the Utah Parks Company. The lodge is on the Register of Historic Places and is very popular; guests should book six months to a year ahead. Day-trippers can get a flavor of the place at the restaurant.

Bryce Canyon receives more than 900,000 visitors per year. The highest numbers arrive from June to September, the lowest December to February.

BELOW LEFT:
Bryce's Pink Cliffs.
RIGHT:
taking in the scenery.

The red blooms of Indian paintbrush.

You can view the park's highly eroded cliffs from your car, or, in summer, park and board a free shuttle that leaves the visitor center every 15 minutes and stops at the lodge, campgrounds, and Sunset, Bryce, Inspiration, and Sunrise points in the main Bryce Amphitheater section. The 18-mile (29km) scenic drive follows the edge of the 8,000ft (2,438-meter) plateau through forests of ponderosa pine and summer wildflowers, such as Indian paintbrush, skyrocket gilia, and penstemon. The highest spot in the park is **Rainbow Point** (9,105ft/2,775 meters). Here, the ponderosa gives way to subalpine conifers, such as white fir and blue spruce. In particularly exposed areas at this high elevation, rare bristlecone pines grow, some more than 1,000 years old.

In the evenings, you will encounter mule deer grazing by the side of the road; in the daytime, rodents like ground squirrels and Utah prairie dogs, an endangered species, are often sighted. The deer are the preferred prey of shy mountain lions. Their numbers are diminished now due to habitat destruction, but their presence is still felt on this wild plateau. The skies are the province of red-tailed hawks and ravens, whose languid, circuitous flight is in sharp contrast to the quick, darting forays of cliff swallows.

In the forests, jays jabber loquaciously in the pines, their iridescent blue feathers flashing among green needles. The wildlife at the 6,600ft (2,010-meter) canyon bottom varies considerably from that on the moister, cooler rim. Pinyon and juniper trees grow alongside sagebrush, clinging tenaciously to pockets of soil in bare rock ledges. Run-off comes and goes swiftly here; there is little to hold it as it courses down steep precipices toward the Paria River, and thence to the Colorado River.

A closer look

Even if you have only a short time, get out of your car and hike down into the amphitheaters along one of the superb intersecting trails, which start from the overlooks. From **Sunrise Point**, you can descend the steep cliffs along

BELOW: Sunrise Point. **BELOW RIGHT:** the sweet-scented evening primrose.

the 1½-mile (2km) round-trip called **Queen's Garden Trail** and, if you wish, join up with the **Navajo Loop Trail** (1½-mile/2km round-trip), which drops down from Sunset Point and proceeds through the clustered formations of Silent City. Don't forget that you are climbing a mountain in reverse.

The steep ascent from Queen's Garden is 320ft (98 meters); from the bottom of Navajo Loop, 520ft (159 meters). Carry water and don't be in too much of a rush. Hiking through these strange carved rocks is one of life's great novelties. You won't soon forget the sight of an out-of-place Douglas fir yearning toward the sunlight from a narrow corridor on Navajo Loop Trail, nor should you miss taking a guided moonlit hike among these phantasmagoric rocks, if you visit at the right time of year.

If you want a longer hike, the strenuous, 5-mile (8km) **Peekaboo Loop** starts at Bryce Point and meanders through the amphitheaters' otherworldly formations. The **Rim Trail** is a fairly flat 5½ mile (9km) hike overlooking the amphitheaters between **Fairyland Point** and Bryce Point.

For overnight trips, the **Under-the-Rim Trail** runs 22 miles (35km) from Bryce Point to Yovimpa Point, through some of the most remote and wildlife-rich country in the park. Be sure to consult the park rangers before attempting long backcountry hikes. Note that permits are required for overnight backpacking.

Although its high elevation made year-round residence here difficult, the region was used by prehistoric Indians – possibly early Basketmaker and Ancestral Pueblo people – who were adept dryland farmers and knew how to utilize the area's plants and animals to survive. These early inhabitants were superseded by nomadic Paiutes, who, like their predecessors, ventured into the high country in summer to hunt game and gather pine nuts and other such edibles.

Mormon settlers, such as Bryce, whose name came to be associated with these spectacular cliffs, generally kept their eyes down and concentrated on wresting a living from the land around **Tropic**, in the Paria Valley. It was left to explorers such as Major

Wranglers lead horseback rides into Bryce Amphitheater along a dedicated horse trail, as well as on the Peekaboo Loop Trail.

BELOW: snowshoers on the move.

From the lofty rim of the amphitheater at Cedar Breaks, you can often see for over 100 miles (160km).

John Wesley Powell to chart the maze of canyonlands in the 1870s and report back on what he had seen. A member of his party labeled the area "one of the wonders of the world." In 1924, the state of Utah pressed National Park Service director Stephen Mather and his assistant Horace Albright to create what was dubbed Utah National Park. Bryce Canyon National Park was created in 1928.

This small park is open year-round and is particularly magical under a fresh snowfall. Snowshoeing and cross-country skiing are encouraged, but snowmobiling is allowed only outside the park limits.

Modern paved roads now make visiting Bryce Canyon easy. You can approach from I-15 via Panguitch, drive up Highway 89 from Kanab, or take the spectacular Scenic Highway 14 from Cedar City. From Highway 89, take State 12 into the park.

Cedar Breaks

You mustn't miss glorious **Cedar Breaks National Monument ⓫**, atop the 10,000ft (3,000-meter) Markagunt

BELOW: looking out over Cedar Breaks.

Plateau, west of Bryce Canyon, which is reached by a short spur (closed from October to May) from Highway 14. This tiny gem preserves another highly eroded amphitheater of Claron Formation rock, but because the amphitheater is deeper, the coloration somewhat different, and descent into it discouraged, it complements a trip to Bryce Canyon rather than takes the place of it.

Cedar Breaks is perhaps best known for its extravagant wildflower displays, including lupine sneezeweed, yarrow, and sunflowers, which begin adorning the meadows in July, shortly after the park reopens.

Summer brings a rush of wildlife, which ranges from scurrying pikas, chipmunks, squirrels, and marmots to stealthy mountain lions and coyotes. Mule deer browse on lush high-country meadows. Ravens and violet-green swallows swoop past colorful cliffs, and chattery Clark's nutcrackers and Steller's jays feast on the seasonal bounty of pine nuts.

A 5-mile (8km) scenic drive follows the rim of the amphitheater and provides many pleasant overlooks from which to view Cedar Breaks. Alpine Pond Trail (2 miles/3km long) takes you through a cool, moist forest of spruce and fir trees.

A completely different hike skirts the rim of the amphitheater, past a large stand of thousand-year-old bristlecones clinging precariously to bare rock at **Spectra Point**, and out along the **Wasatch Ramparts** (4-mile/6km round-trip). Be sure to stay on the marked trails. Cedar Breaks protects a fragile alpine environment; off-trail hiking is discouraged. The park operates a small visitor center and a delightful campground (open during the summer months).

Other campgrounds on national forest lands can be found outside the park limits. Don't hurry through, though; this is some of the most spectacular high country to be found anywhere in the West. ❏

Maintaining the Balance

Mining, pollution, tourism, over-commercialisation: many national parks are under threat from the perils of the modern world

For many people, a visit to a national park offers a respite from the hurly burly of fast-paced and increasingly disconnected modern life, a balm for the soul. But nearly 140 years after Yellowstone was made the USA's first national park, several of America's 392 parks are in crisis – many of them victimized by their own success in attracting visitors; others impacted by human activity just outside their borders.

Mining on the borders of Yellowstone and Arches. Gridlock in Yosemite. Graffiti in Petroglyph Theft of artifacts from Chaco Canyon. Air pollution in Sequoia. Proposed dams on Zion's Virgin River. Loss of native species. Poaching of protected animals. No longer are many national parks islands of calm cut off from the outside world. More and more, they are at the mercy of overcommercialization, which environmental writer Ed Abbey, in *Desert Solitaire*, criticized as "industrial Tourism."

A lot has changed since the National Park Service was founded in 1916. The Vail Agenda, a self-critical report commissioned by the service in 1991, highlighted many of the problems facing park rangers, including excessive paperwork, long hours, low pay, substandard housing, low morale, and an inability to attract qualified staff. Yet, despite these problems, surveys find consistently high ratings for Park Service personnel.

Grand Canyon National Park, with over 4 million visitors annually, has reached crisis point. In 1993, it produced a sophisticated workbook detailing several alternative management plans for the park, and it held town meetings to encourage public input. Other parks are looking for ways to attract more volunteers and better interaction with local communities.

A revival of successful 1930s government programs, such as the Civilian Conservation Corps, which built many of the facilities in the parks, is another possibility. Some parks have also started cooperative ventures with private companies to improve park environments. Grand Canyon, for example, teamed up with Dow Chemical to sponsor a successful recycling program.

The public is already being asked to pay higher charges, to reimburse for expensive search-and-rescues, to stick to quotas in popular backpacking areas in the backcountry, and to submit to a lottery in order to launch private boat trips on the Colorado River through the Grand Canyon.

Kill the cars

Popular parks such as Yosemite, Bryce Canyon, and Grand Canyon now strongly suggest visitors park their cars and use free eco-powered shuttles, bicycles, or their own two feet in order to lessen the impact on park resources; in Zion Canyon, shuttle use is mandatory in summer, a move that has restored the natural quiet in that beautiful spot.

As parks coordinate more closely with neighboring communities, visitors are increasingly finding it easy to base themselves in adjoining gateway towns, a move that could save Grand Canyon and Yosemite national parks, which are in danger of being loved to death by the thousands of tourists who flock there daily.

We may have assumed that our overworked National Park Service can do its job alone, but in the future, we must share the responsibility for these national treasures. ❏

RIGHT: maintenance in the park.

CANYONLANDS

This high-desert park protects a colorful network of sandstone canyons, mesas, buttes, and gorges carved into the Colorado Plateau by the Colorado and Green rivers

Southeastern Utah's **Canyonlands National Park ⑫** sprawls at the heart of the huge geological province known as the Colorado Plateau. Here, across an enormous, tilted, tiered, and carved rock stage, one of nature's longest-running dramas plays every day – an epic in which rock, river, weather, and a perfect cast of well-adapted living things all have equal roles on stage.

The late Stewart Udall, who as Secretary of the Interior was midwife to the congressional bill that created Canyonlands in 1964, described the region as "a vast area of scenic wonders and recreational opportunities unduplicated elsewhere on the American continent or in the world." You will need to plan your trip to this 527-sq mile (1,364-sq-km) park carefully, as it is divided into four equally fascinating units – Island in the Sky, The Needles, The Maze, and the converging Green and Colorado rivers – all located at some distance from each other.

Pick of the park

If you have only a day to explore, the 6,000ft (1,830-meter) plateau of **Island in the Sky**, situated in the northern part of Canyonlands between the Y of the two rivers, offers sweeping views of the entire park, a new visitor center, interpretive talks, a tiny campground (no running water), and short, rugged hikes to salt domes, arches, and other geologic features.

The road to this unit begins 10 miles (16km) north of Moab, then southwest from Highway 191 for another 25 miles (40km). Float trips above the confluence of the Green and Colorado rivers – one of the most pleasurable ways to experience the park – are popular, as are mountain biking and four-wheel driving. Concessionaires, located primarily in Moab or Green River, can arrange these. These

Main attractions

GRAND VIEW POINT
MESA ARCH TRAIL (AT SUNRISE)
GREEN RIVER OVERLOOK (AT SUNSET)
CHESLER PARK TRAIL
SALT CREEK TRAIL
CAVE SPRING TRAIL
HORSESHOE CANYON
THE DOLL HOUSE
MAZE OVERLOOK
GOBLIN VALLEY STATE PARK

PRECEDING PAGES: Mesa Arch in the early morning. **LEFT:** mountain biker.
RIGHT: a juniper tree grows out of solid rock.

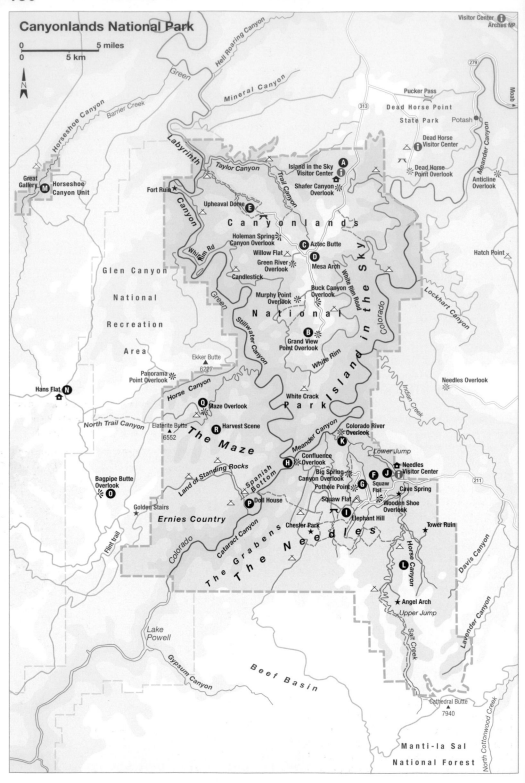

Canyonlands National Park

0 [scale] 5 miles
0 [scale] 5 km

N

Visitor Center
Arches NP

Hell Roaring Canyon

Green

Mineral Canyon

Moab

279

Pucker Pass

313

Dead Horse Point
State Park

Potash

Horseshoe Canyon

Barrier Creek

Labyrinth

Taylor Canyon

Trail Canyon

Island in the Sky
Visitor Center **A**

Shafer Canyon
Overlook

Dead Horse
Visitor Center

Dead Horse
Point Overlook

Anticline
Overlook

Meander Canyon

Great
Gallery

Horseshoe
Canyon Unit **M**

Fort Ruin ★

Canyon

Upheaval Dome **E**

C a n y o n l a n d s

Hatch Point

Holeman Spring
Canyon Overlook

Aztec Butte **C**

Willow Flat **D**

Green River
Overlook

Mesa Arch

Glen Canyon

White Rim Rd

Candlestick

Buck Canyon
Overlook

White Rim Road

Colorado

Lockhart Canyon

National

Murphy Point
Overlook

N a t i o n a l

Recreation

Green

Stillwater Canyon

Grand View
Point Overlook **B**

Area

Ekker Butte
6227

White Rim

Needles Overlook

Panorama
Point Overlook

White Crack

P a r k

I s l a n d   i n   t h e   S k y

Hans Flat **N**

Horse Canyon

Maze Overlook **Q**

Indian Creek

North Trail Canyon

Elaterite Butte
6552

Harvest Scene **R**

Colorado River
Overlook

Meander Canyon

Lower Jump

T h e   M a z e

Confluence
Overlook **H**

K

Needles
Visitor Center

Bagpipe Butte
Overlook **O**

Land of Standing Rocks

Spanish
Bottom

Big Spring
Canyon Overlook

F **J**

211

Pothole Point

G

Squaw
Flat

Cave Spring

Golden Stairs

Doll House **P**

Squaw Flat

Wooden Shoe
Overlook

Ernies Country

Cataract Canyon

Chesler Park

I

Elephant Hill

Tower Ruin ★

Colorado

The Grabens

T h e   N e e d l e s

Horse Canyon

L

Flint trail

Lake
Powell

Gypsum Canyon

Angel Arch ★

Upper Jump

Sal Creek

Davis Canyon

Lavender Canyon

B e e f   B a s i n

Cathedral Butte
7940

North Cottonwood Creek

M a n t i - l a   S a l

N a t i o n a l   F o r e s t

businesses are contracted by the National Park Service to manage a variety of services, including lodging, restaurants, gift shops, and tours.

For an upclose look at Canyon Country, drive south 40 miles (64km) on Highway 191, then another 35 miles (56km) on Highway 211 into the highly rewarding **Needles District**, where a dizzying array of sandstone arches, fins, buttes, spires, and canyons rivals Ancestral Pueblo ruins and rock art for beauty and abundance. The Needles has an attractive visitor center and Squaw Flat Campground (water available year round), primitive backcountry campsites, and popular four-wheel-drive and primitive hiking trails.

The remote **Maze District**, once described as "a 30-sq-mile puzzle in sandstone," can only be reached by foot or four-wheel drive from west of the park (or from the river). If you're well equipped with water, food, and backpacking supplies and willing to spend more time, the pristine Maze contains a rich variety of rocks, desert landscapes, and rock art

For "river rats," there's no better way to go into the heart of this convoluted canyon country than to follow in the wake of John Wesley Powell, who made daring runs down the **Green** and **Colorado** rivers in 1869 and 1871–72. Below the river confluence, the swollen Colorado erupts into roaring white water for the 14 miles (23km) that link sheer-walled **Cataract Canyon** with **Lake Powell**. River running here is carefully monitored by the National Park Service, and only experienced river runners may attempt the trip.

Island in the Sky

Rock is the leitmotif of Canyonlands. In order to try to understand its scope, drive south from **Island in the Sky Visitor Center ❶** to **Grand View Point Overlook ❷**, where a 360-degree panorama unfolds before you. Hidden in the northeast are the soaring red rock spans of Arches National Park. To the

east rise the tall, laccolithic crags (igneous rock) of the **La Sal Mountains**, imposing yet inviting. Closer to the park, beneath **Dead Horse Point State Park**, loop the famous "goosenecks" of the Colorado River, marking the park's eastern border.

To the west, the aptly named Green River winds through **Labyrinth Canyon**, its narrow meanders forming the shared boundary with Glen Canyon National Recreation Area (*see page 164*).

To the southwest, the **Henry Mountains** obstruct the view of Capitol Reef National Park (*see page 171*), their great bulk looming beyond the Maze. The view south absorbs more than 100 miles (160km) of drifting tablelands and swirling canyons, including the junction of the Colorado and Green rivers, bound on either side by the eroded sandstones of The Needles and the tortuous passages of The Maze. Just below this sky island is the **White Rim Road**, a circuitous, 100-mile (160km) dirt trail that was used by prospectors mining uranium in the colorful Chinle Formation in the 1950s. This popular four-wheel-drive route follows a bench

The Canyonlands National Park was established in 1964 "to preserve an area possessing superlative scenic, scientific and archeological features for the inspiration, benefit, and use of the public."

BELOW: tourists walking on the Grand View Point Overlook.

TIP

There are no reliable sources of water anywhere in the park (the Colorado and Green rivers are very silty). Visitors should bring all the drinking water they may need.

of White Rim Sandstone through prime bighorn sheep territory.

The scenic drive offers several places for stopping and hiking. Short trails to **Aztec Butte**  and **Mesa Arch** are clearly marked by rock cairns along the Navajo Sandstone slickrock. Plants struggle to survive in the thin soils found in this arid environment – in cracks in the rock and in fragile, "brown sugar" patches of cryptobiotic soil that will eventually allow pinyons, junipers, blackbrush, and hardy grasses to take hold.

Watch where you walk; your footsteps have a huge impact here. Adaptable reptiles, such as whip-tailed lizards, and ground squirrels, canyon mice, and other gnawing creatures are found on the plateau. They make fine fare for peripatetic coyotes and gray foxes and alert sky patrollers, such as eagles, ravens, and red-tailed hawks.

The rocks in this park contain a color-coded record of sediment deposited over the past 300 million years, in a succession of seas, beaches, deserts, rivers, and streams. But the accounting is not complete; more than a vertical

mile of recent strata has already been borne away by the youthful enthusiasm of the Colorado and Green rivers, which began scouring the land as the massive Colorado Plateau was forced up. The topography is forever changing. As the sediment-laden rivers cut their paths, and ground water, ice, snow, and wind break down the rocks, the eroded beauty of Canyonlands will one day be merely a memory.

To view these geologic processes, hike the trail to **Upheaval Dome** ❺, just off the scenic drive. Below you is a 1,500ft (460-meter) crater filled with a jumble of rocks, which geologists believe is either the site of a meteor impact or a collapsed salt dome. The 11 layers of sedimentary rocks on display sit uneasily on a layer of salt thousands of feet thick – the remnant of evaporated seas that lay trapped here 300 million years ago.

As overlying sediments pressed down on this salt – the Paradox Formation – it liquidized and began to move away from the weight. Highlands blocked it on the east, so it flowed west until it encountered ancient fault blocks that forced the salt to bulge upward, forming the cracked salt domes you see throughout the large Paradox Basin. Ground water began to seep into the fractures, dissolving the salt and deepening the joints through many layers of sedimentary rocks. This weathering of sandstone has created memorable features throughout the park – some of the most spectacular are found among the highly eroded Cedar Mesa Sandstone in The Needles.

The Needles

The turn-off for **The Needles** district lies 14 miles (23km) north of Monticello, on Highway 191, where a paved road follows Indian Creek Canyon to **Squaw Flat** ❻, one of those rare places in Canyonlands blessed with deeper soils that allow Indian rice grass, galleta, and other useful grasses to establish themselves. The road passes **Pothole Point** ❼, where depressions

BELOW: the Needles district.

in the rock trap life-giving rainwater. Good views of the narrow spires of The Needles can be had from here.

The road ends at Big Spring Canyon Overlook, where a trail to the **Confluence Overlook**  begins. From Squaw Flat Campground, a 3-mile (5km) unpaved spur leads to **Elephant Hill** ❶, and thence a dirt road takes you to the collapsing fins of the Grabens near the river, and foot trails enter The Needles themselves. The 5-mile (8km), round-trip **Chesler Park Trail**, through a meadow dotted with eroded rocks, makes a good hike from Elephant Hill. The canyons and meadows of The Needles support many wood rats, chipmunks, squirrels, kangaroo rats, and other rodents, as well as horned larks and black-throated sparrows.

There are a number of places along the scenic drive to turn off and explore. One four-wheel-drive road, beginning at the **Needles Visitor Center** ❶, takes you north to the **Colorado River Overlook** ❿. A short, unpaved spur south of the pavement leads to **Cave Spring Trail**, which preserves a historic cowboy line camp beside a spring. The camp is a reminder that much of Canyonlands was grazed heavily by cattle and sheep from the late 1800s until well into this century. You will need a sturdy pair of legs to explore **Salt Creek** or its main tributary, **Horse Canyon** ❶, a 45-mile (68km) round-trip hike.

Horse Canyon was home to 100 farming families who moved here from overcrowded Mesa Verde in the 1200s. **Tower** and **Keyhole ruins** and the **Thirteen Faces**, red-and-white pictographs painted on the sandstone walls, can still be seen here. They grew their crops along ephemeral washes, now overgrown with willow, tamarisk, and cottonwood, but continued to hunt small game and supplement meals with seeds, nuts, and edible plants. Surplus grain was stored in tightly lidded granaries built into hard-to-reach ledges.

Rock paintings found in these canyons portray large, mysterious-looking, anthropomorphs, both shield-shaped and triangular, bejeweled and brightly painted in red, white, and sometimes blue. (**All-American Man** is one of

TIP

During spring and fall, the demand for backpacking and four-wheel-drive permits frequently exceeds the number available. If you plan to visit the park during peak season, you should make reservations well in advance.

BELOW: rainbows over Pothole Point.

Goblin Valley State Park

Goblin Valley State Park preserves thousands of bizarre hoodoos, spires, and balanced rocks, which erosion has sculpted from soft red-brown Entrada Sandstone. Trails on surrounding BLM land lead to hoodoos, old mines, and views of the Henry Mountains, the Maze, and the San Rafael Swell, a dramatic monocline that runs behind the park. If you look carefully as you explore the San Rafael Swell, you'll see ancient Barrier Canyon-style rock art by Archaic people who hunted and gathered here thousands of years ago; nearby Horseshoe Canyon has the most famous examples of this style of rock art. The park's 21-unit developed campground is very popular with travelers as it has the only developed facilities on the lonesome Highway 24 route west of Canyonlands. Reserve ahead from spring to fall.

The Great Gallery rock art panel in Horseshoe Canyon depicts life-sized human figures.

BELOW: a desert bighorn sheep at home on the rocky terrain. **RIGHT:** Shafer Canyon.

the most famous pictographs.) Images of human figures, game animals, and numerous symbols were also pecked into the walls. Here, as elsewhere, you may look at but not touch rock art. Disturbing artifacts is strictly prohibited. A long drought and increased tensions among villages competing for diminishing natural resources doomed the Ancestral Pueblo way of life in the Four Corners region. By 1300, Pueblo people had moved to farmlands along the Rio Grande and the Little Colorado River in Arizona, where their descendants still live.

The Maze

An even earlier culture has also been identified in Canyonlands: the Archaic people who hunted and gathered here for at least 6,000 years. Dramatic signs of their passage are preserved in 3,000-year-old, ghostly Barrier Canyon-style pictographs found along the 6½-mile (10km), round-trip hike to the **Great Gallery** 🄼 in **Horseshoe Canyon**, a discontiguous park unit north of the Maze District. Horseshoe Canyon offers a taste of the convoluted Maze country

to the south. To get there, turn east off Highway 24, just past the Goblin Valley State Park turn-off, and drive 30 miles (48km) on the sandy road. If you're coming from I-70, a 47-mile (76km) -long dirt road from the town of Green River offers another way in.

Dirt roads like these traverse wild country dotted with strangely named landmarks, which, in true western style, arose from differing perspectives of native people, early adventurers, poetic travelers, and even outlaws like Butch Cassidy and his cattle-rustling cohorts, who hid out at Robber's Roost.

To avoid getting lost, check in at **Hans Flat Ranger Station** 🄽, a 46-mile (74km) ride from Highway 24. After the ranger station, a four-wheel-drive vehicle is essential, preferably a Jeep. The road goes south to reach **Bagpipe Butte Overlook** 🄾, then east along the Flint Trail to Ernies Country and the Land of Standing Rocks. From here, you can hike through the **Doll House** 🄿 above the river confluence and down into Spanish Bottom.

For a look into The Maze, backtrack to the Golden Stairs, then drive northeast to the **Maze Overlook** 🅀 or hike the 14-mile (23km) **North Trail Canyon** to the overlook. A 3-mile (5km) trail leads into The Maze itself, where Archaic pictographs known as the **Harvest Scene** 🅁 reward your efforts.

The Maze is the park's most pristine experience – a dramatic place where kit foxes, coyotes, mountain lions, bobcats, and other desert creatures are bolder, and unexpected seeps deep in the canyons nourish throngs of maidenhair ferns, various mosses, monkeyflowers, and columbines.

This is rugged, beautiful country but it can also be treacherous. You need to be an experienced and well-prepared desert hiker and able to handle any eventuality in a four-wheel-drive vehicle to negotiate exceptionally difficult terrain, where the word "road" is completely foreign. Discuss your plans with the park rangers before attempting a trip, just to be sure. ❏

ARCHES

The sandstone arches that give this park its name are only part of the story. Spires, pinnacles, pedestals, and balanced rocks are among its other extraordinary geological features

he writer Ed Abbey, one of the Southwest's most passionate advocates, marveled: "This is a landscape that has to be seen to be believed and even then, confronted directly by the senses, it strains credulity." Indeed. Yet, one of the pleasures of a trip across the Colorado Plateau is the way its ever-changing topography pushes us to understand our surroundings according to different rules, to change our sense of what is normal. **Arches National Park** ⓭, with its world-renowned population of carved, salmon-colored arches, fins, spires, pinnacles, and balanced rocks, is a case in point. Here, the very landmarks for which this park is famous are windows through which we experience the natural world in a new way.

Red rock giants

This 120-sq-mile (310-sq-km) desert park, 5 miles (8km) north of Moab, Utah, is home to more than 2,000 natural arches and many other strangely eroded red rock giants. Unlike neighboring Canyonlands, which requires many visits to appreciate, Arches is small enough to experience in a day by way of its paved scenic drive, pullouts – where a driver can take a breather and take in the view – and many short trails, but large enough

to warrant longer explorations into the backcountry, where its wild nature becomes apparent.

Arches has the largest number of natural sandstone arches in the world, with many more being formed all the time – the fortuitous result of location, geology, and water erosion. You might think that the explanation for the large number of shape shifting rocks in this place is complicated, but you would be wrong.

The key to this odd convention of geologic landmarks is salt – a common

Maps:
Area 138–9
Park 196

Main attractions
PARK AVENUE
BALANCED ROCK
PANORAMA POINT
DELICATE ARCH
FIERY FURNACE
KLONDIKE BLUFFS
DEVILS GARDEN
LANDSCAPE ARCH

PRECEDING PAGES the Painted Desert.
LEFT: natural sandstone arches.
RIGHT: hiking on the edge.

The rock at Arches offers excellent opportunities for climbers, in spite of its sandy nature. Most climbing routes in the park require advanced techniques.

enough commodity, which here has given rise, quite literally, to this high-relief landscape.

The geologic story

The salt that lies below Arches was deposited 300 million years ago when a succession of large, shallow seas lay landlocked by highlands to the east. As the climate gradually dried, the seawater evaporated, leaving behind salt deposits thousands of feet thick in an enormous depression known as the **Paradox Basin**. Eventually, the highlands (known as the Uncompahgre Uplift) began shedding debris into the basin, which compacted there, cemented by calcium carbonate and other minerals. Its tremendous weight bore down on the underlying Paradox deposits, causing the salt, which is somewhat "plastic," to flow west, away from the burden. The movement stalled when the salt ran up against ancient fault blocks.

One of the most obvious of these faults can be seen near the visitor center, where a 2,500ft (760-meter) displacement along the **Moab Fault**

has exposed the fossiliferous strata of the ancient Honaker Trail Formation on the opposite side of the valley – a rare glimpse of the rocks that make up the park's basement.

Unable to move farther, the salt layer domed up through the 12 layers of rocks lying on top of it, cracking the rocks and weakening the strata. Joints appeared along these fault lines, giving ground water a chance to enter and dissolve the salt.

Undermined by this erosion, the salt domes began to collapse. The low-lying Salt and Cache valleys and the parallel lines of formations sweeping across them are testimony to this ongoing weakening of loosely cemented sedimentary rocks.

It's not difficult to understand what happened next. The evidence can be found everywhere in Arches. Once water, ice, and snow went to work on the rock, deepening and widening joints, all manner of oddly carved stones gradually emerged, of which the delicate spans of reddish-brown sandstone, known as natural arches, are some of the most interesting.

BELOW: blooming mule's ears grow by the Courthouse Towers.

Exploring the Arches

A short orientation presentation, outlining the geology and geography of Arches, is given in the auditorium of the new visitor center on the hour and half-hour. Then, for a look at the many different types of arches and carved phenomena in the park, take the 18-mile (29km) scenic drive from the visitor center to Devils Garden, stopping to hike along the short trails that wind through this oversized Zen garden of standing stones.

The first weathered rocks you come to are the skyscraper-like monoliths in **Park Avenue Ⓐ**, so named because of the way their sheer walls jostle the skyline. Nearby, in the **Courthouse Towers Ⓑ**, are Sheep Rock, the Organ, the Tower of Babel, and the Three Gossips, soaring giants composed of iron-rich Entrada Sandstone, the principal rock layer in the park. Different rates of erosion in the three "members" of Entrada Sandstone are responsible for the majority of features, with the lower Dewey Bridge Member crumbling easily beneath the harder Slick Rock Member.

The uppermost layer, the white Moab Member, can be seen capping some of the higher landmarks. Underlying the Entrada are the swirling beds of cream-colored Navajo Sandstone, whose Sahara-like origins can easily be seen just beyond Courthouse Towers in the humped shapes of "petrified" sand dunes. In this open landscape, you get a great view of the 12,000ft (3,658-meter) snowcapped **La Sal Mountains**, great laccoliths with hearts of lava, exposed by erosion in forested crags and peaks that dominate the eastern sky.

The Windows and beyond

Park rangers recommend that you drive at least as far as the **Windows Section**, for it is here that you can see single and double arches, buttes, windows, and the gravity-defying **Balanced Rock Ⓒ**, sitting beside the 2½-mile (4km) paved spur road. Between May and August, this is a good area to see Indian paintbrush, larkspur, sand verbena, and other wildflowers.

Just beyond The Windows, you can stop and take in much of the park at

BELOW: Turret Arch seen through North Window Arch.

Rangers are located throughout the park to offer a helping hand.

Panorama Point ⓓ. The canyon of the Colorado River is visible on the southeast border of the park. The green belt of willows, tamarisks, and cottonwoods that grows along the waterway seems like a mirage on the other side of this sparsely vegetated salt valley, where only salt-tolerant plants like pickleweed and seepweed can grow.

You can get a better feel for the Colorado River along Highway 128, which parallels the river just outside the park. Travelers on the Spanish Trail in the 1830s and 1840s forded the Colorado River just beyond modern-day **Moab**. This sleepy little community was founded by Mormon missionaries who came to convert the Ute Indians in 1855, although Indian resistance prevented them from settling there before the 1870s. Today, the town makes an excellent jumping-off point for nearby parks.

After Panorama Point, a road turns northeast for 3 miles (5km), crossing an area of collapsed rocks of the more recent Dakota, Morrison, and Mancos formations. The road ends at a view-

BELOW: sun-kissed Fiery Furnace.

point overlooking **Delicate Arch ⓔ**, the world-famous symbol of Utah's red rock country. Delicate Arch is actually not very tall – only 45ft (14 meters) high – but its location on the lip of a slickrock bowl gives it a dramatic bearing. For a close-up look, climb the steep trail to the arch (1½ miles/2km each way) – one of the most rewarding hikes in the park.

Desert fire

The trail begins at a rudimentary cabin, the 1906 **Wolfe Ranch ⓕ**, which was home to a rather antisocial Civil War veteran named John Wesley Wolfe and his son. Wolfe came here for his health in 1888, but it's hard to understand what could have prompted him to settle in such a remote outpost, so far from society. Maybe that was exactly the point. Writer Ed Abbey, who spent several seasons as a backcountry ranger in Arches in the late 1950s, and who wrote eloquently of his experiences in the classic *Desert Solitaire*, apparently relished his isolation. Canyon Country seems to attract loners who value silence and the harmony of the desert.

A few miles farther and you reach the flaming rock fins known as **Fiery Furnace ⑥**. Between April and October, park rangers lead popular twice-daily 3-hour hikes through this deeply eroded rockscape. Group size is limited to 15; reserve online or at the visitor center. Rangers are stationed inside the area to help hikers. Permits are required to hike Fiery Furnace, but it's not a good idea to hike alone: there is no marked trail through the radiating rocks.

Beyond Fiery Furnace, a left turn onto an unpaved road leads 8 miles (13km) across Salt Valley to **Klondike Bluffs ⑪**, whose **Marching Men** formations so impressed prospector Alexander Ringhoffer that he persuaded the railroad to conduct tours to the spot in 1923. Arches was named a national monument just six years later. (It did not officially become a national park until 1971.) Klondike is now one of the least visited places in the whole park.

The scenic drive ends at **Devils Garden ⑫**, where the park's densest array of arches and fins makes a fitting climax to any visit to the park. Several easy trails meander among its soaring spans. Sand Dune Arch shelters a large sand dune at its base; Skyline Arch became famous when a rockfall in November 1940 doubled its size. A 1-mile (1.5km) trail from the road leads to **Landscape Arch ⑬**, a 306ft (93-meter) span of "desert varnished" beige rock, thought to be the longest natural arch in the world.

Fragile soil

You may continue from Landscape Arch along an unimproved trail to two other formations – **Double O Arch** (1 mile/1.5km) and the **Dark Angel** (½ mile/1km). A short side trail leads to massive **Navajo Arch** and the twin openings of **Partition Arch**.

Devils Garden has a pleasant little campground, but you will need to get there early in the day to scoop up a spot. While out hiking, make sure you stay on the trails. The desert floor is dotted with dark patches of cryptobiotic soil, composed of mosses, lichens, fungi, and algae that retain moisture, protect against erosion, and provide

TIP

Always take advice from a park ranger before setting out to drive into the desert. Thunderstorms are common in the summer, and flash floods can make driving hazardous.

BELOW:
Delicate Arch.

TIP

Arches is home to a variety of venomous creatures, including rattlesnakes, scorpions, and black widow spiders. Always watch where you're walking and never put your hand on a surface you can't see.

nitrogen and other nutrients in which plants can grow. Once stepped on, this fragile, new soil, on which so much new life depends, is destroyed for decades.

Temperatures at this 3,960–5,650ft (1,200–1,720-meter) elevation are very hot in summer, and thunderstorms and torrential rain are apt to swoop in suddenly with no warning.

In winter, the climate is surprisingly frigid, with subfreezing night-time temperatures usual. The dry-rocked landscape is occasionally transformed under a glittering white blanket of snow. Colors seem deeper and more intense. The area is subject to dramatic changes in temperature, which can fluctuate by 50°F (28°C) in a 24-hour period.

The secret of survival

Plants and animals must be very choosy about where they live in this difficult environment, jealously guarding their special places in an ongoing bid for survival. Desert creatures are generally nocturnal, venturing out only when the desert cools down. You

BELOW: the soaring Organ formation.
RIGHT: Balanced Rock.

are likely to hear the yip of coyotes at night, as they and their gray fox neighbors trot great distances across the park in search of jackrabbits, cottontails, ground squirrels, and other rodents.

Rattlesnakes, collared lizards, the desert spiny, and other reptiles, which are unable to control body temperatures, doze beneath rocks and bushes at midday. Reptiles, of course, have low metabolic rates, but they also have low energy requirements, as keeping warm in the desert is not difficult. Since reptiles don't sweat or pant, they can't stand very hot temperatures and must seek out some shade. In winter, they hibernate or become inactive.

The sheerest of cliffs make good perches for lazy-winged golden eagles and red-tailed hawks, while, in shadowed canyons, the joyous song of the tiny canyon wren bounces off seeping sandstone walls decorated with colorful water-loving plants.

Hardy junipers do better than pinyon trees on exposed surfaces, clinging tenaciously to naked rocks like drowning men atop life rafts. ❏

Beautiful Bridges

For an interesting comparison with Arches National Park, visit **Natural Bridges National Monument**, off Highway 191, south of Moab. This small park preserves three natural bridges composed of Cedar Mesa Sandstone, which were cut by a tributary of the Colorado River. Sipapu and Kachina Bridges are the world's second- and third -largest natural bridges. Owachomo Bridge is smaller, and only 9ft (less than 3 meters) thick.

To explore Natural Bridges, there's a 9-mile (14km) one-way loop scenic drive, which begins and ends near the visitor center. Overlooks for the three bridges are reached by short walks from parking areas along the drive. Vigorous hikers can complete the 8-mile (13km) loop trail that connects the bridges, following the canyon bottom stream, in about 6 hours.

PETRIFIED FOREST

Fossilized wood that grew 225 million years ago,
the multicolored badlands of the Painted Desert,
ancient Indian rock art, and a pueblo made of
agate make this a unique national park

I f it weren't for the signposts along Interstate 40, it would be easy to drive past **Petrified Forest National Park** ⓯ in northeastern Arizona. For miles, your constant companion is an arid, high desert of scrub and short grasses, crumbling pastel hills, dry washes, distant mesas, and dancing cloud shadows – a place of lingering silences and subtle beauty that inspires daydreams, as mile after mile ticks by.

But don't imagine that these expansive vistas are empty. Far from it. Just beyond the anonymity of the cross-country highway, only slightly hidden from view, lies a compelling landscape filled to bursting with the fossilized remains of ancient plants and animals, the world's largest and most spectacular cache of colorful petrified wood and the scattered artifacts of people who lived here for close to 8,000 years – all of them protected within the 147 sq miles (381 sq km) of the park.

It sits on either side of Interstate 40, east of **Holbrook**, Arizona. Plan on eating and spending the night in Holbrook; no basic lodging or campgrounds are to be found in the park. If you are coming from the west, turn onto Highway 180 at Holbrook and enter from the south entrance (this area contains the greatest concentration of petrified logs). Drivers from the east should exit Interstate 40 and approach the park through the north entrance (where the best views of the **Painted Desert** and important Ancestral Pueblo ruins and rock art are found).

Rainbow rocks

Visitor centers at either end of the park provide information, wilderness camping permits, exhibits, and gifts as well as refreshments. However, the **Painted Desert Visitor Center** (near Interstate 40) is a much better bet. It offers a 20-minute film and a wide range of interpretive activities. About 1½ miles

Main attractions
PAINTED DESERT VISITOR CENTER
PAINTED DESERT INN
PUERCO INDIAN RUIN
NEWSPAPER ROCK
BLUE MESA
JASPER AND CRYSTAL FORESTS
AGATE HOUSE

LEFT: fragments of petrified wood.
RIGHT: fossilized tree trunk section.

Ancient logs long since turned into stone.

(2km) from the visitor center, the restored 1924 **Painted Desert Inn** is an official National Historic Landmark. Historically, it has served as a trading post, an inn, and a restaurant. Today, it is a museum and bookstore.

The only designated trails in the park are short strolls through petrified wood in the southern portion, although you may hike cross-country if you're adequately prepared with a gallon of water (4 liters) per person per day, food, a map, good footwear, and a sense of adventure. It's very exposed here, with summer temperatures soaring near 100°F (38°C), possible thunderstorms and cold winter winds. Always bring protective clothing.

Camping is allowed with a free permit in the Painted Desert Wilderness north of the interstate highway and also in the Rainbow Forest Wilderness at the park's southern end.

A 27-mile (43km) paved scenic drive gives you a good overview of the park. Beginning in the north, the road loops past the **Kachina**, **Chinde**, and other viewpoints that guide the eye directly into the Painted Desert Wilderness,

across the Navajo Nation, to the far-off Hopi Buttes. The screed hillsides, gullied flats, and dark mesas of the Painted Desert are constantly shifting in hue, from charcoal gray to sage green to taupe to pale rose to blood red; the colors are particularly intense after a summer thunderstorm. The rock that is responsible for this rainbow palette is the Chinle Formation, whose sands, silts, and clays make up some of the softest rocks in the Southwest. It's amazing to think that weathering has stripped away thousands of feet of overlying rocks to create this spare landscape.

The Chinle Formation was laid down more than 225 million years ago on a flat plain braided by shallow streams that meandered through the low-lying area. Gradually, several thousand feet of sediment accumulated. The Chinle Formation constantly fascinates geologists, preserving as it does Triassic-era fossils, petrified wood, and abundant materials that give it its distinctive coloration, as well as large amounts of uranium – which provoked a new "gold rush" throughout the Southwest in the 1940s and 1950s.

After about 6 miles (10km), the scenic road goes over the freeway, crosses the Santa Fe Railroad tracks and passes **Puerco Indian Ruin**, a 75-room, 14th-century Ancestral Puebloan village that has been partially excavated. The Puerco River, which roughly follows the railroad, was an important lifeline for Ancestral Puebloan residents and seems to have supported them longer than other water sources in the Four Corners region. This ruin is one of 600 prehistoric sites in the park, which include scatterings of artifacts, pit houses, and masonry pueblos, spanning a period of 8,000 years. Puerco Pueblo was occupied AD 1100–1200 and again AD 1300–1400. It was likely abandoned during the 13th century when a long drought occurred throughout the Southwest.

Ancestral Puebloans wrested a living from this stark environment by sheer adaptability. They knew exactly which desert plants to gather for food and clothing, which soils would yield good clay for pots, how to use every part of a jackrabbit, or deer, and the best way to irrigate small plots of squash, corn, and beans to ensure good crops.

They lived on a cultural frontier, between the Mogollon to the south and other branches of the Ancestral Pueblo culture farther north, and probably traded petrified wood for shells, food, and pottery. It's not clear why the Ancestral Puebloans moved on, but they may have joined the Hopi villages to the north or Zuni Pueblo farther east. After they left, the Navajo moved into the region. Their enormous reservation adjoins the park.

Rock art

Just past Puerco Indian Ruin is **Newspaper Rock**, a sandstone cliff that was once used as a place of inscription by the Ancestral Pueblo people. Then as now, Pueblo people valued creativity greatly, which is evidenced in early baskets and later in decorated pots, as well as crafted implements found wherever the people settled. The exact meaning of the rock art they left behind is still unknown, although this area of archeology is beginning to turn up interesting results. On Newspaper Rock are numerous sheep, lizards, geometric shapes, and eerily anthropomorphic forms,

TIP

For two weeks around the summer solstice, June 21, there are demonstrations of an ancient Anasazi solar calendar at work at Puerco Pueblo (daily at 8am).

BELOW:
the end of the road.

Maps:
Area 138–9

TIP

The park is locked at
night, and visitors must
be in their cars and
driving towards an exit
at closing time (5pm,
later in summer
months).

faint echoes of a culture at whose daily concerns we can only guess. Telescopes at the overlook allow visitors to get a closer look at the images.

At this halfway point, the surrounding country has been carved by wind and water erosion into rocky badlands of mesas, conical hills, and bald hummocks colored by iron (red), manganese (black and purple), and other minerals. They sport names like the **Teepees**, the **Haystacks**, and **Blue Mesa**, but no names seem adequate to describe nature's handiwork in this hot, dry location. A 3-mile (5km) spur road reaches into Blue Mesa, where erosion has left petrified logs balanced precariously on pedestals of soft clay.

How wood became stone

The southern portion of the park is strewn with large quantities of petrified wood, concentrated in the **Jasper** and **Crystal** forests. These stone logs are the preserved remains of 200ft (60-meter) conifers, known as *Araucarioxylon*, that grew on the banks of shallow streams and swamps 225 million years ago. When they toppled,

BELOW: the secrets of the Ancestral Pueblo people are hidden in their petroglyphs.
RIGHT: the beautiful colors of petrified wood.

they were washed into the flood plain, forming great logjams in the shallow rivers. Silty water and mineral-laden volcanic ash covered them, cutting off oxygen and delaying decay; silica gradually seeped into the cells of the trees, hardening into colorful quartz crystals. In some cases, the cell walls were completely dissolved and replaced by jasper, amethyst, and smoky quartz.

Ancestors of modern Pueblo people appreciated the beauty of the stone logs, fashioning them into tools and even building with them. **Agate House** (near Long Logs) is surely one of the most unusual Ancestral Pueblo dwellings in the Southwest. Its sturdy petrified-wood walls are a testament to the utilitarian beauty that was the hallmark of the Ancestral Pueblo people.

The petrified forest lay largely intact for centuries, until the US acquired much of the Southwest through a treaty with Mexico in 1848. Three years later, US Army Surveyor Lorenzo Sitgreaves and fellow officers were sent to chart the new territory, which they found unimpressive, save for gemstones they prized from petrified wood. Word spread quickly and tourism grew in the late 19th century. Hordes of travelers and traders boarded trains and came West to obtain petrified wood for their collections. In no time at all, boxcars of petrified logs were shipped back East for sale, and the Southwest was in danger of losing one of its most remarkable natural assets.

But not everyone was intent on making off with buried treasure. By 1895, a small but vocal group of local residents began to lobby for protection. Petrified Forest National Monument was created in 1906, expanded several times, and redesignated a national park in 1962.

And yet, petrified wood is still disappearing, at the rate of some 12 tons (11 tonnes) a year. Visitor after visitor leaves with "just one little piece," all of which adds up to a continual loss for the park and future generations. One rule: buy your petrified wood in the gift shop, and leave this national park intact. ❑

THE SONORAN DESERT

Torrid and seemingly lifeless, the Sonoran Desert
of southern Arizona is, in fact, home to a unique
variety of plant and animal life. Most obvious are
the signature cacti that gave two parks
their names

The desert must seem an alien place to anyone not used to it – eyeball-scorching, empty moonscapes devoid of water. But, in fact, it is a complex ecosystem, full of living things, each one playing a vital role in maintaining the health of this extraordinary environment.

To truly appreciate the desert, wrote writer and environmentalist Wallace Stegner, "You have to get over the color green; you have to quit associating beauty with gardens and lawns; you have to get used to an inhuman scale; you have to understand geological time."

The desert timetable, with its different seasons and nocturnal emphasis, is different from most others, but no less specific. Give yourself time here, and the unusual rhythms of this place start to have their own logic, and its stubborn character may even become alluring. Once embarked upon, it is a love affair that, for many people, lasts a lifetime.

Southern Arizona sits in the upper half of the Sonoran Desert, which extends southward from the Phoenix Basin into Mexico. Two parks – Saguaro and Organ Pipe Cactus – highlight the Sonoran Desert's unique biological and geological attributes. A third, Chiricahua National Monument, rises 7,000ft (2,100 meters) on the desert's eastern edge. All three are within driving distance of Tucson, Arizona, which makes a good base for your explorations.

Saguaro

The two units of **Saguaro National Park**  are just a stone's throw from Tucson, bellied up to the Tucson and Rincon mountains to the west and east of the city, respectively. The star of this park is the symbol of the Sonoran Desert itself: the many-armed giant cactus known as the saguaro (sa *wah* ro). The east-side **Rincon Mountain District** was set aside in 1933 to highlight

Main attractions
BAJADA LOOP DRIVE (TUCSON MOUNTAIN DISTRICT, SAGUARO)
CACTUS FOREST DRIVE (RINCON MOUNTAIN DISTRICT, SAGUARO)
AJO MOUNTAIN DRIVE (ORGAN PIPE)
PUERTO BLANCO DRIVE (ORGAN PIPE)
BONITA CANYON DRIVE (CHIRICAHUA)
MASSAI POINT OVERLOOK (CHIRICAHUA)
RHYOLITE CANYON TRAIL (CHIRICAHUA)
FARAWAY RANCH (CHIRICAHUA)
FORT BOWIE NATIONAL HISTORIC SITE

PRECEDING PAGES: Bartlett Lake framed by the Sonoran Desert. **LEFT:** giant saguaro cactus. **RIGHT:** blooming ocotillo.

A mature saguaro cactus will reach 35–40ft (11–12 meters) in height and will weigh several tons.

a giant forest of mature saguaros. The **Tucson Mountain District**, added in 1961 for research purposes, contains stands of younger saguaros. Both units have excellent scenic drives and a variety of long and short hiking trails that wind among the saguaros.

Young saguaros establish themselves best on *bajadas* – slopes of rock washed down from desert mountains. This is particularly obvious along the 6-mile (10km) **Bajada Loop Drive** through the Tucson Mountain District, 15 miles (24km) west of Tucson. Here, on the dark slopes of these jagged, volcanic peaks, "nurse" trees, such as mesquite and olive-trunked palo verde, protect saguaro seedlings beneath delicate branches.

Slightly older saguaros form stands here, evenly spaced for optimal survival. In the spring, these cacti sprout glorious white blossoms with heavy pollen centers – a show that rivals that of the wildflowers. More importantly, the creamy blooms attract visiting Mexican long-nosed bats, which pollinate the cactus with their wings as they sup nectar. Come back in late

summer to see the result: ruby-colored fruits that, for centuries, have been harvested and made into syrup and jelly by desert-dwelling Tohono O'odham Indians. The ancestors of the Tohono O'odham – the Hohokam – wandered great distances throughout the desert and left petroglyphs on dark volcanic rocks. These can still be seen in places such as the **Signal Hill** picnic area.

The Rincon District is much more diverse, with hiking trails that take walkers from low desert scrub into woodland and, eventually, to high-country forest, as the elevation varies from 2,600 to 8,666ft (792 to 2,641 meters). The 8-mile (13km) **Cactus Forest Drive** passes through a forest of saguaro elders. Here, dying saguaros have been hollowed out by gilded flicker and Gila woodpeckers for nests. Later, screech owls, elf owls, and cactus wrens will commandeer the cool burrows.

Don't expect to see many creatures in the day; most are nocturnal, waiting for cooler temperatures to exit their burrows and hiding places. You may surprise the hare-like jackrabbit, a colorful collared lizard, or

BELOW: feeding time for the phainopepla family.

Jolly Green Giants

Saguaros may live for more than 150 years, given warm exposure and sufficient rain. Blessed with a shallow but extensive root network, saguaros suck up moisture into barrel-like torsos supported by woody ribs. During a torrential storm, this cactus will swell like an accordion, storing as much as 200 gallons (760 liters) of water for the coming year in gelatinous tissues. The spines of the saguaro and other cacti are specially adapted to deal with temperatures that range between the low 100s°F (around 38°C) in summer and below freezing in winter. Spines protect them from unwelcome intruders, trap cool air, provide shade, and, along with the cacti's waxy coating, offer protection from dehydration. The saguaro uses its arms and trunk to photosynthesize food from sunlight, water, and carbon dioxide.

perhaps one of the hawks nesting in the saguaro's upstretched arms. Go hiking in the early morning or in the evening if you hope to encounter twilight hunters such as kit foxes, coyotes, or pig-like javelinas.

Organ Pipe Cactus National Monument

As you head southwest, the kingdom of the saguaro is joined by that of another many-armed cactus, the organ pipe, which is associated with the 516 sq miles (1,336 sq km) of Sonoran Desert protected as **Organ Pipe Cactus National Monument ⓱**. This park encompasses an area of low mountain ranges, broad plains, and sere salt flats – a juxtaposition of habitats that is home to wildlife of such diversity that the monument was named an International Biosphere Reserve in 1976. Here, the organ pipe cactus and other unusual desert denizens usually found on the Mexican side of the border have unknowingly become United States immigrants in a place where nature, not people, makes the rules. Humans, though, are expected to abide by immigration rules. Border patrol is a constant presence along the adjoining US-Mexico border. Be sure to carry identity papers with you.

Two fairly long scenic drives take you through the park's different habitats, beginning at the visitor center. A campground and the Desert View and Victoria Mine trails are also to be found here.

The Ajo Mountains in the park's eastern section receive the most rainfall, meaning that a spin along the 21-mile (34km) **Ajo Mountain Drive** is one of the most pleasant outings in the park. Organ pipe cacti eagerly gulp in sunlight on mountain *bajadas* and favor south-facing exposures where frost cannot reach them. In spring, the pipes of the cactus sport showy flowers, which open as soon as temperatures drop in the evening. In springtime, when rainfall is adequate, the ground is covered with colorful hordes of lupines, golden poppies, pink owl's clover, and other wildflower extroverts.

In addition to the organ pipe, 28 sharp-spined cacti, including teddybear cholla, prickly pear, and saguaro, are found here – many of them participating in a seasonal round of "you scratch my back, I'll scratch yours" with birds, bats, and other plants that help the cacti reproduce in return for food and shelter. The canyons offer some respite from heat and aridity, providing places where juniper, rosewood, agave, and jojoba trees and animal residents can take refuge. It is here that the Tohono O'odham and their ancestors also retreated from desert extremes, camping in the shade of trees and harvesting the desert bounty.

The western section of the park, in the Lower Colorado Desert zone, is one of the least hospitable areas for residents and visitors alike. You get a strong flavor of the place by taking the 53 mile (85km) **Puerto Blanco Drive**, which skirts the Puerto Blanco Mountains. Creosote and bursage populate 80 percent of the sandy valleys, gradually changing to a mixture of scrub

TIP

The Arizona-Sonora Desert Museum, adjacent to Saguaro West, is an excellent nonprofit-making zoo where you can see many residents of the Sonoran Desert close-up (daily, Oct–Feb 8.30am–5pm, Mar–Sept 7.30am–5pm).

BELOW: lightning over the Ajo Mountains in Organ Pipe Cactus National Monument.

The Sonoran Desert extends west into California: part of Joshua Tree National Park (see page 109) is in a western arm of the Sonoran.

and palo verde on nearby volcanic slopes. The fluorescent-lit landscape shimmers harshly under 105°F (41°C) summer heat, and sensible desert dwellers like bighorn sheep, coyotes, kangaroo rats, desert tortoises, snakes, and high-flying hawks give it a wide berth in the daytime, waiting for the evening to refill empty bellies.

Even more hostile is the salt valley along the Mexican border, where saline soil offers prospects for saltbush but little else. Drive north along the spur road to the **Senita Basin** and an exotic community of Mexican elephant trees, senita cactus, and limberbush appears alongside organ pipe cactus, protected in the lee of two mountain ranges. Signs of ranching and mining can be seen along the border with Mexico, but the area within the park is gradually recovering from man-made intrusions.

Chiricahua National Monument

By now, you may be ready to escape from the baking heat for a while in one of the small mountain ranges that rise enticingly from the desert floor. The rugged Chiricahua Mountains, east of Tucson, make a particularly fine destination. Here, a fascinating combination of strange rock formations, unusual wildlife, and human history is packed into the 19 sq miles (49 sq km) that make up **Chiricahua National Monument** ⓲.

Like other borderland parks, Chiricahua is home to a cosmopolitan mix of Mexican-American flora and fauna, which inhabit the protected corridor provided by these tall and well-watered mountains. But Chiricahua is more than just a haven for exotics; it is also home to a truly bizarre collection of carved-rock features that have been created here by erosion. It was to preserve these strange phenomena that the park was set aside in 1924.

Hundreds of balanced rocks, spires, pinnacles, columns, and other sculpted stones form deep ranks in the northwest section of the Chiricahuas. These are not sedimentary rocks; they are made of grayish volcanic tuff (fused ash), which spewed from nearby **Turkey Creek Caldera** 25 million years ago, forming a 2,000ft (610-meter) plateau. Future geologic activity pushed up the Chiricahuas and left behind horizontal and vertical faults. Duck on a Rock, Totem Pole, Sea Captain, Punch and Judy, and other whimsically named features gradually took shape as wind, water, and ice went to work on areas of weakness.

For an overview, take the 8-mile (13km), winding **Bonita Canyon Drive**, which gradually climbs from the visitor center (5,400ft/1,646 meters) to **Massai Point Overlook** (6,870ft/2,094 meters) through pinyon, juniper, and oak woodland. From here, you can look down into the eroded badlands and out across the crest of the Chiricahuas to Cochise Head beyond the park boundary. On the way back, stop and hike the 3-mile (5km) round-trip to the fire lookout on **Sugarloaf Mountain**, at 7,365ft (2,245 meters) the park's highest peak. From Massai

BELOW: erosion of volcanic rocks on the Echo Canyon Trail, Chiricahua National Monument.

Point, a number of maintained, intersecting trails wind down deep into the canyons to the **Heart of Rocks**, where the most fascinating rock sculptures are found. One good loop trail takes you through **Echo Canyon** (4-mile/6km round-trip), dropping 450ft (137 meters) into the stone galleries. Another way in is to hike the **Rhyolite Canyon Trail** (2 miles/3km) east from the visitor center, a pleasant walk through a cool, riparian habitat.

These eroded uplands are the reason that wildlife of such an unusual variety coexists here. In the moister canyons, you will find Southwestern trees such as dwarf oak, alligator juniper, and Arizona cypress alongside rare Mexican Chihuahua and Apache pine. The high mountainsides are even more lush, supporting Douglas fir, aspen, and ponderosa pine, which, in turn, attract browsing white-tailed deer. What a contrast with the surrounding desert environment, where aridity has hardened the competition. Many exotic birds cross into the park from across the border; sulphur-bellied flycatchers and Mexican chickadees are frequent

visitors. Bring your binoculars; this is birding heaven.

A pleasant, short hike begins at the visitor center and wanders through an open meadow environment, ending at the campground (2-mile/3km round-trip). Turn west, though, and the trail leads to **Faraway Ranch** in Bonita Canyon, the home of the Erickson family for nearly 90 years. The Ericksons moved here two years after the treaty that ended the war between the US Army and the Chiricahua Apaches, to whom these mountains were a much-loved home. The Apaches, led by Cochise and later by Geronimo, held out for years in a valiant attempt to retain their land. But, by 1886, a treaty had been signed; the Apaches were imprisoned and eventually forced to accept reservation living. They are gone but not forgotten. If you're interested in learning more, pay a visit to nearby **Fort Bowie National Historic Site 19**. Established in 1862, the fort was the focal point of military operations against Geronimo. The ruins, set in a 1,000-acre (400-hectare) park, can be reached only by trail. ❑

The Sonoran Desert contains more species of hummingbird than anywhere else in the United States.

BELOW LEFT: graveyard at Apache Pass, near Fort Bowie. **BELOW RIGHT:** Geronimo (crouching), Chiricahua Apache chief.

GUADALUPE MOUNTAINS AND CARLSBAD CAVERNS

From the highest peak in Texas to the country's deepest limestone caves, geology has shaped some wondrous sights in New Mexico's Chihuahuan Desert

There aren't many places in America where you can explore both the outside and inside of what was once a 400-mile (644km) -long barrier reef lying below an ancient shallow sea. But, at the neighboring **Guadalupe Mountains** ⑳ and **Carlsbad Caverns** ㉑ national parks, on the southern New Mexico–Texas border, this is indeed possible. Here, climatic change, geologic activity, and the elements have uncovered a limestone reef formation of startling beauty. Long buried in the past, today they offer a respite from the heat of the surrounding desert and a glimpse of a natural world usually hidden from view.

Guadalupe Mountains

Just a couple of hours north of El Paso, Texas, the towering ramparts of the 50-mile (80km) -long **Guadalupe Mountains** rise up abruptly in the searing Chihuahuan Desert, which extends south from New Mexico and Texas into Mexico. US Highway 62/180 passes through the natural divide of Guadalupe Pass, below the jutting headland of El Capitan and its neighbor, Guadalupe Peak, which, at 8,749ft (2,667 meters), is the tallest mountain in Texas. The sheer limestone walls promise a wilderness, but don't be fooled by appearances: enter these mountains from any of the hiking

trails connecting the desert, interior canyons, and high mountain slopes, and a sanctuary of wildlife opens up.

The best way to explore the backcountry is from a base at **Pine Springs Campground** (5,700ft/1,737 meters), next to the visitor center, from where you can take the long, strenuous Guadalupe Peak, El Capitan, and Tejas trails from the **Pine Springs Trailhead**. About 4 miles (6km) from Pine Springs, the Tejas Trail intersects the **Bowl Trail**, which loops through a high-country, relict conifer forest

LEFT: El Capitan. **RIGHT:** a ranger re-shoes a mule.

The cactus wren makes its nest in the cactus plant, and is protected by the prickly spines.

BELOW: on the road to the Guadalupe Mountains.

2,500ft (760 meters) above the desert floor. Shy bobcats, bears, and mountain lions are found at higher elevations, but you are most likely to find mule deer and elk, which are abundant here.

The 12-mile (19km) Tejas Trail connects Pine Springs with **Dog Canyon**, on the other side of the mountains. Dog Canyon has a ranger station and a campground and may be reached only on foot or via the 70-mile (113km) road that skirts the back of the Guadalupe Mountains just south of Carlsbad. It's a long way but worth the extra mileage.

Guadalupe Mountains is mostly designated wilderness, and wilderness rules are enforced. Everything taken in must be taken out. Remember, too, that, with no modifying influences, deserts tend to be very hot or very cold, depending on season. Wear a hat, sturdy hiking boots, and layered clothing and drink a gallon (4 liters) of water daily.

Guadalupe Mountain hikes

A backcountry trip into the mountains takes planning and stamina, but there are several more moderate day hikes at the lower elevations. Get help in planning your visit from knowledgeable park rangers at the tourist-friendly visitor center, and don't miss one of the excellent evening campfire talks about desert wildlife (some of the subjects of the talks may join you for the show). Cooler morning and evening temperatures enliven the desert, and coyotes and crickets sing a nightly serenade that lulls the senses hypnotically. Emblematic of the Chihuahuan Desert are water-saving species such as lechuguilla, prickly pear, and sotol, which dot the foothills.

Some beautifully marked reptiles, such as collared lizards and mostly harmless snakes, live here, but you will need to be quick to see them in daytime, when they shelter from the heat beneath rocks or burrow into the ground. Equally furtive are large-eared jackrabbits and smaller cottontail rabbits, which dash out suddenly from cover, only to disappear again swiftly.

Just on the other side of the visitor center are the ruins of a horse-changing station of the **Butterfield Stage Line**, which carried the mail cross-

Wild Cave Tours

Lechuguilla Cave is only open to experienced cavers and scientific researchers whose exciting discoveries in the cave include a potential cancer cure derived from previously unknown microbes. The park's ranger-led wild cave tours offer a chance to experience caving, if you're comfortable doing minor crawling, squeezing, ladder, and rope work. The 3-hour Lower Cave tour follows the route used by a National Geographic Society exploratory party in 1924. The 2-hour Lefthand Tunnel tour by candle lantern highlights Carlsbad's history, geology, cave pools, and Permian-age fossils. The most popular off-trail tour is Slaughter Canyon Cave tour, a rugged hike into a cave containing the Monarch, at 89ft (27 meters) high one of the world's largest limestone columns. Make advance reservations for these popular tours.

country in the mid- to late 1800s. A mile and a half (2.4km) north, the whitewashed **Frijole Ranch and Museum**, a pioneer ranch, is open to visitors. From here, the 2-mile (3km) Manzanita and Smith Springs Loop Trail makes a pleasant day hike. The white settlers who moved into the area when it became United States territory in 1849 were subject to attack by Mescalero Apaches, whose detailed knowledge of these desert mountains made them worthy opponents. By 1880, though, the Apaches had been removed from their homelands to a nearby reservation.

The 7 mile (11km), round-trip **McKittrick Canyon Trail** is justifiably the most popular day hike in Guadalupe Mountains. It starts at **McKittrick Canyon Visitor Center**, just off Highway 62/180 to the northeast of Pine Springs. The canyon is famous for the brilliant fall colors of its Texas madrone, bigtooth maple, oak, ash, and walnut trees, which cluster along the only perennial stream in the park. The sweet songs of canyon wrens and tanagers echo musically here; qui-

eter, though, are stealthy bobcats and mountain lions, which pad after mule deer and elk at dawn. More common are small rodents and reptiles, which make their home in lower elevations.

Also beginning at McKittrick Canyon is the 8-mile (13km), round-trip **Permian Reef Geology Trail**, a long day hike that offers an excellent introduction to the park's geology. The steep trail takes you through a cross section of the Permian Reef, which was formed by the limey secretions of calcareous algae, sponges, and other marine organisms that lived in the shallow Permian Sea 250 million years ago. When the sea evaporated, potash, gypsum, salt, and other sediments entombed the reef, until a period of geologic uplift and subsequent erosion again exposed the formation 10 to 12 million years ago.

The Guadalupes continue to be sculpted today by the dissolving action of rainwater made acidic by carbon dioxide and organic matter in the soil. Crystalline calcite deposits have formed pale, marble-like travertine or flowstone around seeps and in

BELOW: the Guadalupes.

streambeds – a taste of the treasures that lie below the surface at nearby Carlsbad Caverns.

The Permian Reef shales contain abundant oil. It was oil exploration in the 1920s that indirectly led to the establishment of the park in 1972. Wallace Pratt, a petroleum geologist who fell in love with McKittrick Canyon and made his home there, donated 5,000 acres (2,000 hectares) of the canyon to the US government. Pratt's stone lodge sits a couple of miles up the canyon. Farther up, you'll find the remains of J.C. Hunter's ranching operation. Both Pratt and Hunter were instrumental in the creation of the park.

But other earlier ranches in the area did not fare well. South of the park, dwarfed by Guadalupe Peak, sit the lonely, boarded-up remains of the **Williams Ranch**, 9 miles (14km) down bone-shaking, unpaved road. The house was built in 1908 by Robert Belcher, who had deluded himself that his new wife would be impressed by this new home. Appalled by the location, she spent one day and one night at the cabin before leaving him. Other small-time ranchers followed; no one stayed long. Today, the cabin is a curiously Western reminder of the folly of human ambition in the face of overwhelming odds.

Carlsbad Caverns

The scorching summer heat can be overwhelming, and there is no better way to cool down fast than to visit world-famous **Carlsbad Caverns**, 35 miles (56km) northeast of Guadalupe Mountains National Park, off Highway 62/180. Carlsbad is as much about ballyhoo as Guadalupe Mountains is about silence, but you should not miss either of them.

Visitors to Carlsbad Caverns may hike the area along 50 miles (80km) of backcountry trails or else take a 10-mile (16km) scenic loop drive through the Guadalupes, but the principal attractions of this national park are the huge, fantastically shaped stalactites, stalagmites, and other precipitated limestone forms that crowd the surfaces of a large underground cave system deep below the Guadalupe Mountains.

BELOW LEFT AND RIGHT: stalagmites and stalactites in Carlsbad Caverns.

Depending on how much time you have, you can descend on foot through the decorated rooms of Carlsbad Cavern on the 1-mile(1.5km) -long **Natural Entrance Route** or make a speedy drop by elevator directly into the 750ft (230-meter) -deep **Big Room**, where the most splendid of these underground features occur. Guided tours are the only way to see the **Kings Palace**, **Queens Chamber**, and **Papoose Room**. Farther along, at the **Green Lake Room**, calcite "lily pads" sit in clear water, and the constant dripping sound is a reminder of what has created this curious place. Some scientists now theorize that fresh water, mixed with hydrogen-sulfide gas seeping into the reef from the oil-rich basin to the south, produced sulfuric acid and accelerated corrosion of the limestone.

One of 110 known caves in the park, Carlsbad Cavern is one of the youngest here, at 4–6 million years old. Most limestone caves are wet, created by surface water flowing through cracks that contains mildly corrosive carbonic acid from organic material.

The caves at Carlsbad Caverns are different. They were not formed by surface water but by the aggressive action of sulfuric acid, created by hydrogen sulfide in oil-rich shales and microbes combining with oxygen at the level of the water table, which dropped as the mountains were uplifted.

Carlsbad's famous decorations began forming several million years ago during a wetter period, as ground water loaded with minerals and gasses from the soil and limestone above percolated into the caves. They have stopped growing now, due to the dry desert air. Carbon dioxide loss from water droplets and evaporation inside the caves yielded calcite crystals that built into odd forms: translucent flowstone and rimstone dams around slow-moving pools, delicate curtains of icicle-like "soda straws," waving helictites, enormous stalagmites rising from the floor, and gravity-defying stalactites hanging from the ceilings. Great columns are created when stalactites and stalagmites join, providing a counterpoint to fragile aragonite formations composed of a different crystalline struc-

TIP

It's possible to tour the Natural Entrance and the Big Room without a guide (8.30am– 3.30pm). At the visitor center, you can rent an electronic device that triggers an audioguide along the trails, providing recorded commentary by rangers, geologists, and cavers.

BELOW:
Inside the Big Room.

The temperature in the Carlsbad Caverns remains a constant 56°F (13°C) all year round.

BELOW: the dazzling White Sands Monument.
RIGHT: soaptree yucca engulfed by drifting gypsum in White Sands Monument.

ture. Rangers stationed throughout the cavern answer questions and give talks at the **Top of the Cross**, in the spectacular Big Room.

Caves of even more marvelous proportions, such as **Lechuguilla Cave**, are being found here constantly. If you have time, you may want to sign up to visit undeveloped **Slaughter Canyon Cave**, which provides a truer caving experience for the physically fit. Carlsbad is also known for another natural phenomenon: bats. As many as 400,000 Brazilian free-tailed bats raise their young inside the Natural Entrance to Carlsbad Cavern during spring and summer. They exit in a long black cloud at dusk and return at dawn, where their re-entry into the cave is marked by a strange whistling sound as they fold their wings and plummet into the darkness. You can watch this mesmerizing summer ritual from an amphitheater seating area at dusk.

Although Indians are known to have used these caves as far back as 12,000 years ago, it was an Anglo cowboy, Jim White, who, among others, popularized the caves in the early 1920s.

He noticed bat droppings (guano), which make fine fertilizer, at the cave entrance and ventured inside – and discovered something that turned out to be much more intriguing. Over the next two decades, White gave unofficial tours of the cavern, unceremoniously dropping visitors into the caves in a guano bucket for a fee. He was a logical choice for chief ranger when the cave was given national monument status in 1923 (Carlsbad eventually became a national park in 1930).

Adjoining White's City has lodging and food, but it's garish and uninspiring. You're better off staying in the town of Carlsbad (20 miles/32km farther north) or camping in Guadalupe Mountains National Park, where you'll find a delightful campground. Get there early: it fills quickly in summer.

Life in the dunes

Although it's west of the Sacramento Mountains, don't miss **White Sands National Monument ㉒**, 15 miles (24km) southwest of Alamogordo. The glaring white dunes, some 60ft (18 meters) high, are formed from gypsum sediments that wash down from the neighboring San Andres and Sacramento mountains and accumulate in lakes in the **Tularosa Basin**. In time, these deposits dry into fine grains that are scooped up by winds and blown into undulating dunes. The dunes support specially adapted mice and lizards that adopt white camouflage to survive, and hardy plants like four-wing saltbush and iodinebush that tolerate the alkaline conditions.

You can drive the 16-mile (26km) round-trip **Dunes Drive**, hike **Big Dune Trail**, and picnic under shelters. The lovely Pueblo Revival-style visitor center is part of a designated historic district. This area is best known, of course, for **White Sands Missile Range**, where the first atomic bomb was tested back in 1945. A visit to "Ground Zero" (available with military escort in April and October) is a powerful experience. ❑

BIG BEND

Mountains contrast with desert within the great bend of the Rio Grande, whose waters meander through deep-cut canyon walls in one of the largest and least-visited parks

Despoblado. The empty land. So the Spanish *conquistadores* named the almost uninhabited territory that borders the Rio Grande in what is now West Texas. Today, we know it as Big Bend Country. It's a dramatic land of contrasts where island-like mountains and deeply etched canyons break up a vast expanse of the Chihuahuan Desert. Named for the great looping curve the Rio Grande makes on its journey to the Gulf of Mexico, **Big Bend National Park ㉓** is still the despoblado – forbidding yet beautiful, an "empty land" that abounds with life.

For most of its history, Big Bend was regarded as an in-between place, a crossing rather than a destination, far from the reach of law and order. Before the arrival of white settlers, Comanche and Apache Indians used its mountain hide-outs to raid villages in northern Mexico. And, even as late as the 1920s, Mexican bandits stole across the border to raid isolated ranches on the American side. Miners and ranchers began trickling into the region in the late 1880s, but most didn't stay long. By the Dust Bowl days of the 1930s, the mines had played out and the range-lands were devastated by drought and overgrazing. The federal government acquired many of these damaged lands,

and, in 1944, more than 700,000 acres (283,300 hectares) were designated as Big Bend National Park, now expanded to 800,000 acres (323,748 hectares).

This is a stark, unforgiving land, broken by lone buttes and naked peaks. Cactus, ocotillo, and greasewood provide sparse cover in the lowlands; agave and lechuguilla rise like daggers from the desert floor. At the center of the park, the **Chisos Mountains**, southernmost in the continental United States, climb to more than 7,800ft (2,377 meters), an oasis of cool breezes

Main attractions
PANTHER JUNCTION VISITOR CENTER
CHISOS BASIN
BOULDER MEADOW TRAIL
WINDOW TRAIL
ROSS MAXWELL SCENIC DRIVE
CASTOLON
SANTA ELENA CANYON
RIO GRANDE VILLAGE
BOQUILLAS CANYON
TERLINGUA/STUDY BUTTE
LAJITAS

PRECEDING PAGES: Big Bend National Park.
LEFT: gazing up at Casa Grande.
RIGHT: coyotes keep watch.

The red peeling bark of the madrone tree.

and shady woodlands in the torrid Chihuahuan Desert. To the south, the Rio Grande, one of the great rivers of the American West, courses through the spectacular gorges of Boquillas and Santa Elena canyons, with walls up to 1,500ft (460 meters) high.

Although it may appear inhospitable to the first-time visitor, Big Bend is among the most biologically diverse sites in the National Park System and has been designated part of the Chihuahuan Desert Biosphere Reserve. It's particularly known as a paradise for birds. More bird species have been sighted in Big Bend than in any other national park (a total of 450 – half the species in North America). The endangered peregrine falcon can still be seen here, as can gray hawks, zone-tailed hawks, and black hawks, rarely spotted north of the park. There are also about 52 species of warblers and, in summer, a variety of hummingbirds, including a few species like the Lucifer's hummingbird, seldom seen elsewhere in the United States. And, of course, there's the more common roadrunner, which you may see chasing after lizards or grasshoppers.

At dusk, some 20 species of bats swoop through the air, hunting insects. Evening is also the best time to catch sight of the shy Carmen Mountains white-tailed deer, a rare subspecies usually found in mountain haunts around the basin. The larger and more common mule deer can be found in the desert surrounding the Chisos Mountains, and a few fleet-footed pronghorn

Big Bend National Park

0   10 miles
0   10 km

N

Marathon, Alpine
Santiago Mountains
Tinaja Mountains
Bear
Dove Mtn 3790
Black Mtn 3629
Guayule
Black Peak 4818
Chalk Draw
385
Park Entrance
Stillwell Mtn 3658
Cupola Mtn 3998
Graytop 4386
Terlingua Creek
Persimmon Gap Visitor Center
Persimmon Gap 3771
Nine Point Mesa
Twin Peaks 6130
Dagger Mtn 4172
Big Brushy Canyon
Black Gap Wildlife Management Area
Chalk Mountains
Rosillos Mountains
Rosillos Peak 5373
Dagger Flat
Stairway Mtn 4172
Sierra del Caballo Muerto
Agua Fría Mtn 4779
Packsaddle Mtn 4661
Christmas Mountains
Corazones Peaks 5281
Texas
Hen Egg Mtn 5002
Fossil Bone Exhibit
Sue Peaks 5857
Telephone Canyon
Christmas Mtn 5719
Croton Peak 4601
Grapevine Hills 3806
Paint Gap Hills 4258
Big Bend
Telephone Canyon Trail
Sawmill Mtn 3758
Wildhorse Mtn 3900
Visitor Center (Park Headquarters)
Roys Peak 3922
National
Strawhouse Trail
Sierra del Carmen
Terlingua
Study Butte
Panther Junction
Dugout Wells
Lajitas
Warnock Environmental Education Center
Burro Mesa
The Window
Chisos Basin
Casa Grande 7325
Chisos Basin
Park
Boquillas Canyon
Well
Alamo
Tule Mtn 3838
Sam Nail Ranch
Emory Peak 7825
Chilicotal Mtn 4052
Boquillas
Boquillas Canyon Overlook
Mesa de Anguila
Chimneys Trail
Sotol Vista Overlook
Dodson Trail
Glenn
Rio Grande Village
Boquillas del Carmen
Santa Elena Canyon
Santa Elena Canyon Overlook
Mule Ears Viewpoint
Elephant Tusk Trail
Hot Springs
Cottonwood
Castolon
Mule Ears Peaks 3881
Elephant Tusk 5240
Talley Mtn 3732
Grande
Cerro del Veinte
Santa Elena
Sierra Ponce
Smoky
Dominguez Mtn 5156
Fresno
Picacho del Centinela 9501
53
San Antonio
Johnson Ranch
Mariscal Mtn 3940
Mariscal Canyon
Mariscal Canyon Trail
MEXICO
Melchor Múzquiz

still roam the flatlands, particularly around upper **Tornillo Creek**. The pig-like javelina, or peccary, is also fairly common. Extremely nearsighted and not a pig at all, it relies on scent to detect intruders and can often be seen blithely munching prickly pear.

Javelina and deer provide food for one of the most elusive predators of the West – mountain lions, or panthers, which have made a strong comeback after decades in which there were no controls on hunting them. They are rarely encountered, but it's not unusual to see their tracks. The park's other large predators, coyotes and bobcats, are also rather shy, although it's not uncommon to hear the coyote's haunting night-time howl.

If this is your first time in Big Bend, your best bet is to start your tour at the visitor center at **Panther Junction ⓐ** in the very heart of the park. From the north, enter on Highway 385 through **Persimmon Gap ⓑ**, a pass through the Santiago Mountains once used by Comanche Indians to run stolen livestock north from Mexico. About 7 miles (11km) past the entrance station, a dirt road leads east to **Dagger Flat ⓒ**, where giant dagger yucca – laden with large white flowers during the springtime bloom – can be seen in their northernmost range. A bit farther south, another turn-off leads to a fossil bone exhibit where ancient mammals once roamed, some 50 million years ago.

The **Chisos Basin ⓓ** is one of the major destinations for park visitors. The road starts about 3 miles (5km) west of Panther Junction and climbs through Green Gulch into the heart of the Chisos Mountains, a cool (sometimes frigid) island of timbered ridges and rugged peaks. As you drive upward, past the jagged profile of Pulliam Ridge (to the right) and Lost Mine Peak (to the left), desert scrub gives way to a belt of grassland and then scattered savanna-like forest. The road crests at **Panther Pass**, breaches an outer wall of peaks, and then makes a winding descent into the basin – an open, mountain-rimmed valley scattered with a relict woodland of Arizona cypress, Douglas fir, quaking aspen, ponderosa, and bigtooth maple, many at the southern limit of their range.

May and June are the hottest months in Big Bend. Afternoon rains often cool the desert from July through October. Spring is warm and pleasant, and winter generally mild – but be prepared for a variety of conditions, even snow.

BELOW: the earless lizard comes out of hiding.

Big Bend's Big Flier

An exhibit in the Panther Junction Visitor Center displays a life-sized replica of the wing bones of an enormous pterosaur (flying dinosaur). The 18ft (5.5-meter) -long specimen was discovered in Big Bend National Park and represents the largest flying creature ever to have existed. In 1971, Douglas A. Lawson, a student at the University of Texas, was doing geological fieldwork in the park for his master's thesis when he discovered a fossil bone protruding out of an arroyo bank. His professor, Dr Wann Langston Jr, determined that this long, hollow, very thin-walled bone could only be from a pterosaur wing. Subsequent excavations revealed more wing bones, but no part of the body. Lawson named his discovery *Quetzalcoatlus* after the Mexican deity Quetzalcoatl, who was worshipped by the Aztecs in the form of a feathered snake. Dr Langston later found other specimens of *Quetzalcoatlus* in another part of Big Bend. Although these were smaller than the original, they were more complete and had an impressive wingspan of at least 18ft (5.5 meters).

Comparison with these complete specimens made it possible to calculate the body size of Lawson's find. This enormous pterosaur had an estimated wingspan of 36–39ft (11–12 meters), making it the largest known flying creature of all time.

TIP

The park is crowded during spring break, when all the campgrounds and lodging may be full. The nearest campgrounds with space available may be 25 miles (40km) away and the nearest available lodging 100 miles (160km) away.

Once damaged by overgrazing, the Chisos Basin has made a strong recovery. Lush grasses have returned to the valley floor and mountain slopes, interspersed with thorny patches of cactus. Wildlife is recovering, too. After decades of absence, a breeding population of black bears is now re-established, having recently returned to the park from Mexico. Two other casualties of the ranching period – the desert bighorn sheep and the Mexican wolf – have not been quite so lucky. Several attempts to introduce bighorn sheep have failed, although there are now some flocks grazing in nearby mountains. However, Big Bend may yet prove to be one of the most promising areas in the Southwest for the reintroduction of Mexican wolves.

The road dead-ends at a collection of visitor facilities at the foot of 7,550ft (2,300-meter) **Casa Grande Peak**, where you'll find a campground, lodge, restaurant, and store as well as a network of trails. For first-time visitors, **Boulder Meadow Trail** is an easy 3-mile (5km) round-trip through pinyon-juniper woodland to a beauti-

ful meadow. Those who have plenty of time and energy can press on to the sweeping vistas at 7,100ft (2,164-meter) **Pinnacle Pass**, and then either make the strenuous journey to the top of 7,825ft (2,385-meter) **Emory Peak** **Ⓔ**, highest in the park, or continue to Boot Spring in densely forested Boot Canyon, the summer home of the rare Colima warbler.

Another good introduction to the basin is the 5-mile (8km) round-trip to **the Window Ⓕ**, a V-shaped notch, or pour-off, on the basin's west side, with gorgeous views of Casa Grande Peak and surrounding mountains. The trail follows a dry creek lined with maples, oaks, and Texas madrone, making for a pleasant and shady stroll. Carmen Mountains white-tailed deer are often seen along this trail. For experienced backpackers, there is a 33-mile (53km) circuit of the rim and mountain flanks that makes an excellent three-day journey.

If you're driving into the park from Alpine, 58 miles (94km) via Highway 118, you can enter the park on its scenic west side, through the old mining town of **Terlingua/Study Butte Ⓖ**.

BELOW: backpackers on a Big Bend trail.

From the entrance gate at Maverick Junction, it's a 26-mile (48km) drive on Highway 118 to reach the main visitor center at **Panther Junction**. The road traverses a landscape of baked tawny bluffs and dry washes sparsely covered with desert shrub and ocotillo. To the north looms **Maverick Mountain**, a dome of intruded magma (molten rock) now exposed by erosion, while to the east, the Chisos Mountains rise like rusty battlements.

Dramatic geology

Halfway between the park's western and eastern entrances is the Castolon/Santa Elena Junction, the start of **Ross Maxwell Scenic Drive**, a 30-mile (48km) road that heads south to Santa Elena Canyon. Along the way, you'll pass **Sam Nail Ranch** ⓗ. With its windmill, water tank, and the remains of the 1916 adobe ranch house, it makes a pleasant stop to birdwatch or picnic. Continuing south, Casa Grande Peak comes into view framed by the gunsight notch of the Window.

Near the southern end of Burro Mesa, three dikes radiate from the Chisos Mountains. These long rock walls were formed by molten lava that was squeezed into a narrow fault. The softer overlying rock gradually eroded, leaving behind freestanding walls of volcanic rock. Watch for **Sotol Vista**, where you'll be treated to glorious views into Mexico. A bit farther, a spur road veers right to Burro Mesa, where you can take a short hike up the dry wash for a firsthand look at desert geology.

In some cases, the dikes have been eroded into fanciful shapes, like **Mule Ears Peaks** ⓘ, which can be viewed from the overlook a few miles farther south. Just beyond the Mule Ears Overlook, the road passes through a narrow canyon of white ash, which was spewed from a volcano about 35 million years ago. Within the bed of ash, near **Cerro Castellan**, are what look like petrified trees; they are really "lava necks," upright tubes of molten rock that have hardened into bizarre shapes.

At **Castolon** ⓙ, you can stop for refreshments and a stroll around the historic army garrison, manned between 1914 and 1918 to protect settlers from Mexican bandits and now

The Rio Grande, Big Bend's southern boundary, is also the US-Mexico border. The National Park Service has jurisdiction only to the center of the deepest channel; the rest of the river lies within the Republic of Mexico, where it is known as the Rio Bravo Del Norte.

BELOW LEFT:
dilapidated windmill at Sam Nail Ranch.
BELOW:
rock formations and desert landscape along Ross Maxwell Scenic Drive.

In 1929, the US Army Air Corps established an airfield at Johnson's Ranch, southeast of Castolon. Rancher Elmo Johnson continued to own the landing field, and his wife, Ada, cooked meals for the pilots.

used as a trading post and ranger station. **Cottonwood Campground**, your best bet for a campground during the crowded spring season, occupies a shady spot on the Rio Grande just beyond the old village.

From Castolon, the scenic drive parallels the Rio Grande for about 8 miles (13km) before coming to a dead end at **Santa Elena Canyon** Ⓚ. A short trail leads into the canyon where 1,500ft (460-meter) limestone cliffs tower over the muddy river. When you're ready, you can either double back to Santa Elena Junction or loop through the backcountry on a 13-mile (21km) dirt road to the park entrance at Maverick Junction.

Rio Grande Village

The 24-mile (39km) drive from Panther Junction to Rio Grande Village passes around the eastern flank of the Chisos Mountains to the cottonwood-shaded Rio Grande. A dirt road heading west just before Dugout Wells leads 9 miles (14km) to **Glenn Spring**, an abandoned village that was the site of a bandit raid in 1916. **Dugout Wells** Ⓛ, another developed spring and old

RIGHT: black bears roam the rugged terrain of Big Bend National Park.
BELOW: bathers in Hot Springs pool at the edge of Rio Grande.

ranch headquarters, is a shady place, ideal for a picnic or a walk along the self-guiding nature trail.

As you descend the long hill toward the Rio Grande, the rugged limestone cliffs of the imposing **Sierra del Carmen** come into sight across the border in Mexico. Much of the Sierra del Carmen is part of a proposed sister park that may unite Big Bend and its Mexican counterpart in an international reserve.

About 3 miles (5km) from Rio Grande Village, another dirt road takes off to the south leading to the now abandoned site of **Hot Springs** Ⓜ, a former health spa and trading post. A stone building still stands on the spot. A short hike takes you to natural hot springs where you can still soak in the 105ºF (40.5ºC) waters that bubble out of the ground.

Cottonwood trees fringe the river near **Rio Grande Village** Ⓝ, which has camping facilities, supplies, gasoline, laundry, and showers. Birdwatching is particularly good in this area, which is a meeting place for river species such as the beautiful vermilion flycatcher, and desert species such as the animated roadrunner.

If you would like to visit the Mexican village of Boquillas, there is usually a nearby ferryman to row you across the river. **Boquillas Canyon Overlook,** at the end of the road, has some marvelous views.

Some 196 miles (315km) of the Rio Grande beyond park borders has received Wild and Scenic River status and are managed as wilderness. Outfitters offer float trips lasting from a day to a week or more. Of these, Boquillas Canyon is best for beginners; Mariscal Canyon, more remote and challenging; and the rugged Lower Canyons only for experienced river runners. Within the park, the float through Santa Elena Canyon offers some white water and long stretches of calmer water. You can put in outside the park at Lajitas, which has luxury accommodations and a spa, and float 20 miles (31km) to the Santa Elena Canyon takeout. For more information, contact the park. ❏

THE ANCIENT ONES

The pithouse communities, elaborate pueblos, and cliff dwellings of the Southwest are not dusty outdoor museums: they form a living link between ancestral Indian people and their modern descendants in New Mexico and Arizona

Stand at the overlook of Cliff Palace in Mesa Verde. Imagine it at night-time, the windows glowing with the warm light of fires within. Once upon a time, ordinary people lived in this "palace." They cooked simple food over the fires and warmed themselves around the hearths on winter nights. They mended sandals, polished pottery, and ground corn, while elders told stories to the young ones.

The prehistoric residents of **Mesa Verde National Park** ㉔ were a branch of the Ancestral Pueblo culture, an Anglo name that supplants the earlier name *Anasazi*, derived from the Navajo word for "enemy ancestors." Their descendants, the Hopi, call them *Hisatsinom*, which means "our ancestors."

From the 1st century AD until the 15th century, three major branches of the Ancestral Pueblo culture – the Mesa Verde, Chaco, and Kayenta cultures – inhabited the Four Corners, where Utah, Arizona, New Mexico, and Colorado meet. A number of fascinating national parks here interpret the preserved remains of the Ancestral Pueblo culture.

Mesa Verde

Mesa Verde National Park protects 13th-century cliff dwellings built at the end of Ancestral Pueblo occupation of the Four Corners. A great introduction to the cliff dwellings is the 2-mile (3km) trail from the **Chapin Mesa Museum** to **Spruce Tree House**. Here, you can stoop through the small doorways, see the soot-blackened ceilings, and feel the cool trickle of the spring that was their lifeblood.

The earliest people here, the Basketmakers, lived in semi-subterranean pithouses. Examples from AD 550 can be seen along **Ruins Road**. By AD 700, residents were building above-ground two-story masonry pueblos of intercon-

Main attractions
MESA VERDE NATIONAL PARK
HOVENWEEP NATIONAL MONUMENT
AZTEC RUINS NATIONAL MONUMENT
CHACO CULTURE NATIONAL
  HISTORICAL PARK
CANYON DE CHELLY NATIONAL
  MONUMENT
NAVAJO NATIONAL MONUMENT
BANDELIER NATIONAL MONUMENT
SUNSET CRATER VOLCANO
WUPATKI NATIONAL MONUMENT
MONTEZUMA CASTLE NATIONAL
  MONUMENT
TUZIGOOT NATIONAL MONUMENT
CASA GRANDE RUINS NATIONAL
  MONUMENT
TONTO NATIONAL MONUMENT
GILA CLIFF DWELLINGS

PRECEDING PAGES: Cliff Palace, Mesa Verde. **LEFT:** multistoried pueblo. **RIGHT:** Catwalk Trail, Gila Wilderness Area.

Ancient domestic artifacts found inside a pueblo.

BELOW: Hovenweep National Monument.

nected living and storage rooms, laying up courses of stone blocks mud-mortared into place and covered in mud plaster. These hamlets formed an arc around a central pithouse, or kiva.

Then as now, kivas were places of special spiritual importance to Pueblo people. Men gathered in kivas to weave, and all the villagers crowded into them to take part in ceremonies. Spruce Tree House alone has eight round kivas, and others are found at nearly every Ancestral Pueblo community.

Residents stalked mule deer and rabbit, gathered the fibers of the yucca plant for woven baskets and sandals, and cultivated small fields and gardens. With only stone or wood hoes and clever water collection systems, they successfully grew crops in this dry environment for centuries. Corn, first cultivated in Mexico, was their earliest and most important domesticated crop, along with squash. Beans were added later, possibly at the same time that Ancestral Pueblo people learned to make pottery, around AD 500. Plain gray, corrugated jars and bowls served for everyday cooking and stor-

age. A finer pottery painted with black designs on white became a Mesa Verde specialty and a popular trade item.

Mesa Verde grew crowded and people were forced away. Fifty miles (80km) west of Mesa Verde, on the Colorado-Utah border, is **Hovenweep National Monument** ㉕. Hovenweep preserves six clusters of multistory towers built at the heads of canyons, perhaps for storage, defense, ceremonies, or skywatching.

Some people went south to what is now **Aztec Ruins National Monument** on the Animas River in northeastern New Mexico. Aztec preserves two large pueblos, only one of which is excavated – **West Ruins** – and a reconstructed great kiva, a larger version of clan and village kivas, that hosted visitors from surrounding communities during social and religious events.

Chaco Canyon

Although its architecture bears the hallmarks of later Mesa Verde occupation, Aztec Ruins was built in the 1100s by people of the Chaco culture, headquartered in **Chaco Canyon**, 60 miles

(100km) south of Aztec. **Chaco Culture National Historical Park** ㉖ is surrounded by the Navajo Nation and can only be reached by a jolting 20-mile (32km) drive over dirt roads. Don't bypass this park, though: within the Ancestral Pueblo world, there has been nothing like Chaco, before or since.

Starting in AD 900, Chacoan astronomer-priest leaders planned and oversaw construction of nine "great houses" in the canyon and on the surrounding cliffs. The most famous is **Pueblo Bonito**, a five-story, 650-room, D-shaped pueblo built using signature Chacoan core-and-veneer tapering walls made of tightly laid, mosaic like masonry.

The great houses are aligned to planetary solstices and equinoxes, vital for farmers whose lives depended on planting and harvesting at the right time of year. It's thought that the priests used windows and markers in the canyon to track the heavens, then sent out word for villagers from throughout the San Juan Basin to come to the canyon to participate in ceremonies.

An elaborate road system radiates from Chaco's great houses to these outlying villages and was apparently used by foot travelers making the journey to Chaco to trade, socialize, and observe seasonal agricultural ceremonies. By the 1120s, Chacoans had dispersed north of the San Juan River and south to the mountains surrounding the Rio Grande, where they mingled with existing populations. Chaco's great houses and kivas can be toured along the paved scenic loop. The road system can be seen on backcountry trails to mesa-top pueblos.

Canyon de Chelly National Monument ㉗ is on Navajo lands in northeastern Arizona. It preserves many ancient cliff dwellings built by people of the Kayenta branch of the Ancestral Pueblo culture. The 1-mile (1.5km) self-guided **White House Ruin Trail**, which begins at White House Overlook on the South Rim Drive, leads to the only site you may visit on your own. You will need to hire a Navajo guide to make trips to view Antelope House, Standing Cow, and other sites. Daily tours into the canyon on special buses with rubber wheels depart from Thunderbird Lodge, the main tourist

The rock walls of Canyon de Chelly served as canvases for Anasazi artwork: hundreds of decorated panels testify to their long occupation here.

BELOW:
Casa Rinconada looking east.

BELOW: view over Tsegi Canyon to Anasazi cliff dwellings in Navajo Monument.
RIGHT: cave dwellings at Bandelier.

lodging in the park. Otherwise, ruins are visible from viewpoints along South Rim Drive, which follows Canyon de Chelly, and **North Rim Drive**, which follows **Canyon del Muerto**, a major tributary.

Another Ancestral Pueblo site on Navajo lands is **Navajo National Monument** ㉘, west of Kayenta, Arizona. From the visitor center, a half-mile (1km) walk on the **Sandal Trail** ends at an overlook above the spectacular alcove pueblo of **Betatakin**, built by the Kayenta branch of the Ancestral Pueblo culture between 1250 and 1300. In summer, rangers lead tours to Betatakin; get there early, as these fill up quickly.

Ancestral Pueblo sites had been abandoned by the time Spanish explorer Coronado made his *entrada* into the Southwest in 1540. Pueblo people had not disappeared, though. Rather, as had happened repeatedly during their early migrations, they had moved on. Drought may have been a driving force, or changes in social and trade networks. Many Pueblo people today say it was prophesied that they should keep moving until they reached

their final destinations – which today are the Hopi Mesas in Arizona and the Zuni lands and villages of the Rio Grande in New Mexico.

Bandelier National Monument ㉙ in northern New Mexico was an important stopping place in the 12th and 13th centuries. Chacoan refugees excavated cave-like dwellings in the volcanic tuff cliffs of Frijoles Canyon and used Frijoles Creek to irrigate crops in the 1100s. They were joined, in the late 1200s, by Mesa Verde families, who built Tyuonyi, a large pueblo on the canyon floor. From the visitor center, the 1-mile (1.5km) -long **Main Loop Trail** follows the creek and accesses some of the ruins via ladders. Unexcavated sites can be seen in Bandelier's 23,000-acre (9,300-hectare) backcountry wilderness. Trails and permits are required for overnight trips.

The Sinagua

The Sinagua were contemporaries of the Ancestral Pueblo culture who, by AD 600, were living in "parks" in northern Arizona, grassy clearings in the ponderosa pine and pinyon-juniper

forests. Beginning in 1064, the eruption of Sunset Crater Volcano, part of the large San Francisco Volcanic Field, forced the Sinagua to move away. Later generations returned to the Sunset Crater area, however, and quickly discovered that the combination of good rainfall and volcanic cinder mulch made for excellent farmlands.

As other immigrants moved into the region, the Little Colorado River quickly become a cultural frontier. The Sinagua adapted pueblo building skills learned from Kayenta Pueblo neighbors but also built ballcourts, a feature of ancient Mexico cultures that had been adopted by the Hohokam culture of southern Arizona. Ballcourts were probably used for socializing, trading, and ceremonial ballgames, much like great kivas were used in great house communities.

Remnants of the Sinagua culture can be seen at **Sunset Crater Volcano National Monument**, 14 miles (23km) northeast of Flagstaff, Arizona, off Highway 89, and a farther 17 miles (27km) north, at **Wupatki National Monument ③**. **Wupatki Pueblo** near the visitor center is the largest and most popular ruin and includes a ball-court. Farther along the scenic road are **Lomaki** and **Wukoki** pueblos, which have been built into the rocks and blend beautifully with their surroundings. The 12,000ft (3,660-meter) San Francisco Peaks, the highest mountains in Arizona, form a photogenic backdrop to these lovely structures.

East of Flagstaff are unique Sinagua cliff dwellings, built directly into alcoves in the limestone cliffs at **Walnut Canyon National Monument**. Early Sinagua residents, in the 1100s, grew corn, beans, and squash on the mesa tops and lived in a small hamlet. By the 1200s, though, they had started building protected dwellings in the cliffs and commuted to the mesa tops to farm. They hunted game and harvested native plants that grew here, including walnuts and grapes along the stream, the fruits wolfberry on the rocky hillsides, and pine nuts from pinyon pines on the mesa tops. The quarter-mile (0.4km) **Island Trail** leads into Walnut Canyon and provides intimate views of many of the rooms.

Hopi Indians of the Bear Clan say that they stopped at Wupatki for a time, building a village and growing corn. But the old men told the people that the land was too rich and that they had to move on before they became too comfortable.

BELOW:
Wukoki pueblo ruins at Wupatki.

The well-preserved four-story Casa Grande ruins, dating from the late Hohokam period.

A southern contingent of Sinagua lived in the **Verde Valley** south of Flagstaff, their golden years dating from 1300 to 1400. Adapting gradually to the environment of the warmer, lower valley, the southern Sinaguans appeared in many ways unlike their northern cousins. Because of their intermediate location between the northland and the deserts, the southern Sinaguans served as middlemen in a brisk trade for salt, cotton, argillite, parrots, and shells. What were first called forts in Sinagua country are now interpreted as possible large storage structures for trade goods. The Sinagua were also expert weavers and skilled jewelers.

Montezuma Castle National Monument 31, just off Interstate 17 (take Exit 289), preserves two multistory cliff dwellings built by the Sinagua just before the year 1000. A short trail along sycamore-lined **Beaver Creek** leads from the visitor center to a view of the castle from below; the ruin itself is off-limits. Nearby **Montezuma Well** is a natural limestone sink fed by artesian springs, which drew prehistoric farmers. By the 14th century, the "well"

supported a community of 150 to 200 residents. It is the only such structure in the National Park System.

In contrast to Montezuma Castle, **Tuzigoot National Monument 32**, about 30 miles (48km) northwest, is a sprawling pueblo perched on an open ridge, with rooms spilling randomly down the hillside. The settlement takes in a full view of the **Verde River**, whose flood plain provided prime farmland. The pueblo was added to over time, and, at its peak, it was home to perhaps 225 souls. Tuzigoot and Montezuma Castle were finally abandoned by the Sinaguan people around 1425. Some of them may have joined the Yavapai who were moving in from the west, while many others resettled at big villages on Anderson Mesa south and east of Flagstaff.

The Hohokam

The Sonoran Desert, land of saguaro cactus and palo verde trees, was home to the Hohokam culture. The Hohokam were well adapted to living conditions in the Sonoran Desert, which receives on average only about

7–10ins (18–25cm) of rain a year. The Hohokam lived in cool pithouse communities, called *rancherias*, which, while sizeable, never reached the size those of their Ancestral Pueblo contemporaries. Their favored building material was caliche, a calcium-rich, rock-hard substance of the valley floors. Mixed with water, caliche turns to a mud that can be daubed over a stick foundation.

The Hohokam were master irrigators. With backbreaking labor, they constructed and maintained a system of dams, headgates, and canals that reached many miles into the surrounding desert. The valleys of two major Southwest rivers, the Gila and the Salt, were their heartland. And, though the Hohokam are most often viewed as a riverine society, their traces have more recently been found in the rocky slopes of the foothills around Tucson, where they cultivated wild plants such as agave. The Hohokam also manufactured extraordinary buff and orange pottery and excellent stone and shell goods.

Around AD 700–900, the Hohokam began building Mesoamerican-style ballcourts and multistoried elite residences atop platform mounds that formed the dwellings of astronomer-priest leaders who used alignments in the buildings themselves to read planetary movements throughout the year.

Casa Grande Ruins National Monument ❸ south of Phoenix is the only national park area now open to the public that is devoted to Hohokam culture. Preserved here is a Hohokam ballcourt. Rising in solitude nearby is the **Casa Grande**, or Big House. This four-story, 11-room structure was built during the early 14th century and protected with a tin roof structure in modern times to preserve the mud walls.

Casa Grande was built in the waning days of the Hohokam. By 1350–1400, the people were gone. Their descendants may be the Pima and Tohono O'odham Indians who live in southern Arizona today.

The Salado

On the higher reaches of the Salt River in central Arizona, a different culture had emerged by 1150, known by their Spanish name: the Salado (the Salt People). Archeologists are divided as to whether they were newcomers to the region or Hohokam who had adapted to the more rugged Tonto Basin.

Tonto National Monument ❸ is the only national park that protects Salado remains. Within the monument, a pair of pueblos, Upper and Lower cliff dwellings, are tucked into caves high in the side of a cliff overlooking **Lake Roosevelt**. From the visitor center, a steep trail leads to the larger Upper Ruin.

The Salado were influenced by neighbors but are known for their gorgeous red, black, and cream (polychrome) ceramics and exquisite woven cotton textiles. They cultivated crops but also excelled at living off the desert's bounty, feeding themselves with the fruits of prickly pear, mesquite, and agave, and hunting rabbit and deer.

By 1200, the Salado had settled into villages along the **Salt River** and

In the walls of Casa Grande are portholes whose edges are struck by the sun's rays on the summer solstice. The Big House may have been home to priests or chiefs responsible for announcing celestial events that signaled planting and harvest times.

BELOW:
Casa Grande Ruins National Monument.

Besh-Ba-Gowah is a reconstructed Salado dwelling near Globe, Arizona. You can walk within the rooms of this 700-year-old pueblo, climb the ladders to the upper floors, and study the pottery and furnishings.

were irrigating fields. When the valley became too crowded, the people moved higher into the hills and built the two pueblos at **Tonto**. For nearly three centuries, the Salado thrived in the Tonto Basin. They outlasted the Hohokam and Ancestral Pueblo cultures, but then they too moved on, perhaps driven out by climate change, salty fields, or outside invaders, leaving the ruins at Tonto silent for 600 years.

The Mogollon

There was nothing flashy about the Mogollon (pronounced *muggy-own*) people who, from the early Christian era until AD 1000, lived in the cool, well-watered mountains of southern New Mexico and Arizona. Due to their proximity to Mexico, they became the first Southwest culture to learn corn cultivation, pottery, and masonry building, technologies developed in Mesoamerica. Early on, the Mogollon made mostly utilitarian brown pottery that served their need for storage, cookware, and containers. They farmed but continued to hunt the abundant game in the highlands,

BELOW: Gila Cliff dwellings.
RIGHT: an ancient petroglyph.

gather plant foods, and live in pit-house villages.

Cliff dwellings were not as characteristic of the Mogollon as they were of other Southwest cultures. Built between 1270 and 1290, **Gila Cliff Dwellings National Monument** ③⑤ in southern New Mexico preserves cliff dwellings built by the Tularosa branch of the Mogollon just before they moved north and merged with Ancestral Pueblo and other cultures in central Arizona.

Gila Cliff Dwellings, near Silver City, New Mexico, is the only site in the park system devoted to the Mogollon. Highway 15 winds north for 44 miles (71km) through the Gila Mountains, providing heart-stopping views of the rugged canyons of the upper Gila River.

Stop at the **visitor center** for information, then drive the short distance up the West Fork of the Gila. From there, a guided 1-mile (1.5km) loop trail leads up **Cliff Dweller Canyon** and into the dwellings 180ft (55 meters) up the canyon wall. Other Mogollon sights, such as rectangular kivas, can be seen to the northwest, on the Mogollon Rim. ❑

Mogollon Traders

The huge territory of the Mogollon included the rolling hills, mountains, and river valleys of the upper Gila and Black rivers in southwest New Mexico and central Arizona, an area that was increasingly on an important trading route. By AD 1000, they were in regular contact with Ancestral Pueblo traders plying their wares along the trade route between Chaco Canyon and Casas Grandes (Paquime) in Chihuahua, Mexico, a large pueblo that specialized in raising scarlet macaws whose feathers were used in Ancestral Pueblo ceremonies. Cultural exchange ensued, and the Mogollon started to build Ancestral Pueblo-style pueblos and adopt other traits. One branch, the Mimbres people of the Mimbres Valley in the Gila Mountains, began to make superb black-and-white pottery that, then as now, was highly prized by collectors and traders.

THE ART OF THE ANCIENT ONES

For thousands of years, American Indians have been producing beautiful objects – and today's visitors can still find art in the traditional style

In 1890, when explorers entered an ancient dwelling at Mesa Verde, Colorado, they found this mug (*pictured left*) and several other mugs tied together with string. Mug House, as the site is now called, is in a region occupied by the Ancestral Pueblo people from about 200 BC to AD 1300. Such fine pottery indicates that these ancient people had a keen sense of esthetics and created beauty even in utilitarian items.

For centuries, Indian groups traded hides, pottery, ornaments, and other useful items among themselves. After European contact, from 1540 on, they did business with whomever happened to be in their territory. When the Navajo were forced onto their reservation in 1868, traders and Indians exchanged goods in a system of barter and credit. Indian-made items made their way to the Eastern states and a national market developed. By the mid-1880s, the railroad had reached the Southwest and many tourists bought direct from Indian artisans. Among the most popular items were pottery, basketry, silver jewelry, and blankets, which Indians modified to heavier rugs in response to the demands of the tourist market.

The remarkable creations of the Southwestern American Indians may still be found in shops and galleries throughout the region. Certain tribes are noted for specific crafts, though most produce an ever-changing variety, using traditional styles even as they bring in new combinations of metals and stones, colors, patterns, and shapes.

ABOVE: Dream catchers, protective amulets made from willow and decorated with beads and feathers, help to eliminate bad dreams.

LEFT: From Pueblo Bonito in Chaco Canyon, this 3in (76mm) frog, made of jet decorated with turquoise, was discovered by the Hyde Expedition in 1900.

BELOW: Ceremonial pipes made from traditional Navajo clay, then fired in an underground pit and coated with pinion sap.

LEFT: Kachina figurines carved from cottonwood roots represent Katsinam, benevolent spirit beings important in Hopi cosmology.

TRADING PLACES

Among the many historic trading posts still operating in the Southwest, Hubbell Trading Post, preserved by the National Park Service, still functions much as it did when John Lorenzo Hubbell established it in 1878. Indians brought livestock, grain, hay, wool, pots, blankets, and other goods to Hubbell, to trade for coffee, tobacco, sugar, flour, canned goods, fabric, metal utensils, and tools.

John Lorenzo Hubbell was largely responsible for popularizing items that continue to delight collectors, particularly rugs. He insisted on high-quality weaving and natural dyes. In 1931, a colleague recalled that he "was the premier trader of them all, and did more to stabilize... the Indian blanket market and industry than anyone else."

For more information, you can call the Hubbell Trading Post National Historic Site: 928-755-3475.

ABOVE: Though most Navajo weavers use commercial yarn, they still employ traditional upright looms.

LEFT AND ABOVE: Hand-spun wool, colored with vegetable dyes, gives rugs and blankets a unique character.

RIGHT: Navajo women in traditional dress with silver and turquoise jewelry.

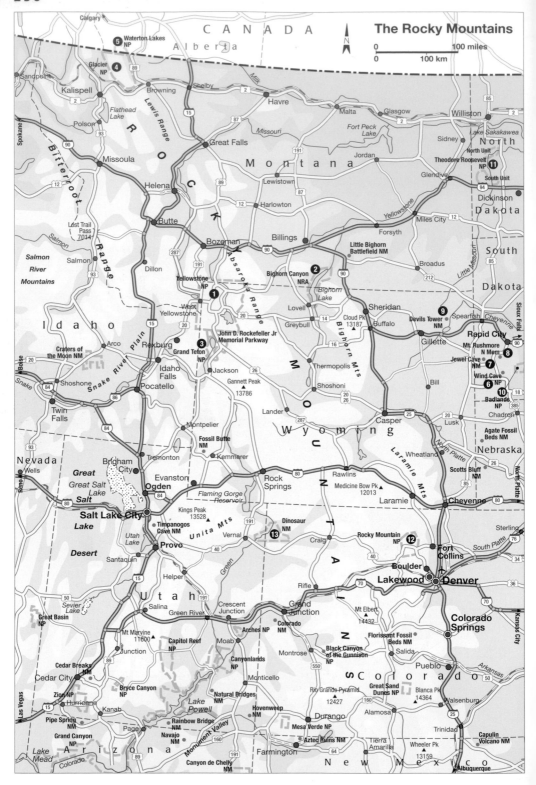

The Rocky Mountains

0   100 miles
0   100 km

CANADA

Alberta

Waterton Lakes NP ⑤

Glacier NP ④

Calgary

Sandpoint

Kalispell

Browning

Shelby

Havre

Malta

Glasgow

Williston

Polson

Flathead Lake

Lewis Range

Milk

Missouri

Fort Peck Lake

Sidney

Lake Sakakawea

Theodore Roosevelt NP ⑪ North Unit

South Unit

North Dakota

Spokane

Missoula

Helena

Great Falls

Montana

Lewistown

Jordan

Glendive

Dickinson

Butte

Bozeman

Billings

Miles City

Forsyth

Broadus

South Dakota

Bitterroot Range

Lost Trail Pass 7014

Salmon River Mountains

Salmon

Dillon

Absaroka Range

Little Bighorn Battlefield NM

Sheridan

Devils Tower NM ⑨ Spearfish Cheyenne

Sioux Falls

Rapid City

Yellowstone NP ①

West Yellowstone

John D. Rockefeller Jr Memorial Parkway

Bighorn Canyon NRA ②

Lovell

Greybull

Bighorn Lake

Cloud Pk 13187

Buffalo

Gillette

Mt Rushmore N Mem ⑧

Jewel Cave NM ⑦

Rapid City

Idaho

Craters of the Moon NM

Arco

Rexburg

Grand Teton NP ③

Idaho Falls

Pocatello

Jackson

Gannett Peak 13786

Shoshoni

Thermopolis

Bighorn Mts

Wind Cave NP ⑥

Badlands NP ⑩

Chadron

Snake River Plain

Twin Falls

Shoshone

Montpelier

Lander

Casper

Lusk

Agate Fossil Beds NM

Nebraska

Nevada

Wells

Reno

Brigham City

Great Salt Lake

Ogden

Evanston

Fossil Butte NM

Kemmerer

Rock Springs

Rawlins

Medicine Bow Pk 12013

Wheatland

North Platte

Laramie Mts

Scotts Bluff NM

North Platte

Salt Lake City

Utah Lake

Great Salt Lake Desert

Flaming Gorge Reservoir

Kings Peak 13528

Uinta Mts

Vernal

Dinosaur NM ⑬

Craig

Laramie

Cheyenne

Sterling

Provo

Santaquin

Helper

Rocky Mountain NP ⑫

Fort Collins

Boulder

Lakewood Denver

South Platte

Timpanogos Cave NM

Rifle

Grand Junction

Mt Elbert 14432

Colorado Springs

Kansas City

Sevier Lake

Salina

Green River

Crescent Junction

Colorado NM

Florissant Fossil Beds NM

Salida

Arkansas

Utah

Mt Marvine 11600

Capitol Reef NP

Moab

Arches NP

Montrose

Black Canyon of the Gunnison NP

Pueblo

Colorado

Great Basin NP

Junction

Cedar Breaks NM

Cedar City

Bryce Canyon NP

Canyonlands NP

Monticello

Rio Grande Pyramid 12427

Great Sand Dunes NP

Blanca Pk 14364

Walsenburg

Zion NP

Hurricane

Kanab

Natural Bridges NM

Hovenweep NM

Durango

Alamosa

Pipe Spring NM

Grand Canyon NP

Page

Rainbow Bridge NM

Navajo NM

Lake Powell

Mesa Verde NP

Aztec Ruins NM

Tierra Amarilla

Trinidad

Capulin Volcano NM

Lake Mead

Arizona

Colorado

Monument Valley

Canyon de Chelly NM

Farmington

Wheeler Pk 13159

New Mexico

Albuquerque

THE ROCKY MOUNTAINS

Ancient peaks and ridges, spectacular lakes
and canyons, hot springs and geysers,
and a wealth of wildlife...

They are known as the backbone of the world. The Rocky Mountains are a crooked spine of peaks and ridges that were thrust skyward more than 50 million years ago and now run through the country's midsection. In Rocky Mountain and Glacier national parks, the mountains were shaped by great sheets of ice, grinding, gouging, and fracturing the bedrock into serrated peaks, bowl-like cirques, "hanging valleys", and enormous mounds of morainal debris.

At Yellowstone, the world's very first national park, an ancient volcanic blast tore open a massive crater where hot springs, geysers, and fumaroles continue to steam and spurt. Immediately to the south, the Teton Range towers grandly over Jackson Hole, a chain of shimmering lakes at its feet.

To the east of the Rockies, a mountainous outlier known as the Black Hills rises from the plains like an island of granite. At their base, the limestone passages of Wind Cave honeycomb the earth beneath prairie and ponderosa forest. In the Dakota Badlands, the plains have been carved by rushing water into a moonscape of gullies, canyons, ravines, and "tables" shared by prairie dogs, bison, pronghorn, and soaring hawks and eagles.

Together, these parks form some of the richest wilderness in the United States, with dense coniferous forests, shady rivers, dazzling wildflower meadows and extensive swaths of alpine tundra. Hikers can explore hundreds of miles of backcountry trails into the realms of mountain goats, bighorn sheep, mountain lions, bobcats, grizzly bears, and wolves. Even motorists are likely to see a variety of large mammals, including bison, elk, mule deer, and pronghorn, not to mention smaller species such as chipmunks, squirrels, and marmots, and a wide variety of birdlife. ❏

PRECEDING PAGES: a river meandering through the Rocky Mountains.
ABOVE LEFT: a red vintage tour bus (jammers) in Glacier National Park.
ABOVE RIGHT: a male elk in the Rocky Mountains.

YELLOWSTONE

The world's first national park is one of the largest in the system. Its famous geysers and hot springs attract millions of visitors, but there are also vast areas of empty wilderness

It is perhaps the world's most famous natural preserve. And yet, despite its renown and its rank as the first national park, **Yellowstone National Park ❶** is capable of surprising even those who know it well, to say nothing of those who visit for the first time.

Most visitors have in mind at least one destination: **Old Faithful Geyser.** Beyond that, they may expect to see wildlife, have a picnic under the pines, or enjoy a meadow of wildflowers. But what they find is so much more. Beyond Old Faithful are more than 10,000 other thermal features half of the known thermal features in the world – including even bigger geysers and several that are more "faithful," erupting more regularly than their celebrated cousin.

The park's 2.2 million acres (890,300 hectares) support approximately 8,000 elk, 1,500 bison, and hundreds of deer, along with moose, bighorn sheep, mountain goats, pronghorn antelope, black bears, grizzly bears, coyotes, trumpeter swans, Canada geese, sandhill cranes, white pelicans, cutthroat trout, and others. After the long-anticipated reintroduction of wolves, the park now represents the entire panoply of Rocky Mountain wildlife.

Yellowstone contains snow-covered mountain peaks, several magnificent high-altitude lakes, numerous rivers and streams renowned for trout fishing, a brightly colored canyon that nearly dwarfs two major waterfalls, one of the most significant volcanic calderas in the world, and layer upon layer of buried petrified forest. None of this came easy. Yellowstone has a history of staggering geologic violence, and it remains one of the most geologically active places in the world.

The lay of the land

Most of Yellowstone occupies a high plateau, which averages 7,000–8,000ft

Main attractions
OLD FAITHFUL GEYSER
OLD FAITHFUL INN
GRAND PRISMATIC SPRING
STEAMBOAT GEYSER
MAMMOTH HOT SPRINGS
FORT YELLOWSTONE
YELLOWSTONE LAKE
YELLOWSTONE RIVER
BIGHORN CANYON NATIONAL RECREATION AREA
PRYOR MOUNTAINS WILD HORSE RANGE

PRECEDING PAGES: Glacier National Park.
LEFT: Yellowstone's Old Faithful Geyser.
RIGHT: family time at Yellowstone.

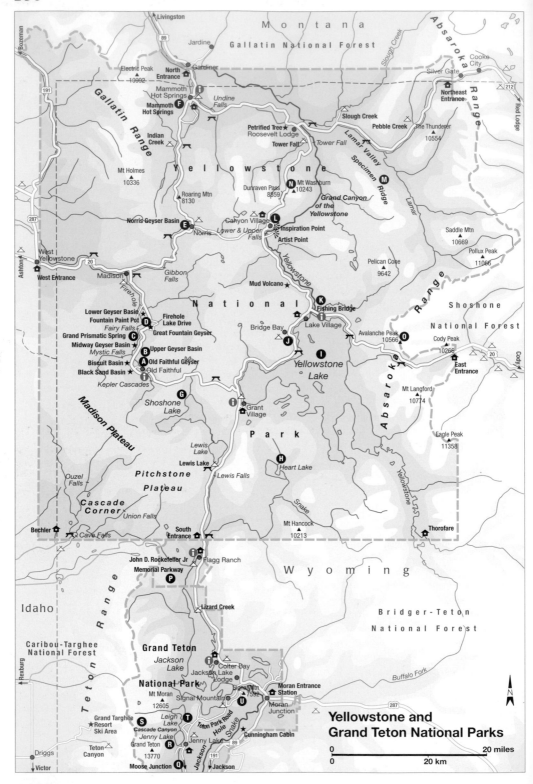

Yellowstone and Grand Teton National Parks

(2,130–2,440 meters) in elevation, ringed by mountains that rise several thousand feet higher. In the northwest, the **Gallatin Range** is capped by Mount Holmes and Electric Peak, both rising over 10,000ft (3,000 meters). To the northeast stands the Beartooth Plateau, a massive Precambrian block where Montana's highest mountain, 12,800ft (3,900-meter) **Granite Peak**, rises a few miles outside the park. Yellowstone's eastern boundary follows the crest of the **Absaroka Range**, a line of rubbly snow-covered volcanic summits that include **Eagle Peak**, which, at 11,358ft (3,460 meters), is the highest point in the park. Lofty terrain continues along the south on Big Game Ridge and the windswept Pitchstone Plateau, while the Madison Plateau holds up Yellowstone's southwest corner.

Winding circuitously across the park's southern third, the **Continental Divide** separates waters flowing toward the Pacific Ocean from streams heading to the Atlantic. Waters from Yellowstone and the surrounding area find their way into many famous rivers, including the Missouri, the Snake, the Bighorn, and the Yellowstone itself. These rivers and their tributaries – the Wind, Sweetwater, Popo Agie, Madison, Gallatin, Clark's Fork, Shoshone, and many others – reverberate through the history of westward exploration and settlement.

Congress established Yellowstone as the world's first national park in 1872. It was an act of foresight brought about largely because of the park's amazing collection of geysers and hot springs, unmatched anywhere else. For years, mountain men and other travelers had told stories of strange doings in the area, so strange that they were disbelieved by most who heard them. Lakes of boiling mud? Gushers of hot water shooting 200ft (61 meters) or more in the air? These could only be tall tales from the imaginations of men who had spent too much time alone in the wilderness.

The stories turned out to be true, and Yellowstone's thermal features are no less wonderful today than they were more than 120 years ago. In the meantime, the park has acquired new significance for other values: wildlife and wilderness. When America was young, the country was rich in wildlife and pristine landscapes. The national occupation was the subduing of wilderness, not its preservation. Forests were being cut down, marshes drained, animals slaughtered.

In 1872, millions of bison still darkened the Great Plains. Who would have guessed that, within 30 years, Yellowstone would become a refuge for the last surviving wild bison in America? Or that, just beyond the start of the 21st century, people from around the world would come here simply to see wild animals in a natural setting? Or that, thanks largely to recovery efforts carried out in Yellowstone, a few remnant herds of bison would survive?

Yellowstone today

In recent years, it has become evident that the park, for all its size, is not nearly big enough to provide safe haven for many of its creatures. As it

By Act of Congress on March 1, 1872, Yellowstone National Park was "dedicated and set apart as a public park or pleasuring ground for the benefit and enjoyment of the people."

BELOW: biking in the park.

happens, Yellowstone is only the heart of a much larger area called the Greater Yellowstone Ecosystem. It shows up clearly from satellite photos, an expanse of high, mostly forested land, punctuated by mountains and bounded on all sides by plains – a region defined by climate and geography, not by administrative decree.

The region is under siege. Chopped into a variety of jurisdictions, sliced by roads and other developments, its best winter range occupied by cattle ranches and towns, the integrity of the ecosystem (that is, its ability to sustain the species that live here) has been compromised.

Yellowstone by itself is not large enough for the bison, which, when snow lies deep in the high country, migrate out of the park to their ancient wintering grounds and into a conflict with ranchers.

The same geographic concerns hold true for any creatures that move with the seasons, or for those that range over large areas, like coyotes and grizzlies. They all need more space than any one administrative unit can provide. It is

toward a coordinated policy throughout the region that conservation efforts are now focused.

The big bang

The Yellowstone landscape was built by a series of volcanoes. Beginning around 50 million years ago, eruptions along the eastern edge of the plateau gave rise to the **Absaroka Range** and continued through cycles of activity for another 20 million years. The following period of relative quiet was marked by such events as the uplift of the **Teton Range**, which began some 10 million years ago and continues to this day. Volcanic activity picked up again some 2 or 3 million years ago.

One event surpasses all – the great Yellowstone volcano, which erupted roughly 600,000 years ago in a cataclysmic explosion. Its scale is difficult to imagine, but some idea can be gained by comparing it with the 1883 eruption of Krakatoa, the South Pacific volcano. According to accounts at the time, the Krakatoa explosion was heard more than 1,000 miles (1,610km) away; its dust rose so high and in such

BELOW: the Absaroka Range.

quantities that it colored the atmosphere around the world for three years, causing what viewers as far away as London called Krakatoa sunsets. It was an enormous event – yet the Yellowstone explosion was far greater, perhaps 100 times larger. Were it to happen again in the near future (geologists say it could happen any time), the eruption would be history's worst catastrophe by a considerable margin.

After the eruption, the center of Yellowstone was a smoking crater, or caldera, 28 by 47 miles (45 by 76km) wide and several thousand feet deep. Subsequent nonexplosive eruptions filled in parts of the caldera and obscured its once-distinct walls. Glaciers further altered its shape when ice covered the Rocky Mountains during the Pleistocene Era. But not all has disappeared. Yellowstone Lake occupies the bulk of the old caldera. The rim itself forms the south slope of Mount Washburn and is traversed by the road near Dunraven Pass to the village of Canyon.

As a footnote to the story, geologists tell us that the eruption was not a singular event. Two others of compa-rable violence occurred in the region 1.3 million and 2 million years ago. In fact, going back some 17 million years, a series of eruptions has made its way across southern Idaho. Moving west to east in a broad curve, the eruptions created the current Snake River Plain – in effect, a geologic burn path that ends, for now, in Yellowstone.

The eruptions have all been caused by the same "hotspot," an upwelling of molten material beneath the earth's crust. The hot spot has not moved; rather, the continent has drifted across it like a sheet of steel over a cutting torch. Currently, the torch burns beneath Yellowstone's many geysers and hot springs.

Exploring the park

There are more geysers and hot springs in Yellowstone than in the rest of the world combined. Many of the thermal features are centered along the **Firehole River**, which rises on the Continental Divide above **Old Faithful Ⓐ**. The river begins much like any mountain stream, its cold clear water tumbling over rhyolite cascades. But once

The Grand Prismatic Spring is located in the Midway Geyser Basin.

BELOW: Geyser Basin. **BELOW LEFT:** Old Faithful.

TIP

Yellowstone's peak period is late June through mid-August, when travel through the park can be slow. Campgrounds and lodgings should be reserved well in advance for this period, and even the first-come, first-served campgrounds are full by late morning.

it hits the geyser basins, it becomes a steaming beauty that never freezes, even on the coldest winter nights.

In its short course (it ends at Madison, just 16 miles/26km north of Old Faithful), the Firehole passes through three concentrations of geysers, called the Upper, Midway, and Lower geyser basins. All are worth seeing, but no one should visit Yellowstone without spending time in the **Upper Geyser Basin B**. Besides Old Faithful, there are several other major geysers that erupt frequently, including Castle, Grand, Beehive, Riverside, and Daisy. In the same area, geysers like Giant, Giantess, Fan, and Mortar erupt irregularly but with spectacular results. Dozens of smaller geysers spout and steam on all sides, in the company of hot pools both large and small. A network of boardwalks and trails makes for easy walking.

If you plan it right, by stopping at the **visitor center** for a list of predicted eruption times, you can catch most of the eruptions in a period of several hours. Early morning is a particularly rewarding time to be out, as is late on

a moonlit night. Don't leave the basin without a visit to the historic **Old Faithful Inn**, a magnificent log structure built during the winter of 1903–4 from local lodgepole pines on a massive base of rhyolite.

Noteworthy farther down the Firehole is **Grand Prismatic Spring C**, more than 300ft (90 meters) across and brilliantly colored. Its neighbor, **Excelsior Geyser**, last erupted in 1983. Apparently, the force of its 300ft (90-meter) eruptions was too much for its plumbing, and it became a simple hot pool – but a most impressive one. A boardwalk leading through dense clouds of steam allows you to get a closer look.

On the **Firehole Lake Loop Drive**, Great Fountain Geyser performs in a manner that certainly lives up to its name, while, at **Fountain Paint Pot D**, a number of large boiling mud cauldrons simmer like immense kettles of viscous sauce. Farther north lies **Norris Geyser Basin E**, the hottest ground in the park. Among its features is **Steamboat**, the largest active geyser in the world, capable of climbing 400ft (120 meters) with a thunderous roar. Seeing such an event, however, is a matter of pure luck; years may pass between eruptions. Quite a few smaller geysers, notably Echinus, Veteran, Little Whirligig, and Minute, erupt frequently or even continuously, making the basin a noisy, active place.

The park's third major thermal area, **Mammoth Hot Springs F**, overlooks old **Fort Yellowstone**, a collection of fine stone buildings built in the years when the United States Army was in charge of the park. Civilian management, lacking funds and poorly organized, had failed to protect the park adequately, so, in 1888, the Army was appointed to what surely stands as one of its most unusual missions. Arresting poachers, guiding tourists, patrolling roads and trails, the soldiers stayed until 1916, when the newly created National Park Service took over the management of Yellowstone.

BELOW: travertine terraces at Mammoth Hot Springs.

There are no geysers at Mammoth. Instead, hundreds of hot springs varying from trickles to small rivers build gleaming white terraces, tier upon tier, brightly painted by bacteria and minerals. The basic material being deposited is calcium carbonate, or travertine, derived from limestone; in the geyser basins, deposits are a different substance – silicon dioxide, or geyserite.

The springs are constantly changing, shifting their vents from one location to another. That change happens quickly is evidenced by stands of trees swallowed up by fresh travertine deposits while nearby, young vegetation thrives in places recently abandoned by scalding waters.

Lakes and rivers

Those interested in seeing thermal features under completely natural conditions should know that thousands of hot springs are scattered throughout backcountry areas of the park. **Shoshone Lake G** and **Heart Lake H** both have attractive thermal areas on their shores. The whole southwest corner of the park, called the **Bechler Region**, is known both for waterfalls and isolated hot springs.

Closer to the road, hikers willing to walk a short distance can find springs and fumaroles (steam vents) in the hills surrounding any geyser basin. Be careful when approaching backcountry thermal ground; it can give way and scald incautious feet, or worse. Also remember that these features are fragile; footprints can last for years. A good rule of thumb is to stay on ground that supports vegetation, a sign that underlying temperatures are not too hot, and stay on marked trails whenever possible.

Other centers of interest include **Yellowstone Lake I**, which is one of the largest high-altitude lakes in the world. Roughly 20 by 14 miles (32 by 23km), with 110 miles (177km) of shoreline, it is filled with clear, icy water. At its deepest point, 390ft (120 meters), temperatures are a constant 42°F (6°C). Yet not even the lake is free of thermal influence. Scattered across the bottom are numerous hot springs and several underwater geysers. These are generally invisible from the surface, but some are

Yellowstone employs more staff than any other park: 730 people work here for the National Park Service, and a further 3,200 for concessionaires.

BELOW: Yellowstone Lake. **BELOW LEFT:** checking out the geysers.

A grizzly bear takes a shower.

strong enough to keep patches of the lake free of ice in the winter.

Yellowstone Lake can be a dangerous place for the unprepared. When a summer storm moves through, the most inviting, mirror-smooth surface can fast become a seething mass of whitecaps. Nonetheless, boating is popular, the fishing is good, and stony beaches offer miles of pleasant walking. The area around **Bridge Bay ❿** is particularly inviting for shore activities. Also worth a visit is **Lake Yellowstone Hotel**, recently restored to its turn-of-the-20th-century beauty. Its lounging areas provide excellent views of the lake and the Absaroka Mountains.

On the north shore, the **Yellowstone River** leaves the lake and slides beneath **Fishing Bridge ❿** – once a famous place for catching native cutthroat trout, now (since fishing is prohibited here) a superb place for watching fish in their natural setting.

A short distance north lies the Grand Canyon of the Yellowstone River. Near **Canyon Village ❿**, the green water explodes into white froth as it tips over the edges of two great

falls into a 1,200ft (370-meter) -deep gorge between brilliant multicolored walls. The canyon is basically a river-eroded geyser basin. The hot acidic water of numerous hot springs in the canyon has altered the volcanic rocks here, coloring and weakening them, and making them vulnerable to rapid erosion. Since the glaciers melted at the end of the last Ice Age, a little more than 10,000 years ago, geologists estimate that the river has deepened the canyon by about 50ft (15 meters).

The northern part of Yellowstone national park stands distinct from the rest. Lower, warmer, and drier than the interior, characterized by sagebrush and open valleys, it is an important wintering ground for large animals – and for sightseers. The road from Gardiner, Montana, to the northeast entrance is the only park road kept plowed in winter.

It is a pity that most visitors never get more than a few hundred yards from their vehicles. So much of experiencing Yellowstone requires contact with the wild world, and this means going some distance – even if not very

BELOW: a bison holds up the traffic.

far – away from vehicles and pavement. Good day hikes include any of the thermal areas. Even the Upper Geyser Basin, subject to midday madness, can be quite deserted at 7am, and this is probably its most beautiful time.

In the north, strong hikers can visit the petrified trees of **Specimen Ridge** or hike up one of the other bare mountain slopes in the Lamar Valley. From Dunraven Pass, a moderate trail up **Mount Washburn** to a fire look-out offers a tremendous panoramic view. In the Grand Canyon area, easy shaded paths follow both rims. On the shore of Yellowstone Lake, a morning beach stroll reveals pelicans, gulls, jumping cutthroat trout, and evaporating mists. From here, you can head to the east entrance, where a steep but rewarding unmarked trail leads to the summit of **Avalanche Peak** .

Watching the wildlife

Yellowstone National Park has a wide range of habitat types that support one of the continent's largest and most varied populations of large mammals. This is a true wilderness, which means that here you meet nature on its terms, not yours. Park regulations exist not only for the protection of natural resources, but also for your safety.

Every year, a number of visitors are injured by wildlife because they approach too close. Wild animals, especially females with young, are unpredictable. But you should have no trepidation, providing you follow some simple guidelines. The park regulations actually prohibit you from approaching on foot within 100yds/meters of bears, or within 25yds/meters of other animals. Use binoculars or a telephoto lens so that you can keep a safe distance. By being sensitive to an animal's needs, you will observe more of its natural behavior. A rule of thumb is: if you cause an animal to move, you are too close.

Bighorn Canyon

East of Yellowstone lies the big, dry and dusty **Bighorn Basin**, where oil pumps oscillate above cattle ranches, and irrigated sugar-beet farms grow green on the edge of vast badlands. The basin reminds us that, despite forested, snow-topped mountains, west-

Following the fires of 1988, thousands of dead trees – known as "snags" – were left standing. These may fall with very little warning, so be alert, especially in campgrounds.

BELOW:
fishing in Soda Butte Creek.

The Great Fire

Over much of Yellowstone, dead trees remind visitors of the fires of 1988, a historic event that, in some areas, dramatically changed the appearance of the landscape. The biggest conflagration to affect the Northern Rockies in 50 years, the fires burned 793,880 acres (321,270 hectares), or 36 percent of the total area of the park. Over the course of the summer, about 25,000 firefighters worked in Yellowstone, while dozens of helicopters and more than 100 fire trucks were deployed to protect developed areas. The total cost ran over $120 million – the most expensive firefighting operation in history

On hot windy days during that unforgettable summer, big fires ran as far as 12½ miles (20km) in a day. Winds gusting over 60mph (100kph) threw embers 1–2 miles (2–3km) ahead of the fire front, triggering yet more blazes. Fires jumped highways, rivers and even the Grand Canyon of the Yellowstone River, not to mention fire lines cleared through the forest to the width of five bulldozer blades.

Yet not one major feature of the park was destroyed. The geysers, waterfalls, herds of wildlife – even the forest – are still here. Many places show no impact at all.

Side by side, burned areas and non-burned areas provide an intriguing study in the causes and effects of fire in wild places.

ern America is predominantly an arid region in which, as the old song puts it, "the skies are not cloudy all day." Places that have abundant water are exceptionally striking, attracting groups of wildlife and people.

One such place is **Bighorn Canyon National Recreation Area ❷**, which was once a deep cottonwood-lined gorge carved into native limestone by the muddy Bighorn River. In 1966, the **Yellowtail Dam** converted the river into a winding reservoir 71 miles (114km) long. The dam and most of the reservoir is in Montana, but road access to the spectacular central section is through the state of Wyoming.

Just outside the town of Lovell, the **Bighorn Canyon Visitor Center** offers exhibits and information, including a three-dimensional model of the region that provides a good orientation. From here, the paved access road heads north, following the canyon rim past numerous scenic points, ending at a campground and boat launch called Barry's Landing on Bighorn Lake.

Along the way, the road traverses a rugged bench separating the sharp

BELOW:
free -roaming mustangs in the Pryor Mountain Range.

escarpment of the **Pryor Mountains** from the vertical depths of the canyon. Several viewpoints provide glimpses into the tawny- and terracotta-colored gorge. Among plants and animals, only desert dwellers thrive at this end of the canyon. In places, vegetation thins out to almost nothing. Scraggly junipers and mountain mahogany pepper the hills, while cottonwood trees line the draws. Sharp-pointed yucca and prickly pear are like little interpretive signs saying "It's dry here." How true: **Horseshoe Bend**, near the head of the canyon, receives an average of only 6 ins (15cm) of rainfall a year.

The river's namesake, bighorn sheep, can sometimes be seen in cliffy areas near the road. The ewes and lambs remain at lower elevations throughout the year; the rams climb into the neighboring Pryor Mountains for the summer and are less often seen. Watch also for peregrine falcons. Young birds have been released here as part of a regional attempt to re-establish the formerly vanished population.

Wild horses

Partway to Barry's Landing, the road passes through the **Pryor Mountain Wild Horse Range**, a 46,800-acre (18,900-hectare) area administered by the BLM to protect wild horses. The herd numbers around 160 animals. Every few years, a roundup is held, and the surplus population is taken away for adoption. How long these horses have lived in this rugged strip of land is uncertain. Some people believe they have been here since the 1700s, when Spanish horses were first introduced to the area. Indeed, they do resemble the horses of the *conquistadores*. If this is true, these animals are a direct link to one of the most important events in the history of the American West. Their arrival gave birth to the great horse cultures of the buffalo plains. Where people had once moved and hunted only on foot, horses brought greater mobility, power, and an entirely new way of life. ❑

Packs Are Back

The howl of Yellowstone's prime predator has returned, but for how long? Wolves are growing in numbers, but their future is uncertain

After an absence of 70 years, the mournful howl of wolves is back in Yellowstone. It's a victory for environmentalists, who have long argued that the park's top hunter is vital to a healthy ecosytem. But, although their numbers are growing rapidly, the future of wolves in the park is not necessarily assured.

Once upon a time, wolves were tracked down and killed by the tens of thousands by bounty hunters equipped with traps, guns, and poison. The last wolves in Yellowstone were killed in 1924, when two pups were shot near Soda Butte. It took decades before the biologists who had encouraged this kind of thing realized the mistake they had made. It was not until 1973 that *Canis lupus*, the gray wolf, was granted protection under the Endangered Species Act.

But, by then, Yellowstone had no wolves to protect – until the US Fish and Wildlife Service hatched a strategy to reintroduce them to the park (and also to central Idaho). After a long and heated debate, in January 1995, 14 wolves captured in western Alberta, Canada, were brought to Yellowstone. They spent their first three months in "acclimation" enclosures at three locations around the Lamar Valley and then more released to roam free. Yellowstone again had three small wolf packs.

Later in the year, it had four, when two of the original wolves paired up and went it alone. All four packs bred successfully during 1995. The following year, despite cutbacks in federal budgets, a further 16 Canadian wolves, this time from British Columbia, were released in Yellowstone.

The original plan had been to import a similar number annually for four or five years. In July 1996, however, faced with continuing opposition from ranchers and some politicians, Secretary of the Interior Bruce Babbitt announced that there would be no more wolves from Canada in 1997. But the Yellowstone population needed no reinforcements. The original 30 immigrants and their offspring adapted so well to their new home that their numbers grew and more packs formed. By the end of 2008, there were 124 wolves in 12 packs in Yellowstone.

But not everyone is entirely happy about their return. Ranchers worried for their livestock forced the government to agree that wolves who preyed upon cattle or sheep could be shot on sight. They would no longer, therefore, be treated as an endangered species but as an "experimental, non-essential" population.

The Wyoming Farm Bureau initially resisted the restoration of wolves to Yellowstone. In December 1997, a Wyoming judge ruled that the government's reintroduction program was illegal and that the wolves in Yellowstone and Idaho should be removed. In effect, this would probably have meant that they would be killed. Fortunately, the Tenth US Circuit Court of Appeals reversed the judge's decision in 2000, for now allowing the wolves to remain.

Whatever the current legal status of Yellowstone's wolves, numerous opinion polls show that American citizens favor their reintroduction. After centuries of unjustly demonizing these fascinating creatures, we at last seem ready to embrace them as natural inhabitants of the Rockies, a valuable component of the food chain and an enduring symbol of the wilderness. ❑

RIGHT: the howl of the wolf is a familiar sound in Yellowstone National Park.

GRAND TETON

Towering above the valley of Jackson Hole,
the Teton peaks are high enough to support
a dozen mountain glaciers. Down in the valley
are lovely lakes and rugged canyons

If any range in America serves as a model for how mountains should look, it's the Tetons. Without warning, these superb peaks rise suddenly from a flat plain to a giddy 13,770ft (4,200 meters). From base to summit, the angle of slope is the same: unrelentingly steep. Anchoring the range, which extends across northwestern Wyoming just south of Yellowstone, is a trio of granite spires – Grand Teton, Middle Teton, and South Teton – flanked by peaks hardly less spectacular, including Mount Owen, Mount Teewinot, and Mount Moran. These are quintessential mountains, rising to sharp, almost delicate points while, at the same time, retaining a sense of massive strength. The rock is hard, clean, and the color of steel. Snowfields and glaciers perch on what appear, from a distance, to be near-vertical cliffs. Up close, they look even steeper.

Glacial lakes strung like watery gems adorn the base of the mountains. Each one – Jackson, Jenny, Leigh, Bradley, String, and Taggart – is filled with icy snowmelt and trout. Beyond the lakes spread the flat reaches of **Jackson Hole**, a valley rimmed by mountains, carpeted by sagebrush, and punctuated by neatly spaced groves of aspens, cottonwoods, and conifers. Pronghorn antelope, bison, and mule deer favor these flats, while large numbers of elk stage a spec-

tacular show during the fall rutting season. The **Snake River**, having grown to size in Yellowstone Park, meanders through Jackson Hole in no evident hurry to leave the Tetons. On either side of the river, willow flats and ponds provide habitat for a variety of wildlife, including beavers, moose, coyotes, trumpeter swans, osprey, bald eagles, sandhill cranes, and many others.

Quintessential mountains

Although the Teton Range consists of very old, very hard rock, these moun-

LEFT: Willow Flats area and Teton Range.
RIGHT: a male elk displays his antlers.

*Heading down to
Jackson Lake for a
spot of swimming.*

BELOW:
a weathered barn
on Antelope Flats at
the foot of the Teton
range.

tains are relatively young, among the youngest in the Rockies. About 9 or 10 million years ago, two blocks of the earth's crust began to shift along a fault line. The western block tilted upwards and became the mountains, while the eastern block swung downward, forming the valley. The movement has not stopped, and, so far, displacement has totaled some 30,000ft (9,000 meters). In the process, the valley block has sunk roughly four times as far as the mountain block has risen. Because rock has eroded from the mountain summits and debris has filled the valley, we see only part of the great escarpment, impressive as that may be.

On their western slope, facing Idaho, the Tetons present a different aspect. The high peaks rise with the same craggy fierceness, but the valleys approaching them are longer and the surrounding country is less steep. Because the range dips in that direction, the slopes are less abrupt and softened by foothills. Seen from this side, it is easier (but only a little) to understand why early French trappers named them *Les Trois Tétons* ("The Three Breasts").

In its 485 sq miles (1,256 sq km), **Grand Teton National Park** ❸ includes most of Jackson Hole, some of the hills to the east, Jackson Lake, and the Teton Range to its crest. Looking from the east, you might assume the crest (defined as the divider of watersheds) follows the line of high peaks, but, in fact, it runs behind them, and all the snow melting from "The Grand" flows eastward into Jackson Hole.

In 1929, when the park was established, it included only the peaks and a few of the morainal lakes at their base. Political wrangling and strong local opposition continued to prevent any enlargement until 1943, when President Franklin D. Roosevelt declared parts of Jackson Hole a national monument and made it possible for the nation to accept a gift of some 33,000 acres (13,350 hectares) of private land from the Rockefeller family. In 1950, Congress joined the monument to the park, essentially forming the single national park we see today. Like Yellowstone to the north, Grand Teton is one part of a larger wild region. National forests, wilderness areas, and wildlife refuges

crowd in on all sides. Notable among them is the **National Elk Refuge**, a 24,700-acre (10,000-hectare) reserve set aside to replace historic wintering grounds that once stretched more than 100 miles (160km) south, to Pinedale, Wyoming, and beyond. Much of that land is now used for cattle ranching or taken up by private homes. In winter, 7,000 to 10,000 elk migrate into the refuge from the surrounding high country. As the snows melt in spring, the herds return to their summer range.

Also worth knowing about is the **John D. Rockefeller Jr Memorial Parkway ℗**, a strip of land between Yellowstone and Grand Teton national parks. Although officially national forest land, this scenic 82-mile (132km) corridor is managed by the National Park Service. It has many of the same values as the adjacent national parks and deserves the same protection.

Touring Grand Teton, visitors have a choice of two main roads. US 89 goes from Jackson to Moran, where it meets US 287 from Dubois, before continuing north to Yellowstone. Most of this route follows the flat, sage-covered terraces above the Snake River, affording superb views of the Tetons. This road is usually chosen by people in a hurry, which is not to say that you can't drive it slowly. Numerous pullouts allow for stopping. Look for antelope and coyote along the way and, in the fall, elk. If you visit on an early fall morning or evening, be sure to walk away from the car for a little distance and listen for bull elk bugling challenges to each other. This eerie, passionate sound, coupled with the crisp, sharp bite of fall air, is one of the Rockies' most powerful and lasting experiences.

The option to Highway 89 is the Teton Park Road, which begins at **Moose Junction ℚ**, where there is a **visitor center** and park headquarters – a good orientation stop. From Moose, the road runs north along the base of the mountains, past **Jenny Lake ℝ** and part of Jackson Lake to a junction with US 89 and 287. Along the way, it

provides access to many of the park's alpine trailheads and the glacial lakes at the base of the mountains. It should be traversed slowly, with frequent stops. A speed of 35 mph (56 kph) seems none too slow, as each turn brings into sight another classic view.

For many, Jenny Lake is the heart of the park. It is certainly the main focus of attention and, crowds notwithstanding, one glimpse of the surrounding country explains why. There are two access points: the **South Jenny Lake Area** is a complex of parking lots and visitor services. A few miles north, the Jenny Lake Road leads to String Lake and various trailheads before skirting the shore of Jenny Lake itself. The section along the shore is one-way for vehicles, two-way for bicycles.

High-country hikes

Grand Teton is a gawking park, the sort of place where you'll want to sit and stare at the shining mountains rising so improbably from the plain. Gawking is a worthwhile activity here. It deserves serious effort. Yet, eventually, many visitors itch to hit the trails, to get *into*

TIP

The charge to Yellowstone National Park also admits you to Grand Teton at no extra cost. If you plan to visit both, be sure to keep your ticket.

BELOW: Jenny Lake.

that amazing scenery; and, once they get away from the roads, they discover the true essence of the park. Choices are many, from trails that follow the valley bottom past morainal lakes with mountains soaring from their opposite shores, to others that strike off among the high peaks. And you don't have to be a mountaineer to get up high. As grand a landscape as this is, it is remarkably accessible.

Most of the mountain hiking in the Tetons is in a number of valleys, called canyons because of their precipitous sides. The most popular of these is **Cascade Canyon** ⑤, reached by an inexpensive boat ride across Jenny Lake. In geologic terms, this is a hanging valley, meaning that it was not carved as deeply by glaciers as the main valley, and is now marked by a steep drop at its lower end. The trail climbs steeply up this drop for half a mile (1km) to **Hidden Falls**, a lovely bridal-veil cascade. A short distance on, the trail emerges from the forest at **Inspiration Point**, giving fine views across the lake to the Gros Ventre Range, which forms the eastern horizon. Most hikers turn

around at this point, yet those who go even a short distance farther up Cascade Canyon find their efforts well rewarded. From open areas, you can see the dividing line on the canyon wall between smooth glaciated rock and the more angular, broken surface that was never reached by the ice. About three hours of hiking will take you to the back side of the central Teton group, where the trail forks.

Heading south on the **Teton Crest Trail**, it is possible to circle the peaks by way of spectacular **Alaska Basin**, which is actually part of the **Jedediah Smith Wilderness Area**, and return to Jackson Hole by way of **Death Canyon**. The entire circuit is a two- or three-day trip, but either canyon is a good choice for day hiking; simply go up until you feel like turning around.

Easy lakeshore trails include the ever-popular circuit of Jenny Lake, which can be shortened by riding partway on the boat. Another trail parallels String Lake and wanders along the east shore of **Leigh Lake** ❶, with spectacular views of Mount Moran and Leigh Canyon. This is also a prime canoeing lake, easily reached by canoe from String Lake and requiring one short portage. No motors are permitted, and, with Mount Moran rising precipitously from the water's edge, this is a spectacular and peaceful place. Nowhere else in the park can one get so quickly and easily into a wilderness setting.

South of Jenny Lake, Bradley and Taggart lakes lie cupped in forested basins with high peaks exposed above them. Getting to either lake involves an interesting walk of several miles through an area burned by a forest fire in 1985.

The wild north

Other highlights in the center of the park include **Signal Mountain** ⓤ, which rises like a grandstand in the middle of Jackson Hole. A paved drive leads to the summit and the best panoramic view of the area. If you can take your eyes off the mountains, you may find your attention drawn to the

THE EPISCOPAL CHAPEL OF THE TRANSFIGURATION

glittering surface of Jackson Lake, a natural lake enlarged by a 39ft (12-meter)-high dam and filled with snowmelt from the mountains. Of course, the biggest supplier of water is the Snake River, pouring southward out of Yellowstone National Park. Although the road parallels the shoreline for some miles, a boat is clearly the best tool for exploring the lake and its surroundings – and is practically the only way of getting into the northern end of the Tetons, the wild, seldom visited chain of peaks rising on the west side of the lake.

This is country for serious hikers only. Getting through it requires following the routes of elk and moose up steep slopes of loose rock and through willow tangles along stream bottoms. Inevitably, game trails vanish into impenetrable thickets, leaving no option but a blind search for another path. For all this effort, the reward is a feeling of being truly remote, in country rarely traveled by any but the native wildlife.

Less heroic walkers interested in exploring the lakeshore area will find pleasant, well-maintained, and largely flat trails in the Colter Bay area. While there, be sure to check out the superb collection in the **Indian Arts Museum** in **Colter Bay Visitor Center**.

A less crowded section of the park lies south of Moose, along the partly paved **Moose-Wilson Road**. The drive is scenic in a low-key way – a good place to see wildlife and the starting point for hikers headed for Death Canyon, Phelps Lake, and Granite Canyon. On the opposite side of the valley, another road goes to the Gros Ventre Campground, the town of Kelly and Slide Lake.

Located just outside the park, **Slide Lake** was created by the Gros Ventre Slide in June, 1925. A cowboy named Huff was herding cattle down the valley when he saw the mountain sliding toward him, trees, rocks, and all. He lost several cattle but managed to get out alive. Behind him, the slide built a dam 225ft (70 meters) high, impounding the Gros Ventre River and creating a large new lake. It took two years for the lake to breach the dam; when it did, a wall of water swept down the canyon, taking the town of Kelly with it, killing six people and doing widespread damage downstream along the Snake River. ❑

Although Snake River has no rapids within the park, the current is always fast, especially during the spring runoff, and can be dangerous for inexperienced boaters.

BELOW:
view of the Tetons over Leigh Lake.

Floating the Snake

During the summer months, the Snake provides good floating through the park and into the Snake River Canyon about 20 miles (32km) south of Jackson. Because the park section lacks rapids, it can be run in rowboats, canoes, and inflatable rafts. Yet the river is deceptively tricky, its channel braided and, in many places, blocked by deadfall. On the other hand, there are few better ways to see the park than by floating silently past towering cottonwoods while the majestic Tetons drift in and out of view. There is always some wildlife to be seen, including moose, elk, and bison. Among the common birds are herons, swans, Canada geese, and mergansers; ospreys and bald eagles nest in treetops along the riverbanks and are often seen with fish in their talons.

GLACIER

This dramatic, mountainous park ranges over a broad and breathtakingly beautiful landscape of sharp-edged peaks, deep evergreen forests, and large, pristine lakes

High in the mountains of north-western Montana, the plunging waterfalls, radiant wildflower meadows, and swirling turquoise streams of **Glacier National Park** ❹ have left millions of visitors slack-jawed with admiration since the 1890s. The naturalist John Muir called it "the best care-killing country on the conti-nent." And Ernie Pyle, the war corre-spondent who saw a bit of the world in his time, said he "wouldn't trade one square mile of Glacier for all the other parks put together."

Celebrated not only for the beauty of its land but also for its abundant wildlife and excellent network of hik-ing trails, Glacier lies at the center of a sprawling territory of protected lands. Huge national forests extend to the west and south of the park, embracing wild and scenic river corridors and immense wilderness areas. To the north lies Cana-da's **Waterton Lakes National Park** ❺ and more forest preserves.

History of the rock

Scan the flanks of any mountain in Glacier and you will soon see that it is composed of layer upon layer of sedi-mentary rock. These layers are the pages of the park's early geologic history, and their story reaches back approximately 1.6 billion years to a time when this land was flat. Mud, sand, and silt, which washed out onto this plain for several hundred million years, accumulated to depths of 3–5 miles (5–8km) and turned to stone — much of it very colorful; vivid red and blue-green mudstone are the most notable deposits. The rock layers preserved ripple marks, mud cracks, and even impressions made by raindrops that fell more than a billion years ago. (You can pass your hand over some of these marks beside St Mary Lake.)

This thick sheet of strata remained buried until just 70 million years ago,

Main attractions
GLACIER PARK LODGE
GOING-TO-THE-SUN ROAD
ST MARY LAKE
HIDDEN LAKE OVERLOOK
JACKSON GLACIER
LAKE MCDONALD
MANY GLACIER HOTEL
WATERTON LAKES NATIONAL PARK
PRINCE OF WALES HOTEL

PRECEDING PAGES: Hidden Lake.
LEFT: Lake Josephine, Glacier National Park.
RIGHT: touring round the park.

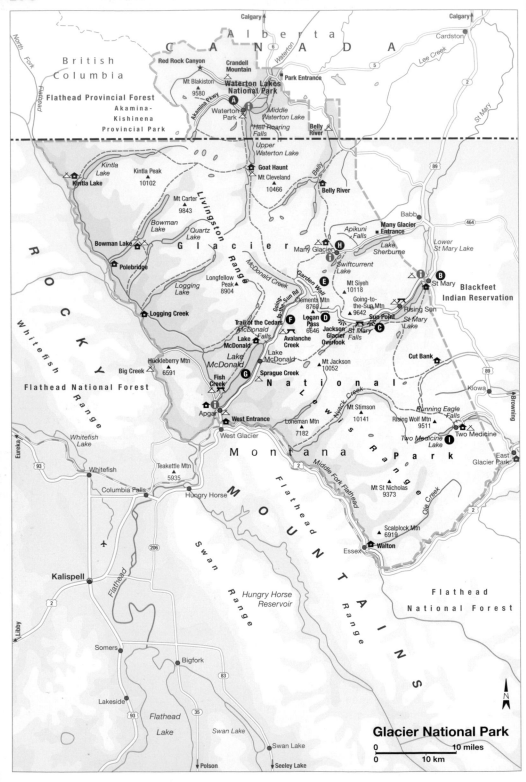

Glacier National Park

then rose through the surface as the earth's crustal plates collided along the western edge of North America. Like a fender bender in slow motion, the western portion of the continent crumpled, gradually elevating chains of mountains. Here, though, the strata did not simply rise in place. It broke away in pieces and slid more than 35 miles (56km) eastward before coming to rest in what are now Glacier and Waterton parks. The mountains that rise abruptly on the east side of the parks represent the leading edge of that colossal slab.

For tens of millions of years, erosion carried away the upper layers until all that remained were the oldest tiers of rock. Then came the great Ice Ages. At least three times in the past 200,000 years, enormous glaciers formed in the upper ramparts of the mountains and plowed their way down to the plains and river valleys. These great masses of ice sometimes exceeded depths of 2,000ft (600 meters), and their effects can be seen at every turn. The steep, semicircular walls and flat floors of the park's spacious valleys trace the outlines of the largest glaciers. Huge mounds of morainal debris confine the park's big lakes.

There are knife-edged ridges, horn-shaped peaks, cirques, and hanging valleys. All were created in one way or another by glaciers, but not by the 25 or so remaining dwarfs that nibble away at the peaks today. The last of the titanic glaciers that shaped the park melted away about 7,000 years ago. By that time, people had been living in and around Glacier for at least 2,500 years.

The first settlers

They probably came from the northeast corner of Asia, walking over the land bridge that formed in the Bering Strait during the Ice Ages. They fished the lakes and rivers along the eastern slopes of the mountains and hunted bison, elk, bighorn sheep, and deer. Then came the powerful Blackfeet confederation, expanding south from the North Saskatchewan River. Superb horsemen,

the Blackfeet became the most powerful military force on the northwestern plains. By the end of the 19th century, though, they were laid low by small-pox epidemics and illicit alcohol, by-products of the westward expansion of Anglo civilization. Eventually, they were confined to a reservation that included the eastern half of what is now Glacier. But, when miners found traces of minerals in the mountains, the tribe sold that portion to the US government.

Boomtowns sprouted in the St Mary and Many Glacier valleys, and, in Waterton, roughnecks drilled for oil. Meanwhile, conservationists in the US and Canada were trying to convince their respective governments to preserve the lands as national parks. The mining claims soon played out, and objections to creating the parks were dropped. Waterton was set aside in 1895 and Glacier was designated in 1910.

Sensing that the region could rival the Alps as a resort, owners of the Great Northern Railway built a series of Swiss-style lodges with a network of horse trails and roads. Many of the buildings have been torn down, but

The people who migrated from Asia to the Glacier area were probably the ancestors of the Kootenai, Flathead, and Kalispel tribes.

BELOW: the way to the woods.

The hoary marmot, a large relative of the squirrel, lives in the Glacier's subalpine highlands.

BELOW: the historic Many Glacier Hotel at the base of Mt Grinnell.

three of the grand old lodges still put up guests. The **Glacier Park Lodge**, in East Glacier, was built in 1912–13 on a frame of massive, unpeeled logs cut from cedar and Douglas fir trees 500 to 800 years old. The largest of these posts and beams stand in the hotel's three-story central lobby and support the roofs of the hotel's verandas. The **Many Glacier Hotel** was erected in 1914–15 on the shores of Swiftcurrent Lake, directly across the water from some of the park's most spectacular mountain scenery. Like the Glacier Park Lodge, it has a rustic central lobby built with large timbers and native stone. Across the border, in Waterton, stands the **Prince of Wales Hotel**.

Flora and fauna

All over this primitive country roam some of the most impressive and beautiful animals in North America. Glacier abounds with typical Rockies animals – elk, moose, black bear, and mountain lion. Grizzlies wander the high country basins, digging up ground squirrels and munching on roots, grasses, and berries. And a colony of gray wolves has

returned to the park after an absence of wolves for over 40 years.

You will find wetlands throughout Glacier, thick with marsh grasses, cattails, reeds, and a cornucopia of insects, fish, amphibians, waterfowl, and semi-aquatic mammals such as beaver, muskrat, and mink. The wetlands also attract osprey and some large mammals, including moose.

Arms of prairie grass stretch into many of the eastern valleys, and grasslands appear as isolated pockets in the forests of the west side. The meadows support elk and deer as well as many types of small rodents, which attract predators such as wolves, mountain lions, hawks, coyotes, and badgers.

Groves of aspen, cottonwood, and other deciduous trees shade the edges of meadows and give way at higher elevations to evergreens. The middle slopes of the park's mountains consist mainly of lodgepole, spruce, and fir. However, warm Pacific air masses stall out on Glacier's western slopes and drop enough moisture to support stands of cedar and hemlock.

Among the small valleys and basins that dot Glacier's high country, forests of Engelmann spruce, whitebark pine and subalpine fir grow alongside sprawling meadows carpeted with wildflowers, sedges, and grasses. Thickets of berry bushes crowd the avalanche slopes. Known as the subalpine zone, this niche is home to grizzly bears, bighorn sheep, wolverines, marmots, weasels, ground squirrels, and, far up in the highest reaches, mountain goats.

Finally, along the crest of the mountains, the trees give out almost entirely. Those that survive here hug the ground and seek cover from wind by twisting and bending around rocks. Few animals besides mountain goats and pikas (tiny hares) spend much time here.

Going to the Sun

Most visits to Glacier start with a trip over Logan Pass on **Going-to-the-Sun Road**. Aptly named, this amazing 50-mile (80km) strip of switchbacked

pavement climbs over the spine of the park's mountains and, hugging the cliffs below the Continental Divide, connects two of its most spectacular valleys. Many scenic turnouts and wayside exhibits allow you to stop and enjoy the route at your own pace. You can start the trip from either side of the park, but it is perhaps best to begin from the east-side village of **St Mary ❸** in the morning, with the sun at your back.

The road skirts the shore of **St Mary Lake**, a 10-mile (16km) body of crystal-clear water that occupies an enormous depression gouged out by one of the huge valley glaciers thousands of years ago. At the head end of the lake, **Sun Point ❸** offers a great view of the lower valley and the surrounding peaks.

Soon, you plunge into deep forest and begin the long climb to Logan Pass. A roadside exhibit identifies **Jackson Glacier**, one of the few active glaciers visible from the road. It has shrunk to 30 percent of its original size.

Logan Pass ❹ (6,646ft/2,026 meters) was formed by two glaciers gnawing away on either side of the ridge. Eventually, they chewed clear through the intervening rock and created this relatively low spot along the Continental Divide. It is a stunning place. Valley walls plunge from sight, and row upon row of summits reach off in all directions. Jagged peaks loom directly overhead. Waterfalls spill over cliffs just a hundred yards from the visitor center parking lot, and broad meadows of wildflowers spread at your feet.

Park naturalists offer two guided walks from Logan (between mid-June and Labor Day). One passes through the wildflower meadows above the visitor center to **Hidden Lake Overlook**, on the rim of a spectacular cirque of peaks towering over a beautiful lake. The other hike follows the Highline Trail across cliffs and avalanche slopes to grassy meadows overlooking **McDonald Valley**. Chances of seeing mountain goats are good on both hikes.

From Logan Pass, the road slants down the side of the **Garden Wall ❺**,

a knife-edged ridge that runs north through the heart of Glacier's most popular backcountry areas. A 1967 fire cleared much of the wall, opening the slope to various types of shrubs, including berry bushes, which attract bears in late summer and the fall.

On the valley floor, you follow McDonald Creek, a lovely watercourse that curls through the ancient cedar and hemlock, forest of the park's warmer, moister west side. At **Red Rock Point**, the creek zigzags between tilting blocks of vermilion mudstone and whirls into a deep turquoise pool. A bit farther along, **Trail of the Cedars ❻** loops through a cathedral stand of ancient cedar, hemlock and cottonwood trees. The mossy forest floor, the banks of ferns, the sunlight slanting through the mist – all lend an air of the primordial to the grove.

Before long, you find yourself along the shores of **Lake McDonald ❼**, the largest body of water in the park. Lined with cedar trees and warm enough to swim in during late summer, the lake has colorful pebble beaches that offer sweeping vistas of the mountains. Going-

Roughing It

Hiking and camping are popular activities in the West. Before starting out, check weather and road conditions and obtain the required permits. If possible, hike with a partner. Tell someone where you're going and when you'll return. Wear 30-plus SPF sunscreen, sunglasses, hat, sweater, jacket, hiking boots or waterproof hiking sandals, and thick, breathable socks to protect against blisters. Eat high-carbohydrate snacks and drink a gallon of water (4 liters) per person a day. Filter all water from streams: Giardia bacteria is common and causes cramps and diarrhea. Observe wilderness ethics and "pack it in, pack it out." Bury human waste in a cat hole 6ins (15cm) deep and at least 100ft (30 meters) from water, and pack out used toilet paper. Do not build campfires – fire rings scar the land for years. Instead, bring a backpack stove for hot drinks and meals. Keep a clean camp to prevent encounters with wildlife, such as bears. Hang food at least 100yds/meters from camp, and avoid fragranced products. In the desert, be careful where you place your hands: snakes and scorpions hide under boulders during the day. If you're bitten by a snake, don't panic. Most venomous snakebites are not fatal. Get to a doctor immediately. Shake out shoes and clothing before putting them on and avoid unrolling your sleeping bag before you're ready to use it.

to-the-Sun Road stops just beyond the southwest end of Lake McDonald, with a fine overview of the park.

Back on the park's east side, the **Many Glacier**  area lies in a striking, high-country basin carved out by glaciers, ringed by mountains, and dotted with chains of small lakes. It is the hub of a large trail network offering everything from an afternoon's stroll to week-long treks, and it is an excellent area for spotting bears, bighorn sheep, and mountain goats. The road ends at **Swift-current Lake**, where you'll find the Many Glacier Hotel. The railroad stalled the dismantling of a sawmill across the lake until 1925, when the director of the Park Service lost patience. In the most spectacular interpretive event in the park's history, he had crews place dynamite charges, then invited hotel guests out on the veranda to watch him blow up the offending structure.

Like Going-to-the-Sun Road, Many Glacier attracts throngs of visitors. You'll find a much quieter and only slightly less impressive glacial basin at **Two Medicine Lake** ❶, between East

BELOW: taking in the sights on one of the park's many peaks.

Glacier and St Mary. The area got its name from a tradition of two Blackfeet tribes, who held their annual sun dance in adjacent medicine lodges.

Across the border

Waterton Lakes National Park ❺ is just a seventh the size of Glacier, but well worth the visit into Canada. You may need a driver's license, a visa, or a passport to cross the border; check before you leave home. The park embraces three beautiful and very different valleys and, as in Glacier National Park, its mountains rise abruptly from the Great Plains. Waterton enjoys a rich and varied climate in which moist Pacific air battles with frigid Arctic weather. This turbulent mix kicks up high winds, drops plenty of rain and snow, and accounts, in part, for the tremendous variety of plants that thrive here – 1,300 species all told.

Squeezed between two rows of mountains, **Upper Waterton Lake** occupies a long, narrow trough at the head end of the park's main valley. The **Prince of Wales Hotel** commands a fabulous view of the surrounding peaks, the town of Waterton, and the narrow waters of the lake, which extends south across the international border into Glacier. A bit more formal and graceful than its American counterparts across the lake, the seven-story hotel stands on a spit of land extending between **Upper** and **Middle Waterton** lakes. Never visited by its namesake, the Prince of Wales offers a wonderful, and wind-free, view of Waterton's mountains.

Excursion boats cruise across Upper Waterton Lake to **Goat Haunt**, in Glacier. There, naturalists lead hikes into the **Kootenai Lakes**, a common hangout for moose. Red Rock Parkway follows Blakiston Creek up the floor of another of the park's valleys, ending at a gorge cut through red mudstone by turquoise water. Akamina Parkway follows a chasm into Waterton's third valley, climbs through the park's highest forests and dead-ends at **Cameron Lake**, a small lake ringed with cliffs. ❏

Disappearing Glaciers

They may still sparkle and glisten in the highest ranges, but many of the national parks' icecaps are receding at an alarming rate

U ntil 10,000 years ago, the end of the last Ice Age, much of North America was covered in ice sheets several miles thick. As the climate warmed the ice sheets melted. Today, all that remains are ice fields filled with glistening glaciers atop the highest mountain ranges in northern latitudes.

Glaciers form when more snow falls in winter than evaporates in summer and the snow compacts into deep, heavy ice. Gravity slowly sets the glacier in motion down the mountain, carrying abrasive boulders and debris with it in a sort of conveyor-belt motion.

The aftermath of glaciation is distinctive. Glaciers gouge U-shaped valleys, with broad bottoms and narrow high sides of polished, striated rock; knife-edged aretes, where two glaciers meet; hanging valleys and, often, waterfalls, where one glacial valley overtakes a side valley; bowl like cirques in mountain sides that fill with sparkling lakes, or tarns; and huge stranded boulders known as glacial erratics, that are often as large as an average house.

As the glacier slows it drops its load of till, or moraine. Lateral moraines line the lower valley sides, while a terminal moraine forms below the glacier. The snout of a glacier ebbs and flows with the seasons, usually leaving behind a large tarn at the terminus, filled with turquoise glacial meltwater refracting light through fine glacial rock powder. It's a beautiful sight.

North America's glaciers began forming about 7 million years ago and have advanced and receded repeatedly. The Little Ice Age of AD 1300–1850, when the global climate cooled, led to a glacial advance. But since 1850, the start of the Industrial Revolution, which introduced man-made pollutants into the atmosphere, and a global warming trend, glaciers have been in retreat worldwide.

The effects of former glaciation are evident in many western parks. They can be seen as far south as Utah's Cedar Breaks National Monument and the Kolob Canyons district of Zion National Park, and most famously, in the polished granite landmarks and tumbling waterfalls of Half Dome and El Capitan in California's renowned Yosemite National Park.

Living glaciers are most visible in Alaskan parks, from Glacier Bay to Kenai Fjords. While most are in retreat, some on Glacier Bay's west side are advancing, fed by copious snowfall in the Fairweather Mountains.

In the Lower 48, many people are surprised to learn that the largest number of glaciers is not in Montana's Glacier National Park but in Washington North Cascades National Park, which has a record 312 glaciers.

As elsewhere, North Cascades glaciers are in significant retreat, but nowhere is the situation more critical than at Glacier National Park. Glacier had 37 ice fields with 150 glaciers when the park was designated in 1910; since then, however, record heat and summertime drought have led to a shocking decline.

In April 2010, the park announced that the park has just 25 remaining glaciers – the same number as can be found on a single Washington peak: Mount Rainier. At the current rate of loss, geologists expect that all the park's glaciers will have disappeared by 2020. ❑

RIGHT: the icy wilderness of Glacier Bay National Park and Preserve, Alaska.

THE DAKOTAS

The Black Hills and Badlands of Dakota are not
as barren and monotonous as they first appear.
The land of the prairie dog is also a land
of bizarre beauty

T he Great Plains are a land of liberating and, some would say, ter-
rifying space. Endless miles of
grasslands sprawl beneath a pale-blue
dome. The earth stretches in every
direction as flat and featureless as a tide
of forgetting. "Outsiders have considered this prairie place barren, desolate,
monotonous, a land of more nothing
than almost any other place you might
name," writes William Least Heat-
Moon. For those who know them well,
however, these plains can form a land
of subtle enchantment. Take a good
look and you'll find that sky and grass
can produce fascinating variations and
that the prairie – seemingly endless – is
punctuated with landforms of extraordinary ruggedness and beauty.

The high plains of North and South
Dakota are such a place. Here, in the
semi-arid country west of the Missouri
River, the rolling prairie abruptly gives
way to the Badlands and the Black
Hills. Three national parks – Wind
Cave, Badlands, and Theodore Roosevelt – highlight the natural and cultural features of these extraordinary
places. Wind Cave and Badlands are
separated by about 100 miles (160km)
and are within easy driving distance of
Rapid City, South Dakota, on the eastern edge of the Black Hills. Theodore
Roosevelt National Park is near Dick-

inson, North Dakota, and is a full day's
drive from Rapid City.

Cave of the Wind

Two worlds are preserved at **Wind
Cave National Park** ❻. On the surface, this 28,295-acre (11,459-hectare)
park is a sanctuary of rolling grasslands and ponderosa forest snuggled
against the foot of South Dakota's
fabled Black Hills. Below ground,
it's a hidden world of dark and silent
passages honeycombed through an
ancient bed of limestone.

Main attractions
GARDEN OF EDEN TOUR, WIND CAVE NATIONAL PARK
RANKIN RIDGE TRAIL, WIND CAVE NATIONAL PARK
LANTERN TOUR, JEWEL CAVE NATIONAL MONUMENT
EVENING ILLUMINATIONS, MOUNT RUSHMORE NATIONAL MEMORIAL
BIGFOOT PASS, NORTH UNIT, BADLANDS NATIONAL PARK
CEDAR PASS TRAILS, NORTH UNIT, BADLANDS NATIONAL PARK
STRONGHOLD TABLE, SOUTH UNIT, BADLANDS NATIONAL PARK
WIND CANYON TRAIL, THEODORE ROOSEVELT NATIONAL PARK
NORTH UNIT SCENIC DRIVE, THEODORE ROOSEVELT NATIONAL PARK

PRECEDING PAGES: fog over the Badlands.
LEFT: camping in the wilderness.
RIGHT: a ranger leads a cave tour.

Alvin McDonald mapped the first ten miles of Wind Cave by candlelight.

BELOW: exploring underground at Wind Cave.

People who think of caves as cold, damp holes in the ground suitable only for bats and hibernating bears will find Wind Cave surprisingly hospitable. It's a relatively dry cave, the temperature hovers around 53°F (12°C) year-round, and, with the exception of a few bats, mice, and insects, it is virtually lifeless. With more than 132 miles (213km) of explored passages, it's the third-longest cave in the United States and the fourth-longest cave in the world.

Formation of this subterranean labyrinth began about 50 million years ago. Water, made acidic by carbon dioxide in the air and soil, began trickling through the limestone, widening the joints and cracks that were created during the uplift of the Black Hills. When the water table dropped, it left behind a tortuous network of caverns and crawlways that are still largely unexplored.

The cave's most conspicuous feature is the wind that streams in and out of its narrow mouth, sometimes as fast as 70 mph (113 kph), equalizing air pressure on either side of the surface. The Lakota Indians were the first to take notice of the mysterious winds. According to Lakota mythology, the Cave of the Winds is a sacred place where bison, pronghorn, and other creatures emerged from the underworld.

Probably the first white men to discover the cave were the Bingham brothers, Jesse and Tom, who stumbled across the entrance in 1881. Attracted by a whistling noise, one of them peered into the narrow mouth and was amazed when the wind blew his hat off. He was even more amazed when, on a return trip with friends, he held his hat over the hole and it was sucked into the cave.

Systematic exploration didn't start until nine years later, when 17-year-old Alvin McDonald began a short but remarkable career as the self-appointed "Permanent Guide of Wind Cave." Alvin's father brought the family to the cave in 1890, and, together with John Stabler, they created the Wonderful Wind Cave Improvement Company, hoping to attract tourists from nearby Hot Springs. Although several family members were involved in the project, Alvin was the most committed,

recording his adventures in a diary that is still on display at the **visitor center**. With nothing but a candle, a hammer, and a ball of twine to mark his path, he logged more than 1,000 hours of exploration. Visitors can still see the letters Z.U.Q. that he burned into the cave walls – although nobody knows exactly what they mean.

What Alvin McDonald discovered was a cave of remarkable beauty and complexity. Among his most significant finds was the abundance of boxwork, a mineral formation made of crisscrossing calcite fins found almost exclusively in Wind Cave. In some places, the fins are no more than an inch or so, giving the appearance of an intricate crystal web embedded in a limestone matrix. Elsewhere, the fins protrude as much as 10 or 12 inches (25 or 30cm), creating spectacular crystal "crates." Alvin also came across an abundance of other delicate formations such as popcorn, frostwork, and branching, antler-like helictites, all created by the gradual accretion of calcite crystals in seeping water. He found gypsum needles as fine as hair

and patches of hard, diamond-shaped crystals known as dogtooth spar.

Unfortunately, Alvin didn't live to see Wind Cave get the attention it deserved. He died of typhoid fever when only 20 years old. Ten years after his death, following several long and bitter ownership disputes, the federal government took possession of the cave. It was designated a national park in 1903.

Going underground

All cave tours start at the visitor center, where you'll find books, maps, a cafeteria (summer only), and a schedule of nature walks, campfire talks, and other special events. The 1-hour **Garden of Eden Tour** is offered year-round and introduces visitors to the cave's human and natural history on a short paved trail accessed via elevator. Longer tours are offered in summer; they last from 1 to 2 hours and require varying levels of fitness. The **Candlelight Tour** (reservations strongly recommended due to popularity and limited group size) re-creates cave exploration back in Alvin's day when visitors saw

BELOW: boxwork calcite formation inside Wind Cave.

The Maah Daah Hey Trail

The 96-mile (153km) Maah Daah Hey Trail begins 20 miles (32km) south of Watford and traverses the North and South units of Theodore Roosevelt National Park, ending at Sully Creek State Park, south of Medora. The trail passes through magnificent badlands surrounded by expanses of gently rolling prairie and offers the chance for an intimate, multiday experience within the Badlands for backcountry bikers, hikers, and horseback riders. Look out for mule deer, coyotes, golden eagles, prairie falcons, and, if you're lucky, reintroduced bighorn sheep and elk. Within Theodore Roosevelt National Park, look out for bison and feral horses. The trail's name is a reference to the area's original Mandan inhabitants, who called the region *Maah Daah Hey*, meaning "an area that has been or will be around for a long time."

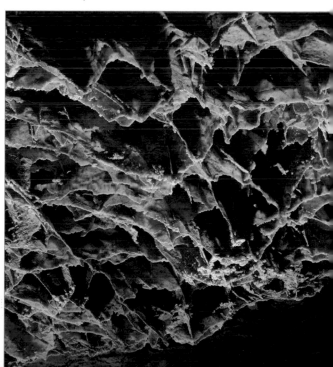

Prairie flowers in Custer State Park.

"Wonderful Wind Cave" by the dim light of makeshift lanterns. This strenuous tour lasts 2 hours and includes a (1.6km) mile of rough terrain.

For a more intimate look at the cave, the park also offers the longer **Wild Cave Tour** (reservations required) in which small groups are suited up in caving gear and taken off-trail. The tour lasts 4 hours and is very strenuous. There's lots of crawling and climbing, so expect to get good and dirty.

But the cave is only half the story here. The park is also a wildlife sanctuary, an ecological crossroads where the Great Plains meet the mountains. The park encompasses a transitional zone between high-country ponderosa forest and the surrounding sea of mixed-grass prairie. Here, where the solitary Black Hills rise from the plains, eastern and western species overlap. Ponderosa pine, reaching its eastern boundary, shares the park with American elm, at its westernmost range. The western wood pewee and pinyon jay share the skies with the eastern bluebird and phoebe.

Starting at the park's northern boundary, Highway 87 winds through a forest of ramrod-straight ponderosa pines that finger into swells of grassland fringed here and there by deciduous trees that grow along creeks and ravines. Bison, pronghorn, and mule deer often graze near the road, and there are several roadside prairie-dog towns where you can watch these highly social rodents pop in and out of their complex network of tunnels. You may even see a coyote scouting nearby for an early-morning or evening meal. Elk and mule deer find daytime cover in the woods but venture into the grasslands to graze in the evening. If you visit in early fall, listen for the haunting bugle of bull elk establishing territory during the yearly rut.

About 2 miles (3km) from the park boundary, you'll find sweeping vistas at **Rankin Ridge Trail**, a steep mile-long (1.6km) loop along the edge of a forested ridge. At the top, a fire tower affords views of the Black Hills scrawled against the horizon and, to the south, **Buffalo Gap**, a natural corridor into the high country once used by bison, Indian hunters, and mountain men like Jedediah Smith.

For a closer look at the backcountry, you can pick up the **Centennial Trail** about 4 miles (6km) farther south on Highway 87. The trail follows **Beaver Creek** into a lovely shaded canyon for about 2 miles (3km) and then heads north into wooded hills and rolling meadows. You can loop back to the parking area on **Lookout Point Trail** for a 3-mile (4.8km) round-trip or hook up with the Highland Creek or Sanctuary trails for longer and more strenuous backpacking trips.

For hikers competent with a compass and topographical map, cross-country travel is permitted throughout the park. Remember to steer clear of prairie-dog towns, and never try to feed the animals. Give bison a wide berth, too. They look placid and slow-moving but have been known to charge hikers who get too close.

Back in the car, Highway 87 winds through the high country toward

Highway 385. The first right off 385 takes you past **Elk Mountain Campground**, where a short self-guiding trail loops through the surrounding woods and prairie. Back on the highway, Highway 385 dips into **Bison Flats**, where the great beasts can often be seen grazing, wallowing in the dust or nourishing themselves at a nearby mineral lick.

True eekers of solitude may prefer the two gravel roads (NPS 5 and 6) that cross the park's less-traveled eastern flank. Especially lovely is **Boland Ridge Trail**, off NPS 6, which strikes out on a 3-mile (5km) journey up and over the sage-colored ridge into a prairie world where lone bison munch on grassy hillsides, golden eagles glide on columns of air, and the wind whispers incessantly through a scattering of hardy pines.

Wind Cave is a handy jumping-off point for sites throughout the Black Hills. **Custer State Park** adjoins the park's northern boundary and has hiking trails, lakes, and a route into some of the most stunning sections of the Black Hills.

Jewels and presidents

If you're in the mood for more underground adventures, **Jewel Cave National Monument ❼** – named after the layer of calcite crystals that adorn its walls – is about 35 miles (56km) west of Wind Cave. Jewel Cave is slightly smaller than its more famous neighbor and does not have the same richness of wildlife above ground, but its beautiful subterranean formations fully justify its fanciful name. Various tours are offered, including, in summer, the Lantern Tour and the Spelunking Tour, a strenuous trek involving hiking, climbing, and crawling.

The dramatic Iron Mountain Road leads from Wind Cave through tunnels and over picturesque bridges to **Mount Rushmore National Memorial ❽**, where sculptor Gutzon Borglum blasted his colossal presidential portraits out of the granite mountainside. Work on the project began in 1927 and was still unfinished when Borglum died in 1941. His studio can be visited, and the nightly lighting ceremony that concludes a ranger talk and film (Memorial Day through Labor Day) is dramatic.

Devils Tower was the USA's first national monument to be declared by Theodore Roosevelt in 1906.

BELOW:
Mount Rushmore's heads of Presidents Washington, Jefferson, Roosevelt and Lincoln.

Black-Tailed Prairie Dogs

There are five species of prairie dogs, but only the black-tailed prairie dog is protected within Theodore Roosevelt National Park, its native habitat. Prairie dogs are not dogs at all; they are rodents in the squirrel family. Early French explorers called them "*petit chiens*" (little dogs) because of their "bark." The distinctive yip is used by male lookouts, perched very charmingly on their hindlegs, and serves as a warning to family members in the 50 or so associated burrows known as "towns." Prairie dogs have a lifespan of just 5–7 years. Like bison and their sworn enemy, black-footed ferrets, they were extirpated from their range by overzealous ranchers and are now being reintroduced. Look for prairie dogs in three "towns" along roadways and other areas in the park's South Unit.

Devils Tower National Monument ❾, an 865ft (264-meter) column of volcanic rock near Sundance, Wyoming, is a 3-hour drive from Wind Cave. The nearly vertical monolith, a popular rock-climbing site, is set in rolling hills covered with pine forests, deciduous woodlands, and prairie grasslands.

The bad lands to cross

About 60 air miles (100km) east of Wind Cave, the prairie takes on a completely different aspect. This is the Badlands, an immensely rugged country of furrowed cliffs, gnarled spires, and deep, branching ravines that were torn from the plains of South Dakota by a half-million years of soil erosion.

In the early 19th century, French fur traders called the area *les mauvaises terres à traverser* – "the bad lands to cross" – because of the maze of twisting canyons that blocked their passage to the White River basin. John Evans, a government geologist dispatched to Dakota Territory in 1849, likened the area to a "magnificent city of the dead, where the labor and genius of forgotten nations had left… a multitude of

monuments of art and skill." He marveled at the well-defined layers of rock that striped the canyon walls and, like many explorers before him, was fascinated by the "ponderous character" and "strange physiognomy" of the ancient creatures whose bones lay exposed on the eroded earth.

First-time visitors to **Badlands National Park** ❿ may very well agree with Evans's initial impression: this is indeed a city of the dead, as stark and barren as any ancient ruin. The effect is especially chilling in the light of the midday sun, when short shadows exaggerate the landscape's fractured lines and give the Badlands a threatening, almost sinister, look. Ridges twist like crooked spines; grass-capped buttes or "tables" rise to dizzying heights; turkey vultures hang on the wind; and, here and there, the bones of long-dead creatures poke through crumbling earth.

But, in the evenings, when the light softens, the air of desolation begins to lift, and the Badlands become a different place, warmer, more inviting. As the sun goes down, delicate shadows creep along broken ridges, softening

BELOW: Devil's Tower.
BELOW RIGHT: coyote on the prowl for his next meal.

folds and crevices that look severe in full daylight. The long rays bring out the deep bruise-colors that stripe the cliffs, and, where the sun's full glare reflects only gray and white, the more forgiving light of evening shows shades of red, umber, and burning violet.

The evening also brings a rush of life. Eagles circle overhead scanning for a final meal. Chipmunks dash between the shadows. Bighorn sheep clamber to higher ground. Out on the prairie, owls, bobcats, coyotes, and prairie rattlers begin their nocturnal hunt.

Scenic drive

Entering the North Unit of the park from the northeast, Highway 240 passes the **Big Badlands Overlook**, your first grand view of the country's ravaged landscape, and then descends through the Badlands Wall, a 100-mile (160km) -long barrier between the upper prairie and the jumbled landscape below.

The road bottoms out near the recently renovated **Ben Reifel Visitor Center**, where exhibits, maps, and books – as well as rangers – will help acquaint you with the park; be sure to inquire about ranger-guided nature walks and other special programs held at the nearby Cedar Pass Campground and elsewhere. The road continues along the base of the Badlands Wall for a short stretch and then makes a winding ascent toward **Big Foot Pass Overlook**.

Here, the cliffs face northwest over **Bigfoot Pass** with nothing but broken land between you and the horizon. Dusk is particularly dramatic. The sun sets as it must have on the first day of creation, over an unfinished world still imperfectly shaped. The pass is named after Chief Bigfoot, who led a band of Minniconjou Sioux through the Badlands in the winter of 1890 in order to escape United States troops. The Indians were captured and brought to a place called **Wounded Knee** about 50 miles (80km) south, where the infamous massacre of more than 200 of Bigfoot's people took place.

From Bigfoot Pass, the road climbs to the upper prairie over arid grasslands where homesteaders worked "starvation claims" during the land boom after

Wild horses roam in the Badlands.

BELOW:
Yellow Mounds
overlook.

1910. This final stretch of paved road is spectacular, with wide-open views of jagged peaks, sheer-sided buttes, and chromatic, low-lying humps laid bare by more than a half-million years of wind and water. The Yellow Mounds, Pinnacles, and Hay Butte overlooks are especially stunning.

If time and weather permit, you can continue on an unpaved road along the edge of the **Sage Creek Wilderness Area**. The road passes a prairie-dog town, and bison, pronghorn, and mule deer can often be seen nearby. There are no marked trails, but hikers can strike out cross-country from the Sage Creek Campground. Motorists should follow the Sage Creek Rim Road to Highway 44 and then turn left toward the Ben Reifel Visitor Center in a 90-mile (145km) loop.

For a closer look at the backcountry, try the maintained trails in the developed Cedar Pass area near the visitor center. The most challenging is the 1½-mile (2.4km) **Notch Trail**, which leads to a chink in the cliffs overlooking the Badlands' southern border. To get there, you have to walk a half-mile

(1km) trail across rugged terrain. At the end, a 40ft (12-meter) ladder leads up a canyon face.

The trail continues along the edge of a cliff toward the viewing area. From here, the Badlands seem to melt into the White River basin, where rain and countless rills and rivulets wash them away. The jagged peaks gradually grow smaller and less defined, until there is nothing left but bluffs and hollows stretching to the horizon like the folds of a rumpled blanket.

Two other short, easy trails start at this parking area. The **Door Trail** makes a three-quarter-mile (1.2km) round-trip into a moonscape of branching canyons and gullies. The quarter-mile (400-meter) **Window Trail** leads to a fenced viewing area overlooking a dramatic mudstone canyon. Farther down the road, the steep, half-mile (0.8km) **Cliff Shelf Nature Trail** circles a depression created by a massive slump of the cliff above. The hollow collects water, creating an oasis of plant and animal life in the stark Badlands Wall. A short drive brings you to the **Fossil Exhibit Trail**, which makes a flat quarter-mile (400-meter) loop. Replicas of fossils are displayed under plastic domes; most are ancient mammals dating from 23 to 35 million years ago.

For longer hikes, try the **Castle Trail**; the trailhead is directly across the road. It's a fairly easy 10-mile (16km), round-trip walk through prairie and mudflats, past eroding mudstone castles and flat-topped rain pillars. You can lengthen the hike by sidetracking onto the 4-mile (6.4km) **Medicine Root Trail** or the quarter-mile (400-meter) extremely steep **Saddle Pass Trail**.

Mountains of sheep

The balance of beauty and desolation is nowhere more precarious or powerful than at **Sheep Mountain Table**, a high plateau on Pine Ridge Indian Reservation overlooking a labyrinth of barren canyons. A rutted dirt road (which can be partially driven before

BELOW: viewing area at the Window Trail.

requiring you to hike or bike) veers off County Road 589 (NPS 27) and crosses white alkali flats to the hill. Squat, mushroom-shaped formations stand like guardians on either side of the road as you pass.

At the top, the table is broad and flat and surprisingly lush. A thick growth of prairie grass, prickly-pear cactus, and yucca blankets the ground, and scattered groves of juniper stand near the edge. This is one of the least-traveled parts of the Badlands, and the best place to go if you're looking for solitude. Head to the very end of the table, where unmarked trails lead to stark panoramas of interlocking cliffs and canyons. It wasn't always so quiet out here. During World War II, ranchers were forced to relocate when the military used the area as a gunnery range. Apparently, a few bombs went astray. According to a roadside display, one old settler was interrupted during breakfast when "an errant shell crashed through her roof, her bed, and the bedroom floor."

To the southwest of Sheep Mountain Table is a vast undeveloped area of prairie and tablelands known as the **South or Stronghold Unit**, within Pine Ridge Indian Reservation. The main attraction here is Stronghold Table, a slender finger of high ground where Lakota Ghost Dancers gathered in December 1890. Hungry, desperate, impoverished by war and reservation life, they came to the Stronghold to dance, "die", and dream of a new world washed clean of white men.

The only way to the Stronghold is a gravel road about 7 miles (11km) off County Road 589, and then you must hike or drive another 2 miles (3km) or so until you reach the "narrows," the eroding land-bridge that connects the table with the "mainland." It doesn't appear on the park map. You will need to get directions and ask about road conditions at the **White River Visitor Center**, open only in summer.

The plateau itself is flat and featureless. There are no signs or monuments to mark the spot, just a lonely swath of prairie grass and cactus. Sitting on the cliffs is like dangling your feet over the edge of the world, with only an occasional meadowlark and a few

The evolution of animals such as the horse, sheep, pig, and rhinoceros can be seen in the Badlands fossil beds, the world's richest from the Oligocene period (23–35 million years ago).

BELOW LEFT:
Sheep Mountain Table.
BELOW:
Little Missouri River in Theodore Roosevelt National Park.

A white-tailed deer.

BELOW: a wild
stallion leads his
herd in Theodore
Roosevelt National
Park.

semi-wild horses to keep you company. At times, the only thing that stirs is the wind, coursing like a restless spirit through the canyons and ravines. Its ceaseless whispering is a slender defense against the powers of silence, but it does remind you that, despite the stark surroundings, this is not "a city of the dead."

Roosevelt and the Badlands

In 1883, a young New Yorker headed west to hunt bison in North Dakota. During his two-week stay, the energetic young man became absorbed with the cattle industry and, being well off financially, invested some of his money in the Maltese Cross Ranch.

He was future US president Theodore Roosevelt (TR), and he returned the following year to set up his own operation, the Elkhorn Ranch, on the banks of the Little Missouri River. Alas, it was a short-lived affair. The range was exhausted by overgrazing and couldn't sustain the herds through the severe winter of 1886–7.

Roosevelt's herd was virtually wiped out, like those of most other ranch-ers on the northern plains, and the Elkhorn went under. Nevertheless, the brief time spent "among the barren, fantastic and grimly picturesque deserts of the so-called Bad Lands" left a deep impression on TR and how he conceived of conservation – the need to balance use and protection of natural resources. Today, much of the land that Roosevelt knew and loved is protected in the three units of **Theodore Roosevelt National Park** ⓫: the 72-sq-mile (186-sq-km) South Unit immediately off Interstate 94 at Medora, the 38-sq-mile (98-sq-km) North Unit, south of Watford City on Highway 85, and the undeveloped site of the erstwhile Elkhorn Ranch.

Union Army General Alfred Sully, who conducted campaigns against the Plains Indians, described the North Dakota Badlands in 1864 as "Hell with the fires out." It is a harsh and inhospitable land, broken into countless ridges, coulees, and fluted bluffs. Water has shaped the landscape. Pelting summer rains collect in rivulets and ravines, cutting through layers of sediment laid down by ancient seas, swamps, and volcanoes. The runoff carries debris to the **Little Missouri River**, which winds lazily along a wide floodplain.

But there's a softer side, too. Laid bare by erosion, the slump-shouldered hills are brightened by patches of brick-red "scoria" *(see page 296)*, bluish bentonite clay, and thin veins of lignite coal. On cooler, moister, north-facing slopes, dense stands of juniper and ash provide cover from the sun, as do groves of cottonwood trees along the Little Missouri. Elsewhere, the park is home to rolling mixed-grass prairie, rabbitbrush, prickly-pear cactus, spiky yucca, and thick patches of aromatic sage.

The park sustains bison, wild horses, prairie dogs, mule deer, white-tailed deer, elk, pronghorn, and a variety of predators – coyotes, bobcats, badgers, and rattlesnakes. Songs of meadowlarks, sparrows, and towhees carry through

woodlands and prairies. Golden eagles ride air currents overhead; bald eagles migrate through the fall.

The South Unit

A leisurely driving tour of either unit takes about a half-day and features breathtaking views of multihued gullies, coulees, and canyons, and, more often than not, a close-up look at wandering bison, pronghorn, and prairie dogs. Seven miles (11km) east of Medora, exit 32 off Interstate 94, you'll find **Painted Canyon Visitor Center** (Apr–Nov only), which has views, a nature trail, grazing bison, exhibits, bookstore, and a ranger-staffed information desk. The main **South Unit Visitor Center**, at the Medora turn-off, has ranger information, a film about TR, exhibits on natural history, and artifacts from TR's ranching days. You can also view Roosevelt's tiny **Maltese Cross Cabin**, moved here from the ranch. It has been restored with period furnishings.

The first leg of the 36-mile (58km) **Scenic Loop Drive** takes you to the **Medora Overlook**, with a grand view

of the tiny frontier town founded by the Marquis de Mores, a French aristocrat who came to the Badlands in 1883 intending to establish a cattle empire. The marquis built his home, the Chateau de Mores, on a bluff overlooking the town, which he named after his wife.

Back on the road, you pass several prairie-dog towns, then get a first proper look at the Badlands from **Skyline Vista**. The road winds down to the **River Woodland Overlook**. It passes through a dense grove of cottonwoods crowding the Little Missouri River, which is surrounded by tawny bluffs peppered with stands of juniper. A little farther on, the Cottonwood Campground occupies a relaxing and shady spot along the river.

Turning right at the intersection, the next 10 miles (16km) twist through bluffs and valleys into the ravaged heart of the Badlands, with glorious, sweeping vistas at the North Dakota Badlands, Buck Hill (requires a short steep walk) and Boicourt overlooks. Two self-guiding nature trails do a fine job of introducing visitors to the park's varied ecology. The

There are guided tours of Theodore Roosevelt's Maltese Cross Cabin in summer, self-guided in winter.

BELOW: Maltese Cross Cabin.

The South Unit was designated a national memorial park in 1947, and the North Unit added the following year. Together, they achieved national park status in 1978.

BELOW: the secluded North Unit.
BELOW RIGHT: a cowboy hits the open trail.

Ridgeline Trail is just under half a mile (1km) long and quite steep in places. The **Coal Vein Trail** is about a mile (1.5km) long and is also rather steep. A coal seam burned here from 1951–77, baking overlying clay into the reddish brick-like substance known locally, but incorrectly, as scoria.

The trail loops through shady stands of juniper, along a canyon rim and across patches of prairie grass before returning to the parking lot. Have you noticed that signposts and tree trunks look worn around the edges? Bison walk these trails, too, and often use trees and posts to scratch themselves.

The Scenic Loop Drive comes to a visual crescendo at **Wind Canyon Trail**, a quarter-mile (400-meter), steep climb along the rim of a dramatic side-canyon of the Little Missouri River. The view is glorious. It's a short drive past another prairie-dog town to historic **Peaceful Valley Ranch**, where horseback riding is available between Memorial and Labor days. You'll also find several trailheads on this final stretch of the scenic loop.

Ambitious hikers can try the 16-mile (26km) **Petrified Forest Loop Trail** into the heart of the South Unit's wilderness area, where they'll find the largest and most plentiful samples of petrified wood; a cutoff on the **Lone Tree Loop Trail** along Knutson Creek covers much of the same ground.

To the east, the **Paddock Creek Trail** is a one-way, 11-mile (18km) hike across the scenic loop and into the stunning **Painted Canyon** area, where the park maintains a small herd of wild horses. Backpackers can make it a round-trip on the **Talkington Trail**, which loops back toward the trailhead. The **Jones Creek Trail** is shorter but no less interesting – perfect for a leisurely day hike. It cuts a 4-mile (6km) path through the grassy folds of Jones Creek valley, occasionally skirting the edge of a deep ravine. Although there are a few gradual slopes, most of the trail is flat and grassy.

The North Unit

The North Unit is even farther off the beaten path and offers wonderful seclusion during the off-season. The 14-mile (23km) **Scenic Drive** runs

roughly parallel to the Little Missouri for the first 5 miles (8km) or so. Just beyond the visitor center, you may see a few head of Texas longhorns, maintained by the park as a reminder of the area's ranching history. At the Slump Block Pullout, you'll get an explanation of "slumping" – the way an entire block of earth slides down a hillside, keeping its sedimentary layers intact and giving the hills a characteristic slope-shouldered profile.

There's another geologic curiosity at the **Cannonball Concretions Pullout**, where hard sandstone spheres eroded away from softer deposits. From the river bottom, the road winds to the plateau above, passing overlooks and pullouts with gorgeous views of the river, prairie, and rugged canyons. Views from the River Bend and Oxbow overlooks are particularly spectacular.

Two self-guiding nature trails – the **Squaw Creek Nature Trail** and the **Caprock Coulee Nature Trail** – are fairly short and easy. Leaflets available at the trailheads explain the complex relationship between water, fire, earth, plants, and animals that makes up Badlands ecology. If you're feeling ambitious, you can continue on the **Upper Caprock Coulee Trail** for a 4-mile (6km) loop. The trail makes a gradual 400ft (120-meter) ascent through the Badlands, alternating between the hotter, drier, north-facing slopes and the ash and juniper groves of the wetter south-facing slopes. It tops out on the prairie, offering magnificent views of the Badlands, then crosses the Scenic Drive onto a steep, deeply eroded bentonite cliff. (Be careful if you walk here: bentonite clay is extremely slippery, even when dry.)

The trail follows a ridgeline overlooking the Little Missouri, crosses the **River Bend Overlook** and then descends through grasslands and juniper groves to the parking area.

For longer hikes, the 16-mile (26km) **Achenbach Trail** heads up and over the Achenbach Hills, crosses the Little Missouri (ask rangers about river cross-

ing conditions), and then rises steeply to the magnificent **Oxbow Overlook** before returning to Juniper Campground along the river bottom. The 11-mile (18km) **Buckhorn Trail** loops around the eastern portion of the park, with long stretches on Squaw Creek to the upper prairie and then back into the Badlands to the river bottom.

Roosevelt's Ranch

Adventurous travelers may also want to consider a trip to the undeveloped site of Roosevelt's **Elkhorn Ranch**, about 20 miles (32km) from the South Unit along a dirt road. Be sure to ask a ranger about road and river crossing conditions before striking out. For those who prefer floating to walking, the Little Missouri winds gracefully through all three units. The 120-mile (190km) trip takes about three days and is usually best in April and May. The park is open year-round, but snowfall, usually between October and March, can limit travel. Weather changes quickly in the Badlands, and nights can be chilly even in summer. Be prepared for some foul weather, including high winds and

The two units of Theodore Roosevelt National Park are 70 miles (113km) apart, via I-94 and Highway 85.

BELOW: the North Unit.

ROCKY MOUNTAIN

Straddling the Continental Divide, the park
contains sky-scraping peaks, 150 lakes, rushing
mountain streams, alpine tundra, pristine forests,
and an amazing array of wildlife

When Pope John Paul II journeyed to Denver in 1993, he asked to see **Rocky Mountain National Park ⑫**. The pontiff's hiking outfit was a bit unusual (His Holiness wore a white cassock, gold pallium, and sneakers with matching gold shoelaces), but the visit confirmed what lovers of the park already knew: Rocky Mountain can truly be considered a religious experience. Like John Paul, millions of pilgrims have thrilled at this sea of mountain peaks since the park was created in 1915. Many of the peaks within Rocky Mountain's 414 sq miles (1,072 sq km) soar over 12,000ft (3,660 meters). "There are higher peaks elsewhere," author Freeman Tilden wrote in 1951. "But for a sheer sense of towering density, of closely packed mountaintops, I know of nothing like this."

By the time Zebulon Pike set eyes on the Rockies in 1807, Indians had been venturing into the high country for at least 7,000 years. Later, mounted hunters of the Ute, Arapaho, Cheyenne, and Shoshone tribes tracked deer and buffalo in the foothills and bighorn sheep on the alpine slopes. Late in the 19th century, a flood of trappers, miners, and ranchers tried to tap the mountains' natural wealth. Mining camps such as Lulu City sprang up overnight and disappeared just as quickly. Hunting campaigns drove grizzly bears, wolves, elk,

and bison to the brink of extinction.

Among the pioneers was a different breed, too – people like Enos Mills, who mined peace and rejuvenation from the mountains and made a living sharing them with others. Hailed as the "John Muir of the Rockies," Mills hatched the idea for the park and spent years rallying support and lobbying Congress, which finally gave its consent in 1915.

Estes Park to Grand Lake

The **Trail Ridge Road**, the park's main thoroughfare, is perhaps the most

Main attractions
BEAVER MEADOWS VISITOR
   CENTER
TRAIL RIDGE ROAD
MANY PARKS CURVE
TUNDRA NATURE TRAIL
NEVER SUMMER RANCH
GLACIER LAKE
LONGS PEAK
DINOSAUR QUARRY, DINOSAUR
   NATIONAL MONUMENT
HARPERS CORNER SCENIC DRIVE,
   DINOSAUR NATIONAL MONUMENT
ECHO CANYON, DINOSAUR
   NATIONAL MONUMENT

LEFT: snowboarding on the slopes.
RIGHT: an Aspen-lined mountain trail.

Rocky Mountain National Park

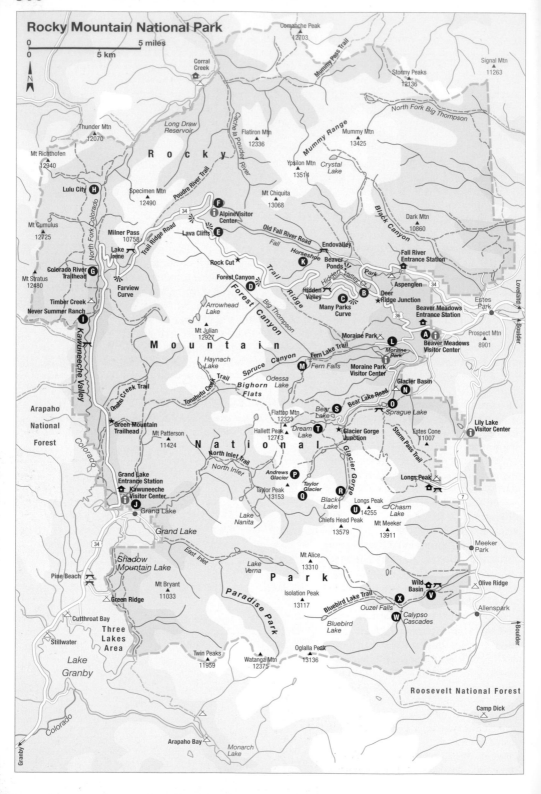

0 _____ 5 miles
0 _____ 5 km

N

Comanche Peak
12703

Signal Mtn
11263

Corral Creek

Mummy Pass Trail

Stormy Peaks
12136

North Fork Big Thompson

Thunder Mtn
12070

Long Draw Reservoir

Flatiron Mtn
12336

Mummy Range

Mummy Mtn
13425

R o c k y

Mt Richthofen
12940

Specimen Mtn
12490

Poudre River Trail

34

Ypsilon Mtn
13514

Crystal Lake

Dark Mtn
10860

Lulu City H

Mt Chiquita
13068

F AlpineVisitor
Center

i

Mt Cumulus
12725

Milner Pass
10758

Lava Cliffs E

Old Fall River Road

Endovalley

Fall River Entrance Station

Lake Irene

Rock Cut ★

Fall

Horseshoe
K

Beaver Ponds

Aspenglen

34

Estes Park

Colorado River Trailhead G

Forest Canyon D

Hidden Valley

C

Deer
★ Ridge Junction

B

Mt Stratus
12480

Farview Curve

Arrowhead Lake

Many Parks Curve

Beaver Meadows Entrance Station

Loveland

Timber Creek

Never Summer Ranch I

M o u n t a i n

Mt Julian
12921

Fern Lake Trail

Moraine Park

L A

Beaver Meadows Visitor Center i

Prospect Mtn
8901

Haynach Lake

Spruce Canyon

Fern Falls

Moraine Park

Moraine Park Visitor Center

Boulder

Bighorn Flats

Odessa Lake

M

Glacier Basin

N

Lily Lake Visitor Center i

Green Mountain Trailhead

Mt Patterson
11424

Flattop Mtn
12323

Bear Lake S

Bear Lake Road

Sprague Lake

O

Estes Cone
11007

N a t i o n a l

Hallett Peak
12713

Dream Lake

T

Glacier Gorge Junction ★

Storm Pass Trail

North Inlet Trail

Andrews Glacier

P

Taylor Glacier

Longs Peak

7

Grand Lake Entrance Station

Kawuneeche Visitor Center i

J Grand Lake

Taylor Peak
13153

Q

R

Black Lake

Longs Peak
U 14255

Chasm Lake

Meeker Park

Grand Lake

Lake Nanita

Chiefs Head Peak
13579

Mt Meeker
13911

Shadow Mountain Lake

Pine Beach

East Inlet

Lake Verna

Mt Alice
13310

Wild Basin

V

Olive Ridge

Green Ridge

Mt Bryant
11033

Isolation Peak
13117

Bluebird Lake Trail

X

Ouzel Falls

Calypso Cascades

Allenspark

Cutthroat Bay

Three Lakes Area

W

Stillwater

Bluebird Lake

Boulder

Lake Granby

Twin Peaks
11959

Watanga Mtn
12375

Oglalla Peak
13136

P a r a d i s e   P a r k

P a r k

Roosevelt National Forest

Colorado

Granby

Arapaho Bay

Monarch Lake

Camp Dick

scenic drive in North America. Open from mid-May until the first heavy snowstorms blanket the interior in October, it features well over a dozen spectacular overlooks and exposes visitors to a large expanse of alpine tundra, one of the rarest ecosystems in the lower 48 states.

Starting at the **Beaver Meadows Visitor Center Ⓐ** in Estes Park, Highway 36 climbs gently through foothills scattered with ponderosa pine and sagebrush. At Deer Ridge Junction, Trail Ridge Road veers left and makes an abrupt ascent along **Hidden Valley Creek Ⓑ**, dammed in several places by beavers who usually emerge from their lodges in the early evening. The creek is also home to rare greenback cutthroat trout; a roadside exhibit provides information on them.

Just beyond, the overlook at **Many Parks Curve Ⓒ** perches over deep valleys cut by Pleistocene glaciers more than 13,000 years ago. (Several diminishing glaciers remain in Rocky Mountain, most straddling the eastern edge of the Continental Divide in the park's central area.) Overhead, a red-tailed hawk or golden eagle may be scanning the "parks," or meadows, for an opportunity to snatch a small rodent or even a marmot sunning itself on a rock.

Trail Ridge Road passes through stands of fir and Engelmann spruce that are common in the subalpine zone and then, beyond the stunning overlook at **Forest Canyon Ⓓ**, enters alpine tundra. One of the highest overland routes on the continent, Trail Ridge Road stays above the tree line for 11 miles (18km), cresting at 12,183ft (3,713 meters) near **Lava Cliffs Ⓔ**.

Alpine tundra

A treeless, windblown realm, alpine tundra exists only in the highest reaches of the Rockies, North Cascades, and Sierra Nevada. For a closer look, walk the self-guiding **Tundra Nature Trail** near **Rock Cut**.

As you walk the trail, look closely for camouflaged ptarmigan, a member of the grouse family whose plumage changes from snowy white in winter to mottled brown in summer. You may also spy a water pipit foraging for insects, or pudgy yellow-bellied marmots scampering across a talus slope, or perhaps bighorn sheep, elk, or mule deer grazing warily in a distant meadow.

Be sure to bring along a jacket for these altitudes. The temperature here can be 20°F (11°C) cooler than at Estes Park. Remember, too, that you are more than 4,000ft (1,220 meters) higher. The air is thin and it's not uncommon for lowlanders to feel short of breath, light-headed, or nauseated.

Only the hardiest plants can survive in these Arctic-like conditions. Stunted by wind and cold, gnarled whitebark pine hugs the ground; although no larger than bushes, some are as much as 200 or 300 years old. Silver-dollar-sized patches of lichen (actually an alga and fungus that grow symbiotically) can be centuries old as well. A bouquet of wildflowers – including lupines, yellow snow buttercups, shooting stars, daisies, and blue Colorado columbines, among others – sends a blush through

The alpine tundra is an extremely fragile environment; it's imperative to stay on the trails at all times. Trampling delicate tundra plants can cause damage that takes decades, if not centuries, to repair.

BELOW:
a hovering humming bird among the blooms.

TIP

The Rocky Mountain Nature Association has books for sale in each visitor center and also runs summer seminar programs on the ecology of the park. Call 800-816-7662 for details.

the meadows in late June and often lasts until the first snowfall of fall. For more information about alpine tundra ecology, you should stop at the **Alpine Visitor Center** , which is just a short drive from the Tundra Nature Trail.

Trail Ridge Road dips about 1,000ft (300 meters) in 4 miles (6km) and then, at Milner Pass, crosses the **Continental Divide**, which runs diagonally through the park from northwest to southeast. From Milner Pass, the road zigzags several dizzying miles and then heads south toward the **Colorado River Trailhead** , where you can start a 2-mile (3km) hike to the tumbled-down cabin of Joe Shipler, a miner who tried his luck here in the 1870s. About 2 miles (3km) farther north, a few old shacks are all that remain of **Lulu City** , where hundreds of prospectors, hearing stories of gold and silver strikes, came to make their fortunes in the early 1880s. The trail follows the North Fork of the Colorado River, which here is hardly more than a trickle. Believe it or not, this is the beginning of one of the mightiest rivers in the West – the same rushing waters that flow through the

Grand Canyon several hundred miles away.

About 2 miles (3km) farther south, a short trail leads to the **Never Summer Ranch** , a dude ranch founded in the 1920s and now operated as a "living history" exhibit, with guides in period costume. The final stretch of Trail Ridge Road descends into Kawuneeche Valley to the **Kawuneeche Visitor Center** . Coniferous forests grow thick here, and the Colorado River is fringed with aspens and willows that explode with fall colors. Moose and elk are a common sight, and the birdwatching, especially for neotropical songbirds such as warblers, thrushes, and finches, is generally excellent.

For a more intimate experience of the western slope, seasoned backpackers can make a leisurely two-day, 17-mile (27km) round-trip on the **Tonahutu Creek Trail** between the Green Mountain trailhead and Haynach Lake, or a 15-mile (24km) round-trip on the **North Inlet Trail** between Grand Lake and North Inlet Falls.

Horseshoe Park

If time allows, plan a side trip to **Horseshoe Park** , a popular area for wildlife-watching northwest of Estes Park. From the visitor center, take Highway 36 into the park, then turn right at the junction with Highway 34 to **Sheep Lakes**, where naturally occurring mineral licks attract bands of bighorn sheep. The **Old Fall River Road**, a one-way unpaved lane open only in summer, starts at Endovalley and makes a 9-mile (14km) climb, much of it above the tree line, to the Alpine Visitor Center. Notice the rocky debris scattered along the road; it was deposited by a dam break in 1982 that sent a flood of mud, rocks, and water downslope as far as Estes Park.

Bighorn sheep are frequently seen in this area. About 200 bighorns graze on the lush meadows and rocky slopes around Horseshoe Park. During the winter breeding season, males vie for dominance, using their massive cork-

BELOW:
fun among the leaves in the fall.

screw horns in dramatic head-butting contests. The report can be heard echoing through the mountains. Elk are frequently spotted here, too, never far from the forest edge.

Another option is to explore **Moraine Park ❶** and Bear Lake Road, which leads into one of the most picturesque and heavily used regions of the park. The area is laced with interconnecting trails, and it's possible to spend a day or more hiking from one mountain lake to another and experiencing a variety of life zones. Hikers can spend the morning wandering among tree-ringed glens and turquoise lakes, then make a push towards the Continental Divide, where glaciers and snowfields send meltwater cascading down the eastern slope.

You can get your bearings at the **Moraine Park Visitor Center**, where exhibits and a short interpretive trail explain the area's cultural and natural history, and then strike out on any number of possible tours.

A short drive to the **Cub Lake Trailhead** enables you to explore Moraine Park or to make the gentle 4-mile (6km) climb to Cub Lake, **Fern Falls ⓜ**, and

Fern Lake; an extension trail makes a steep connection to the stark shoreline of Odessa Lake. Farther south, a free summer shuttle bus runs from **Glacier Basin ⓝ** to the end of Bear Lake Road.

An easy nature trail around **Sprague Lake ⓞ** makes a pleasant stroll through a storybook mountain setting. Farther down, a steep 4-mile (6km) round-trip takes hikers up to and around the forested shore of Bierstadt Lake. You'll find tougher hikes at Glacier Gorge Junction, which has branches that go to the foot of **Andrews Glacier ⓟ** and **Taylor Glacier ⓠ** via Loch Vale as well as a 5-mile (8km) scramble through Glacier Gorge to frigid **Black Lake ⓡ**, well above the tree line.

The most traveled and possibly the most beautiful route is the short trail from **Bear Lake ⓢ** to **Dream Lake ⓣ**, which is cupped in a magnificent high-country basin with the snow-dusted summits of Flattop Mountain and Hallett Peak rising grandly from behind.

Longs Peak and Wild Basin

Farther south, an ascent of **Longs Peak ⓤ** is a challenge even for the most

TIP

Hi-Country Stables, located at Moraine Park and Glacier Creek, offers guided horseback riding. For more information, call 970-586-1206.

BELOW: stunning scenery in the Rocky Mountains.

The Continental Divide

A raindrop that falls on the western side of the Continental Divide flows toward the Pacific Ocean; water that falls on the eastern side of the Divide runs toward the Atlantic. Known as the "backbone of America," the Divide also has a profound effect on climate. Trapped behind mountain peaks, clouds blowing in from the Pacific Ocean dump rain and snow on the western slopes, supplying the headwaters of the Colorado River. Half as much moisture falls east of the Divide, much of it evaporating due to the incessant, drying winds. The lush riparian environment of the western side sustains moose, river otter, Colorado River trout, and a profusion of conifers. The more arid, eastern landscape supports Abert's squirrel, endangered greenback cutthroat trout, ponderosa pine, prickly pear, and wood lily.

A skeleton of Tyrannosaurus rex at Dinosaur National Monument.

BELOW: a lonesome pine in Dinosaur National Monument.
BELOW: fossils are the big draw at Dinosaur

ambitious and physically fit hikers. At 14,255ft (4,345 meters), Longs Peak towers over the eastern side of the park; its flat summit and nearby **Chasm Lake** are considered by many to be the most magical destination in the park. And, although technical equipment isn't necessary to make the climb, it's a mistake to underestimate just how arduous the 16-mile (26km) round-trip, taking from 12 to 15 hours, can be.

Hikers should be prepared for high winds, biting cold, and some hand-and-foot scrambling. It is essential to start your hike well before daybreak to avoid dangerous afternoon lightning storms; many hikers stay at nearby Longs Peak Campground the night before. Greenhorns can inquire at the **Colorado Mountain School** in Estes Park about climbing lessons and guide services.

To escape the crowds, try the **Wild Basin V** region, off Route 7 just southeast of Longs Peak. Cut off from the rest of the park by a crescent of surrounding mountains, this isolated pocket of mountain lakes and exuberant waterfalls is still recovering in places from a 1978 forest fire.

Hikers can spend a leisurely for noon on the moderate, 3-mile (5km) trail leading to **Calypso Cascades W** and **Ouzel Falls X**, named for the tiny river-faring bird that John Muir found so enchanting. The trail branches a bit farther on, following a string of lakes into the highlands.

A Jurassic park

The highlight at 210,000-acre (85,000-hectare) **Dinosaur National Monument 13**, straddling the Colorado–Utah border, is a unique deposit of dinosaur fossils laid down during the Jurassic era, when more than 1,500 dinosaur bones were deposited in an ancient riverbed and turned to stone. The embedded fossils form one wall of the **Dinosaur Quarry Visitor Center**, a big draw for families when it is open in summer and accessible by free tram. Currently, the visitor center and fossil wall are closed for major reconstruction. Quarry visitors can walk the half-mile (800-meter) **Fossil Discovery Trail** and view fossils at a temporary visitor center.

Dinosaur has two spectacular scenic drives. Tour of the Tilted Rocks, on the Utah side near Dinosaur Quarry, is a 22-mile (35km) round-trip that parallels the Green River, prehistoric petroglyph sites, the upturned rocks of Cub Creek and the shaded historic Josie Morris Cabin.

For spectacular scenery, you can't beat the Journey Through Time tour (62 miles/100km round-trip), which begins at Canyon Area Visitor Center, just east of Dinosaur, Colorado. The final 12 miles (19km) offer breathtaking views of canyon country cut by the conjoining Yampa and Green rivers. The road dead-ends at **Harpers Corner**, where there's a 2-mile (4.5km) trail. Adventurous travelers will want to turn off before the end of the drive and descend the steep, 13-mile (21km) dirt road to historic **Echo Canyon**, the heart of Dinosaur.

The road passes frontier cabins and ends at a lovely riverfront campground.   ❏

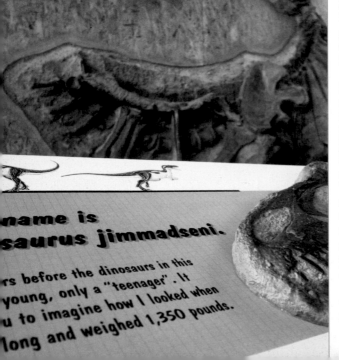

name is saurus jimmadseni.

rs before the dinosaurs in this young, only a "teenager". It u to imagine how I looked when long and weighed 1,350 pounds.

WILD AND WONDERFUL

For many people, the appeal of the West's national parks is the wildlife they protect. And no region has a more diverse animal population than the Rockies

The Rocky Mountains cross both the northern and southern borders of the United States. Along this jagged ridge lie some of our great wildlife parks – Glacier, Yellowstone, Rocky Mountain – along with lesser parks that have abundant and extraordinary wildlife: White Sands with its kangaroo rats and rattlesnakes, Carlsbad Caverns with its bats, Big Bend with its *javelinas*. Of federally managed lands, only national parks attempt to preserve complete ecosystems, allowing soil, water, and living creatures to interact unimpaired. Such efforts call for large sections of wilderness, but the health of these natural refuges provides a baseline by which we can measure the health of the country's biology. Several of the parks have been designated biosphere reserves – major ecosystems protecting the diversity of life.

As the characteristics of the Rockies change from northern to southern latitudes, so do the animals that live there. Some, like moose, live only in the northern climes, while others, black-tailed jackrabbits among them, settle in lower, drier lands. Coyotes, pronghorns, and mountain lions are at home almost anywhere. Semidesert shrub and woodlands are the domain of the ringtail a beguiling nocturnal creature. Its tail accounts for about half of its 2ft (60cm) length and gives it exquisite agility.

ABOVE: Male elk use their antlers to establish dominance and occasionally for defense. A set of antlers, shed annually, can weigh up to 40lbs (18kg).

BELOW: The coyote sometimes lives in packs but is often solitary. Its high-pitched yipping, barking and quivering howl are the Song of the West and a ritual enjoyed by many.

LEFT: The sure-footed Rocky Mountain Goat.

BIRDLIFE IN THE ROCKIES

About 80 percent of North American bird species migrate seasonally. The Rockies invite and channel migration, and the birds present a mosaic of movement as they ebb and flow north and south. Most Rocky Mountain parks have between 250 and 300 bird species: about one-fifth are year-round residents, about half stay only for the nesting and breeding season, and the remainder are just passing through.

Hummingbirds are found throughout the Rockies, but many, because they depend on blossoms for nectar, begin to move south by midsummer to prepare for migration to Central America. Illustrated above is a black-chinned hummingbird (a female – since only the males live up to their name).

Wings give birds the freedom to wander, but not aimlessly. Most are specific about where they feed and breed. One species of duck feeds in water up to 6ins (15cm) deep; another, in water from 12 to 24ins (30–60cm) deep; another prefers water 20–40ft (6–12 meters) deep. Some birds prefer dense shrub thickets, others nest on the ground, others high in the tops of trees.

LEFT: The black-tailed jackrabbit uses the visibility afforded by grasslands to spot predators and escape in 10ft (3-meter) bounds.

BELOW: Male bears weigh up to 450 lbs (200kg) and can run at 30 mph (48kph).

RIGHT: The yellow-bellied marmot can be found on the rocky subalpine slopes. Here they excavate networks of burrows and will hibernate from September to spring.

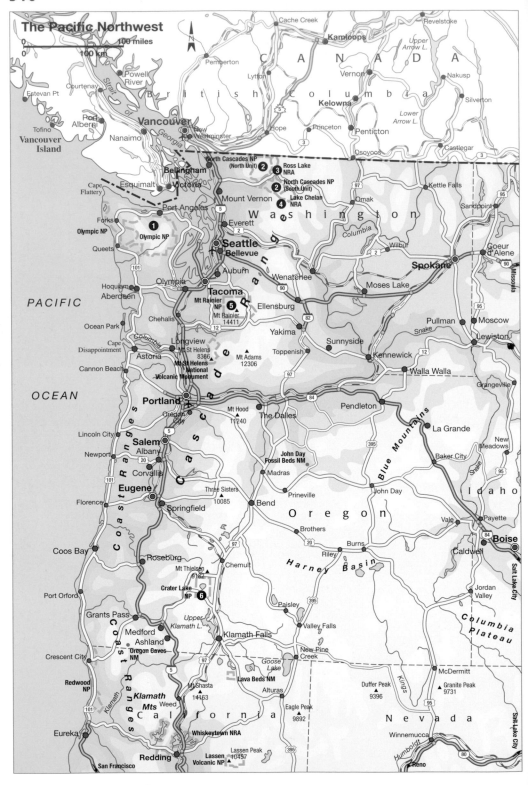

The Pacific Northwest

100 miles
0
0
100 km

N

CANADA

Cache Creek
Revelstoke
Kamloops
Upper
Arrow L.
Pemberton
Lytton
Vernon
Nakusp
Powell
River
Courtenay
Silverton
Estevan Pt
British Columbia
Kelowna
Lower
Arrow L.
Port
Alberni
Nanaimo
Hope
Princeton
Penticton
Castlegar
Vancouver
New
Westminster
Osoyoos
Tofino
**Vancouver
Island**
Esquimalt
Bellingham
Victoria
North Cascades NP
(North Unit)
Ross Lake
NRA
Kettle Falls
Cape
Flattery
Port Angeles
Mount Vernon
North Cascades NP
(South Unit)
Omak
Sandpoint
Forks
Olympic NP
Olympic NP
Lake Chelan
NRA
Washington
Coeur
d'Alene
Queets
Everett
Columbia
Wilbur
Seattle
Bellevue
Spokane
PACIFIC
Hoquiam
Aberdeen
Olympia
Auburn
Wenatchee
Moses Lake
Moscow
Ocean Park
Tacoma
Mt Rainier
NP
Mt Rainier
14411
Ellensburg
Pullman
Cape
Disappointment
Chehalis
Yakima
Snake
Lewiston
Astoria
Longview
Mt St Helens
8366
Mt Adams
12306
Toppenish
Sunnyside
Kennewick
OCEAN
Cannon Beach
Mt St Helens
National
Volcanic Monument
Walla Walla
Grangeville
Portland
Oregon
City
Mt Hood
11240
The Dalles
Pendleton
La Grande
New
Meadows
Lincoln City
Salem
Albany
John Day
Fossil Beds NM
Baker City
Newport
Corvallis
Madras
Blue Mountains
Eugene
Three Sisters
10085
Bend
Prineville
John Day
Idaho
Florence
Springfield
Brothers
Vale
Payette
Boise
Coos Bay
Roseburg
Chemult
Burns
Riley
Caldwell
Oregon
Harney Basin
Port Orford
Mt Thielsen
9182
Crater Lake
NP
Paisley
Jordan
Valley
Grants Pass
Upper
Klamath L.
Valley Falls
**Columbia
Plateau**
Medford
Ashland
Klamath Falls
New Pine
Creek
Oregon Caves
NM
Goose
Lake
McDermitt
Crescent City
Lava Beds NM
Duffer Peak
9396
Granite Peak
9731
**Redwood
NP**
**Klamath
Mts**
Mt Shasta
14163
Alturas
Eagle Peak
9892
Nevada
Eureka
Weed
California
Whiskeytown NRA
Lassen Peak
10457
Winnemucca
San Francisco
Redding
Lassen
Volcanic NP
Reno
Salt Lake City

THE PACIFIC NORTHWEST

This is where glaciers continue to shape
the landscape, and where the forests
grow dense and tall

The Pacific Northwest sustains a riotous profusion of life. For sheer biomass, its old-growth forests are virtually unsurpassed in the American West. The Cascade Range forms the region's western flank, catching moisture that blows in from the Pacific Ocean and casting a long rain shadow over the eastern plateau. Evidence of the range's volcanic origins is everywhere. In Oregon, the caldera of Mount Mazama, a dormant volcano that last erupted 7,700 years ago, cups the blue waters of Crater Lake, the deepest in the country.

To the north, the giant bulk of Washington's Mount Rainier rises like a titan. The greatest single-peak glacial system in the US radiates from the summit and slopes of the ancient volcano, and its shoulders are draped with dazzling wildflower meadows and deep-green ancient forests.

In North Cascades National Park, adjoining the Canadian border, a chaotic jumble of high craggy peaks, glaciers, lovely waterfalls, sparkling lakes, and lush forests supports a wild diversity of flora. Throughout this remote mountain wilderness, mountain goats, black bears, mountain lions, lynx, eagles, and hawks range freely.

To the west, the snow-dusted peaks of the Olympic Peninsula seem to float above the wild, wave-battered Pacific Coast, where bald eagles soar over waters populated by seals, sea otters, and migrating whales. Lush temperate rainforest cloaks Olympic's western slope, where annual rainfall in excess of 200ins (500cm) on high peaks nourishes an emerald cathedral of Douglas fir, Sitka spruce, western red cedar, and thick growths of mosses and ferns.

North of Canada, Alaska contains over 85,000 sq miles (220,000 sq km) of National Park System lands. From the frigid peak of Mount Denali, the highest in North America, to the vast tundra of Gates of the Arctic and Kobuk Valley, Alaska's parks can be described only in superlatives. ❑

PRECEDING PAGES: Whiskey Bend Trail, Olympic National Park. **TOP:** Mount McKinley, Denali National Park and Preserve. **ABOVE LEFT:** hiking Hoh Rain Forest Trail, Olympic National Park. **ABOVE RIGHT:** Wizard Island, Crater Lake National Park.

OLYMPIC

Often referred to as "three parks in one," Olympic has three distinct ecosystems – glacier-capped mountains, wild Pacific coastline, and the world's largest temperate rainforest

t was in 1788 that British Captain John Meares gave them their name. Awestruck by the snowcapped pinnacles that loom over the rugged Washington coast, he dubbed the tallest peak Mount Olympus, "home of the gods." Today, 7,980ft (2,432-meter) Mount Olympus stands at the center of **Olympic National Park ❶**, a 922,651-acre (373,384-hectare) sanctuary of glacier-clad mountains, lush temperate rainforest and miles of wild shoreline. It is such an exemplary reservoir of ecological diversity that the UN has designated Olympic a World Heritage Site and an International Biosphere Reserve.

Remarkably, the sawtooth summits that crown the Olympic Mountains were once at the bottom of the Pacific Ocean. Scratch away the mantle of snow and ice, and you'll find marine fossils entombed in alpine rock and 50-million-year-old volcanic "pillow basalts." About 30 million years ago, as the Pacific plate collided with North America, the upper layers of the ocean floor were planed off and thrust upward, creating the jigsaw of basalt and sedimentary rocks that now make up the Olympic Mountains.

Glaciers finished the job. They carved signature U-shaped valleys, fracturing and polishing bare rock, scooping out lakebeds, and transporting boulders, or erratics, miles from their origin. Glaciers also bulldozed Puget Sound and the Strait of Juan de Fuca, isolating the Olympic Peninsula from inland species. The result is several evolutionary detours, and 24 endemic species, from the Olympic pocket gopher and Olympic Mazama marmot to the Flett's violet, found only on the peninsula.

Some 266 glaciers remain atop the Olympic Mountains, fed by moist Pacific breezes that dump over 200ins (500cm) of precipitation on the crest each year. It's not uncommon to have

Main attractions
OLYMPIC NATIONAL PARK VISITOR CENTER, PORT ANGELES
HURRICANE RIDGE
MOUNT OLYMPUS
ELWHA RIVER TRAIL
LAKE CRESCENT
HALL OF MOSSES TRAIL, HOH RAIN FOREST
QUINAULT VALLEY
ENCHANTED VALLEY TRAIL
KALALOCH BEACHES
LA PUSH
POINT-OF-ARCHES, RIALTO BEACH
CAPE ALAVA
OZETTE
MAKAH NATION, NEAH BAY

PRECEDING PAGES: grey whale off Westport.
LEFT: making a splash at Lake Crescent.
RIGHT: walking in the rainforest.

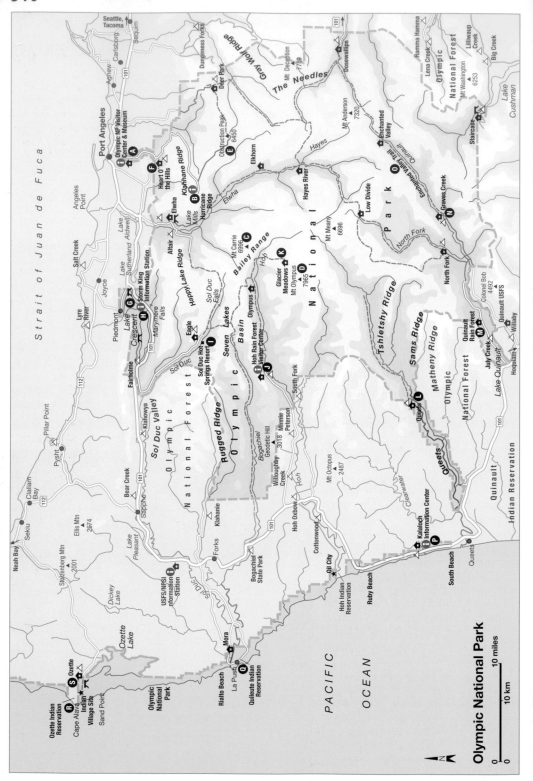

Olympic National Park

Strait of Juan de Fuca

PACIFIC OCEAN

0   10 miles
0   10 km

20 overcast days per month on the west side of the park, or several weeks of nearly constant drizzle. Thirteen major rivers drain the high country, including the Queets and Hoh rivers, which cascade down mountainsides toward the Pacific. Oddly, only miles to the east, on the opposite side of the mountains, parts of the park are among the driest spots on the West Coast. Nevertheless, a traveler's best friend in Olympic is a rain jacket and an extra pair of dry shoes.

Exploring the wilderness

Olympic contains one of the largest tracts of roadless land in the US. Highway 101 wraps around three sides of the park. Spoke roads give limited access to the interior, but no roads cross these high peaks; this is a backpacker's paradise. For an introduction to this spectacular park, visit the **Olympic National Park Visitor Center Ⓐ** in Port Angeles (on the north side of the park), where exhibits, maps, books, and rangers will help organize your journey. From here, you can drive a counterclockwise circuit that takes you to Olympic's three con-

trasting regions – the mountains, the rainforest, and the wild coast.

The mountains

Beyond the visitor center is 5,757ft (1,755-meter) **Hurricane Ridge Ⓑ**, the highest point you can reach by car. Steep and winding, the scenic road alone climbs nearly 5,000ft (1,520 meters) in 17 miles (27km), suggesting just how abruptly the mountains rise from the sea. Pull out binoculars at the Hurricane Ridge Visitor Center for a close-up look at the park's mightiest, glacier-saddled peaks. At nearly 7,000ft (2,130 meters), **Mount Carrie Ⓒ** and her ringlet of glaciers dominate the foreground, while 7,965ft (2,428-meter) **Mount Olympus Ⓓ**, clothed in the pearly white robe of **Blue Glacier**, rises from behind. Seven glaciers hang from Olympus; its massive shoulders have been draped in ice for thousands of years, but although annual snowfalls can reach 200ins (500cm) the glaciers continue to decrease in size. Heavy snowfalls often keep the steep gravel road from Hurricane Ridge to 6,450ft (1,966-meter) **Obstruction Peak Ⓔ**.

TIP

Hurricane Ridge and Hoh visitor centers are open all year (when road and weather conditions allow), though they may be self-service during the winter months.

BELOW:
the Elwha river.

Peninsula Reservations

The Hood Canal Twana (Skokomish), north-shore Jamestown and Port Gamble S'Klallam and Elwha Klallam, and coastal Queets, Hoh, Makah, Quinault, and Quileute tribes have lived on the peninsula for millennia, harvesting record runs of salmon, whales, seals, game, roots and berries, and red cedar and other forest products. Tribes alternately warred and traded and used elaborate potlatch (gift-giving) ceremonies to maintain the power balance, traveling to neighboring villages in ocean-going cedar canoes. A renaissance in native pride began with the discovery in 1970 of a 450-year-old Makah whaling village entombed in a mudslide at Ozette. Longhouses and nearly 500,000 artifacts of outstanding beauty and utility are now on display at the Makah Cultural and Resource Center at Neah Bay near Cape Flattery.

Among the 300 species of bird at Olympic National Park is the Golden Eagle.

BELOW: the Hall of Mosses in the Hoh Rain Forest.

closed until early July, but intrepid motorists will find the trip worth their time and patience.

The **Elwha River Trail**, which follows the stream through the Elwha Valley at the foot of Mount Olympus, is magical in solitude and beauty. The route links summer ranger stations at Elkhorn, Hayes River, and Low Divide, then connects with the North Fork Trailhead on the southern end of the park. In 1889, James Christie led an expedition along this route and emerged at Quinault Lake – six months later.

From Hurricane Ridge, you can backtrack through the **Heart O' the Hills Entrance ⑤** and then continue west on Highway 101 to the shores of **Lake Crescent ⑥**, a misty tarn that was scooped out by glaciers about 10,000 years ago. Set near an ancient landslide that divided the lake in two, the **Storm King Information Center ⑪** is a great place to catch a sunset or to watch storm clouds gather above the coast. A short walk on the **Marymere Falls Trail** leads to a lovely 90ft (27-meter) cascade, just one of dozens that gush over mountain ridges throughout the park.

Continue on the highway along the southern shore of Lake Crescent and then turn left about 2 miles (3km) past Fairholm toward **Sol Duc**. Notice that the trees are getting bigger. This is the western front of the Olympic Range, one of the rainiest spots in the country.

The road passes rustic **Sol Duc Hot Springs Resort ❶**, which was built in 1911 and still caters to travelers who want to soak away their aches and pains after a long day of hiking.

At the height of the spring runoff, cataracts such as **Sol Duc Falls** tumble with a roar. Located about a mile (1.5km) from the end of the road, the falls are a watery gateway to the hard scrabble **Seven Lakes Basin Trail**, which makes a 17½-mile (28km) loop at the headwaters of the Sol Duc and Bogachiel rivers, an area of subalpine forest, meadows, and deep-blue lakes.

The rainforest

Rejoin Highway 101 and make the 3-hour drive west, then south through Forks to the **Hoh Rain Forest Visitor Center ❶**. Olympic National Park protects the world's largest temperate rainforest – one of only three in the entire world. The perpetual mist and showers, together with a deep layer of decaying organic matter, produce subalpine fir, and other trees of truly gargantuan size.

Two short interpretive loops start near the Hoh Visitor Center, the **Spruce Nature Trail** and the **Hall of Mosses Trail**. Here, a leafy canopy of western hemlock, bigleaf maple, Sitka spruce, and red cedar casts an emerald twilight of shade and sunbeams. Fallen trees, called nurse logs, provide a fertile spot for seedlings to sprout. The endangered spotted owl makes its home here, and black bear, black-tailed deer, and Roosevelt elk are occasionally seen feeding in the underbrush.

Those who want to penetrate deeper into the forest can hike all or part of the one-way 17-mile (27km) Hoh River Trail to **Glacier Meadows ⓚ**, the staging ground for most climbs of Mount Olympus. (The ascent can be hazard-

ous.) Fishing is excellent in the Hoh River and the other watercourses that tumble toward the ocean.

Olympic is 95 percent wilderness. To explore further, drive to the **Queets ①** or **Quinault Rain Forest ⑩** districts in the southwestern corner of the park. About 80 miles (130km) from the Hoh Rain Forest Visitor Center, the Queets Campground in the Quinault Valley is the jumping-off point for either a moderate 3-mile (5km) loop trail through the rainforest or a demanding one-way 18-mile (30km) backpacking trip along the Queets River. The Quinault district offers three short hikes – the half-mile (1km) Maple Glade Rain Forest Trail, the 1-mile (1.5km) loop at **Graves Creek ⑩**, and a 3-mile (5km) stretch of the **Enchanted Valley Trail ⓪** from the Graves Creek Ranger Station to the canyon at Pony Bridge. Several other, tougher, trails follow Graves Creek, the North Fork of the Quinault River, and Skyline Ridge into the park's interior.

The coast

Set apart both physically and spiritually from the main body of the park, Olympic's 57-mile (92km) coastline occupies a narrow strip of land that is constantly pummeled by surf and wind and blessed with an abundance of marine life. There are more than 600 miles (970km) of backcountry trails in Olympic, but nothing quite compares to hiking on beach wilderness. Veiled in mist, a scattering of rock arches, "sea stacks", and tiny islands gives the coast a dreamy, otherworldly quality. Harbor seals haul out on the rocks; bald eagles prowl the skies; otters float on their backs in kelp beds, using stones to crack shellfish; raccoons, skunks, and an occasional black bear wander toward the water looking for a meal.

Highway 101 leads to the popular developed southern beaches of Ruby Beach to South Beach. Rangers at the **Kalaloch Information Center ⓟ** lead summer nature hikes. Solo explorers must pick up a tide table, as incoming tides can trap hikers between head-

lands, leaving them stranded on the rocks for hours, or worse. Watch out, too, for large floating tree trunks. Huge winter waves can send logs hurtling toward the beach like missiles, destroying anything in their path.

The miles of forest and wilderness coastline in the vicinity of First Beach and Rialto Beach are a hiker's paradise. Spur roads from Highway 101 lead to the Quileute Indian village of **La Push ⓠ** and nearby **Mora**, where you can head south on the 17-mile (27km) South Coast Wilderness Trail that connects La Push and Oil City, or north on the 20½-mile (33km) North Coast Wilderness Trail from Rialto Beach. Day visitors will want to walk as far as Point-of-Arches, a 1½-mile (2.5km) stroll to a coastal arch that shelters many tidepools. To reach **Cape Alava ⓡ**, the westernmost point in the continental US, turn off Highway 101 at Sapho and follow Highway 112 to **Ozette ⓢ**, then hike the 3-mile (5km) Cape Alava Trail across a patch of coastal forest to the point. Campgrounds are located along the coast at Kalaloch, Mora, and Ozette and fill quickly in summer. Get there early. ❏

The islets off the Olympic coast are critical breeding sites for seabirds. Most are national wildlife refuges and strictly off-limits to visitors.

BELOW: waters wash over Second Beach, the Olympic Peninsula.

NORTH CASCADES

Most of this park is wilderness area, and startlingly beautiful wilderness at that – high jagged peaks, deep valleys, shimmering lakes, more than 300 glaciers, and, of course, countless waterfalls

North Cascades National Park Complex ❷ is often overlooked by travelers. A relative newcomer to the National Park System (it was established in 1968), North Cascades is tucked away in the northwestern corner of Washington state adjoining the Canadian border. "Nowhere do the mountain masses and peaks present such strange, fantastic, dauntless and startling outlines as here," declared Henry Custer after surveying the region for the government in 1859.

North Cascades has razor-edged summits, massive blue glaciers, primeval forests, and, true to its name, hundreds of cascades, fed by storms that blow in from the Pacific. Its snow-draped peaks are compared to the Swiss Alps; its long, deep lakes are said to resemble Norwegian fjords; and its broad expanse of alpine tundra is ecologically akin to conditions in the Arctic. In the mid-19th century, explorers found the terrain impenetrable, giving the peaks names such as Mount Challenger, Mount Fury, Mount Terror, and Mount Despair.

Though laced with a well-maintained network of hiking trails, North Cascades remains a remote mountain wilderness that is best known by the mountain goats who wander its highest peaks, and by the black bears and mountain lions that range across dense forests and subalpine meadows.

Some 93 percent of the 684,313-acre (276,932-hectare) park is managed as the Stephen Mather Wilderness. Its borders are buffered by surrounding wildlands – including the Pasayten, Mount Baker, Noisy-Diobsud and Glacier Peak wilderness areas – that ensure solitude for creatures requiring vast open spaces and for backpackers who want to immerse themselves in wilderness. Nature seems to be responding to the protection. Grizzlies and gray wolves, both severely reduced by bounty hunters 60 years ago, have recently been sighted in the park.

Main attractions
STATE ROUTE 20 (NORTH CASCADES SCENIC HIGHWAY)
NORTH CASCADES VISITOR CENTER, NEWHALEM
GORGE CREEK FALLS
DIABLO LAKE
SOURDOUGH MOUNTAIN TRAIL
ROSS LAKE
CASCADE PASS TRAIL
LAKE CHELAN
STEHEKIN
AGNES GORGE TRAIL
RAINBOW FALLS TRAIL

LEFT: hiking in North Cascades.
RIGHT: identifying birds with a ranger.

Geologic history

The rugged appearance of the North Cascades was shaped by Ice Age glaciers that retreated north about 10,000 years ago. They sheared mountaintops into arêtes and dagger-like horns, gouged bowl-shaped cirques, depositing mounds of debris, or moraines, and widened valleys. Some 312 glaciers remain here – more than found in any national park in the lower 48 states. Glaciers advance or retreat seasonally, grinding the underlying rock into a glacial "flour" that washes into waterways like the Skagit River, turning them a lovely shade of turquoise.

North Cascades is actually three parks managed as a complex by the National Park Service. **Ross Lake National Recreation Area ❸** divides the national park into two units – north and south – and **Lake Chelan National Recreation Area ❹** forms a southern appendage. There's only one main road into the park complex: North Cascades Highway (State Route 20), which crosses the North Cascades to the Methow Valley via Winthrop and is dubbed "the most scenic moun-

The western slopes of the Cascade Range receive more than 100ins (250cm) of rain a year. Blocked by mountain peaks, few storm clouds reach the eastern side, which receives scarcely one-fifth of that amount.

BELOW: Ross Dam on the Skagit river.

tain drive in Washington." The park's annual 450,000 visitors primarily travel this road, explore trails and sights close to the highway, and take boating tours of the park's three largest lakes – Diablo Lake, Ross Lake, and Lake Chelan.

Getting oriented

State Route 20 starts out in the Skagit River Valley, the fertile bottomlands adjoining Puget Sound. Park headquarters is in **Sedro Woolley**, just east of Interstate 5, where you can pick up visitor information. The highway follows the **Skagit River ❹**, a favorite wintering spot for bald eagles, which arrive here to gorge on salmon after the fall spawning season, and passes through the gritty logging communities of Concrete, Rockport, and Marblemount.

About 55 miles (88km) from Sedro Woolley is **Newhalem**, one of the villages created by Seattle City Light in the 1920s to house workers who built the three dams that stand farther upstream – the Gorge, Diablo, and Ross. Today, a quarter of Seattle's energy needs are drawn from the Skagit's glacier-driven waters. Turn right to reach the attractive

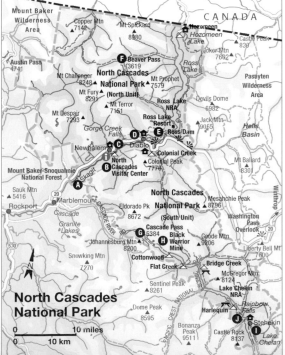

wood-and-glass **North Cascades Visitor Center B**. Here, you can watch a film, view exhibits, pick up maps and books, and inquire about weather, hiking, camping, nature walks, and cruises on the lake offered by Seattle City Light.

Adjoining Newhalem Creek Campground are two short interpretive trails – **To Know a Tree Trail** and **Trail of the Cedars** – which introduce hikers to native lodgepole pine, Douglas fir, western red cedar, yew, and western hemlock, some of them several hundred years old. The trees account for only a small portion of more than 1,500 plant species that flourish in the park's cool, damp forest.

Back on the highway, stop at **Gorge Creek Falls C**, one of hundreds of cataracts that tumble down the mountains, then continue to the little town of **Diablo D** across the Diablo Dam, where you can catch a 2½-hour Seattle City Light tour (reservations recommended) during summer, enjoy stunning views of waterfalls and wildlife, or limber up on one of the trails. For hikers in top physical condition, a strenuous 10-mile (16km) round trip on **Sourdough Mountain Trail** leads to a gorgeous panorama of lakes, glaciers, and surrounding peaks. A more moderate alternative is a tugboat ride to **Ross Dam E** and then a fairly easy 4-mile (6km) hike along Diablo Lake Trail back to your car.

Beyond Diablo, the highway dips south toward Colonial Creek Campground, where the short but steep **Thunder Woods Nature Trail** takes you on a 1-mile (1.5km) loop into the realm of giant cedars. For a longer hike, try a portion of 19-mile (31km) **Thunder Creek Trail**, which passes through a densely forested valley beneath Neve, Klawatti, and Boston glaciers before climbing toward 6,063ft (1,848-meter) **Park Creek Pass**.

If arduous hiking isn't your cup of tea, drive to the **Diablo Lake Overlook** for an upclose view of some of the park's highlights. A reflection of Sourdough Mountain shimmers on the lake, and

the glacier-carved pinnacles of Colonial Peak and Ruby Mountain, both over 7,000ft (2,130 meters), rise to the south. Before reaching the park boundary, you will pass a short interpretive boardwalk at the Happy Crest Forest Walk and, just beyond, the **Ross Lake Overlook**, where you'll get a fine view of the park's largest lake and where, on spring and fall nights, you may be lucky enough to hear a loon's eerie yodel echo off the water.

Ross Lake

To explore the northern reaches of the park, base yourself at the "floating cabins" of rustic **Ross Lake Resort** (seasonally open; reservations required well in advance), reached only by passenger ferry or by hiking trails from Diablo or Ross Dam. Here, you can rent canoes, kayaks, or motorboats, or hire a water taxi, to one of several camping areas or trailheads. Backpackers can pick up **Big Beaver Trail**, which traces the lakeshore for about 2½ miles (4km) before veering into Big Beaver Creek valley, where river otter, beavers, black-tailed deer, and other wildlife are often sighted amid one of the most extensive stands

TIP

The park is open year-round, but heavy snowfall closes the highway as early as mid-October, leaving the interior sealed off until late spring. Most of the campgrounds are closed in winter.

BELOW: atmospheric Ross Lake.

The leaves on a sugar maple tree at Lake Chelan turn bright orange and yellow as fall approaches.

BELOW: Lake Chelan National Recreation Area.

of gigantic, ancient, western red cedar. The trail toils over 3,619ft (1,100-meter) **Beaver Pass** and then intersects Little Beaver and Brush Creek trails at the toes of the Picket Range, which shoulders the park's largest glaciers. From here, backpackers can choose to return the way they came, to make the difficult 11-mile (18km) trek to **Ross Lake**, or to continue exploring the park's wild northwestern corner.

Stehekin Valley

The southern area of the park (including Lake Chelan National Recreation Area) is equally remote. The only road access is bumpy, gravelly **Cascade River Road**, which makes a winding 30-mile (48km) climb from Marblemount's Wilderness Information Center toward **Cascade Pass** . A parking lot sits directly below Johannesburg Mountain, a dramatic peak rising above the trailhead that frequently thunders with the sound of glacial ice falling from hanging valleys created by Johannesburg Glacier. From here, the switchbacks head up historic Cascade Pass Trail, used in 1811 by Alexander Ross, a fur trader

working for John Jacob Astor, and later by gold and silver miners. This is not a beginner's trail; the pass is steep, rugged, and often besieged by wind and cold, which, thankfully, helps deter biting insects in summer. But even if you go just a short way, you'll be amply rewarded with stunning views of Johannesburg Mountain, Boston Peak, Sahale Mountain, Boston Glacier, and Doubtful Lake, not to mention hardy stands of stunted high-elevation trees known as krummholz, whitebark pine, and cheerful throngs of alpine wildflowers in summer.

A steep side trail leads about 4 miles (6km) past 15 waterfalls to Horseshoe Basin, where you can poke around the abandoned **Black Warrior Mine** . Be extremely careful. Old structures and mine shafts can be dangerous. Tread lightly and stay on the trails throughout the area; alpine meadows are fragile and have been damaged by careless hikers.

Cascade Pass Trail eventually loops down to **Cottonwood Campground**, where you can catch a bus (make reservations in advance) on a bumpy old mining road that follows the **Stehekin**

North Cascades Geology

The jumbled peaks and steep ramparts of the North Cascades have a different appearance from the rest of the Cascades, a volcanic range that appeared within the past 40 million years. In fact, the North Cascades are much older than their surrounding brethren. They were born 400 million years ago as volcanic islands in the Pacific Ocean just off the coast of Washington (roughly where eastern Washington is now). They accreted to North America as the oceanic ridge spread eastward, widening the ocean and creating what is now western Washington. It surprises many people to learn that, although the 35-million-year-old volcanoes of 10,775ft (3,284-meter) Mount Baker and Glacier Peak lie nearby, the North Cascades are themselves not volcanic: they are a mosaic of crumpled terranes forced up by seismic forces.

River to Lake Chelan's isolated but busy north shore. The ride takes about two hours. There are stops at backcountry campgrounds where you can pick up a short segment of the **Pacific Crest National Scenic Trail**, which snakes along the Cascade Range from the Canadian border on its way to Mexico.

An easier way into the Stehekin Valley is either by floatplane or one of two ferries that leave from the little town of **Chelan** on Highway 97 at the lower end of Lake Chelan (daily May to October; 3–4 days weekly the rest of the year). The 4 hour ride takes you through a glacier-gouged trench surrounded by forest-clad mountains. Enlarged by the Chelan Dam, **Lake Chelan** is one of the deepest freshwater lakes in the country, with a depth of about 1,500ft (460 meters).

As the boat approaches Stehekin Landing, you begin to see why this region is called the "Wilderness Alps of the Stehekin." Tourists have been finding refuge in this remote pocket of natural beauty since the late 1800s, when the first hotel was built. Modest accommodations (reservations recommended well in advance) as well as campgrounds, stores, and a restaurant are available at **Stehekin ①**, which is operated by some of the nearly 100 permanent residents.

Rangers at the seasonal Golden West Visitor Center can help you decide which hiking trails are best for you. The short **Imus Creek Nature Trail** is a good introduction to the variety of plants you're likely to see in the valley. A longer walk on **Lakeshore Trail** heads south from the visitor center and features lovely views of Lake Chelan. Farther afield, you can take the bus (mid-May to mid-October) to High Bridge for a moderate 5-mile (8km) round trip to **Agnes Gorge**, or, for an extremely tough workout, you can make the 6,000ft (1,830-meter) climb up 8-mile (13km) **McGregor Mountain Trail**. For something a bit more relaxing, consider strolling up the road a few miles for a picnic at the 312ft (95-meter) **Rainbow Falls ②** on the eastern edge of the valley. Remember, though, you will need to spend the night at Stehekin if you plan on hiking, due to the limited ferry schedule. ❏

Visit the historic Buckner Homestead at Stehekin for a revealing illustration of the hardships and pleasures of life in the wilderness.

BELOW LEFT:
Stehekin Landing.
BELOW LEFT:
relaxing by Lake Chelan.

MOUNT RAINIER

The greatest single-peak glacier system in the United States radiates from the summit of this ancient volcano, with dense forests and flower-filled subalpine meadows below

On a clear day, you can see Mount Rainier from 100 miles (160km) away. Its peak towers 14,410ft (4,392 meters) into the sky, making it the highest in the Cascade Range and the fifth highest in the contiguous United States. Its glacial crown shines in the sun like a studded pearl. Even cloaked in mist, its presence is commanding, a nearly perfect volcanic cone, standing among the clouds in majestic solitude. Rainier's volcanic fires have been dim for more than a century, but its allure is as bright as ever.

The Nisqually, Cowlitz, Yakama, Puyallup, and Muckleshoot Indians who summered on Rainier's slopes called it Tahoma, "The Great Mountain." They shared the forests and alpine crags with bountiful wildlife, including Roosevelt elk, mountain goats, black bears, and whistling picas. Today, much of the same land is contained within the 368 sq miles (953 sq km) of **Mount Rainier National Park ⑤**. It is a sanctuary of forests, waterfalls, lakes, and wildflower meadows that sustains nearly 1,000 species of plants and animals. A giant among mountains, Rainier is nonetheless a geologic infant. Although eruptions beginning 40 million years ago built ancestral stratovolcanic cones that were precursors to the modern Cascades, including the Tatoosh Pluton beneath Mount Rainier, "the Mountain," as it is known in the region, only appeared a million years ago. Thousands of lava flows have increased the height and mass of the cone, the last occurrence about 150 years ago. Mount Rainier is not extinct; it is dormant. Sulfurous steam is perpetually present in the twin summit craters. Even small eruptions trigger deadly mudflows, or lahars, due to the large number of glaciers. Rainier is considered the most dangerous volcano in the whole Cascade Range.

PRECEDING PAGES: towering Mount Rainier.
LEFT: all aboard for a steam ride.
RIGHT: climbing Camp Muir.

Admiral Peter Rainier (1741–1807), the British sailor for whom Washington state's Mount Rainier is named.

Fire and ice

Meanwhile, ice continues to break down what fire has already built up. Rainier is mantled with 25 permanent glaciers, the largest number for any single peak in the Lower 48. From above, they look like a frozen flower, a sunburst, with fingers of ice radiating down the slopes in every direction. Buried under nearly 57ft (17 meters) of snow annually, the great frozen rivers can move as much as a foot (30cm) per day, depositing boulders and debris in morainal mounds.

Touring the park requires at least a full day. To get properly acquainted, you should plan on two or three days or more, preferably during the week in order to beat the crowds. Entering the park from the west, you are immediately swept away by Rainier's grandeur. Route 706 between the Nisqually Entrance and Paradise truly deserves its reputation as one of America's most breathtaking drives. With views of the mountain and the glistening mass of Nisqually Glacier crowding your windshield, the road passes through a cathedral of aged Douglas fir, western hemlock, and red cedar, climbing 3,400ft (1,036 meters) in 18 miles (29km).

A major flood in November 2006 swept away Sunshine Point Campground and Picnic Area at the Nisqually entrance, the park's only year-round campground. It remains closed indefinitely. Camping is available between June and September at Cougar Rock, between Paradise and Longmire; at Ohanapecosh on the southeast side, at White River on the east side, and Mowich Lake, at the northwest entrance.

Make your first stop at **Longmire ⒶA**, 6 miles (10km) from the entrance. This National Historic District is the oldest settlement in the park and is named for James Longmire, who opened the Mineral Spring Resort here in 1885. The village is now occupied by the **National Park Inn**, a rustic, 25-room hotel, a store, the Longmire Museum, and the Transportation Museum.

The nearby **Wilderness Information Center** is the best place to inquire about weather, road and trail conditions, and obtain backcountry permits for overnight hikes along the park's 300 miles (483km) of trails. A short

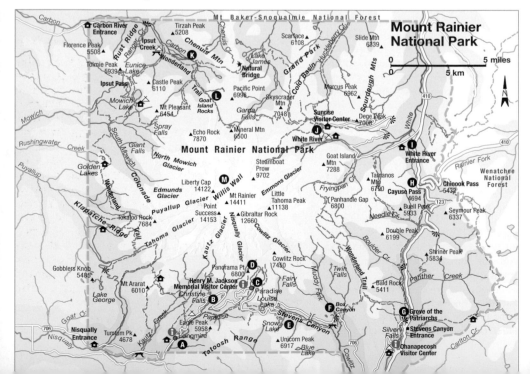

Mount Rainier National Park

jaunt on the **Trail of the Shadows** will help acquaint you with the park's fragile meadow ecology; the walk passes the mineral springs that James Longmire promoted as a wonder cure in the late 19th century and a pioneer cabin built by his son. Longmire also makes a good starting point for backpacking trips on all or part of the **Wonderland Trail**, which makes an epic 93-mile (150km) loop around Mount Rainier. It is hailed as one of the premier trails in the National Park System, a rugged up-and-down passage through a variety of animal and plant communities, skirting glaciers, meadows, lakes, and rivers over the course of a two-week hike.

From Longmire, the road continues along the **Nisqually River**, winding and switchbacking up the grade past **Christine Falls ❸**, just one of several cascades in this area that send glacial runoff plunging down the mountain. To the south, you'll begin to see the jagged peaks of the **Tatoosh Range**, a small mountain spur that outdates Rainier by more than 30 million years. Keep your eyes peeled for **Ricksecker Point Road**, a short loop about 6 miles (10km) from Longmire where you'll be treated to dazzling views of Nisqually Glacier clinging to Rainier's southern face. The icy juggernaut is slipping in your direction, but don't worry. In May 1970, Nisqually made one of the swiftest advances ever recorded – 29ins (74cm) in a single day.

Life in Paradise

As the road climbs into alpine meadows filled with a stunning array of wildflowers, you'll understand why Martha Longmire, upon first seeing the area in 1885, proclaimed: "This must be what Paradise is like!" **Paradise ❸** is cross-hatched with trails that are perfect for an afternoon or a full day of hiking. If you plan on staying longer, consider making reservations (as much as a year in advance) at the renovated historic **Paradise Inn**, a rustic gem built of local cedar in 1916. Be sure to stop at the new **Paradise Jackson Visitor Center** (daily

in summer, weekends and holidays in winter) to see the new park film and exhibits on natural history, purchase books and maps, and check the schedule of ranger-guided nature walks.

If you want to start with an easy hike, the self-guiding **Nisqually Vista Trail** makes a 1-mile (1.5km) loop past glorious splashes of Indian paintbrush, shooting star, and dozens of other wildflowers that follow the retreating melt line up the slope. The 1½-mile (2km) **Alta Vista Trail** is also quite manageable, meandering through wildflowers to a view of Rainier's explosive southern neighbor, Mount Saint Helens, some 45 miles (72km) away. For a tougher hike, the **Skyline Trail** makes a 5-mile (8km) loop to the 6,800ft (2,070-meter) **Panorama Point ❶**, where you'll enjoy fine views of Nisqually Glacier with the Cascade Range trailing off into the southeast. The 5-mile (8km) **Lakes Trail** leads to Reflection Lakes and Louise Lake, both placid tarns that, on still days, reflect Rainier as well as any mirror.

Paradise is also a staging area for most attempts on Mount Rainier's summit. The first well-documented ascent was

TIP

In summer, Mount Rainier gets very busy at weekends: large crowds arrive early and parking lots are full before noon. Try to schedule your visit for a weekday.

Ancient Forests

How do we both use something and simultaneously preserve it? This dilemma is at the heart of the fierce battle being waged over the Northwest's old-growth forests. At the center of the controversy is the diminutive Northern spotted owl, now a threatened species. Spotted owls require the type of layered canopy and diverse ecology found only in old-growth forests. Biologists view the owl as an "indicator species" and say the reason for its decline is loss of habitat. Only 10 percent of the old-growth forests in the Lower 48 remain, most in national parks, while clear-cutting has been permitted on surrounding US Forest Service lands. In 1991, a federal judge restricted Northwest timber sales until the forest service, the timber industry, and environmentalists could formulate a plan to protect the owl. For loggers, the ban meant major job losses, double-digit unemployment, and escalating social ills in hard-hit logging towns. In 1994, a compromise under President Clinton reduced the sale of old-growth timber to less than one-third and established protection zones around critical watersheds and stands of ancient forest. It also provided a $1.2 billion package to help logging communities make the transition to a more diversified economy. Sadly, though, spotted owl populations continue to decline by some 3.7 percent a year, probably due to an influx of barred owls. As a result, the controversy over logging and owls remains.

TIP

The park's 147 miles (237km) of roads are usually accessible from late May into October, when they are closed by snowfall. The road from the Nisqually Entrance to Paradise is open year-round, although snow or avalanches may cause temporary closures.

completed by Hazard Stevens and P.B. Van Trump in 1870, although curious Indians may have done it earlier. John Muir made the climb in 1888, and **Camp Muir**, a climber's outpost, is named in his honor. These days, 10,000 climbers attempt to climb to the summit every year. The 18-mile (29km), two-day trek is extremely strenuous and potentially life-threatening. More than 50 people have died on Mount Rainier. If you would like to make the climb, the National Park Service strongly recommends you hire a guide through Rainier Mountaineering, Inc., a climbing school and outfitter service operated by the famed mountaineer Lou Whittaker. Stop in at the Climbing Information Center in the Guide House, next to Paradise Inn, for permits and information.

Sunrise

From Paradise Jackson Visitor Center, the road loops around Paradise Valley and then runs past Reflection Lakes along the base of the Tatoosh Range, which cradles the glistening waters of Bench and Snow lakes at its feet.

The road enters the sheer, glacier-carved walls of **Stevens Canyon E**. At the end, a short nature trail leads to the **Box Canyon F** gorge, a narrow slot about 100ft (30 meters) deep, sliced out of the rock by the Muddy Fork of the Cowlitz River. About 10 miles (16km) farther, a second nature trail, the delightful **Grove of the Patriarchs G**, loops beneath a canopy of ancient cedar, hemlock, and fir, some as much as 1,000 years old. Turn left at the Stevens Canyon Entrance and swing north on Highway 123 beneath Shriner, Double, and Buell peaks. Continue north on Highway 410 at **Cayuse Pass H** and then take the first left toward the **White River Entrance I** on a winding mountain road that quickly climbs above the timberline. At an elevation of 6,400ft (1,950 meters), **Sunrise Visitor Center J** (early July–mid-Sept, weather permitting), on the park's east side, offers lush wildflower meadows and an intimate look at Rainier's icecap. The closest is **Emmons Glacier**, the largest in the contiguous United States. Take an easy walk on Emmons Vista Trail for the best views. The **Sourdough Ridge Trail** is about 1½ miles (2km) long and steep in places, but a great introduction to the plant life on the drier side of the mountain. Hardier hikers can climb into alpine tundra on the 7-mile (11km) **Burroughs Mountain Trail**. If snow remains, only hikers experienced with an ice axe and crampons should attempt the slippery slopes.

To get off the beaten path, visit the **Carbon River K** region in the park's northwestern corner, 17 miles (27km) from the town of Wilkeson. The Carbon River Road to **Ipsut Creek Campground** was washed out by the 2006 flood. Foot and bike camping are permitted, but car camping is no longer allowed. This is a jumping-off point for day hikes into temperate rainforest and overnight trips to Mowich, Eunice, or James lakes or to the foot of Carbon Glacier. High above the craggy **Goat Island Rocks L** is the headwall of a glacial cirque known as **Willis Wall M** – a Mecca for rock climbers. ❑

BELOW: taking a break in the Grove of Patriarchs.

Danger on the Mountain

The volcano of Mount Rainier is potentially the most dangerous in the Cascades, with 25 major glaciers, and constant geothermal activity

Mount Rainier towers over a population of 2.5 million residents in the Seattle Tacoma metropolitan area, and its drainage system via the Columbia River impacts an additional 500,000 residents in southwest Washington and northwest Oregon. With the greatest single-peak glacial system in the United States – along with Paradise's record winter snowfalls – the Mountain is the most potentially dangerous episodically active volcano in the Cascades.

There are 25 major glaciers on Mount Rainier and numerous unnamed snow or ice patches. The glaciers radiate from the summit, like spokes on a wheel, creating deep-cut valleys. Climate change is already changing snowfall patterns and the shrinking glaciers throughout the Lower 48, creating unstable geology in seismically active volcanoes.

Geothermal activity, as evidenced by sulfurous steam in the twin summit craters, is perpetually present. Eruptions melt glacial ice rapidly. The Mountain would barely have to clear its throat to cause a catastrophic Mount St Helens-type avalanche mudflow, or lahar. It's happened at least 60 times since the Ice Age ended, and will certainly happen again.

By far the largest lahars in Rainier's million-year-old history were the concurrent Osceola and Paradise mudflows, 5,600 years ago. These lahars collapsed 2,000ft (600 meters) of the old mountain top and swept a 70ft (21-meter) deep wall of debris through the White River and Nisqually river valleys to the park's northern boundary.

The mudflows significantly altered the Puget Sound coastline, pushing it out several miles. The scar from this collapse is a horseshoe-shaped basin some 1.2 miles (2km) wide, open to the northeast. Communities like Puyallup (PEW-allup), west of the park, are built on the mudflow. In 1947, a similar mudflow devastated Kautz Creek, near the Nisqually Entrance.

Even more frequent, and of concern, are smaller glacial outburst flows, stream capture, and floods in glacial valleys have caused debris flows. Filled

with glacial ice blocks and boulders, these debris flows reshape the valleys. Fifteen such flows have raced down river valleys since 1986 alone.

The Great Flood of 2006

Heavy rainfall and flooding are a constant danger in the Northwest. Pacific storms blow moisture-laden clouds onshore that rapidly drop their heavy load as they meet high mountain ranges like the Olympics and the Cascades.

In November 2006, 18ins (45cm) of rain falling over 36 hours turned into a nightmare of epic proportions for Mount Rainier National Park. In what has been called The Great Flood of 2006, the Nisqually, Carbon, Stevens, Ohanapecosh, and White rivers and Kautz Creek, exiting the park through steep glacial valleys, overflowed their banks. The floodwaters caused mudslides; wiped out levees and filled reservoirs with debris; washed away roads and campgrounds; damaged part of the park's main circular Wonderland Trail and other trails; and downed telephone, electrical, and sewer systems. Flooding affected the whole park, but was particularly destructive in the heavily visited Paradise area, destroying sections of the Nisqually Road and cutting off Longmire and Paradise from the Nisqually entrance. The whole park was forced to close for an unprecedented six months to assess damage, repair, and rebuild. Mother Nature had spoken. ❏

RIGHT: parked cars partially submerged in floodwater.

CRATER LAKE

Oregon's only national park is centered on a wall of volcanic cliffs encircling a lake of indescribable blue. Even in a region of volcanic wonders, there's nothing quite like this caldera

Main attractions
CRATER LAKE
STEEL VISITOR CENTER
SINNOTT MEMORIAL OVERLOOK
   GEOLOGY EXHIBITS
HISTORIC CRATER LAKE LODGE
RIM DRIVE
WIZARD ISLAND BOAT TOURS
MOUNT SCOTT TRAIL
THE PINNACLES
CASTLE CREST WILDFLOWER
   GARDEN TRAIL
GODFREY GLEN TRAIL
PACIFIC CREST NATIONAL SCENIC
   TRAIL SEGMENT
RANGER-LED SNOWSHOE WALKS ON
   WINTER WEEKENDS

Crater Lake has been called "the bluest lake on earth" and "the shimmering jewel of the Cascades." It's a picture of nature in repose, a lake so round, so blue, so perfectly tranquil that it seems unearthly. Its waters are cupped like a chalice offered to the sky. Stars reflect on its surface like a thousand torches. How odd, then, that such an enchanting place, such flawless composure, is the by-product of a violent explosion. It occurred some 7,700 years ago when **Mount Mazama** erupted and collapsed. The event was catastrophic, filling nearby canyons with hundreds of feet of ash and sending debris as far downwind as Alberta, Canada. The 1980 eruption of Mount Saint Helens pales by comparison.

According to a Klamath Indian legend, Mazama's demise was caused by a fierce battle between Llao and Skell, the spirits of the underworld and sky. Spurned by a human female, Llao rushed to the peak of Mount Mazama and rained fire on her people in punishment. Skell took pity on the humans and, after an earth-shaking confrontation, drove Llao back into the bowels of the volcano and buried him under a torrent of rock and flame.

Geologists tell a similar story in a slightly more dispassionate way. Like other volcanic peaks in the Cascade Range, they say, Mazama is the product of a tectonic process that causes the ocean floor to be forced under the North American plate. As the ocean bedrock is driven deeper into the earth, it's transformed by heat and pressure into molten magma, which, in some cases, wells up to the surface in great gushes of mountain-building, or mountain-destroying, lava and ash. The eruption probably lasted only a few days, but so much magma was ejected from reservoirs beneath Mount Mazama that its walls buckled inward, leaving a gaping maw.

LEFT: Crater Lake.
RIGHT: Wizard Island.

Natural volcanic spires.

Not dead: just sleeping

Snow and rain blowing in from the Pacific took about 800 years to fill the caldera, which, at a depth of 1,943ft (592 meters), now contains the deepest freshwater lake in the US. Small eruptions have followed the collapse, and warm springs still flow far below the lake's surface. But in recent years, Mazama has been relatively quiet. Not dead, geologists warn, just sleeping.

Today, the lake sits at the bull's-eye of **Crater Lake National Park ❻**, created in 1902 at the urging of William Gladstone Steel. A tireless campaigner, Steel became enchanted by the lake as a boy. Thanks to his enthusiasm, the lake is circled by a lovely 33-mile (53km) road known as **Rim Drive**, which is punctuated by more than two dozen scenic overlooks and several trailheads.

Travelers on the main north-south Interstate 5 artery may prefer to access the park from its quiet North Entrance (only open in summer). The park's main visitor hub is on the southwest side of the caldera, reached via State Route 62 from Klamath Falls. Seasonal visitor services are located at Mazama Village, Park Headquarters, and Rim Village. Mazama Motor Inn and the recently renovated historic **Crater Lake Lodge** in Rim Village are open from May to October.

Steel Visitor Center next to park headquarters has year-round information, exhibits, a film about the park, and an onsite post office. **Rim Village ❶** is the center of activity for food, lodging, and guest services during the tourist season. Stop at **Rim Visitor Center** for information on hiking, campfire talks, and guided nature walks. Exhibits about geology and lake research are located at nearby **Sinnott Memorial Overlook**, where sweeping views will help you get a feel for the lay of the land. The caldera is ringed with a blanket of conifers that drop to the water's edge and envelop the mountain in every direction but north, where the ash-smothered **Pumice Desert** remains stark and treeless. A few of Mazama's sister peaks, including Mount Scott and Union Peak, flank the caldera, and 9,182ft (2,800-meter) Mount Thielsen towers to the north.

Driving northwest from Rim Visitor Center, you'll encounter several

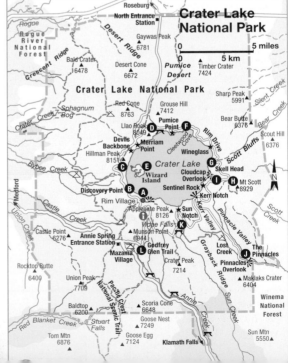

landmarks. The first, **Discovery Point B**, is believed to be the spot where, in 1853, the first white men – a group of prospectors searching for the fabled "Lost Cabin" gold mine – set eyes on the lake, which they promptly named Deep Blue Lake. About 2 miles (3km) up the road, a second peak, the 8,013ft (2,442-meter) **Watchman**, towers over the caldera. A short, steep trail leads to a fire tower atop the peak, affording the best views on the western shore. With binoculars in hand, you'll see scores of soaring birds in summer and the fall – falcons, hawks, and, if you're lucky, bald or golden eagles.

Almost directly north, **Hillman Peak C** is one of Mazama's ancient volcanoes, now sheared in half by the mountain's collapse. Farther along the caldera wall, a formation known as the Devils Backbone – a wall of volcanic rock – juts into the water. Beyond that, **Llao Rock D** is an ancient lava flow that hangs from the rim. Keep your eyes open for protected peregrine falcons, which build eyries in the cracks and overhangs.

The most prominent landmark on this stretch of the rim is **Wizard Island E**, a cone-shaped "volcano within a volcano." It rises more than 700ft (210 meters) above water level like a wizard's cap. The Wizard Island Overlook offers the best view. If time allows, you can also catch a concessionaire-run tour boat to the island from **Cleetwood Cove F** on the northeast lakeshore. The mile-long (1.5km) trail from Cleetwood Cove Overlook to the boat landing is extremely steep. If you are in poor health, or simply out of shape, you may not want to try it.

Boat tours are first come, first served. They last for one hour and 45 minutes and are led by a park naturalist. Along the way, you may spot waterfalls cascading toward the lake, cormorants and gulls skimming the water, a bald eagle circling over the cliffs, or a variety of waterfowl bobbing peacefully on the surface. On the island, the fairly strenuous **Wizard Island Summit Trail** leads about a mile (1.5km) to its crater, which stands at an elevation of 6,940ft (2,115 meters).

Back on the road, the eastern side of the lake features three extraordinary viewpoints. The first, **Skell Head G**,

Rim Drive would be closed by snow for most of the year were it not for a massive clearing operation that begins in April. Most of the road is covered by more than 20ft (6 meters) of snow, but this is all cleared by the beginning of July.

BELOW: boat tour docking at Wizard Island.

Crater Lake in Winter

Average winter snowfall at Crater Lake is approximately 45ft (13.7 meters), making it one of the snowiest places in the Pacific Northwest. Cross-country skiing, snowshoeing, and snow camping attract winter sports enthusiasts prepared for the conditions. Ranger led snowshoe walks on weekends are a good introduction to winter ecology. Group limit is 30, and advance reservations are required. Check with Steel Visitor Center. Highway 62 and Munson Valley Road are plowed in winter and kept open as far as Rim Village. Rim Drive and North Entrance start to be plowed in late April, but areas such as East Rim Drive and Pinnacles Road typically aren't snowfree until July. Services at Mazama Village and Rim Village are closed from October to late May, except for a café/gift shop at the rim.

BELOW: feet up at Crater Lake Lodge.
BELOW: the Pacific Crest National Scenic Trail.

is an ancient volcanic formation that bulges toward the water. About 2½ miles (4km) farther on, a steep, 2½-mile (4km) trail climbs to the summit of 8,929ft (2,722-meter) **Mount Scott** ⓗ, the park's highest peak. The path makes a switchback ascent through dense stands of subalpine fir and clusters of wildflowers before rising above the timber line, where gnarled whitebark pine manage to eke out an existence under brutal conditions. Mount Scott is the finest visual perch in the park. Keep your eyes peeled for red-tailed hawks, golden eagles, and other raptors soar on the air currents that curl up the mountain like invisible waves.

Beyond the Mount Scott trailhead, a spur road leads to **Cloudcap** ⓘ, the highest overlook on the rim, where you can get good views of Phantom Ship, an island of tough volcanic rock that pokes through the surface just offshore. For a closer look, stop at **Kerr Notch**, a classic U-shaped valley carved by glaciers well before Mazama's catastrophic eruption. If time allows, you can pick up the 7-mile (11km) spur road that shoots out to **The Pinnacles** ⓙ, spiky,

fang-like formations – some 100ft (30 meters) tall or more – that have eroded out of a bed of volcanic ash.

Return to Rim Drive and turn left. The last leg of the journey takes you past **Vidae Falls** ⓚ, where you can picnic next to a stepped 100ft (30-meter) cascade. About 3 miles (5km) farther on, the **Castle Crest Wildflower Garden Trail** takes you on a half-mile (1km) stroll through a medley of blossoming flowers during the summer months. Interpretive signs point out the names of species that grow beneath the cool understory of old-growth fir and hemlock as well as those that prefer the sunny meadows. A variety of hummingbirds summer in this area, and you can often see or hear them zipping through the underbrush.

Beyond the rim

The park doesn't end with Rim Drive. Areas beyond the caldera are quieter, and you're more likely to glimpse the shy wildlife, such as elk, black-tailed deer, pronghorn, and black bear. About 2 miles (3km) south of park headquarters, for example, the **Godfrey Glen Trail** ⓛ makes an easy 1-mile (2km) loop through a dense stand of fir and hemlock that grows at the edge of a weirdly eroded canyon of volcanic ash. A bit farther down the road, at the seasonal Mazama Campground, 2-mile (3km) **Annie Creek Canyon Trail** enters yet another canyon carved out of ancient beds of ash, which are now embroidered with wildflowers.

For longer hikes, a segment of the **Pacific Crest National Scenic Trail** runs the length of the park, swerving around the lake to the west and then flanking the stark, ash-covered Pumice Desert, reclining beneath Mount Thielsen just north of the park boundary. Several spur trails make interesting side trips along the way. It takes two to three days, possibly more, to cover the entire 33 miles (53km), but short stretches are accessible from Highway 62 west of Annie Spring Station and the North Entrance Road. ❏

ALASKA

The USA's largest state is a land of superlatives:
its enormous national parks contain the
continent's tallest mountain, the largest sub-polar
ice field, and a glacier larger than Rhode Island

here it stands, thrusting mightily
against the sky. At 20,320ft (6,194
meters) above sea level, **Mount
McKinley** is the perfect symbol of
Alaska. In a land of superlatives and
extremes, this granite monolith is the
49th state's most dominating feature.
It is also the centerpiece of **Denali
National Park and Preserve ❶**. Towering above its Alaska Range neighbors, Mount McKinley – also known
by its Athapaskan name meaning "The
High One" – is a wild, desolate world
of ice, snow, and extreme cold, much
different from the semi-wilderness
that most park visitors experience.

Cold mountain

Mount McKinley's great height, combined with its subarctic location, makes
it one of the coldest mountains on the
planet. And the peak is so massive, it
creates its own weather systems; some
storms have produced winds greater
than 150mph (240kph). No wonder
Denali has earned a reputation as the
ultimate challenge in North American
mountaineering. But the great peak's
magnetism also tugs on those who'll
never climb its slopes. Denali is the
most popular of Alaska's federal parklands. And the majority of visitors have
two main goals: first, to see Denali; second, to see Alaska's wildlife.

Unfortunately, the chances of seeing the continent's highest peak are
not very good. Mount McKinley is visible only one out of every three days
between Memorial Day and Labor
Day, Denali's main tourist season.
But opportunities to view wildlife
are much greater. Nearly everyone
who travels into the 6-million-acre
(2.4-million-hectare) park sees at least
one of Alaska's "big four": grizzly bear,
Dall sheep, moose, or caribou. Wolves
have also become increasingly visible
in recent years.

Main attractions
DENALI NATIONAL PARK AND PRESERVE
WRANGELL-ST ELIAS NATIONAL
  PARK AND PRESERVE
KENAI FJORDS NATIONAL PARK
LAKE CLARK NATIONAL PARK AND
  PRESERVE
ANIAKCHAK NATIONAL MONUMENT
  AND PRESERVE
GLACIER BAY NATIONAL PARK AND
  PRESERVE
KLONDIKE GOLD RUSH NATIONAL
  HISTORIC PARK
SITKA NATIONAL HISTORICAL PARK
GATES OF THE ARCTIC NATIONAL
  PARK AND PRESERVE
KOBUK VALLEY NATIONAL PARK
BERING LAND BRIDGE NATIONAL
  PRESERVE

PRECEDING PAGES: hiking in Denali.
LEFT: catch of the day at Homer harbor.
RIGHT: fishing south of Anchorage.

TIP

For advance camp–
ground or shuttle
reservations in Denali
National Park, you
should call 800-622-
7275.

Abundant wildlife

It's not by chance that Denali offers such wildlife riches. Situated 120 miles (193km) southwest of Fairbanks and 240 miles (386km) northwest of Anchorage, the park was established in 1917 to protect the region's large mammals, especially Dall sheep, from hunting. Because wildlife viewing is a key ingredient of most people's "Denali experience," and because most visitors don't leave the park's single 92-mile (148km) road, travel restrictions have been enacted to ensure that uncontrolled traffic doesn't drive wildlife from the road corridor.

Trip planning begins at **Denali National Park Visitor Center**, which has exhibits, a park film, and books and maps. The park road is paved as far as Savage River and may be driven by cars, but the majority of visitors who "explore" Denali via the road system use the park's pricey shuttle-bus service. Green shuttle buses begin leaving the Wilderness Access Center at milepost 1 early in the morning and continue on a regular schedule through mid-afternoon. Suggested items to

bring: food, drink, and warm clothes, none of which is available beyond the park entrance. Midsummer temperatures range between 40°F (4°C) and 85°F (29°C). Those seeking guided tours may travel on buses operated by a park concessionaire. Drivers describe the park's wildlife, plants, geology, and history on 5- to 8-hour excursions (advance reservations recommended).

Beyond the road corridor are millions of acres of scenic wildlands. Backcountry explorers wishing to camp overnight must obtain a permit, issued at the visitor center. Denali's backcountry areas have been divided into 87 units; many have visitor quotas to prevent crowding. Wilderness travelers are cautioned that backcountry trips require careful planning and a knowledge of bears, minimum-impact camping, river crossings, route finding, and wildlife-viewing ethics.

The park also has six road-accessible campgrounds, plus one at Morino, near the railroad depot. In peak season, they fill quickly. Lodging is available at privately operated lodges in the Katishna area at the end of the park road or outside the park along the George Parks Highway.

Accessible by railroad, bus, or private vehicle, Denali National Park is often filled to overflowing in July and August. Visitors who haven't made advance reservations will need to allow at least two days to get a campground site or shuttle seat. Registration for shuttle-bus seats and campground sites can be made in person at the visitor center up to two days in advance.

New discovery

Thirty years ago, **Wrangell-St Elias National Park and Preserve ❷** was an overlooked and undervalued mountain wilderness. Created in 1980, the nation's largest park – at 13 million acres (5.3 million hectares), the size of six Yellowstones – was also one of its least known. But some time in the late 1980s, Wrangell-St Elias was "discovered." And Kit Mullen, a park

BELOW: the abandoned mining camp of Kennicott.

staffer from 1981 to 1992, guesses that this park abutting the Canadian border "will become the next Denali, in terms of visitor use. There's so much access, probably more than any other national park in Alaska; you've got two roads into the park and airstrips all over."

The northern entry is the 42-mile (67km) -long gravel **Nabesna Road** (generally passable for two-wheel-drive vehicles in summer, but high-clearance and/or four-wheel drive may be needed), which connects Alaska's highway system with the tiny mining community of Nabesna. The main access into Wrangell-St Elias is **McCarthy Road**. Sixty miles (98km) long and also unpaved, it stretches from Chitina, at the park's boundary, to the gateway community of **McCarthy**. (To enter McCarthy, visitors must leave their vehicles and cross the Kennicott River on hand-pulled trams.)

The number of people traveling McCarthy Road has grown from 5,000 in 1988 to 65,000 in 2009. Only a fraction of those who drive McCarthy Road visit the backcountry. Most spend time in McCarthy – for decades

a haven for Alaskan recluses, but now a tourist town – hike to the nearby **Kennicott** and **Root** glaciers, or travel the 4½ miles (7km) to the now abandoned Kennicott copper-mining camp.

The park's real treasures, however, lie beyond such roadside attractions, in a wild and magnificent alpine world that guide Bob Jacobs calls "North America's mountain kingdom." It's a kingdom that includes four major mountain ranges and six of the continent's 10 highest peaks, including 18,000ft (5,500-meter) **Mount St Elias**. Here, too, is North America's largest sub-polar ice-field, the Bagley, which feeds a system of gigantic glaciers; one of those, the **Malaspina**, is larger than Rhode Island. Rock walls rise thousands of feet above glacially carved canyons, like the Chitistone and Nizina. And rugged, remote coastline is bounded by tidewater glaciers and jagged peaks. The park's alpine superlatives, along with those of neighboring **Kluane National Park ❸** in Canada and Glacier Bay National Park, have prompted their combined designation as a World Heritage site.

TIP

There are several private lodges and bed and breakfast establishments along the McCarthy Road, especially in McCarthy, Kennicott, and the highway communities.

BELOW:
falling tidewater glaciers.

The Murie Center

Olaf and Margaret (Mardy) Murie were early pioneers in the wilderness movement. Mardy's passionate testimony to Congress helped pass the landmark 1980 Alaska Lands Act, which protected many pristine Alaska lands. Murie Science and Learning Center, at milemarker 1.4 in Denali National Park, is part of a national effort to increase the amount of scientific research in the parks. The center represents eight of Alaska's Arctic and subarctic national parks and teams with a growing number of partners in research and educational activities. The building is open to visitors and features an exhibit area, classroom, and office space for visiting scientists. It offers educational activities and seminars during the summer and serves as Denali's winter visitor center, from late September until May 14 every year.

The alpine forget-me-not, the state flower of Alaska.

There's a certain irony to the new-found interest in Wrangell-St Elias: much of what's been "discovered" by modern-day explorers was known to local residents centuries ago. One of the park's best-known overland routes, the primitive and rugged **Goat Trail**, was traditionally used by Athapaskan people for hunting and trading. Most of Wrangell-St Elias's natural wonders are inaccessible to those who remain along the road system. Air-taxi services provide transportation into the park, and guide outfits offer river rafting, climbing, and trekking opportunities. Increasingly popular are "flightseeing" tours out of McCarthy or communities that neighbor Wrangell-St Elias.

Kenai Fjords

The third (and only other) federal parkland connected to Alaska's highway system is 670,000-acre (270,000-hectare) **Kenai Fjords National Park** ❹, located on the Kenai Peninsula in south-central Alaska. As its name suggests, this unit is dominated by coastal fjords: long and steep-sided glacially carved valleys now filled with seawa-ter, and accessible only by floatplane or boat. High above the rugged coastline is the 300-sq-mile (780-sq-km) **Harding Icefield**, whose eight tidewater glaciers calve icebergs into the fjords, creating thunderous booms audible 20 miles (32km) away.

The best-known fjord is **Aialik Bay**, simply because it's the closest to the park's gateway community, **Seward**. A favorite of sea kayakers, Aialik and neighboring **Harris Bay** are also vis-ited daily by commercial tour boats, weather and seas permitting, during the summer. Only rarely explored, the park's outer fjords are ideally suited to wilderness travelers seeking solitude. Though they barely touch the tip of the park's coastal wilderness, full-day boat tours nevertheless offer quite a show: calving glaciers, rugged scenery, and abundant marine life – whales, porpoises, sea otters, sea lions, seals, and thousands of seabirds.

Despite all of Kenai Fjord's coastal splendors, its chief attraction is an inland, road-accessible glacier about 130 miles (200km) by road from Anchorage. In 1997, about two-thirds

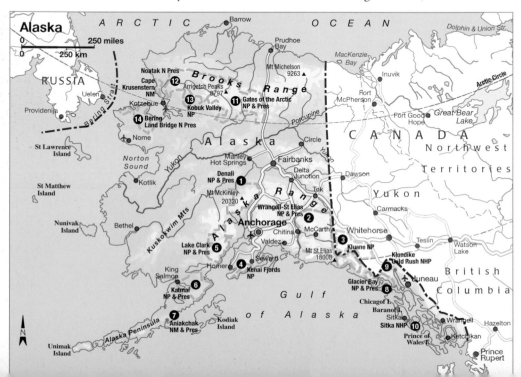

of the park's 306,000 visitors traveled the 9-mile (14km) gravel road (open to vehicles from late May–early Oct) to **Exit Glacier**. A gentle trail leads to the glacier's snout, while a steeper trail follows the glacier's edge and allows visitors to peer into caverns beneath the ice and hear its groaning movements.

Like most Alaskan parks, Kenai Fjords has a limited number of facilities both along the road system and in the backcountry. Park headquarters in Seward is open year-round. A visitor center at Exit Glacier offers exhibits, a bookstore, and nature walks and interpretive programs between Memorial Day and Labor Day. A small walk-in campground is located nearby.

Lake Clark

With abundant wildlife and wilderness, **Lake Clark National Park and Preserve ❺** epitomizes wild Alaska. Indeed, this 4-million-acre (1.6-million-hectare) unit may be the quintessential Alaskan parkland. Within its boundaries lie two active volcanoes, including one that erupted from 1989–1990. The cliffs along its rugged coastline serve as rookeries for multitudes of seabirds. Two major mountain systems, the Aleutian and Alaska ranges, join to form the Chigmit and Neocola mountains, whose pristine snowcapped peaks are mostly unclimbed. The park embraces a remarkably diverse mix of plant communities: from coastal rainforest to boreal forest typical of interior Alaska, and several varieties of tundra.

Several river and lake systems, including three designated wild rivers, offer world-class fishing. And Lake Clark's recreational opportunities appeal to a wide variety of user groups, from hunters and anglers to river runners, kayakers, hikers, mountaineers, and wildlife enthusiasts. Located on the western side of **Cook Inlet**, Lake Clark can easily be reached by air from several different communities: Anchorage, Kenai, Homer, and Iliamna.

Here, then, is a national park with fantastic scenery, easy access, and diverse recreational opportunities. Yet Lake Clark remains among Alaska's least appreciated national parks for a variety of reasons. First, it doesn't have a focus, like Katmai's bears, Denali's

Lake Clark's various ecosystems support more than 100 species of birds and nearly 40 species of mammals.

BELOW LEFT: a creek-side cabin near Anchorage. **BELOW:** Exit Glacier's outwash plain, Kenai Fjords National Park.

Grizzly Bears

While their numbers dwindle in other states, in Alaska, grizzlies thrive. But do they deserve their bad reputations as ruthless killers?

Alaska is often called the last stronghold of North America's grizzly bears, and for good reason: this is where *Ursus arctos horribilis* has been given its last, best chance to survive. Tens of thousands of grizzlies once roamed the lower 48 states. Now, there are fewer than 1,000, distributed in isolated groups in Montana, Wyoming, Idaho, and Washington.

In Alaska, meanwhile, the population of grizzlies and their coastal counterparts, brown bears, is estimated to be about 40,000. Powerful carnivores equipped to kill other large mammals, grizzlies deserve our respect. When surprised or threatened, they'll do whatever it takes to protect themselves. That may mean fleeing. Or attacking.

Teddy bears with teeth

Bear attacks on humans are, in fact, fairly rare, yet grizzlies have been portrayed as ruthless, marauding killers. "We've been raised with an ingrained fear of bears that's out of proportion to reality," says an Alaska biologist, Mike McDonald. "We've been taught that if you see a bear, you're gonna get eaten."

Several precautions can be taken to minimize the chances of an unwanted encounter. Whenever possible, walk in open country, during daylight hours. When passing through forested areas or thick brush, make noise. Sing, talk loudly, clap your hands. Keep alert and look for signs of bears: fresh tracks, bear scat, claw marks on trees, matted vegetation, or animal carcasses.

Traveling in groups is recommended: no grizzly bear assault has ever been reported on a group of six or more people. Cook all meals away from tents and hang food out of reach. After fishing, change clothes before entering your tent and store the fish away from camp.

You should put garbage in airtight containers and pack it out. When establishing camp, stay away from trails and berry patches. And avoid areas where scavengers have gathered, or which smell rotten. A bear's food cache may be nearby.

If you encounter a bear, talk to it. But don't yell. "That might be interpreted as aggression," McDonald says. "Don't growl." And don't run. That will almost certainly trigger a bear's predatory instincts. When dealing with a sow and cubs, avoid getting between mother and young. As a rule, bigger is better: with two or more people, stand side by side or stretch out a piece of clothing.

Climb a tree or play dead!

In forested areas, it may help to climb a tree. But young grizzlies can climb and even adults can pull their way quite high. Learn to recognize when a bear is stressed.

Warning signs include yawning, salivating, huffing, growling, flattened ears, stiff-legged walk, swatting vegetation, or jaw popping. Many threatening displays end with a bear walking away. And even when a bear charges, often it's a bluff. But if a grizzly does make contact, the best thing to do is play dead. Lie on your stomach or curl into a ball with your hands behind your neck.

Playing dead, though, isn't appropriate if a bear shows predatory behavior: instead of charging in a rush, such a bear will show intense interest and may circle or stalk you. If you are sure that you're being treated as prey, never play dead. Luckily, such occurrences are very rare. ❑

LEFT: time for a take-away supper.

"High One" and wildlife viewing, or Kenai Fjords' Exit Glacier and coastal tours. Second, it's not accessible by road. Third, it lacks visitor facilities. There's little apart from a field head-quarters at Port Alsworth, a small community on the shores of 42-mile (68km) Lake Clark.

The National Park Service largely depends on the private sector to pro-vide amenities. Several privately owned wilderness lodges are located within, or near, Lake Clark, and more than three dozen guide services operate in the park. Those who explore the park on their own should be wholly self-suf-ficient and prepared for cool and often wet weather. Storms commonly delay backcountry flights, so it's best to have a flexible schedule.

Katmai

An annual ritual begins in early July, as thousands of bright, silvery sockeye salmon push upstream toward **Brooks Lake**. As they near their spawning grounds, the salmon face one final obstacle: 5ft (2-meter) -high **Brooks Falls**. It's not high enough to stop the fish, but it's enough to stall them.

Following the salmon to Brooks Falls is *Ursus arctos*, the brown bear. Coastal equivalents of grizzlies, brown bears are usually solitary animals. But here, in the presence of abundant salmon, they've learned to tolerate each other. As many as a dozen bears may gather at the falls in July, with 35 to 40 inhabiting the 1½-mile (2km) -long Brooks River drainage. The bears, in turn, attract humans. When bears are fishing, people can be found at the Brooks Falls viewing platform from dawn to dusk.

Located in 4.7-million-acre (1.9-million-hectare) **Katmai National Park and Preserve ❻**, 300 miles (483km) southwest of Anchorage, Brooks Falls and nearby **Brooks Camp** have become one of Alaska's fastest-growing visitor destinations, thanks to the park's more than 2,000 easy-to-see bears. But only in the last

decade has Katmai become renowned for its bears. For most of its existence, Katmai's primary appeals have been sportfishing and the **Valley of 10,000 Smokes**, formed in 1912 by a giant volcanic eruption.

The eruption caused the collapse of Mount Katmai, devastated the sur-rounding landscape, and created thou-sands of steaming fumaroles (only a few active vents remain). Scientific expeditions to the area led to the crea-tion of Katmai National Monument in 1918; the monument was enlarged and elevated to park status in 1980.

Katmai received little attention until entrepreneur Ray Petersen established five remote fishing camps within the unit during the 1940s. The largest was Brooks, where clients fished for rainbow trout and salmon and visited the valley.

Now, as then, seasonally open Brooks Camp is Katmai's premier attraction. But bears, not fishing or volcanic devastation, are what lure most people. Visitors must fly in, using plane services based in **King Salmon**. Those who stay overnight use the park

There are at least 14 active volcanoes in Katmai – more than in any other national park. The eruption of Novarupta in 1912 was the largest volcanic event of the 20th century.

BELOW:
catch of the day.

Detail of a totem pole at Sitka National Historical Park.

BELOW: exploring a glacier.
BELOW RIGHT: carving on a tree trunk at Glacier Bay National Park.

campgrounds or Brooks Lodge cabins. Reservations are essential for either. But a large and growing number of visitors are day-trippers who stay for only a few hours.

Beyond Brooks is the "unseen" Katmai: vast untrammeled wilderness that includes a multitude of destinations, from the Valley of 10,000 Smokes (daily bus tours offer sightseers a glimpse of the barren landscape) to glacier-covered mountains, the **Alagnak Wild River**, and rugged fjord-like coastal areas.

Southwest of Katmai, on the Alaska Peninsula, **Aniakchak National Monument and Preserve ❼** was established in 1978 to protect Aniakchak Caldera, one of the world's great craters. Aniakchak, in the volcanically active Aleutian Mountains, formed 3,500 years ago and last erupted in 1931. The 6-mile (9.5km) -wide, 2,500ft (762 meter) -deep crater includes lava flows, cinder cones, explosion pits, and Surprise Lake, the source of the Aniakchak River. The river cascades through a 1,500ft (460-meter) gash in the crater wall known

as The Gates. Remote and with notoriously bad weather, Aniakchak is one of Alaska's least-visited parks.

Glacier Bay

Much has changed since John Muir found an "icy wilderness unspeakably pure and sublime" during his 1879 visit to Glacier Bay. **Grand Pacific Glacier**, which carved the bay, has receded 20 miles (32km). Cruise ships and tour boats annually bring more than 400,000 visitors. The bay, its glaciers, wildlife, and surrounding landforms are now protected by 3.3-million-acre (1.3-million-hectare) **Glacier Bay National Park and Preserve ❽**.

Yet, for all its changes, Glacier Bay remains an icy wilderness still largely unspoiled and, by most standards, remote. Sixty miles (97km) northwest of Juneau in Alaska's Panhandle, the park can be reached only by boat or plane. And, except for a short stretch of road and limited facilities (including visitor center, campground, trail system, lodge, and restaurant) at **Bartlett Cove**, Glacier Bay is undeveloped. It is, in essence, a backcountry "marine

park" with a glacial landscape that is best explored by boat.

Sixty-two miles (100km) long and surrounded by a horseshoe rim of mountains, Glacier Bay is best known for its 17 tidewater glaciers and whale watching: in summer, the bay is frequented by orcas, minkes, and humpbacks. Porpoises, sea otters, sea lions, harbor seals, and seabirds also populate its waters, while bears, wolves, moose, and mountain goats inhabit its shores. The landscape also shows the stages of plant succession left by a retreating glacier: lush coastal forests give way to fields of willow and alder, soft shrubby mats, and, finally, bare rock and blue ice. The bay has about a dozen inlets or arms to explore – one reason it's considered a kayakers' paradise. But most visitors visit Glacier Bay in the comfort of cruise ships or charter boats, which make daily sightseeing trips.

Beyond Glacier Bay itself, the park encompasses miles and miles of rugged, rarely visited outer coastline. Inland are huge ice fields, dozens of glaciers, legions of unnamed and unclimbed mountains, and a portion of the spectacular **Alsek River**, born in neighboring British Columbia.

The discovery of gold in Canada's Yukon brought thousands of hopeful prospectors to Skagway and Dyea, Alaska. Their gold-hungry stampede is commemorated by **Klondike Gold Rush National Historic Park** ❾, 80 miles (130km) by air north of Juneau, at the northern end of Alaska's Inside Passage. The park includes historic buildings and museum exhibits in Skagway and portions of Chilkoot and White Pass trails, all prominent in the 1898 gold rush.

On Baranof Island in Alaska's Southeastern Panhandle, the small **Sitka National Historical Park** ❿ the state's first federal park, commemorates the 1804 Battle of Sitka, the last major conflict between Europeans (Russians) and the natives of the northwest coast (Tlingit Indians). The 113-acre (46-hectare) park contains a temperate rainforest, a scenic coastal trail, Tlingit totem poles and crafts, and the Russian Bishop's House, built in 1842 and the oldest intact piece of Russian-American architecture.

TIP

The best time to explore Glacier Bay is mid-May through mid-September, but, even in summer, you should come prepared for rainy, cool weather.

BELOW LEFT: all aboard a sightseeing trip round the bay.
BELOW: a harbor seal on Glacier Bay.

Gates of the Arctic

In 1929, while exploring the North Fork of the Koyukuk River in Alaska's Brooks Range, wilderness advocate Robert Marshall encountered "a precipitous pair of mountains, one on each side" of the stream. The eastern peak Marshall named **Boreal Mountain**; its western neighbor he christened **Frigid Crags**. Together, they became the Gates of the Arctic.

A half-century later, in 1980, Boreal Mountain, Frigid Crags, and several million acres of Arctic landscape were forever protected in **Gates of the Arctic National Park and Preserve ⓫**. Four times larger than Yellowstone, Gates of the Arctic girdles the central **Brooks Range**, the Rocky Mountains' northernmost extension. Billed as America's "ultimate wilderness," the 13,200-sq-mile (34,200-sq-km) unit lies entirely above the Arctic Circle and has some of the continent's wildest, most fragile, ecosystems. Its forests, alder thickets, and tundra are home to 36 species of mammals, including grizzly and black bears, wolves, moose, Dall sheep, caribou, and wolverines.

Capping the range are wave upon wave of mountain ridges and jagged peaks – most of them nameless – that seem to stretch forever. The mountains are dissected by expansive U-shaped valleys that magnify the sense of wide-open spaces. Among the streams knifing through the park are six officially designated "wild rivers." Chief visitor attractions, besides "the Gates," include 8,510ft (2,594-meter) Mount Igikpak, Walker Lake, and a group of towering granite spires called the Arrigetch Peaks.

Since park managers are required to manage Gates of the Arctic as wilderness, no maintained trails or other visitor facilities have been developed within its boundaries. The only easy access is by plane, though it's also possible to enter by boat or walk in from the **Dalton Highway**, which roughly parallels the park's eastern edge. Most visitors fly into the park from **Bettles**, the regional supply center and ranger station site.

Visitors are warned that they should be "fully competent in outdoor skills" and totally self-sufficient. The best time to visit is from June through August. Even then, be prepared for occasional freezing temperatures. A few wilderness lodges or cabins located near the park offer some degree of Arctic comfort, and several locally based outfitters conduct reasonable guided trips.

Adjoining Gates of the Arctic to the west is **Noatak National Preserve ⓬**, a pristine, mountain-ringed river basin, which includes the 65-mile (105km) Grand Canyon of the Noatak (a migration route for animals between Arctic and subarctic environments) and an array of flora as diverse as anywhere in the earth's northern latitudes.

Kobuk Valley

To the south of Noatak can be seen one of the strangest sights anywhere in America: 100ft (30-meter) -high sand dunes in Arctic Alaska. Surrounded by more typical boreal forest, the 25-sq-mile (65-sq-km) **Great**

BELOW: many moose roam Gates of the Arctic.

Kobuk Sand Dunes are the provocative centerpiece of **Kobuk Valley National Park** ⓭. At 2 million acres (800,000 hectares), Kobuk Valley is one of Alaska's smallest national parks and almost certainly its least known. Centered around the Kobuk River Valley, it's accessible by either boat or air. Most visitors begin their trips in **Kotzebue**, an Eskimo village 75 miles (120km) to the west.

Summer temperatures may exceed 90°F (32°C) in the ever-shifting dunes, made of ancient glacial sand carried to the Kobuk Valley by wind and water. They're most easily reached at their northern end, where they come closest to the **Kobuk River**. (Also within the park are two smaller dunes, the **Little Kobuk** and **Hunt River**.)

The Kobuk is the region's major travel corridor, for both humans and caribou. Its valley is an important fall and winter range for the Western Arctic caribou herd; the animals can be seen crossing the Kobuk River from late August through October, during their annual migration. Caribou are an important food source for the region's native residents, who have lived along the Kobuk for at least 12,000 years. Eskimos still hunt caribou at a well-known archeological site called **Onion Portage**.

Bordering the Kobuk Valley on the north and south are the **Baird** and **Waring** mountains, respectively. Born in the Baird Mountains, the **Salmon River** flows through the park's western region; a wild and scenic river, it's popular with river floaters. As at Gates of the Arctic, park facilities are minimal and visitors must be prepared to be self-sufficient.

Bering Land Bridge

Located on the Seward Peninsula to the west is **Bering Land Bridge National Preserve** ⓮, a remnant of the land bridge that connected Asia with North America more than 13,000 years ago, allowing native people to travel south. There are ash explosion craters and lava flows (both rare in the Arctic), as well as plentiful paleontological and archeological resources and large seasonal populations of migratory birds. ❑

During the glacial epoch, the Bering Land Bridge was a migration route for people and animals. It was by this route that humans first passed from Asia to the Americas.

BELOW: polar bears wander the sea ice in a constant search for food.

Inupiat Heritage Center

▌Inupiat Heritage Center is a National Park Service unit in Barrow, Alaska, the northernmost community in the United States. Its mission is to interpret Inupiat Eskimo culture and the role of Inupiat Eskimos in 2,000 commercial whaling voyages into Arctic waters from New Bedford, Massachusetts, during the late 19th/early 20th centuries. In addition to crewing on ships, Inupiat Eskimos hunted for food for the whalers, provided fur clothing, and sheltered crews that were shipwrecked on the Alaska coast. The center houses exhibits, artifacts, library, gift shop, and a room where Inupiat people can demonstrate and teach traditional crafts in Elders-in-Residence and Artists-in-Residence programs. It is affiliated with New Bedford Whaling National Historical Park in Massachusetts. Access is by air. It is open year-round.

✕ INSIGHT GUIDES — TRAVEL TIPS
US NATIONAL PARKS WEST

A-Z

A HANDY SUMMARY OF PRACTICAL INFORMATION, ARRANGED ALPHABETICALLY

Admission Charges

Charges and Park Passports

Most parks charge an entrance fee, usually around $20–25, which allows unrestricted vehicle entry for a car and up to four passengers for one week.

If you plan on visiting several parks on your vacation, or to return within a year, you should buy **America the Beautiful Annual Pass** ($80), available at any park that charges an entrance fee, or by calling 888-ASK-USGS. The pass entitles you and the passengers in your vehicle unrestricted admission to all parks for a year. *(See page 369.)*

You can purchase the pass at any park that charges an entrance fee (the park you choose will benefit directly from the sale, an added incentive). You can also purchase the pass by logging on to www.store.usgs.gov/pass or by telephoning 888-ASK-USGS. The pass offers access to all public lands managed by the National Park Service, US Forest Service, US Fish and Wildlife Service, Bureau of Land Management, and Bureau of Reclamation.

Golden Years

If you are aged 62 or older and a US citizen (or permanent resident in the United States), you can apply for an **America the Beautiful Senior Pass**. For a one-time, inexpensive processing charge, this admits you and your family, or any accompanying passengers in your car, to all national parks, monuments, recreation areas, etc, that charge an entrance fee. It also provides a 50 percent discount on fees for services and facilities such as camping, parking, or guided interpretive tours. You must apply in person, with proof of age and residency, at any park that charges an entrance fee.

US citizens or permanent residents who are 62 years or older (with appropriate identification) may purchase an America the Beautiful – National Parks and Federal Recreational Lands Pass – Senior Pass – Cost $10. The pass entitles the holder to free admission and a 50-percent discount on facility fees

for camping, boating, and interpretive tours except those offered by independent concessionaires. *(See page 373.)*

Permanently disabled travelers may obtain a free **America the Beautiful Access Pass**, which entitles the holder to free admission to any park and a 50-percent discount on camping, facility, and interpretive tour fees except those offered by private concessionaires.

Budgeting for Your Trip

The US remains a good buy for travelers. This is especially true when it comes to visiting national parks, where entrance and use fees are a bargain and gateway communities, usually in the kind of remote settings where parks are found, are set up to offer a range of inexpensive food, lodging, and other visitor services.

In general in the US, allow $80–100/day for good-quality hotels for two people, although really memorable hotels and bed-and-breakfasts tend to run you closer to $150/night and up.

At the other end of the spectrum,

you'll find an array of hostels and campgrounds with full facilities for $16–18/night; bare-bones motel lodgings in rural areas can be found for less than $50; and reliable chains are in the $60–80 range (look for AAA discounts and online deals at chains like Best Western and La Quinta). Try to choose lodgings that include a hot breakfast (many do) to save money. Budget travelers can probably get away with $30/day per person for basic meals if you stick with diners, cafes, markets, and inexpensive restaurants, eat lightly, and don't drink alcohol. If you eat a substantial breakfast in a restaurant or café (and you should if you are out touring parks), you'll pay $6–10; lunch entrees run around $10–15 and dinner around $18–30 in an average restaurant.

Note: In-park lodgings and restaurants are run by concessionaires under renewable contracts with the National Park Service. Costs are fixed annually with the park service, specifically to offer a range of prices to suit every price point. Even so, in-park lodging is limited and still pricey, particularly at big-name parks like Yosemite and Grand Canyon; you should book a year ahead to guarantee a stay. Gateway communities tend to be a bit cheaper but don't have the same cachet or views.

Gas (petrol) in 2010 ran around $3/gallon. Many parks offer free shuttles now, either within the park or from a gateway community. The golden age of travel is still alive and well in some parks, such as Grand Canyon, where you can take a Harvey Tour of the park or ride into the heart of the Grand Canyon Village on the South Rim on the historic Grand Canyon Train from Williams.

It goes without saying that transportation to and within Alaska's huge, spread-out national parks requires a lot of planning and can be expensive.

To reach Katmai, for example, you must fly there on a small plane with a bush pilot. You can drive to other Alaska parks, such as Denali, but once there must ride the mandatory and costly shuttle system (advance reservations required).

If you are visiting Southeast Alaska, consider taking the Alaska Marine Ferry system from Seattle or British Columbia up the Inside Passage to Haines, a good way to enjoy a relaxing multiday cruise, sea air, and view marine life and astonishing vistas.

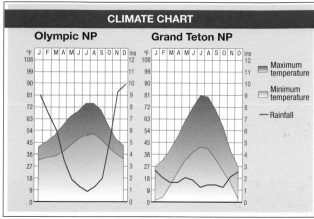

Camping Reservations

Most tent and RV sites in the parks are available on a first-come, first-served basis. Arrive as early as possible to reserve a place. Campgrounds fill early during the busy summer season (spring, fall, and winter in the desert parks). A limited number of campgrounds in the most popular parks can be reserved in advance (see park listings section). Fees are usually charged for campgrounds. Backcountry permits may be required for wilderness hiking and camping.

Children

Children love the parks, but it is important to take precautions. First, take everything you need. Some parks are quite remote and supplies may be limited. If you need baby formula, special foods, diapers (nappies), or medication, carry them with you.

It's also a good idea to bring a general first-aid kit for minor scrapes and bruises. Games, books, and crayons help kids pass time in the car. Carrying snacks and drinks in a day pack will come in handy when kids (not to mention adults) get hungry and there are no restaurants or campgrounds nearby.

Inquire about campfire talks, guided nature tours, and special children's programs. Some 290 parks offer the Junior Ranger program where kids pick up interpretive booklets and fill in answers to receive a Junior Ranger certificate and a patch or badge. Rangers do a fine job of interpreting the natural and cultural features of the parks and kids usually find these presentations fascinating. Park bookstores now have a range of publications, coloring books, jigsaws, and games aimed specifically at park interpretation for children.

The parks can be dangerous. Children need close supervision. Ask a ranger if a specific trail or region is suitable for children. Are there steep slopes, cliffs, river crossings, other

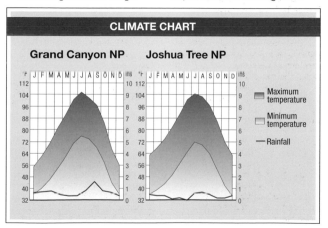

hazards? Is the trail too strenuous for a child? Are there special precautions to take?

Avoid dehydration by having children drink plenty of water before and during a hike, even if they don't seem particularly thirsty. Make sure kids are properly protected from sun exposure, a given in parks. Have them wear a wide-brimmed hat, long pants and shirts that can be rolled down to protect bare skin from sun and stickers, sturdy athletic shoes or hiking sandals, polarized sunglasses, and, most important, sun lotion with a 30+ SPF. Don't push children beyond their limits. Rest often, provide plenty of snacks, and allow for extra napping.

Give yourself plenty of time. Remember, kids don't travel at the same pace as adults. They're a lot less interested in traveling from point A to point B than in exploring their immediate surroundings.

Climate

Climate in the national parks varies dramatically by region, season, and elevation. Bad weather, including violent rain, snow, lightning, or dust storms, can kick up unexpectedly. A change in elevation can cause temperatures to fall or rise by more than 20°F (11°C). It may be warm and sunny in low-lying areas but frigid in the mountains.

In some parks, daytime temperatures can top 90°F (32°C) and then plummet below freezing during the night. Similarly, a day may start clear and sunny but end with cold, drenching rain. Snowfall may close roads in some mountain parks as much as nine months a year. Flash floods may temporarily close roads in desert areas and can make hiking dangerous.

It is imperative to call the parks in advance for up-to-date weather, road, and trail conditions. For specific weather information, see the separate park listings.

When to Visit

The parks – especially the popular mountain parks – tend to be crowded in summer. Traffic jams, inadequate parking, and crowded facilities are common at Grand Canyon, Yellowstone, Yosemite, Mount Rainier, and many other parks during the peak of the season. To beat the rush, consider visiting in late spring or early fall. The weather may not be quite as balmy, there may even be snow on the ground, but it's worthwhile to see the

parks without the crowds. Weekends are the busiest times, so try to visit on weekdays. Some park roads and most trails may be closed in winter, but snowshoeing, cross-country skiing, and other winter activities are often permitted and give visitors a unique perspective on the parks.

In desert parks such as Canyonlands, Death Valley, Joshua Tree, Organ Pipe Cactus, Saguaro, Guadalupe Mountains, and Big Bend, fall, spring, and winter are the busy seasons. With summer temperatures in excess of 100°F (38°C), it is too hot to do much sightseeing or hiking.

What to Wear

Weather can change unpredictably in any season, so be prepared for just about anything. The best plan is to dress in layers so that they can be pulled off or put on as conditions dictate. Bringing rain gear is always a good idea.

If you plan on hiking any distance, consider investing in a sturdy pair of hiking boots. Properly broken in, they will prevent painful blisters and protect your feet from bumpy trails, jagged rocks, cacti, thorns, and other hazards. Two pairs of socks – a polypropylene inner and a heavy outer – will also help keep your feet dry and comfortable.

Day hikers should also consider bringing a small backpack or waistpack (or, in American parlance, "fanny pack") to carry essentials. Include a compass, a topographical map, a flashlight, mirror, sunglasses, a pocket knife, a lighter or waterproof matches, a candle, a minimum of a liter of water per person, high-energy food, water-purification tablets or filter, a first-aid kit, a broad-brimmed hat, a sweater, rain gear, and space blanket. Wear pants and shirts that

can be rolled down to protect skin from exposure and apply a 30+ SPF sunblock, even if the day starts out cloudy. The sun can be merciless, especially in desert areas where there is little shade.

Crime and Safety

Don't be lulled into complacency by the beautiful surroundings. Crime is on the rise in the highly used national parks, but a few common-sense precautions will help keep you safe.

For starters, don't carry large sums of cash or wear flashy or expensive jewelry. Keep them locked in your trunk (car boot) or in a hotel safe. Lock unattended cars and keep your belongings in the trunk. If possible, travel with a companion.

If you are a witness to or victim of a crime, or need to report an emergency situation of any kind, immediately contact the nearest ranger or call park headquarters.

Following changes in the law in 2010, firearms are permitted to be carried into national parks now, but they must be broken down, unloaded, encased, and kept in your car out of sight. Hunting is prohibited at all but a few special times and areas. Unless hunting is explicitly allowed by the park superintendent, assume that it is forbidden. Poaching is a federal offense and is severely punished by fines and/or prison.

Fishing may be allowed in some areas depending on the site and the season. Permits and state licenses may be required. Inquire in advance at park headquarters.

Backcountry permits (often free) and trailhead registration are required in many parks. Speak with park rangers before heading into the backcountry.

BELOW: riding the Golden Canyon Trail in Death Valley.

A few parks have restrictions on carrying and/or drinking alcohol. Contact the park in advance if you intend to bring alcohol. State and local liquor laws apply.

Customs Regulations

All people entering the US must go through US Customs. Be prepared to have your luggage inspected and keep the following guidelines in mind:
• There is no limit to the amount of money you can bring into the US. But, if the amount exceeds $10,000 (in cash and other negotiable instruments), you must file a special report with customs.
• Any objects brought for personal use may enter duty-free.
• Adults may enter with a maximum of 200 cigarettes or 50 cigars (not Cuban) or 2kg (4.4lbs) of tobacco and/or 1 liter of alcohol duty-free.
• Gifts valued at less than $800 can enter duty-free (US citizens) or $100 (foreign travelers).
• Meat and meat products, dairy products, seeds, plants, and fruit are prohibited and will be confiscated if you try to bring them in (note: many airports now use airport sniffer dogs to find these items and illicit drugs, so it's not worth trying to hide them). Live animals are subject to complex quarantine laws.
• Illicit drugs and drug paraphernalia are strictly prohibited. If you must bring narcotic or habit-forming medicines for health reasons, ensure that they are properly identified, bring only the quantity you will need and have either a prescription or a letter from your doctor.

For additional information, contact **United States Custom Service**, PO Box 407, Washington, DC 20044, tel: 877-227-5511; www.cbp.gov.

D isabled Travelers

The passage of the 1995 Americans With Disabilities Act brought sweeping changes to facilities across America. Accommodations with five or more rooms must be usable by persons with disabilities. Older and smaller inns and lodges are often wheelchair-accessible.

Public lands, such as state and national parks, are required to accommodate travelers with disabilities. Although accessibility varies from park to park, it's common for visitor centers, exhibits, some campgrounds, and short, level, paved nature trails to be "barrier free" or "accessible."

Braille and CD recordings may also be available in some parks. For information on handicapped accessibility, contact the parks directly (see listings) and ask for the accessibility coordinator.

Some parks, such as Grand Canyon, produce a special park newspaper specifically aimed at accessible trip planning for the park. For general information on travel for the handicapped, contact the Society for Accessible Travel and Hospitality (tel: 212-447-7284; www.sath.org), which publishes a quarterly magazine on travel for the disabled.

E lectricity

Standard American electric current is 110 volts. An adapter is necessary for European appliances, which run on 220–240 volts.

Embassies and Consulates

Foreign Embassies in the United States
Australia: 1601 Massachusetts Avenue NW, Washington, DC 20036, tel: 202-797-3000.
Belgium: 3330 Garfield Street NW, Washington, DC 20008, tel: 202-333-6900.
Canada: 501 Pennsylvania Avenue NW, Washington, DC 20001, tel: 202-682-1740.
Denmark: 3200 Whitehaven Street NW, Washington, DC 20008, tel: 202-234-4300.
France: 4101 Reservoir Road NW, Washington, DC 20007, tel: 202-944-6000.
Germany: 4645 Reservoir Road NW, Washington, DC 20007, tel: 202-298-4000.
Great Britain: 3100 Massachusetts Avenue NW, Washington, DC 20008, tel: 202-462-1340.
Greece: 2217 Massachusetts Avenue NW, Washington, DC 20008, tel: 202-939-1300.
India: 2107 Massachusetts Avenue NW, Washington, DC 20008, tel: 202-939-7000.
Israel: 3514 International Drive NW, Washington, DC 20008, tel: 202-364-5500.
Italy: 3000 Whitehaven Street NW, Washington, DC 20008, tel: 202-612-4400.
Japan: 2520 Massachusetts Avenue NW, Washington, DC 20008, tel: 202-238-6700.
Mexico: 1911 Pennsylvania Avenue NW, Washington, DC 20006, tel: 202-728-1600.
Netherlands: 4200 Linnean Avenue

NW, Washington, DC 20008, tel: 202-244-5300.
New Zealand: 37 Observatory Circle NW, Washington, DC 20008, tel: 202-328-4800.
Norway: 2720 34th Street NW, Washington, DC 20008, tel: 202-333-6000.
Portugal: 2125 Kalorama Road NW, Washington, DC 20008, tel: 202-328-8610.
Republic of Korea: 2320 Massachusetts Avenue NW, Washington, DC 20008, tel: 202-939-5653.
Singapore: 3501 International Place NW, Washington, DC 20008, tel: 202-537-3100.
Spain: 2375 Pennsylvania Avenue NW, Washington, DC 20037, tel: 202-452-0100.
Taiwan: 4201 Wisconsin Avenue NW, Washington, DC 20016, tel: 202-895-1800.

Emergencies

Most towns and cities have 24-hour pharmacies (often called drugstores) and Urgent Care walk-in clinics for minor injuries, Emergency Rooms at hospitals, and poison control centers. Look in the Yellow Pages or the inside cover of the telephone book. Or **dial 411** for telephone operator assistance.

If you need to call for help, such as an ambulance or the police, dial the US **emergency number 911**. A dispatcher will answer your call, provide immediate first-aid information if needed, and send help. **If you can't get through, dial 0** for the telephone operator. In national parks, **contact a ranger** immediately. Most rangers, especially those working the backcountry, have training in CPR and Wilderness First Responder (EMT) skills.

Environmental Ethics

The old saw is good advice: "Take nothing but pictures, leave nothing but footprints."

The goal of low-impact/no-impact backpacking is to leave the area in the same condition as you found it, if not better. If you're camping in the backcountry, don't break branches, level the ground, or alter the landscape in any way. Parks in cooler, moister areas of the country may still allow you to build fires in designated firepits, but out West many parks are dry as a bone and only portable stoves are allowed.

When nature calls, dig a cat hole 6ins (15cm) deep and at least 100ft

A – Z

CALIFORNIA AND THE PACIFIC

THE SOUTHWEST

THE ROCKY MOUNTAINS

THE PACIFIC NORTHWEST

(30 meters) from water, campgrounds and trails. Whatever you pack in, pack out, including trash and used toilet paper. For more information on backcountry camping, see *Roughing It* on page 279.

Etiquette

Visitors often associate the US with relaxed manners. While that may be true up to a point, particularly in dress and table manners, you should also be prepared for many Americans, particularly those who live in conservative rural areas of the West, to be surprisingly polite and formal, both in speech, dress, and the intricate dance of social interaction.

Americans, as a rule, are positive, curious about others, generally accepting of differences, warm, effusive, and tactile. This being a nation of immigrants, care is generally taken in polite society not to give offence to any one group, and chauvinism and racism, though evident, are not tolerated in most social situations, so be careful about making off-color jokes or making assumptions about different regions of the country.

Visiting Indian reservations, which are sovereign lands within the US with their own laws and moral code, calls for unique sensitivity and cultural awareness. Make an effort to blend in, dress conservatively, behave modestly – particularly at Indian dances, which are religious rituals – and never enter a home without being invited (nor refuse a meal if invited on a feast day, as that is considered rude). Many tribes rely on tourism for their income and have developed luxury resorts on their scenic lands to rival any in Las Vegas.

In remote areas, you will usually be asked to pay a small fee to take photos of family members.

Care for Your Feet

Even if you plan to do only short day hikes, it's worth investing in a sturdy pair of hiking shoes or boots. Consider buying them a half or full size larger than usual and be sure to break them in properly before arriving.

A thin, inner polypropylene sock and a thick, outer sock will help keep your feet dry and comfortable. If blisters or sore spots develop, quickly cover them with moleskin, available at just about any pharmacy or camping supply store.

G ay and Lesbian Travelers

On the whole, urban areas in the US are safer places to visit for gay and lesbian travelers than rural destinations away from the cities. Keep a low profile in such areas, particularly in the conservative rural areas in the West, to avoid problems. Having said that, the lucrative GLBT market is one of the hottest targeted markets in the US, and most states now offer information on gay-friendly travel within their communities. Major cities like Seattle, San Francisco, Los Angeles, Phoenix, Albuquerque, and Tucson roll out the red carpet. Smaller arts and university towns, such as Santa Fe, Boulder, and Flagstaff, also have surprisingly large gay communities.

For more information, check out www.queeramerica.com and the Gay and Lesbian Yellow Pages (tel: 800-697-2812; www.glyp.com). Damron Company (tel: 415-255-0404, 800-462-6654; www.damron.com) publishes guides aimed at gay travelers and lists gay-owned and gay-friendly accommodations nationwide.

H ealth and Medical Care

Most accidents and injuries are caused by inattentive or incautious behavior. You may be on vacation but your brain shouldn't be. Pay attention to where you are and what you are doing. Keep your eyes on the road when driving. If you want to gaze at the scenery, use an overlook or pullout. Better yet, get out of the car and walk. Don't take unnecessary chances on the trail. You have nothing to prove to yourself or your companions. Heed all posted warnings and, when in doubt, seek the advice of rangers.

Fitness and Altitude Sickness

Use common sense. Don't attempt trails that are too strenuous for your level of fitness. Ask rangers how long and steep the trail is before beginning. You may want to "warm up" on a shorter, less strenuous trail before starting a long hike.

Concentrate on what you're doing and where you're going. Even well-trod trails can be dangerous.

Air is thinner at higher elevations. Unless properly acclimatized, you may feel uncharacteristically winded. If you experience nausea, headache, vomiting, extreme fatigue, light-headedness, or shortness of breath, you may be suffering from altitude sickness. Although the symptoms

may appear to be mild at first, they can develop into a serious illness. You should return to a lower elevation and try to acclimatize gradually.

Water

It's essential in the bone-dry West to carry a little more water than you think you'll need and drink it before you feel thirsty. The rule of thumb is 1 gallon (4 liters) a day per person, more in extreme conditions. Drink at least a quart (1 liter) at the start of a hike, and prevent dehydration by drinking at regular intervals while you're on the trail, even if you don't feel particularly thirsty. To avoid hyponatremia, an electrolyte imbalance caused by drinking too much water and not eating enough high-energy food, be sure to eat salty high-energy foods as well as drinking water. If you start to feel light-headed, weak and unwell while exerting yourself in extreme conditions, try drinking slightly salted water to help balance your adrenal system.

All water taken from natural sources must be purified before drinking. Giardia is found in water (even crystal-clear water) throughout the West and can cause severe cramps and diarrhea. The most popular methods of purifying water are using a water-purification tablet or a water-purification filter, both available from camping supply stores; some water-bottles have built-in filters now for convenience. Or boil water for at least 15 minutes.

Frostbite and Hypothermia

Hypothermia – the potentially fatal loss of core body temperature – can be prevented. First, dress appropriately. It's best to dress in layers so that you can take clothes off or put them on as required. The first layer should be made of fabrics that keep moisture away from the skin such as silk, wool, or synthetics like polypropylene or fleece. Avoid being both cold and wet. Bring along extra layers in case you get soaked. Keep your body well fueled and hydrated with food and water. Be prepared to turn back or seek shelter if weather turns bad. It's a very good idea to carry a small space blanket package with you whenever you are hiking that will allow you to get warmed up fast.

Keep in mind that it doesn't have to be freezing for you to get hypothermia. The telltale signs are extreme shivering, loss of coordination, and inability to reason (an outdoor writer calls these symptoms "the umbles," or

Hiking Sense

Avoid solitary hiking. The best situation is to hike with at least two other partners. If one person is injured, one member of the party can seek help while the other two remain behind.

If you must hike alone, be sure to tell someone your intended route and time of return or leave a note in your car at the trailhead. Overnight backcountry hiking usually requires a free permit; some day hikes into popular backcountry areas require a permit, too. Ask a ranger before setting out and be sure to self-register at the trailhead.

Above: hikers check the miles in Yosemite National Park.

stumbling, fumbling, mumbling).

If a member of your party is hypothermic, set up camp and establish a stable, warm environment as quickly as possible. Put up a tent, build a fire, or light a portable stove. Remove the victim's wet clothes and put him or her into a prewarmed sleeping bag. In extreme situations, remove your own clothes, get into the bag with the victim and maintain skin-to-skin contact. Try to reduce all heat loss from wind or moisture. If conscious, have the victim drink sweet, warm fluids. If one person is hypothermic, others may be, too.

Frostbite occurs when living tissue freezes. Symptoms include numbness, pain, blistering, and whitening of skin. The most immediate remedy is to put frostbitten skin against warm skin. Simply holding your hands for several minutes over another person's frostbitten cheeks or nose, for example, may be sufficient. Otherwise, immerse frostbitten skin in warm (not hot) water.

Refreezing will cause even more damage, so get the victim into a warm environment as quickly as possible. If one person is frostbitten, others may be, too. Check all members of your party for frostbite.

Swimming

Even the strongest swimmers can drown. Check with park rangers before swimming in any body of water. Strong currents and cold water can quickly overcome even an experienced swimmer. Wear a life vest when boating, and avoid hypothermia by staying out of frigid water.

Sunburn

Protect yourself from the sun. Always use a high-SPF sunscreen and wear a wide-brimmed hat, a cotton bandanna that can be wetted and placed around the neck, clothing that can be rolled down to protect exposed skin, and polarized sunglasses, even if the day starts out cloudy. Avoid hiking during the midday hours. Be careful to avoid dehydration and overexposure to the sun. In the desert, or at high altitude, this can happen rapidly even on cloudy days. Avoid excess alcohol, caffeine, and sugar to cut down on dehydration. Pace yourself at high altitude. Allow a day or two to gradually acclimatize to elevation changes. Even the fittest person at sea level should expect to be affected when exerting themselves at high elevations, as Search and Rescue rangers in parks will attest.

Creepy-Crawlies

The bite or sting of a **spider**, **ant** or **scorpion** is not usually fatal but it can cause a lot of pain and itching, and the area round it may swell. In most cases, discomfort gradually subsides.

If extreme symptoms such as numbness, tingling, shooting pain, abdominal cramps, low blood pressure, high temperature, spasms, breathing difficulty, or problems focusing the eyes occur, see a physician at once. Bringing the insect (dead or alive) with you will greatly help the doctor.

There is not much you can do if you are bitten by a **chigger** or "red bug." A salve from the drugstore may help relieve the itching, but you will just have to wait for it to go away. The same is true of the bite of the **mosquito**, found by the million around the water in low-lying areas anywhere from Texas to Alaska.

Lyme disease is carried by tiny **ticks** no larger than a poppy seed. To protect yourself from ticks, wear long pants tucked into your socks and a long-sleeved shirt. Insect repellent will help, too.

In Southwest desert parks, such as Canyonlands, be prepared for tiny no-see-ums in areas with juniper trees at the start of the breeding season in May. They get into hair, eyes, and ears and produce nasty bites. Wear a fine-mesh net, keep tents closed up and try repelling them with a herbal repellent containing pennyroyal.

Insurance

Most visitors to the US will have no health problems during their stay. Even so, you should never leave home without travel insurance to cover both yourself and your belongings. Your own insurance company or travel agent can advise you on policies, but shop around since rates vary. Make sure you are covered for accidental death, emergency medical care, trip cancelation, and baggage or document loss.

Maps

Free maps of the national parks, national forests, and other public lands are handed out at park entrance stations when you pay your fee or may be obtained from National Park Service and other agency regional offices (see listings for telephone numbers and addresses). Excellent digital maps can be downloaded free from the National Park Service's website: www.nps.gov

Free city, state, and regional maps as well as up-to-date road conditions and other valuable services are available to members of the American Automobile Association (AAA). If you plan on driving any distance, the service is well worth the price of membership. In the Southwest, the AAA map "Indian Country" offers the

National Park Service

The National Park Service is administered by the US Department of the Interior.

For general information about the parks, contact the **Office of Public Inquiries, National Park Service**, National Park Service, 1849 C Street NW, Washington, DC 20240. tel: 202-208-3818, www.nps.gov.

Information is also available from the appropriate regional offices:
Midwest Region, National Park Service, 601 Riverfront Drive, Omaha, NE 68102-4226, tel: 402-661-1736.

Intermountain Region, National Park Service, 12795 Alameda Parkway, Denver, CO 80225, tel: 303-969-2500.

Pacific West Region, National Park Service, One Jackson Center, 1111 Jackson Street, Suite 700, Oakland, CA 94607, tel: 510-817-1300.

Alaska Area Region, National Park Service, 240 West 5th Avenue, Suite 114, Anchorage, AK 99501, tel: 907-644-3510.

National Trails Program, National Park Service, Conservation and Outdoor Recreation, 1849 C Street NW, Washington, DC 20240, tel: 202-354-6900.

Other wilderness and public land areas are administered by:
Bureau of Land Management, US Department of the Interior, 1849 C Street NW, Room 5665, Washington, DC 20240, tel: 202-208-3801, www.blm.gov.

US Fish and Wildlife Service, US Department of the Interior, 1849 C Street NW, Washington, DC 20240, tel: 800-344-WILD, www.fws.gov.

US Forest Service, US Department of Agriculture, 1400 Independence Avenue SW, Agriculture Building, Washington, DC 20250, tel: 800-832-1355, www.fs.fed.us.

most complete map of the Navajo reservation and surrounding areas; in fact, it is so detailed, many Navajos use it themselves to navigate. It may be bought at many gas stations. Free maps are also available from city and state tourism bureaus *(see listings)*.

High-quality topographical maps of the national parks and other natural areas are available from **National Geographic Maps**, PO Box 4357, Evergreen, CO 80437-4357, tel: 800-962-1643 or tel: 303-670-3457.

Topographical maps produced by the **US Geological Survey** are available from map dealers throughout the United States. For more information, and the location of dealers, contact the USGS at PO Box 25286, Denver, CO 80225, tel: 303-202-4700 or 888-ASK-USGS, or on their website www.usgs.gov.

Media

Books and Magazines

The parks offer a variety of free flyers, brochures, and maps. Additional books can be purchased at visitor center bookstores run by park nonprofit cooperating associations. Many associations produce their own visitor publications, which are sold in the park and through their website *(see separate listings)*.

The following magazines often feature articles about the national parks, natural history, environmental issues, and outdoor recreation:

Arizona Highways, 2039 West Lewis Avenue, Phoenix, AZ 85009, tel: 800-543-5432, www.arizonahighways.com.
Audubon, 700 Broadway, New York, NY 10003, tel: 800-274-4201, www.audubonmagazine.org.
Backpacker, Rodale Press, Inc., 33 East Minor Street, Emmaus, PA 18098, tel: 800-666-3434, www.backpacker.com.
National Geographic and National Geographic Traveler, 1145 17th Street NW, Washington, DC 20036, tel: 800-638-4077, www.nationalgeographic.com.
National Parks, 1300 19th Street NW, Suite 300, Washington, DC 20036, tel: 800-NATPARK, www.npca.org.
National Wildlife, 11100 Wildlife Center Drive, Reston, VA 20190-5362, tel: 800-822-9919, www.nwf.org.
Natural History, American Museum of Natural History, 36 West 25th Street, 5th Floor, New York, NY 10010, tel: 646-356-6500, www.naturalhistorymag.com.
Outside Magazine, 400 Market Street, Santa Fe, NM 87501, tel: 800-678-1131, www.outsidemag.com.
Sierra, 85 Second Street, 2nd Floor, San Francisco, CA 94105, tel: 415-977-5500, www.sierraclub.org.

See our list of recommended books at the end of Travel Tips (page 405).

Money

Currency

The basic unit of American currency, a dollar ($1), is equal to 100 cents. There are four common coins, each worth less than a dollar: a penny or 1 cent (1¢), a nickel or 5 cents (5¢), a dime or 10 cents (10¢), and a quarter or 25 cents (25¢).

There are several denominations of paper money: $1, $5, $10, $20, $50, $100, and, rarely, $2. Each bill is the same basic color, size, and shape; be sure to check the dollar amount on the face of the bill.

It is advisable to arrive with at least $100 in cash (in small bills) to pay for ground transportation and other incidentals.

Travelers' Checks

Foreign visitors are advised to take US dollar travelers' checks since exchanging foreign currency – whether as cash or checks – can be problematic. A growing number of banks offer exchange facilities, but this practice is not universal.

Most shops, restaurants, and other establishments accept travelers' checks in US dollars and will give change in cash. Alternatively, checks can be converted into cash at the bank.

Credit Cards

These are very much part of daily life in the US. They can be used to pay for pretty much anything, and it is also common for car rental firms and hotels to take an imprint of your card as a deposit. Some rental companies may oblige you to pay a large deposit in cash if you do not have a card.

You can also use your credit card to withdraw cash from ATMs (Automatic Teller Machines). Before you leave home, make sure you know your PIN and find out which ATM system will accept your card. The most widely accepted cards are Visa, American Express, MasterCard, Diners Club, Japanese Credit Bureau, and Discovery.

Money may be sent or received by wire at any **Western Union** office (tel: 800-325-6000) or **Travelers Express MoneyGram** office (tel: 800-666-3947).

Tipping

As elsewhere, service industry personnel (but not National Park Service employees) who work in and around the parks depend on tips for a large part of their income.

With few exceptions, tipping is ultimately left to your discretion; gratuities are not automatically added to the bill. In most cases, 15–20 percent is the going rate for tipping

Park Listings

From pages 370–404 are listings for each of the national parks, giving information on everything from opening hours to lodgings and disabled access. The parks are listed under the following regional headings:

- California and the Pacific
- The Southwest
- The Rocky Mountains
- The Pacific Northwest

waiters, taxi drivers, and barbers. Porters and bellmen usually get about 75¢–$1 per bag, but never less than $1 total.

Opening Hours

Banks: 9/10am–3/4pm Monday–Friday (although most have drive-through lanes that stay open longer). **Offices**: 8am–5pm Monday–Friday. **Museums**: many are closed on Monday.
National parks: Hours at park facilities vary from site to site and season to season. During peak months, park facilities tend to stay open 8.30am–6pm, seven days a week; some desert park visitor centers may open earlier in the summer to allow visitors to get a start during the cooler time of day.

Hours may be limited during the off-season and some mountain parks suspend facilities completely during winter. Holiday closings, if any, may include Thanksgiving, Christmas and New Year's Day.
Retail shops: 10/11am–5/6pm Monday–Friday, except in large shopping malls, where hours are extended to 8, 9, or 10pm and weekends.

Pets

Except for seeing eye dogs (guide dogs), it's not a good idea to bring dogs into a national park. Pets and wildlife in parks don't mix, and restrictions on where you can take your dog in the park are very stringent. Generally, dogs must be on a 6ft (1.8-meter) or less leash at all times and are only allowed in parking lots, in your car, or within 50 to 100ft (45 to 90 meters) of the road.

Parks usually allow dogs in campgrounds and in developed areas, but there can be exceptions to these rules. Dogs are prohibited on all trails, beaches, or inside buildings. Some parks offer kennels. Inquire in advance.

Postal Services

Even the most remote towns are served by the US Postal Service. Smaller post offices tend to be limited to business hours (Mon–Fri 9am–5pm), although central, big-city branches may have extended weekday and weekend hours. Many of them are open for at least a couple of hours on Saturday mornings, but they are all closed on Sunday.

There may also be coin-operated machines that dispense stamps whether the office is open or not. Rates are usually listed nearby. Stamps are also sold at some convenience stores, service stations, hotels, and transportation terminals, usually in vending machines.

There are US Post Office Information numbers in the phone book, or call 411 and ask the operator.

For reasonably quick delivery at a modest price, ask for first-class or priority mail. Second- and third-class mail is cheaper and slower.

For expedited deliveries, often overnight, try **USPS Express Mail**. The most reliable domestic and international courier services are **Federal Express** (tel: 800-463-3339) and **United Parcel Service** (tel: 800-PICK-UPS).

Poste Restante

Visitors can receive mail at post offices if it is addressed to them, care of "General Delivery," followed by the city name and (very important) the zip code. You must pick up this mail in person within a week or two of its arrival and will be asked to show some form of valid personal identification.

Public Holidays

Banks, federal, state, county and city offices and private businesses often close during public holidays. Many stores remain open during weekends and holidays. Most visitor centers in the national parks close on Thanksgiving Day, Christmas Day, and New Year's Day.

New Year's Day January 1
Martin Luther King Jr's Birthday January 15, although observed the third Monday in January
Presidents' Day Third Monday in February
Easter Sunday Late March/early April
Memorial Day Last Monday in May
Independence Day July 4
Labor Day First Monday in September
Columbus Day Second Monday in October
Veterans Day November 11
Thanksgiving Day Fourth Thursday in November
Christmas Day December 25

BELOW: climber access trail signs at Joshua Tree National Park.

ABOVE: Alaska float planes, ready for take off, near Anchorage.

Spain	34
Sweden	46
Switzerland	41
United Kingdom	44

Western Union (tel: 800-325-6000) can arrange telegram, mailgram, and telex transmissions. Check the local phone directory or call information for local offices.

Fax machines are available at most hotels and even some motels. Printers, copy shops, stationers, and office-supply shops may also have a machine, as well as a few of the convenience stores around.

R eligious Services

The US Government officially observes separation of Church and State. In practice, though, since its founding, America has attracted numerous immigrants fleeing religious persecution in their home country, and religious freedom is an aspect of American life that is never taken for granted and taken quite seriously. The majority of Americans believe in God and many attend religious or spiritual services regularly in their communities. Both high- and low-church Christianity is usually the most visible religious expression across the US, but you'll also find Jewish temples, Mormon tabernacles and temples, Baptist chapels, Quaker meeting houses, Buddhist zendos, pagan Wicca ceremonies, evangelical tent revivals on Indian reservations, and other religious gathering places in the unlikeliest places, even remote national parks. Visitors are welcome at most church services. The homegrown American Church of Jesus Christ of Latter-day Saints, otherwise known as the LDS or Mormon Church, welcomes visitors to its tabernacles but non-Mormons may not enter a Mormon temple. Many national parks offer Christian or interfaith worship services on Sundays and holidays, such as Easter sunrise services, either in dedicated churches or other locations around the park.

T elephones

In this era of cell phones, you'll find fewer public telephones in hotel lobbies, restaurants, drugstores, garages, roadside kiosks, convenience stores, and other locations. The cost of making a local call from a payphone for three minutes is 25–50¢. To make a long-distance call from a payphone, use either a prepaid calling card, available in airports, post offices, and a few other outlets, or your credit card, which you can use at any phone: dial 1-800-CALLATT, key in your credit-card number, and wait to be connected. In many areas, local calls have now changed to a 10-digit calling system, using the area code. Watch out for the in-room connection charges in the more upmarket hotels; it's cheaper to use the pay phone in the lobby. Ditto: wireless and broadband internet connections in your room: many hotel lobbies offer free wireless but charge for it in guest rooms. Inquire ahead of time.

Dialing Abroad

To dial abroad (Canada follows the US system), first dial the international access code 011, then the country code. If using a US phone credit card, dial the company's access number below, then 01, then the country code.

Sprint, tel: 10333.

AT&T, tel: 10288.

Country codes:

Australia	61
Austria	43
Belgium	32
Brazil	55
Denmark	45
France	33
Germany	49
Greece	30
Hong Kong	852
Israel	972
Italy	39
Japan	81
Korea	82
Netherlands	31
New Zealand	64
Norway	47
Singapore	65
South Africa	27

Time Zones

The continental US is divided into four time zones. From east to west, later to earlier, they are Eastern, Central, Mountain, and Pacific, each separated by one hour. Most of Alaska is situated in the Alaska Time Zone, an hour earlier than the Pacific Coast. Hawaii is in its own time zone, two hours earlier than the Pacific Coast. Thus, when it is 8pm Greenwich Mean Time, it is 3pm in New York City, 2pm in Chicago, 1pm in Denver, noon in Los Angeles, 11am in Anchorage and 10am in Honolulu. Note: Be aware in your travels around the Southwest that Arizona, while in the Mountain Time Zones, does not observe Daylight Savings Time, and nor does the Hopi Reservation. This means that during the summer, Arizona and the Hopi Reservation are, effectively, in the Pacific Time Zone. Just to complicate things, though, the Navajo Nation, which spans Arizona and New Mexico, does observe Daylight Savings Time.

National parks situated in the different time zones include:

Mountain Time Zone: Arches, Badlands, Bryce Canyon, Canyonlands, Capitol Reef, Carlsbad Caverns, Glacier, Grand Canyon, Grand Teton, Guadalupe Mountains, Mesa Verde, Rocky Mountain, Theodore Roosevelt, Wind Cave, Yellowstone, and Zion.

Pacific Time Zone: Crater Lake, Death Valley, Joshua Tree, Lassen Volcanic, Mount Rainier, North Cascades, Olympic, Redwood, Sequoia-Kings Canyon, Yosemite.

Alaska Time Zone: Denali, Gates of the Arctic, Glacier Bay, Katmai, Kenai Fjords, Kobuk Valley, Lake Clark, and Wrangell-St Elias.

Hawaii Time Zone: Haleakala and Hawaii Volcanoes.

In spring, many states move the clock ahead one hour for daylight savings. In fall, the clock is moved back one hour to return to standard time.

Tourist Information

State Tourism Offices

See listings under National Parks for regional tourism offices or chambers of commerce.

Alaska Travel Industry Association, 2600 Cordova Street, Suite 201, Anchorage, AK 99503-2745, tel: 800-327-9372, www.travelalaska.com.

American Samoa Office of Tourism, PO Box 1147, Pago Pago, American Samoa 96799, www.amsamoatourism.com.

Arizona Office of Tourism, 1100 West Washington, Suite 155, Phoenix, AZ 85007, tel: 866-275-5816 or 602-364-3700, www.arizonaguide.com.

California, Travel and Tourism Commission, 980 9th Street, Suite 480, Sacramento, CA 95814, tel: 877-225-4367, www.visitcalifornia.com.

Colorado Tourism Office, 1625 Broadway, Suite 1700, Denver, CO 80202, tel: 800-265-6723 or 303-892-3885, www.colorado.com.

Hawaii Visitors and Convention Bureau, 2270 Kalakaua Avenue, Suite 801, Honolulu, HI 96815, tel: 800-464-2924 or 808-924-0200, www.gohawaii.com.

Idaho Division of Tourism Development, 700 West State Street, Boise, ID 83720, tel: 800-635-7820 or 208-334-2470, www.visitid.org.

Kansas Travel and Tourism, 1000 SW Jackson Street, Suite 100, Topeka, KS 66612, tel: 785-296-2009, www.travelks.com or www.kansascommerce.com.

Travel Montana, 301 South Park, PO Box 200533, Helena, MT 59620, tel: 800-847-4868 or 406-841-2870, www.visitmt.com.

Nebraska Travel and Tourism, 301 Centennial Mall South, PO Box 94666, Lincoln, NE 68509-4666, tel: 888-444-1867, www.visitnebraska.gov/tourism.

Nevada Commission on Tourism, 401 North Carson Street, Carson City, NV 89701, tel: 800-NEVADA-8 or 775-687-4322, www.travelnevada.com.

New Mexico Tourism Department, Lamy Building, 491 Old Santa Fe Trail, Santa Fe, NM 87503, tel: 800-545-2070 or 505-827-7400, www.newmexico.org.

North Dakota Tourism Division, Century Center, 1600 East Century Avenue, Suite 2, PO Box 2057, Bismark, ND 58502, tel: 800-435-5663 or 701-328-2525, www.ndtourism.com.

Oregon Tourism Commission, Economic Development Department, 670 Hawthorne Avenue SE, Salem, OR 97301, tel: 800-547-7842, www.traveloregon.com.

South Dakota Office of Tourism, Capitol Lake Plaza, 711 East Wells Avenue, Pierre, SD 57501, tel: 800-952-3625 or 605-773-3301, www.travelsd.com.

Texas Tourism, PO Box 12728, Austin, TX 78711, tel: 800-888-8839, www.traveltex.com.

Utah Office of Tourism, Council Hall, Capitol Hill, Salt Lake City, UT 84114, tel: 800-200-1160, www.utah.com.

Washington State Tourism Division, PO Box 42525, Olympia, WA 98504-2525, tel: 800-544-1800, www.experienceWA.com.

Wyoming Travel and Tourism, 125 at College Drive, Cheyenne, WY 82002, tel: 800-225-5996 or 307-777-7777, www.wyomingtourism.org.

Tour Operators

The following nonprofit organizations offer a variety of park tours. Some feature horseback riding, backpacking, field seminars, bird trips, skiing, river running, photography ,and other special activities:

Audubon Nature Odysseys, tel: 800-967-7425, www.travel.audubon.org

Canyonlands Field Institute, PO Box 68, Moab, UT 84532, tel: 800-860-5262 or 435-259-7750, www.canyonlandsfieldinst.org

Desert Institute at Joshua Tree National Park, 74485 National Park Drive, Twentynine Palms, CA 92277, tel: 760-367-5535, http://desertinstitute.homestead.com

Grand Canyon Field Institute, PO Box 399, Grand Canyon, AZ 86023, tel: 866-471-4435, www.grandcanyon.org/fieldinstitute

National Wildlife Federation, 11100 Wildlife Center Drive, Reston, VA 20190-5362, tel: 800-822-9919, www.nwf.org/expeditions

North Cascades Institute, 810 State Route 20, Sedro Woolley, WA 98284, tel: 360-854-2599, www.ncascades.org

Olympic Park Institute, Olympic National Park, 111 Barnes Point Road, Port Angeles, WA 98363, tel: 360-928-3720, www.yni.org/opi

Sierra Club, 85 Second Street, 2nd Floor, San Francisco, CA 94105, tel: 415-977-5500, www.sierraclub.org

Yellowstone Association, PO Box 117, Yellowstone National Park, WY 82190, tel: 406-848-2400, www.yellowstoneassociation.org

Yosemite Association, PO Box 230, El Portal, CA 95318, tel: 209-379-2646, www.yosemite.org

Transportation

Historically, there has been very little public transportation to national parks, which tend, by their very nature, to be a long way from population centers. Gradually, though, there is beginning to be a more integrated public transportation system at some parks for those who do not drive. Amtrak and historic trains and commercial shuttle buses now offer access to the park or adjoining gateway community. Once you enter the park, you will increasingly find a free shuttle bus system (sometimes mandatory, as at Zion Canyon in peak season) and a variety of bus tours by concessionaires. You may also find more unusual forms of transportation, from mule rides, horsepacking and llama trekking to mountain bicycle hire and houseboat rentals. Remote Alaskan parks are usually reached by commercial jet, bush plane, ferry, tour boat, or, where there is highway access, by car.

Getting There By Air

If driving directly to the parks is impractical because of distance, the next best way to get there is to fly to a nearby city and rent a car. The major hubs closest to the western parks are:
California: San Diego, Los Angeles, San José, Oakland, San Francisco. Inquire about connections to air terminals at Palm Springs, Crescent City, Fresno, Visalia, and Merced, California.
Southwest: Albuquerque International Sunport, Santa Fe Airport (daily American Eagle flights from Dallas–Fort Worth and Los Angeles), Las Vegas-McCarran, Phoenix Sky Harbor, Tucson, El Paso, Salt Lake City. Inquire about connections to air terminals at Moab, Bryce Canyon, St George, and Cedar City, Utah; Flagstaff, Page, and Grand Canyon, Arizona; Grand Junction, Colorado; and Carlsbad, New Mexico.
Northwest: Portland, Seattle-Tacoma, Spokane. Inquire about connections

Hitchhiking

Hitchhiking is illegal in many places and ill-advised everywhere. It's an inefficient and dangerous method of travel. In a word, don't!

to air terminals at Medford, Oregon, and Port Angeles, Washington.

Alaska: Anchorage. Inquire about connections using small regional carriers to Fairbanks, Homer, and Juneau. Note: Alaska has very little highway. You should plan on flying to your destination.

Rocky Mountains: Billings-Logan, Missoula, Great Falls, Bozeman, Denver, Salt Lake City. Inquire about connections to air terminals at Rapid City, South Dakota; Jackson Hole and Yellowstone, Wyoming; and Kalispell and Glacier Park, Montana.

Getting There By Train

Amtrak offers services to more than 500 destinations across the US, but it services only one national park directly. The Empire Builder between Chicago and Seattle stops seasonally at Glacier National Park. Other lines make stops near several parks where you can rent a car or arrange another mode of transportation. Generally speaking, the trains are comfortable and reliable, with lounges, restaurants, snack bars, and, in some cases, movies and live entertainment.

Amtrak's Southwest Chief runs from Chicago to Los Angeles, with stops near park areas at Raton, Santa Fe, Albuquerque, and Gallup, New Mexico; Winslow, Flagstaff (Open Road Tours bus service serves the South Rim of the Grand Canyon) and Kingman, Arizona; and Needles and Barstow, California. Note: the **New Mexico Rail Runner Express** train runs frequently between Albuquerque and the Santa Fe Depot in downtown Santa Fe. From here, you can rent a car or join a tour to nearby parks.

The Sunset Limited runs from Orlando to Los Angeles, with stops

RV Rentals

No special license is needed to operate a motor home (or RV – recreational vehicle), but they aren't cheap. If you add up the cost of rental fees, insurance, gas, and campgrounds, you may find that renting a car and staying in motels or camping is cheaper.

RVs are also large and slow and may be hard to handle on mountain roads. If parking space is tight, driving an RV can be very inconvenient. Also, access to some park roads may be limited. For more information, call the **Recreational Vehicle Rental Association**, tel: 800-336-0355 or visit www.rvra.org.

near park areas at Alpine and El Paso, Texas; Deming, New Mexico; Tucson and Maricopa, Arizona; and North Palm Springs, California.

The California Zephyr runs from Chicago to San Francisco, with stops near park areas at Denver and Grand Junction, Colorado; Green River, Provo, and Salt Lake City, Utah; Reno, Nevada; and Sacramento, California.

The Empire Builder runs from Chicago to Seattle, with stops near park areas at Williston, North Dakota; East Glacier Park, Montana; and Seattle, Washington.

The Coast Starlight runs from Seattle to Los Angeles, with stops near park areas at Tacoma, Washington; Klamath Falls, Oregon; Redding, Sacramento, and Santa Barbara, California.

The San Joaquins line runs from Oakland to Bakersfield, with stops near park areas at Merced (Amtrak Thruway bus service to Yosemite) and Fresno, California.

Be sure to ask about two- or three-stopover discounts and deals for senior citizens, military veterans, AAA members, students, and children.

Visit www.amtrak.com or call **800-USA-RAIL** or your local Amtrak representative for more information.

Getting There By Bus

One of the least expensive ways to travel in America is by bus. The biggest national bus company is **Greyhound** (tel: 800-231-2222, www.greyhound.com), which has agencies overseas. Greyhound buses are comfortable, air conditioned and even have electrical outlets and free Wi-fi on board these days.

The company routinely offers discounts as low as a $99 go-anywhere fare and special Web-only fares. Call the Greyhound office nearest you for information on special rates and package tours.

Greyhound generally does not service national parks. A car rental, shuttle bus, or other mode of travel is necessary from the major hubs.

Getting There By Car

Driving is by far the most flexible and convenient way of traveling to the national parks.

Major roads are well maintained, although backcountry roads in or near the parks may be unpaved. If you plan on driving into remote areas or will be encountering heavy snow, mud, or severe weather, it's a good idea to use a four-wheel-drive vehicle with high clearance.

Your greatest asset as a driver is a

good road map. These can be obtained from state tourism offices, gas stations, supermarkets, and convenience stores. Although roads are maintained even in remote areas, you should listen to local radio stations and check with highway officials or park rangers for the latest information on weather and road conditions, especially if you plan on leaving paved roads.

Driving conditions vary greatly, depending on elevation. During fall, winter, and early spring, your car should be equipped with snow tires or chains, a small collapsible shovel and an ice scraper. Be prepared for the extra time required to drive along winding, narrow mountain roads.

If you plan to drive in desert areas, carry extra water – at least 1 gallon (4 liters) per person per day (5-gallon containers are easily available in supermarkets) – and take some food, too. Flash floods may occur during the rainy season, from early summer to fall. Be very cautious about driving across dry washes; unseen storms upstream can send floodwaters down a canyon rapidly and wash away your car.

Service stations can be few and far between in remote areas. Not every town has one and many close early. Check your gas gauge often. It's always better to have more fuel than you think you will need. If possible, carry a spare gallon of gas with you, and spare tires in remote desert areas.

If your car breaks down on a backroad, do not attempt to strike out on foot, even with water. A car is easier to spot than a person and gives shelter from the elements. Sit tight and wait to be found. Use a mirror or CD to signal for help.

Finally, if you intend to do a lot of driving, it's a good idea to join the **American Automobile Association**. The AAA offers emergency road service, maps, insurance, bail bond protection, and other services, such as hotel discounts (AAA, 1000 AAA Drive, Heathrow, FL 32746; tel: 407-829-5500; www.aaa.com).

Car Rental

National car rental agencies are located at all airports, cities, and large towns. In most places, you must be at least 21 years old (25 in some states) to rent a car, and you must have a valid driver's license and at least one major credit card. Foreign drivers must have an international driver's license. Check that you are properly insured for both collision and personal liability. Insurance may not be included in the base rental fee. Additional cost varies depending on the car and the type of coverage but usually ranges between $10 and $20 per day. You may already be covered by your own auto insurance or credit card company, so check with them first.

You should also inquire about an unlimited mileage package. Otherwise, you may be charged an extra 10–25¢ or more per mile over a given limit. Rental fees vary depending on time of year, how far in advance you book and if you travel on weekdays or weekends. Be sure to inquire about discounts or benefits for which you may be eligible, including corporate, credit card or frequent-flyer programs.

Rental Agency Numbers
Alamo: tel: 800-327-9633, www.go alamo.com.
Avis. tel. 800-831-2847, www.avis.com.
Budget: tel: 800-527-0700, www. budget.com.
Dollar: tel: 800-800-4000, www.dollar. com.
Enterprise: tel: 800-325-8007, www. enterprise.com.
Hertz: tel: 800-654-3131, www.hertz. com.
National. tel. 800-227-7308, www. nationalcar.com.
Thrifty: tel: 800-367-2277, www.thrifty. com.

Shuttle System

Free park shuttles, often running on green fuels, are now operating in and around many national parks, allowing you to park and ride. They run on a series of loops all day long and make stops at the most popular attractions within the park. Most, such as the shuttles at Yosemite and Bryce Canyon, are optional, and you can still drive around the park, if you wish, although you will run into traffic jams and parking at the most popular parks in summer. During the high season, parks like Grand Canyon and Zion have instituted mandatory shuttle use on the most popular routes in their parks (West Rim Drive at Grand Canyon, Zion Canyon in Zion). Alaska's Denali National Park requires visitors to use a concessionaire-run shuttle system to get around. Advance reservations are required.

V isas and Passports
Visas and Entry

A machine-readable passport, a passport-sized photograph (note: the

ABOVE: take the steam train round Mount Rainier National Park.

size required in Britain is different from that in a US passport), a visitor's visa, proof of intent to leave the US after your visit, and (depending upon your country of origin) an international vaccination certificate, are required of most foreign nationals for entry into the US.

Visitors from the UK staying less than 90 days no longer need a visa (visa waiver); however, non-US residents from VWP countries are required to submit information about themselves online to the Department of Homeland Security and be pre-approved for travel to the US at least three days before they travel. It is compulsory for short-term visitors to the US to register via the website of the Electronic System for Travel Authorization (www.csta.us/travel_ authorization.html) before traveling.

Vaccination certificate requirements vary, but proof of immunization against smallpox or cholera may be necessary.

US citizens traveling by air between the US, Canada, Mexico, the Caribbean, and Bermuda must present a current passport; a birth certificate and photo ID are no longer valid proof.

Up-to-date details on entry requirements and machine-readable passports may be found on the US State Department's website: www.travel. state.gov/visa/visa_1750.html.

Extension of stay

Non-US citizens should contact US Immigration and Naturalization Service at 425 I Street, Washington, DC 20536
Tel: 202-501-4444
Toll free: 888-407-4747

W eights and Measures

Despite efforts to convert to metric, the US still uses the Imperial System of weights and measures.

1 inch	= 2.54cm
1ft	= 30.48cm
1 yard	= 0.9144 meter
1 mile	= 1.609km
1 pint	= 0.473 liter
1 quart	= 0.946 liter
1 ounce	= 28.4 grams
1 pound	= 0.454kg
1 acre	= 0.405 hectare
1 sq mile	= 259 hectares
1 centimeter	= 0.394 inch
1 meter	= 39.37 inches
1 kilometer	= 0.622 mile
1 liter	= 1.057 quarts
1 gram	= 0.035 ounce
1 kilogram	= 2.205 pounds
1 hectare	= 2.471 acres
1 sq km	= 0.386 sq mile

Wildlife

Never approach wild animals. Don't try to feed or touch them, not even the "cute" ones like chipmunks, squirrels, and prairie dogs (they may carry diseases). Some animals, such as bison, may seem placid and slow-moving but will charge if irritated. People who have tried to creep up on bison or moose in order to get a better photograph have been seriously injured. Buy a telephoto lens.

Store your food in airtight bags or containers, especially in bear country. Hang food at least 15ft (5 meters) above the ground and several hundred yards/meters from camp. Be careful with deodorants, colognes, perfumes, and anything else that a bear might think has an interesting odor.

ABOVE: tuning up in Santa Fe.

Wild and Scenic Rivers and National Seashores

In addition to the parks and monuments covered in the color section of this book, the National Park Service and other federal land management agencies administer a system of protected, free-flowing streams and rivers, designated as wild and scenic rivers, and stretches of beach named national seashores. Contact these units directly for information on hours, seasons, access, recreational opportunities, weather and road conditions.

Alagnak Wild River, c/o Katmai National Park and Preserve, PO Box 245, King Salmon, AK 99613, tel: 907-246-3305, www.nps.gov/alag.
Alatna Wild River, Gates of the Arctic National Park and Preserve, 201 First Avenue, Fairbanks, AK 99701, tel: 907-692-5494, www.nps.gov/gaar/alat.
Aniakchak River, c/o Aniakchak National Monument and Preserve, PO Box 245, King Salmon, AK 99613, tel: 907-246-3305, www.nps.gov/ania.
Charley River, Yukon-Charley Rivers National Preserve, Eagle Visitor Center, PO Box 167, Eagle, AK 99738, tel: 907-547-2233, www.nps.gov/yuch.
Chilikadrotna River, Lake Clark National Park and Preserve, 240 West 5th Avenue, Suite 236, Anchorage, AK 99501, tel: 907-644-3626, www.nps.gov/lacl.
Flathead River, Flathead National Forest, 650 Wolf Pack Way, Kalispell, MT 59901, tel: 406-758-5200, www.fs.fed.us/r1/flathead.
John Wild River, Gates of the Arctic National Park and Preserve, 201 First Avenue, Fairbanks, AK 99701,

tel: 907-692-5494, www.rivers.gov/wsr-john.html.
Kern River, Sequoia/Kings Canyon National Park, 47050 Generals Highway, Three Rivers, CA 93271, tel: 559-565-3341, www.rivers.gov/wsr-kern.html.
Kings River, Sequoia/Kings Canyon National Park, 47050 Grants Highway, Three Rivers, CA 93271-9700, tel: 559-565-3341, www.rivers.gov/wsr-kings.html.
Kobuk Wild River, Gates of the Arctic National Park and Preserve, 201 First Avenue, Fairbanks, AK 99701, tel: 907-692-5494, www.rivers.gov/wsr-kobuk.html.
Merced River, Yosemite National Park, PO Box 577, Yosemite National Park, CA 95389-0577, tel: 209-372-0200, www.nps.gov/yose.
Missouri National Recreational Rivers, 508 East Second Street, Yankton, SD 57078, tel: 605-665-0209, www.nps.gov/mnrr.
Mulchatna River, Lake Clark National Park and Preserve, 4230 University Drive, Suite 311, Anchorage, AK 99508-4626, tel: 907-644-3626, www.nps.gov/lacl.
Niobrara National Scenic River, PO Box 319, Valentine, NE 69201, tel: 402-376-1901, www.rivers.gov/wsr-niobrara.html.
Noatak River, Gates of the Arctic National Park and Preserve, 201 First Avenue, Fairbanks, AK 99701, tel: 907-692-5494, www.nps.gov/gaar.
North Fork of the Koyukuk Wild River, Gates of the Arctic National Park and Preserve, 201 First Avenue, Fairbanks, AK 99701, tel: 907-692-5494, www.nps.gov/gaar.
Point Reyes National Seashore, 1 Bear Valley Road, Point Reyes

Station, CA 94956, tel: 415-464-5100, www.nps.gov/pore.
Rio Grande Wild and Scenic River, Big Bend National Park, PO Box 129, Big Bend National Park, TX 79834-0129, tel: 432-477-2251, www.nps.gov/rigr.
Salmon Wild River, Kobuk Valley National Park, Western Arctic National Parklands, PO Box 1029, Kotzebue, AK 99752-1029, tel: 907-442-3890, www.nps.gov/noaa.
Tinayguk Wild River, Gates of the Arctic National Park and Preserve, 201 First Avenue, Fairbanks, AK 99701, tel: 907-692-5494, www.nps.gov/gaar.
Tlikakila Wild River, Lake Clark National Park and Preserve, 4230 University Drive, Suite 311, Anchorage, AK 99508-4626, tel: 907-644-3626, www.nps.gov/lacl.
Tuolumne River, Yosemite National Park, PO Box 577, Yosemite National Park, CA 95389-0577, tel: 209-372-0200, www.nps.gov/yose.

Nonprofit Cooperating Associations and Organizations

Books, maps, seminars, tours, and other services are available from the following nonprofit educational organizations:
Alaska Geographic, 810 East Ninth Avenue, Anchorage, AK 99501, tel: 877-AKPARKS or 907-274-8440, www.alaskageographic.org.
Arizona Memorial Museum Association, 1 Arizona Memorial Place, Honolulu, Hawaii 96818, tel: 808-422-5664, www.arizonamemorial.org
Badlands Natural History Association, PO Box 47, Interior, SD 57750, tel: 888-433-5584 or 605-433-5489, www.badlandsnha.org.
Black Hills Parks and Forests Association, 26611 US Highway 385, Hot Springs, SD 57747, tel: 605-745-7020, www.blackhillsparks.org.
Big Bend Natural History Association, PO Box 196, Big Bend National Park, TX 79834, tel: 432-477-2236, www.bigbendbookstore.org.
Bryce Canyon Natural History Association, PO Box 640051, Bryce Canyon, UT 84764, tel: 435-834-4783, www.brycecanyon.org.
Canyonlands Natural History Association, 3015 South Highway 191, Moab, UT 84532, tel: 800-840-8978 or 435-259-6003, www.cnha.org.
Capitol Reef Natural History Association, HC 70 Box 15, Torrey, UT 84775, Tel: 435-425-3791 ext. 106, www.capitolreefnha.org.
Carlsbad Caverns-Guadalupe Mountains Association, PO Box

1417, Carlsbad, NM 88221, tel: 575-785-2486, www.ccgma.org.
Colorado Mountain Club, 710 10th Street, Suite 200, Golden, CO 80401, tel: 303-279-3080, www.cmc.org.
Crater Lake Natural History Association, PO Box 157, Crater Lake, OR 97604, tel: 541-594-2211, www.nps.gov/archive/crla/nha.htm.
Discover Your Northwest, 164 South Jackson Street, Seattle, WA 98104, tel: 877-874-6775, www.discovernw.org.
Death Valley Natural History Association, Hwy 190-Panamint, Death Valley, CA 92328, tel: 760-786-2146, www.dvnha.org.
Glacier Natural History Association, PO Box 310, West Glacier, MT 59936, tel: 406-888-5756, www.glacierassociation.org.
Glen Canyon Natural History Association, PO Box 1835, Page, AZ 86040, tel: 877-453-6296 or 928-608-6358, www.gcnha.org.
Golden Gate National Parks Conservancy, Building 201, Fort Mason, San Francisco, CA 94123, tel: 415-561-3000, www.parksconservancy.org.
Grand Canyon Association, PO Box 399, Grand Canyon, AZ 86023, tel: 800-858-2808 or 928-638-2481, www.grandcanyon.org.
Grand Staircase-Escalante National Monument, 190 East Center Street,

Kanab, UT 84741, tel: 435-644-4388, www.gsenm.org.
Grand Teton Association, PO Box 170, Moose, WY 83012, tel: 307-739-3403, www.grandtetonpark.org.
Hawaii Natural History Association, PO Box 74, Hawaii Volcanoes National Park, HI 96718, tel: 808-985-6051, www.hawaiinaturalhistory.org.
Intermountain Natural History Association, 1291 East Highway 40, Vernal, UT 84078-2830, tel: 800-845-3466, www.inhaweb.com.
Joshua Tree National Park Association, 74485 National Park Drive, Twentynine Palms, CA 92277, tel: 760-367-5525, www.joshuatree.org.
Lassen Association, PO Box 220, Mineral, CA 96063, tel: 530-595-3399, www.lassenassociation.org.
Mesa Verde Museum Association, Inc., PO Box 38, Mesa Verde, CO 81330, tel: 800-305-6053 or 970-529-4445, www.mesaverde.org.
Mount Rushmore History Association, 13030 Hwy 244 Keystone, SD 57751, tel: 800-699-3142, mtrushmorebookstore.com.
Mount St Helens Institute, 42218 NE Yale Bridge Road, Amboy, WA 98601, tel: 360-449-7883, www.mshinstitute.org.
Point Reyes National Seashore Association, 1 Bear Valley Road, Building 70, Point Reyes Station,

CA 94956, tel: 415-663-1200, www.pointreyes.org.
Redwood Park Association, 1111 2nd Street, Crescent City, CA 95531, tel: 707-464-9150, www.redwoodparkassociation.org.
Rocky Mountain Nature Association, PO Box 3100, Rocky Mountain National Park, Estes Park, CO 80517, tel: 970-586-0108, www.rmna.org.
Sequoia Natural History Association, 47050 Generals Highway, Suite 10, Three Rivers, CA 93271, tel: 559-565-3759, www.sequoiahistory.org.
Theodore Roosevelt Nature & History Association, PO Box 167, Medora, ND 58645, tel: 701-623-4884, www.trnha.org.
Western National Parks Association, 12880 North Vistoso Village Drive, Tucson, AZ 85737, tel: 520-622-1999, www.wnpa.org.
Yellowstone Association, PO Box 117, Yellowstone National Park, WY 82190, tel: 406-848-2400, www.yellowstoneassociation.org.
Yosemite Association, PO Box 230, El Portal, CA 95318, tel: 209-379-2321 or 209-379-2646, www.yosemite.org.
Zion Natural History Association, Zion National Park, Springdale, UT 84767, tel: 800-635-3959 or 435-772-3265, www.zionpark.org.

National Trails System

The National Park Service, in association with other state and federal agencies, manages a system of scenic, historic, and recreational trails, many of which pass through or between national parks and monuments. Contact these regional offices for maps and information on access, recreational activities, and weather conditions.

Ala Kahakai National Historic Trail, 73-4786 Kanalani Street, Suite 14, Kailua-Kona, HI 96740, tel: 808-326-6012, www.nps.gov/alka.
California National Historic Trail, NPS National Trails System Office, 324 South State Street, PO Box 30, Salt Lake City, UT 84111, tel: 801-741-1012, www.nps.gov/cali.
Continental Divide National Scenic Trail, US Forest Service, Northern Region, Federal Building, PO Box 7669, Missoula, MT 59807, tel: 303-275-5054, www.fs.fed.us/cdt/admin.htm.
El Camino de los Tejas National Historic Trail, National Trails Intermountain Region, PO Box 728,

Santa Fe, NM 87504-0728, tel: 505-988-6098, www.nps.gov/elte.
El Camino Real de la Tierra Adentro National Historic Trail, National Trails Intermountain Region, PO Box 728, Santa Fe, NM 87504-0728, www.nps.gov/elca.
Iditarod National Historic Trail, Anchorage District, Bureau of Land Management, 4700 BLM Road, Anchorage, AK 99507, tel: 907-267-1246, www.blm.gov/ak/st/en/info/directory.html.
Juan Bautista de Anza National Historic Trail, Pacific West Regional Office, National Park Service, 1111 Jackson Street, Suite 700, Oakland, CA 94607, tel: 510-817-1323, www.nps.gov/juba.
Lewis and Clark National Historic Trail, 601 Riverfront Drive, Omaha, NE 68102, tel: 402-661-1804, www.nps.gov/lecl.
Mormon Pioneer National Historic Trail, NPS National Trails System Office, 324 South State Street, Suite 200, Salt Lake City, UT 84111, tel: 801-741-1012, www.nps.gov/mopi.

Nez Perce National Historic Trail, US Forest Service, 2730 Highway 12, Orofino, ID 83544, tel: 208-476-8334, www.fs.fed.us/npnht.
Old Spanish National Historic Trail, National Trails Intermountain Region, PO Box 728, Santa Fe, NM 87504-0728, tel: 505-988-6098, www.nps.gov/olsp.
Oregon National Historic Trail, NPS National Trails System Office, 324 South State Street, Suite 200, Salt Lake City, UT 84111, tel: 801-741-1012, www.nps.gov/oreg.
Pacific Crest National Scenic Trail, US Forest Service, Pacific Southwest Region, 1323 Club Drive, Vallejo, CA 94592, tel: 707-562-8881, www.fs.fed.us/pct.
Pony Express National Historic Trail, NPS National Trails System Office, 324 South State Street, Suite 200, Salt Lake City, UT 84111, tel: 801-741-1012, www.nps.gov/poex.
Santa Fe National Historic Trail, National Trails Intermountain Region, National Park Service, PO Box 728, Santa Fe, NM 87504-0728, tel: 505-988-6888, www.nps.gov/safe.

C ALIFORNIA AND THE PACIFIC

PRACTICAL INFORMATION ON CALIFORNIA, INCLUDING DEATH VALLEY, YOSEMITE, AND REDWOOD

Accommodations

The price guide indicates approximate room/cabin rates:
$ = $110 or less
$$ = $110–250
$$$ = more than $250

CALIFORNIA

Cabrillo National Monument

Address 1800 Cabrillo Memorial Drive, San Diego, CA 92106-3601, tel: 619-557-5450, www.nps.gov/cabr.
Access Ten miles (16km) from San Diego: follow Highway 209 south from I-5 and I-8 to the tip of Point Loma.
Seasons and Hours Open daily 9am–5.15pm.
Charge Yes.
Handicapped Access Visitor center, plus ramps throughout much of the park. Audio Station Programs available in six languages.
Activities Scenic drives, hiking, bicycling, wildlife watching, interpretive programs.
Special Events *December–March*: Gray whale migration.
Late September: Cabrillo Festival – cultural dances, food, and re-enactment of Juan Rodríguez Cabrillo's 1542 landing.
Camping No camping within the park.
Permits and Licenses Permits required for film shoots, weddings, group tide pool visits, memorial services, and other events.
Gateway Community San Diego.
Accommodations None within the park. Plentiful food, gas, and lodging

in San Diego. For information, contact the San Diego International Visitor Information Center, 1040 West Broadway, San Diego, CA 92101, tel: 619-236-1212, www.sandiego.org.
Weather Mediterranean climate, with summer temperatures 80–100°F (27–38°C), winter temperatures 35–75°F (2–24°C).
General Information The monument offers programs and a small museum about Juan Rodríguez Cabrillo, a superb view of San Diego harbor, and whale-watching in winter. The Old Point Loma Lighthouse, Fort Rosecrans coastal defense remains, a coastal sage scrub ecosystem, and the Cabrillo tide pools are preserved by the National Park Service.

Channel Islands National Park

Address 1901 Spinnaker Drive, Ventura, CA 93001-4354, tel: 805-658-5730, www.nps.gov/chis.
Access The islands can be reached by boat from park headquarters in Ventura. The authorized park concessionaire is Island Packers, 3600 Harbor Boulevard, Ventura, CA 93035, tel: 805-382-1779, www.island packers.com. For air transport to Santa Rosa Island, contact Channel Islands Aviation, 305 Durley Avenue, Camarillo, CA 93010, tel: 805-987-1301; www.flycia.com. If possible, you should reserve well in advance. To get information and permits to visit The Nature Conservancy (TNC) lands on western Santa Cruz, contact The Nature Conservancy, Santa Cruz Island Preserve, 201 Mission Street, San Francisco, CA 94105, tel: 415-777-0487; www.tnc.org.
Seasons and Hours The park is open

daily year-round. Visitor center: daily 8.30am–5pm; closed Thanksgiving and Christmas.
Charge No, but concessionaire charges a fee for boat trips.
Handicapped Access Visitor centers and boat and plane tours are wheelchair accessible; the islands are undeveloped and do not offer accessible trails.
Activities Backpacking, camping, scuba diving, snorkeling, swimming, boating, kayaking, sailing, bird-watching, whale watching, interpretive programs.
Camping Reservations and permits required, tel: 877-444-6777 or www. recreation.gov, up to 5 months in advance. Experienced kayakers and boaters may camp on Santa Rosa Island beaches.
Permits and Licenses Free permit required for private boaters to hike beyond the ranger station on San Miguel (tel: 805-658-5711). Private boaters must have a permit to land on Western Santa Cruz (allow 10 days for processing). Contact TNC, tel: 415-777-0487, www.tnc.org/cruzpermit.
Gateway community Ventura.
Accommodations No lodging in the park. Food, gas, and lodging are available in Ventura. Contact Ventura

Keep Your Distance

Visiting tide pools, beaches, and other areas on the Channel Islands may inadvertently disturb some endangered species, including the Californian brown pelican, or seals and sea lions. These animals are protected by federal law: stay far enough away so as to not disturb them.

Visitors & Convention Bureau, 101 South California Street, Ventura, CA 93001, tel: 800-483-6214, www.ventura-usa.com.

Food and Supplies No stores or restaurants in the park. Food and supplies available in Ventura.

Weather Summer is extremely dry on the islands, with temperatures usually 55–80°F (13–27°C). Winter temperatures usually 45–65°F (7–18°C). Be prepared for high winds, fog, and sea spray at any time.

General Information Backcountry users should carry all necessary food and water.

Death Valley National Park

Address PO Box 579, Death Valley, CA 92328, tel: 760-786-3200, www.nps.gov/deva.

Access Death Valley is about 150 miles (240km) from Las Vegas, Nevada. Follow I-95 north to Highway 373. Drive south to Death Valley Junction, then take Highway 190 into the park. If you're entering from California, enter the park on Highway 190 from the little town of Olancha or Highway 178 from Ridgecrest.

Seasons and Hours The park is open daily year-round. The visitor center is open daily 8am–5pm.

Charge Yes.

Handicapped Access Visitor center, Salt Creek Nature Trail and some campgrounds.

Activities Scenic drives, backpacking, camping, hiking, bicycling, wildlife watching, interpretive programs, backcountry roads, golfing, and horseback riding.

Special Events *November:* The Death Valley '49ers Encampment features special tours, presentations, art shows, and other festivities. *March/April:* Easter week is celebrated during the Spring Fling at Furnace Creek Inn with fun Easter egg hunts, a colorful parade, and a golf tournament.

Camping All campgrounds are first-come, first-served, except for Furnace Creek and group sites, which must be reserved by contacting 877-444-8777 or www.recreation.gov.

Permits and Licenses Free backcountry permits may be obtained at Furnace Creek Visitor Center or Stovepipe Wells Ranger Station.

Gateway Communities: a number of desert communities in Nevada and California east of the park lie just outside park boundaries. Along Interstate 95 in Nevada are Tonopah, Goldfield, Beatty, Indian Springs, and Las Vegas; Amargosa Valley and Stateline are on Highway 373; and Pahrump, a hot springs resort, is between Death Valley and Las Vegas. Closest to the park along Highway 127 in California are Death Valley Junction, Shoshone, Tecopa, and Baker.

Accommodations The park contains three lodges, ranging from a full-service resort to a modest motel: **$$$** *Furnace Creek Inn,* tel: 760-786-2345. **$$** *Furnace Creek Ranch,* tel: 760-786-2345. **$** *Stovepipe Wells Village Motel,* tel: 760-786-2387.

Make reservations well in advance. Additional lodging is available outside the park at the Panamint Springs Resort, tel: 775-482-7680. Inexpensive lodgings may be found in communities listed above, along Highway 95 and 373 in Nevada and Highway 127 in California.

Food and Supplies Restaurants and limited supplies are available in the park at Furnace Creek, Scotty's Castle and Stovepipe Wells and nearby communities, such as Baker.

Weather Summer temperatures commonly exceed 120°F (49°C) in the valley. Winter is milder, with snowfall in higher elevations. Flash floods can occur in any season.

General Information Carry water for yourself and your car at all times. Carry and drink at least a gallon (4 liters) per person per day (5-gallon water containers with built-in taps to carry in your car are available at all supermarkets). Do not underestimate the heat and aridity. Plan on visiting cooler, higher-elevation sites during summer. Flash floods are dangerous. Do not walk or drive in low-lying areas during or immediately after a rainstorm. Do not attempt to cross a flooded road. Abandoned mines are extremely dangerous. Contact rangers before entering.

Devils Postpile National Monument

Address PO Box 3999, Mammoth Lakes, CA 93546, tel: 760-934-2289, www.nps.gov/depo.

Access The monument is about 13 miles (21km) from Mammoth Lakes, California, along a winding narrow road. Follow Highway 395 south from Bridgeport or north from Bishop. Note: a mandatory shuttle has been introduced and operates between mid-June and Labor Day between Mammoth Mountain Main Lodge Adventure Center and Reds Meadow Valley. Visitors may drive in before 7am or after 7.30pm in their own vehicles. All park visitors pay the transportation fee to enter the valley, whether using their own car or not.

Seasons and Hours Open daily, mid-June–October. Call ahead to confirm opening.

Charge Yes. (America the Beautiful Passes and other passes are not currently accepted.)

Handicapped Access Ranger station, toilets, and picnic tables.

Activities Guided walks, hiking, camping, wildlife watching, interpretive programs, fishing.

Camping First-come, first-served.

Permits and Licenses California fishing license.

Gateway Community Mammoth Lakes.

Accommodations None in the park. Lodging is available in Mammoth Lakes and Reds Meadow. Contact Mammoth Lakes Visitors Bureau, PO Box 48, Mammoth Lakes, CA 93546, tel: 888-GO-MAMMOTH, www.visitmammoth.com.

Food and Supplies None in the park.

BELOW: scrap mining equipment in Death Valley National Park.

Restaurants and supplies are available in Mammoth Lakes and Reds Meadow.
Weather The park is closed in winter. Expect cool nights and summer thunderstorms.
General Information Located between Yosemite and Sequoia national parks, this seasonally open 798-acre (323-hectare) park protects dramatic basalt columns, Rainbow Falls, and a section of the John Muir Trail.

Golden Gate National Recreation Area

Address Fort Mason, Building 201, San Francisco, CA 94123-1307, tel: 415-561-4700, www.nps.gov/goga.
Access The park is at the headlands of the Golden Gate in San Francisco and Marin County. It can be reached by car from Highway 101 or by public transportation.
Seasons and Hours Access to the recreation area daily year-round. Facilities vary in their opening hours, between 8 and 10am, and most close between 4.30pm and sunset; closed Thanksgiving, Christmas, and New Year's Day.
Charge For select tours and facilities.
Handicapped Access Visitor center, Muir Woods Nature Trail, Alcatraz tour.
Activities Hiking, biking, swimming (Stinson Beach only), golf, wildlife watching, interpretive programs, tours of Alcatraz, museums and historic ships.
Camping Contact 877-444-6777 or www.recreation.gov to reserve campgrounds at Kirby Cove; all other campgrounds, reserve through Marin Headlands Visitor Center, tel: 415-391-1540.
Permits and Licenses None.
Gateway Community San Francisco/Bay Area communities.
Accommodations None in the actual park. Lodging is available in the Bay Area. Contact San Francisco Convention & Visitors Bureau, 900 Market Street, San Francisco, CA 94102, tel: 415-391-2000, www.onlyinsanfrancisco.com.
Food and Supplies Food service is available at some facilities and throughout the surrounding area.
Weather Cool and breezy. Make sure you take a jacket in summer. Expect rain in winter and spring, and some fog in summer.
General Information This urban park includes beaches, coastal wildlands, hiking trails, Alcatraz Island, military sites, and Fort Mason cultural center.

Joshua Tree National Park

Address 74485 National Park Drive, Twentynine Palms, CA 92277, tel: 760-367-5500, www.nps.gov/jotr.
Access The park is about 140 miles (225km) east of Los Angeles. To enter from the north, take I-10 east to Palm Springs, then Highway 62 to either Joshua Tree or Twentynine Palms. To enter from the south, take I-10 east to the Cottonwood entrance.
Seasons and Hours Open daily all year round. The park is open 24 hours; visitor centers are open daily 8am–5pm.
Charge Yes.
Handicapped Access Visitor centers, Cap Rock, Bajada, and Oasis of Mara nature trails.
Activities Scenic drives, backpacking, camping, hiking, bicycling, rock climbing, wildlife watching, interpretive programs, and backcountry roads.
Camping Black Rock and Indian Cove may be reserved from September to Memorial Day, up to six months in advance, tel: 877-444-6777 or log on to www.recreation.gov. All other campgrounds are open on a first-come, first-served basis.
Permits and Licenses Self-registration at backcountry clipboards. Contact park for details.
Gateway Community Twentynine Palms.
Accommodations None in the park. Inexpensive lodging is available in Twentynine Palms, Joshua Tree, Yucca Valley, Palm Springs, and Indio. Contact local chambers of commerce for information.
Food and Supplies Restaurants and supplies are available in Twentynine Palms, Joshua Tree, Yucca Valley, Palm Springs, and Indio.
Weather Summer temperatures exceed 100°F (38°C). Winter lows 35–45°F (2–7°C).
General Information Carry water for yourself and your car during hottest months. For people, carry at least a gallon (4 liters) per person per day (5-gallon water bottles with taps are available at supermarkets to carry in the car). Do not enter abandoned mine shafts; they are dark and extremely dangerous.

Lassen Volcanic National Park

Address PO Box 100, Mineral, CA 96063-0100, tel: 530-595-4480, www.nps.gov/lavo.
Access The park is 48 miles (77km) east of Redding via Highway 44, 51

Hot Spots

Take great care when walking in Lassen Volcanic or Hawaii Volcanoes national parks. Always stay on the marked trails near hot springs, lava flows, and other geothermal areas. The ground may be thin and easily broken, which can cause severe burns.

miles (82km) east of Red Bluff via Highways 36 and 89.
Seasons and Hours The park is open daily year-round. Sections of Lassen Park Road are usually closed by snow from late October to mid-June. The visitor center is open daily 8am–5pm (until 6pm in summer); closed public holidays.
Charge Yes.
Handicapped Access Visitor center and select campgrounds.
Activities Scenic drives, backpacking, camping, hiking, cross-country skiing, snowshoeing (January–March), boating, wildlife watching, naturalist programs (June–August).
Camping Eight campgrounds are open June–September. Four are open on a first-come, first-served basis, and four may be reserved ahead of time by contacting 877-444-6777 or www.recreation.gov.
Permits and Licenses Free wilderness permit required for backcountry camping.
Gateway Community Mineral.
Accommodations
$$ *Drakesbad Guest Ranch* (rustic lodge and cabins); call 530-529-1512 for information and reservations. Additional inexpensive lodging is available in Mineral, Chester, Redding, and Red Bluff. Contact Shasta Cascade Wonderland Association, 1699 Highway 273, Anderson, CA 96007, tel: 530-365-7500, www.shastacascade.org.
Food and Supplies The Manzanita Lake Camper Store offers food and gifts daily during the summer months. Additional services at Mineral, Chester, Red Bluff, and Redding.
Weather Summer temperatures usually 40–80°F (4–27°C), colder in higher elevations. Winter temperatures usually 15–45°F (-9–7°C), with abundant snowfall. Snow covers much of the park mid-October through mid-June.
General Information The thin air of high altitude makes hiking in the high country difficult for most lowlanders. Check road and weather conditions before visiting.

Lava Beds National Monument

Address 1 Indian Well Headquarters, Tulelake, CA 96134, tel: 530-667-8100, www.nps.gov/labe.
Access The monument is off Highway 139 about 30 miles (48km) from Tulelake, California, and 60 miles (97km) from Klamath Falls, Oregon.
Seasons and Hours The park is open daily year-round. The visitor center is open 8.30am–5pm in winter, 8am–6pm in summer; closed Christmas.
Charge Yes.
Handicapped Access Visitor center and select campgrounds.
Activities Backpacking, camping, hiking, cave tours (summer only), wildlife watching, prehistoric sites, interpretive programs.
Camping First-come, first-served. Fee charged for campgrounds, no fee for backcountry camping, but checking in at the visitor center is appreciated.
Permits and Licenses No.
Gateway Community Tulelake.
Accommodations None in the park. Inexpensive lodging available in Tulelake and Klamath Falls. Contact Shasta Cascade Wonderland Association, 1699 Highway 273, Anderson, CA 96007, tel: 530-365-7500, www.shastacascade.org.
Food and Supplies None in the park. Nearest stores are at Tionesta and Tulelake.
Weather Generally unpredictable. Summer temperatures usually 40–85°F (4–29°C). Winter temperatures usually 15–40°F (-9–4°C). Freezing temperatures and snow are possible at any time.
General Information Located in Northern California near the Oregon border, this 46,600-acre (18,858-hectare) park preserves a rugged volcanic landscape where Modoc Indians clashed with the US Army in 1872–3. Be sure to notify park rangers before exploring backcountry caves or lava tubes, for your own safety.

Mojave National Preserve

Address 2701 Barstow Road, Barstow, CA 92311, tel: 760-252-6100, www.nps.gov/moja.

Accommodations

Access The Mojave National Preserve is approximately 60 miles (97km) southwest of Las Vegas and 60 miles (97km) east of Barstow, CA, accessible via I-15 and I-40.
Seasons and Hours The preserve is open year-round 24 hours a day. Kelso Depot Visitor Center is open 9am–5pm daily.
Charge No.
Handicapped Access All information centers and some trails.
Activities Scenic drives, camping, hiking, hunting, wildlife watching, interpretive programs.
Permits and Licenses California state hunting regulations apply.
Camping Two campgrounds in the preserve, on a first come basis. Also roadside camping is permitted in areas that have been traditionally used for that purpose.
Gateway Community Barstow is park headquarters. Other surrounding communities include Baker, Ludlow, Nipton, Baker, Searchlight, and Needles.
Accommodations None in the preserve. Towns with inexpensive lodging include Ludlow, Nipton, Baker, Primm, Searchlight, Barstow, and Needles.
Food and Supplies Small stores with limited supplies in Cima and Nipton.
Weather Temperatures above 120°F (49°C) are common in summer. Winters can bring freezing temperatures.
General Information The Mojave National Preserve is 1.6 million acres (650,000 hectares) of desert, encompassing rolling sand dunes, volcanic cinder cones, Joshua tree forests, vast panoramic vistas, and mile-high mountains. The spring wildflower bloom in early March brings many visitors from all over America and beyond.

BELOW: Joshua Tree National Park.

Pinnacles National Monument

Address 5000 Highway 146, Paicines, CA 95043-9762, tel: 831-389-4485, www.nps.gov/pinn.
Access The West District of the monument is located off Highway 101 about 12 miles (19km) east of Soledad. The East District is about 35 miles (56km) south of Hollister via Routes 25 and 146. There is no connecting road between the two districts.
Seasons and Hours The monument is open for day-use year-round. The East Side is open 24 hours; the West Side entrance gate is open 7.30am–8pm. Visitor centers are open daily 9am–5pm.
Charge Yes.
Handicapped Access Visitor centers and some campgrounds.
Activities Hiking, caving, interpretive programs, wildlife watching.
Camping Pinnacles Campground is the park's only campground and is very popular. It adjoins Pinnacles Visitor Center near the east entrance from Highway 25 on Route 146. Reserve through 877-444-6777 or www.recreation.gov.
Permits and Licenses No.
Gateway Communities Soledad and Hollister.
Accommodations None In the park. Lodging is available in Soledad, San Juan Bautista, King City, Hollister, and Salinas. Contact Salinas Valley Chamber of Commerce, 119 East Alisal Street, PO Box 1170, Salinas, CA 93902, tel: 831-424-7611, www.salinaschamber.com.
Food and Supplies None in the park. Services available in Soledad, Hollister, San Juan Bautista, King City, Salinas. Also (weekends only) at Pinnacles Campground near the east entrance.

Weather Summer temperatures can exceed 100°F (38°C). Spring and fall are mild. Low rainfall, mainly in winter and spring.

General Information This 26,480-acre (10,720-hectare) park features dramatic rock spires more than 1,000ft (300 meters) tall. Rock climbing and caving should be attempted by experienced people only. Be sure to carry an adequate supply of water. The park is often filled to capacity at weekends. Due to limited parking, visitors are encouraged to visit the monument on weekdays if possible.

Redwood National and State Parks

Address 1111 Second Street, Crescent City, CA 95531-4198, tel: 707-464-6101; www.nps.gov/redw.

Access The park is about 40 miles (64km) north of Eureka and about 20 miles (32km) south of Crescent City via Highway 101.

Seasons and Hours The park is open daily year-round. Information centers are open daily 9am–5pm, until 6pm in summer; closed Thanksgiving, Christmas, New Year's Day, and, in some cases, all winter.

Charge State park picnic areas only.

Handicapped Access Information centers, Tall Trees shuttle bus and select trails. Prairie Creek Redwoods State Park contains Revelation Trail, specially designed for blind visitors.

Activities Scenic drives, backpacking, biking, camping, hiking, fishing, boating, wildlife watching, interpretive programs.

Permits and Licenses California fishing license and free backcountry camping permits required.

Camping Three developed campgrounds in the redwoods and

one on the coast. Although there are first-come, first-served campgrounds available, reservations are accepted and strongly recommended for camping at the Jedediah Smith, Mill Creek, and Elk Prairie campgrounds between May 1 and September 30. Reservations must be made at least 48 hours in advance by contacting 877-444-7275 or www.recreation.gov.

Gateway Communities Crescent City, Eureka and Klamath.

Accommodations None in the park. Lodging is available in Crescent City, Klamath, and Eureka. Contact the Humboldt County Convention and Visitors Bureau, 1034 2nd Street, Eureka, CA 95501, tel: 800-346-3482, http://redwoods.info.

Food and Supplies Food service and supplies available in Crescent City, Requa, Orick, Klamath, and Eureka.

Weather Temperatures vary depending on location. On the coast, summer daytime temperatures range 55–70°F (13–21°C), winter temperatures 30–40°F (-1–4°C). Inland, summer highs reach 80–100°F (27–38°C), winter lows dip below freezing. Expect heavy rain and fog October–April.

General Information Access to the Tall Trees Grove is limited; summer shuttle bus transports visitors down the rugged 7-mile (11km) road to the trailhead. Otherwise, a limited number of private-vehicle permits are distributed on a first-come, first-served basis. Backpackers must secure a free permit at any information center. Animal-proof food canisters are available to borrow free of charge at Thomas H. Kuchel Visitor Center. Swimming can be extremely dangerous. Ocean water is very cold, the currents are strong, and there are no lifeguards on duty.

Santa Monica Mountains National Recreation Area

Address 401 West Hillcrest Drive, Thousand Oaks, CA 91360, tel: 805-370-2301, www.nps.gov/samo.

Access This huge sprawling wild urban park is west of Griffith Park in Los Angeles County and can be reached on Highways 101 and 1.

Seasons and Hours Park is open year-round. The visitor center in Thousand Oaks is open 9am–5pm, closed Thanksgiving, Christmas, and New Year's.

Charge No.

Handicapped Access Visitor center. Some sites accessible to some degree.

Activities Hiking, mountain-biking, swimming, surfing, wildlife watching, interpretive programs.

Permits and Licenses California fishing license.

Camping First come, first served. Family and group campgrounds at Malibu Creek, Point Magu, and Leo Carrillo state parks may be reserved by contacting 877-444-6777 or www.recreation.gov. Reserve NPS Circle X Group Campground by calling the park in advance.

Gateway Communities Thousand Oaks, Malibu, Topanga and Santa Monica.

Accommodations Lodging is available throughout the Los Angeles metro area. Thousand Oaks and Santa Monica are good options. Contact Los Angeles Convention and Visitors Bureau, 333 South Hope Street, 18th Floor, Los Angeles, CA 90071, tel: 800-228-2452 or 213-624-7300, www.discoverlosangeles.com.

Food and Supplies Within the park in the community of Topanga and Malibu and nearby Santa Monica and Thousand Oaks.

Weather Mediterranean climate, with summer temperatures 80–100°F (27–38°C), winter temperatures 35–75°F (2–24°C). In summer, the coastal side of the mountains is generally 10 degrees cooler than the inland side; in winter, this pattern is reversed.

General Information The national recreation area is a cooperative effort that joins federal, state, and local

BELOW: hikers take a break in Yosemite National Park.

Accommodations

The price guide indicates approximate room/cabin rates:
$ = $110 or less
$$ = $110–250
$$$ = more than $250

park agencies with private preserves to protect the natural and cultural resources of this mountain range and seashore.

Sequoia and Kings Canyon National Parks

Address 47050 Generals Highway, Three Rivers, CA 93271-9700, tel: 559-565-3341 (recorded information), www.nps.gov/seki.

Access The south entrance of Sequoia is 35 miles (56km) from Visalia via Highway 198. The Grant Grove entrance of Kings Canyon is 55 miles (89km) from Fresno via Highway 180.

Seasons and Hours The park is open daily year-round. Sections of the Generals Highway and side roads within the park are closed by snow in winter; tel: 559-565-3341 for road and weather conditions.

Charge Yes.

Handicapped Access Visitor centers, paved trails in Grant Grove and Giant Forest, select campgrounds.

Activities Scenic drives, backpacking, camping, hiking, horseback riding, rock climbing, mountain climbing, fishing, cross-country skiing, snowshoeing, wildlife watching, interpretive programs, backcountry roads.

Special Events *April:* The Jazz Affair in Three Rivers brings music-lovers to a little town just outside the park. *May:* Red Bud Festival in Three Rivers is a two-day arts and crafts fair. *December:* Caroling and ecumenical Christmas service at the base of the General Grant Tree, known as the Nation's Christmas tree.

Camping Mostly first come, first served. Only the Dorst Creek and Lodgepole campgrounds may be reserved up to 6 months in advance by contacting 877-444-6777 or www.recreation.gov. Sites fill early in summer.

Permits and Licenses Backcountry camping permits ($15) required. California fishing license.

Gateway Communities Three Rivers, Visalia, and Fresno.

Accommodations Kings Canyon Park Services (tel: 866-KCANYON, www.sequoia-kingscanyon.com) manages accommodations in Kings Canyon, ranging from cabins to comfortable lodges. Delaware North Park Services (tel: 866-807-3598, www.visitsequoia.com) manages a rustic lodge in Sequoia:
$–$$$ *Wuksachi Lodge* (all year).
$$ *Cedar Grove Lodge* (summer only).
$$ *Grant Grove Lodge* (cabins).
$–$$ *John Muir Lodge.*

$$ *Stony Creek Lodge.*
Additional accommodations are available in Three Rivers, Visalia and Fresno. Contact the Visalia Chamber of Commerce, 220 N. Santa Fe Street, Visalia, CA 93292, tel: 559-734-5876, www.visaliachamber.org.

Food and Supplies In summer, supplies are available at Cedar Grove, Lodgepole, and Stony Creek (Sequoia National Forest). Groceries, meals, and gift shop at Grant Grove year-round. Outside the park, services in Three Rivers, Visalia, and Fresno.

Weather Summer temperatures 50–95°F (10–35°C), colder in higher elevations. Winter temperatures 15–45°F (-9–7°C), with abundant snowfall.

General Information Thin air makes hiking in the high country difficult for lowlanders. If possible, give yourself several days to adjust. Rivers are cold and swift; use caution when hiking near waterways. Check road and weather conditions before visiting in winter.

Whiskeytown National Recreation Area

Address 14412 Kennedy Memorial Drive, PO Box 188, 14412 Kennedy Memorial Drive, Whiskeytown, CA 96095-0188, tel: 530-246-1225, www.nps.gov/whis.

Access The three units of this recreation area can be reached via Highways 5 and 299 from Redding.

Seasons and Hours The recreation area is open daily year-round. The visitor center is open daily 9am–6pm summer, 10am–4pm winter, closed Thanksgiving, Christmas, and New Year's Day.

Charge Yes.

Handicapped Access Visitor center, parts of some trails.

Activities Backpacking, camping, hiking, fishing, wildlife watching, swimming, water-skiing, horseback riding, interpretive programs.

Permits and Licenses Free backcountry permits.

Camping Campsites at Dry Creek Group Tent Campground can be reserved in advance by contacting 877-444-677 or www.recreation.gov. Campsites in the RV, primitive, and tent campgrounds available on a first-come, first-served basis.

Gateway Community Redding.

Accommodations None in the park. Lodging is available in Redding. Contact Shasta Cascade Wonderland Association, 1699 Highway 273, Anderson, CA 96007, tel: 530-365-7500, www.shastacascade.org.

Food and Supplies Beach snack bars and Marina Stores operate daily through the summer. Additional services available in Redding.

Weather Summer temperatures 60–100°F (16–38°C), colder in higher elevations. Winter temperatures 20–50°F (-7–10°C).

General Information The park features backcountry forest and a wide variety of water sports on the large man-made reservoir. The Whiskeytown unit is administered by the National Park Service. The other two units are administered by the National Forest Service.

Yosemite National Park

Address PO Box 577, Yosemite National Park, CA 95389, tel: 209-372-0200, www.nps.gov/yose

Access The park is about 75 miles (120km) northeast of Merced via Route 140, about 100 miles (160km) east of Modesto via Routes 108/120, about 65 miles (105km) north of Fresno via Route 41 and 125 miles (200km) south of Carson City, Nevada, via Highway 395 and Route 120.

YARTS (tel: 877-989-2787) offers bus

BELOW: follow the sign.

Accommodations

The price guide indicates approximate room/cabin rates:
$ = $110 or less
$$ = $110–250
$$$ = more than $250

service from Mammoth Lakes and Merced. Yosemite Via Adventures, Inc. (tel: 800-727-5287) offers a bus service from Merced. Once you're in the park, an excellent free shuttle bus system, running all year, links the main attractions in Yosemite Valley, Tulomne Meadows, (summer only), Wawona-Mariposa Grove of Giant Sequoias, and Badger Pass (in winter). Concessionaire-run sightseeing/hiking bus tours of the Valley, Tuolomne Meadows, and Glacier Point are also available for a fee. For more information, tel: 209-372-1240.

Seasons and Hours The park is open 24 hours a day, year-round. Visitor centers are open daily in summer 8am–5pm, extended hours in some locations, reduced hours in winter. Tuolumne Meadows Visitor Center is open summer only. Tioga Road, Mariposa Grove Road, and Glacier Point Road are closed by snow mid-November–late-May.

Charge Yes.

Handicapped Access Visitor centers, nature center, art center, and select trails and campgrounds.

Activities Scenic drives, bus tours, backpacking, camping, hiking, fishing, boating, horseback riding, biking, swimming, float trips, cross-country skiing, ice skating, snowshoeing, art workshops, wildlife watching, interpretive programs. Call Yosemite Mountaineering School for rock and mountain climbing instruction and guide service, tel: 209-372-1000.

Special Events *January:* Chefs' Holidays bring well-known chefs to the Ahwahnee hotel for a gourmet banquet and demonstrations.
November–December: Vintners' Holidays, wine-tasting and seminars at the Ahwahnee.
December: Historic Bracebridge Dinner Pageant held at the Ahwahnee Hotel. Yosemite Pioneer Christmas re-creates an old-fashioned yuletide at Pioneer Yosemite History Center.

Permits and Licenses California fishing license required. Wilderness permit required for overnight travel into the park's backcountry, tel: 209-372-0740.

Camping Seven of Yosemite's 13 popular campgrounds may be

reserved in advance; other sites are first-come, first-served. For reservations, contact 877-444-6777, www.recreation.gov. Sites fill early between April and September. Make reservations well ahead of time or get here early am.

Gateway Communities El Portal, Oakhurst, Mariposa, Lee Vining, and Groveland.

Accommodations Delaware North Parks & Resorts at Yosemite Inc., (tel: 559-253-5635, www.yosemitepark.com) manages accommodations in the park ranging from cabins to full-service, historic hotels:
$$$ *The Ahwahnee.*
$–$$ *Curry Village.*
$$ *High Sierra Camps (annual lottery only).*
$$ *Tuolumne Meadows Lodge.*
$$ *Wawona Hotel.*
$$ *White Wolf Lodge.*
$$$ *Yosemite Lodge at the Falls.*
Just outside Yosemite, between Wawona and Mariposa Grove, Delaware North also operates Tenaya Lodge at Yosemite, a luxury spa resort open all year. Other accommodations are available in Oakhurst, El Portal, Mariposa, Lee Vining, and Groveland. Contact Yosemite Sierra Visitors Bureau, 41969 Highway 41, Oakhurst, CA 93644, tel: 559-683-4636, www.yosemitethisyear.com.

Food and Supplies Food service and supplies are available in the park at Yosemite Valley, Wawona, Tuolumne Meadows, and White Wolf.

Weather In the valley, summer temperatures are usually 50–95°F (10–35°C), winter temperatures 20–50°F (-7–10°C). Summer temperatures are considerably cooler in the high country, 30–70°F (-1–21°C). Expect summer thunderstorms, and heavy snowfall November–May.
Motorists are required to carry tire chains in their vehicles from November to March.

General Information The park's website is very informative. If you need additional information, write to the Public Information Office, Yosemite National Park, address as above, or tel: 209-372-0200. A ranger is available to answer questions daily 8.30am–5pm (closed for lunch).

HAWAII

Haleakala National Park

Address PO Box 369, Makawao, HI 96768, tel: 808-572-4400,

www.nps.gov/hale.

Access The main entrance of the park is about 19 miles (31km) from Pukalani via roads 377 and 378. The coastal Kipahulu District is about 15 miles (24km) from Hana via Highway 36 (the scenic Hana Highway).

Seasons and Hours The park is open daily year-round. Park headquarters visitor center is open daily 6.30am–4pm, Haleakala Visitor Center open daily 5.15am–3pm, Kipahulu Visitor Center open daily 9am–5pm (all subject to staff availability).

Charge Yes.

Handicapped Access Visitor center, park headquarters, and Hosmer Grove picnic area.

Activities Scenic drives, camping, hiking, biking, backpacking, wildlife watching, swimming, interpretive programs.

Permits and Licenses Free permits required for camping in two wilderness campgrounds.

Camping Two large wilderness campgrounds have campsites available on a first-come, first-served basis. Three cabins (accessible only by foot) in crater available by reservation (call the headquarters well in advance); three nights per month limit.

Gateway Communities Pukalani, Hana, and Kahului.

Accommodations None in the park, except for wilderness cabins. Lodging is available in Hana, Kahului, and Pukalani. Contact Maui Chamber of Commerce, 313 Ano Street, Kahului, HI 96732, tel: 808-871-7711, www.mauichamber.com.

Food and Supplies There is none in the park, and there is no drinking water at Kipahulu. Food and supplies are available in Hana, Pukalani, and Kahului.

Weather At high elevations, the weather changes rapidly and unpredictably – intense sunshine, thick clouds, heavy rain, and high winds are possible in the same day. The Kipahulu district is warmer and more moderate but also subject to heavy rains.

General Information The thin air at high elevations can make hiking difficult. Come prepared for sudden changes in weather.
Note: the scenic coastal route along the Hana Highway is the only access to remote Kipahulu. It is extremely slow and winding and can cause car sickness. Flash flooding of pools and streams can be hazardous to swimmers and hikers at Kipahulu. Check with park rangers before entering pools.

Hawaii Volcanoes National Park

Address PO Box 52, Hawaii National Park, HI 96718-0052, tel: 808-985-6000, www.nps.gov/havo.
Access The Kilauea Visitor Center is 29 miles (47km) southwest of Hilo and 82 miles (132km) southeast of Captain Cook via Highway 11.
Seasons and Hours The park is open daily year-round. The visitor center is open daily 7.45am–5pm. Jaggar Museum is open 8.30am–7.30pm.
Charge Yes.
Handicapped Access Visitor center, museum, overlooks, and nature trails.
Activities Scenic drives, camping, hiking, backpacking, wildlife watching, interpretive programs.
Permits and Licenses Free back-country camping permits required in certain areas. Apply at Kilauea Visitor Center at least 24 hours before.
Camping Two free drive-in campgrounds. First-come, first-served.
Gateway Community Hilo.
Accommodations
$$ *Volcano House*, PO Box 53, Hawaii Volcanoes National Park, HI 96718, tel: 808-967-7321. $ *Namakanipaio Cabins*, PO Box 53, Hawaii Volcanoes National Park, HI 96718, tel: 808-967-7321.
Note: Volcano House and Namakanipaio Cabins are both currently closed for renovations and are expected to reopen under a new concessionaire in 2011. Contact the park for status updates. The closest lodging is currently in Hilo; Kailua-Kona, on the other side of the island, also has gas, food, and lodging. Contact Hawaii Island Chamber of Commerce, 106 Kamehameha Avenue, Hilo, HI 96720, tel: 808-935-7178, www.hicc.biz.
Food and Supplies There is a restaurant at Volcano House (see above note about current closure). Food and supplies available in Volcano Village and Hilo.
Weather Summer highs tend to be in the low 80s °F (high 20s °C), while winter temperatures occasionally dip into the low 40s °F (4–7°C). At high elevations, weather fluctuates wildly; it can be rainy and chilly at any time of the year. The coastal plain is often dry and windy. For up-to-date weather forecasts, tel: 808-935-8555.
General Information Stay on marked trails. Hardened lava flows are easily broken. Consult rangers before approaching active lava flows. For eruption information, tel: 808-985-6000. Note: due to high fire danger, campfires are strictly banned.

AMERICAN SAMOA

The National Park of American Samoa

Address Pago Pago, AS 96799-0001, tel: + 684-633-7082, www.nps.gov/npsa.
Access Flights from Honolulu to Pago Pago International Airport on American Samoa's largest island, Tutuila. Regular scheduled flights serve park areas of Ofu and Tau.
Seasons and Hours The park is open year-round.
Charge No.
Handicapped Access Visitor center and a trail.
Activities Wildlife watching, backpacking, swimming, scuba diving, and snorkeling.
Permits and Licenses None.
Camping Land is leased from private landowners, from whom permission should be sought for camping.
Gateway Community Pago Pago on Tutuila Island.
Accommodations None in the park. Lodging is available in Pago Pago. Since this is a cultural park, it is highly recommended that you stay with a Samoan family in a village. Contact American Samoa Office of Tourism, PO Box 1147, Pago Pago, American Samoa 96799, tel: + 684-699-9411, www.amsamoatourism.com.
Food and Supplies None in park, but food available in neighboring villages.
Weather Expect hot, rainy, tropical weather year-round.
General Information Do not expect mainland facilities: these are undeveloped tropical islands with difficult access to interior. Solar radiation is intense. Don't hike without water. Take insect repellent. Other dangers: sharp coral, falling coconuts.

National Historic Sites and Historical Parks

California

Eugene O'Neill National Historic Site, PO Box 280, Danville, CA 94526, tel: 925-838-0249, www.nps.gov/euon. The playwright wrote some of his best-known works at this home from 1937–44.
John Muir National Historic Site, 4202 Alhambra Avenue, Martinez, CA 94553-3883, tel: 925-228-8860, www.nps.gov/jomu. Muir's home and gravesite commemorates his life and career as a naturalist, organizer, and writer.
Port Chicago Naval Magazine National Memorial, PO Box 280, Danville, CA 94526, tel: 925-228-8860, www.nps.gov/posh. On July 17, 1944, 320 men were instantly killed when the munitions ships they were loading at Port Chicago blew up. Visits to this new NPS site are by reservation only.
San Francisco Maritime National Historical Park, Fort Mason, Building E, San Francisco, CA 94123-1315, tel: 415-447-5000, www.nps.gov/sfr. Several historic ships and a maritime museum on the San Francisco waterfront.

Hawaii

Kalaupapa National Historical Park, PO Box 2222, Kalaupapa, HI 96742, tel: 808-567-6802, www.nps.gov/kala. The park protects the still occupied historic Hansen's disease (leprosy) settlement (1866–1969) on remote Molokai Island; areas relating to early settlement, including sites associated with recently beatified Father Damien; and habitats for rare and endangered species.
Kaloko-Honokohau National Historical Park, 73-4786 Kanalani Street, Suite 14, Kailua-Kona, HI 96740-2000, tel: 800-320-9057, www.nps.gov/kalo. The park preserves several interesting pre-European archeological sites.
Pu'uhonua o Honaunau National Historical Park, PO Box 129, Honaunau, Kona, HI 96726-0129, tel: 808-328-2326, www.nps.gov/puho. An ancient Hawaiian refuge for native people who had broken the Islands' elaborate taboo system, the park preserves prehistoric sites and a lovely coastal landscape with black sand beaches. The premier Hawaiian culture park.
Puukohola Heiau National Historic Site, 62-3601 Kawaihae Road, Kawaihae, HI 96743, tel: 808-882-7218, www.nps.gov/puhe. The park has the ruins of a temple built on the Big Island by King Kamehameha the Great in 1791.
USS Arizona Memorial, 1 Arizona Memorial Place, Honolulu, HI 96818-3145, tel: 808-422-3300, www.nps.gov/valr. A haunting underwater memorial at the site on the island of Oahu where the USS *Arizona* was sunk during the explosive 1941 attack on Pearl Harbor. This is the most visited NPS site in Hawaii, with up to 4,000 visitors a day.

T HE SOUTHWEST

INFORMATION ON ARIZONA, NEVADA, NEW MEXICO, TEXAS, UTAH, AND THE GRAND CANYON

Accommodations

The price guide indicates approximate room/cabin rates:
$ = $110 or less
$$ = $110–250
$$$ = more than $250

ARIZONA

Canyon de Chelly National Monument

Address PO Box 588, Chinle, AZ 86503-0588, tel: 928-674-5500, www.nps.gov/cach.
Access The park is on the Navajo Nation. The visitor center is 3 miles (5km) from Route 191 in Chinle.
Seasons and Hours The monument is open daily year-round. The visitor center is open 8am–5pm winter, closed Christmas.
Charge No.
Handicapped Access Visitor center and some overlooks on scenic drive.
Activities Wildlife watching, hiking, horseback riding, jeep tours, interpretive programs, scenic drive.
Special Events *September:* Navajo Nation Fair celebrates Navajo life and culture with food, dancing, rodeo, arts and crafts at Window Rock.
Camping Cottonwood Campground near Thunderbird Lodge has first-come, first-served campsites.
Permits and Licenses Backcountry travel by hiking, horseback, or vehicle (except for White House Ruin Trail) with permit and authorized Navajo guides only. Ask for list of authorized guides at the visitor center or Thunderbird Lodge.

Gateway Community Chinle.
Accommodations
$–$$ *Thunderbird Lodge*, PO Box 548, Chinle, AZ 86503, tel: 928-674-5841, www.tbirdlodge.com.
Motels and hotels available outside the park in Chinle as well as Kayenta, Window Rock and Gallup. Contact Navajo Nation Tourism, PO Box 663, Window Rock, AZ 86515, tel: 928-871-6436, www.discovernavajo.com.
Food and Supplies Cafeteria and limited supplies are available at Thunderbird Lodge in the park. A supermarket is located in nearby Chinle.
Weather Summer is hot and dry with highs above 90°F (32°C); winter is cold with occasional snowstorms; temperatures commonly dip below freezing.
General Information Situated on the Navajo Nation and occupied by several traditional Navajo families, Canyon de Chelly National Monument encompasses four canyons and features dramatic 13th-century Ancestral Pueblo cliff dwellings, including White House Ruin, Antelope House, and Mummy Cave. Respect the privacy of resident Navajos. Their hogans, corrals, and fields are off-limits. Disturbing ruins in any fashion is strictly prohibited. March through November, the Navajo Nation observes **Mountain Daylight Savings Time** when the time will be the same as Colorado, New Mexico, and Utah. The rest of Arizona observes Mountain Standard Time all year round.

Chiricahua National Monument

Address 12856 East Rhyolite Creek Road, Willcox, AZ 85643, tel: 520-824-3560, www.nps.gov/chir.
Access The park is 120 miles (193km) east of Tucson, and 36 miles (58km) southeast of Willcox, AZ. From I–10, take Highway 181 to park entrance.
Seasons and Hours Open daily year-round. The visitor center is open 8am–4.30pm; closed Christmas.
Charge Yes.
Handicapped Access Visitor center, campground, and Faraway Ranch.
Activities Interpretive programs, hiking, camping, scenic drive, wildlife watching.
Special Events *Mother's Day:* Ice Cream Social, Faraway Ranch. *Christmas:* Open House, Faraway Ranch. Both are fun and festive.
Camping First-come, first-served, on campground only (no backcountry camping).
Permits and Licenses No.
Gateway Community Willcox.
Accommodations None in the park; hotels and motels are available in Willcox, contact Willcox Chamber of Commerce, 1500 North Circle I Road, Willcox, AZ 85643, tel: 520-384-2272, www.willcoxchamber.com
Food and Supplies None in the park; restaurants and stores are available in Willcox.
Weather Summer temperatures usually 70–95°F (21–35°C), cooler at high elevations; thunderstorms are common July–September. Winter temperatures often dip below freezing with highs in the upper 50s°F (14°C) and occasional snowfall.
General Information There is no public transportation to the park. Fill up with gas at Willcox, as none is available nearer the park. For a short visit, take the 8-mile (13km) scenic

Year-Round Program

Glen Canyon National Recreation Area hosts numerous special events during the year, including:
January: Hole-in-the Rock Commemoration.
March/April: Lake Powell Hot Air Balloon Regatta; Lake Powell Marathon.
July: Fireworks displays at Wahweap and Bullfrog
November: Parade of Boat Lights (Bullfrog).
December: Parade of Boat Lights (Wahweap).

drive to Massai Point, hike the Echo Canyon Loop trail (3½ miles/6km), and take a tour of Faraway Ranch (daily).

Glen Canyon National Recreation Area

Address PO Box 1507, Page, AZ 86040-1507, tel: 928-608-6200, www.nps.gov/glca.
Access The main entrance is in Page on Highway 89 in northern Arizona. Backcountry areas can be reached via Highways 276 and 95 in southeast Utah and via boat across Lake Powell.
Seasons and Hours The park is open year-round. Carl Hayden Visitor Center adjoining Glen Canyon Dam and Lake Powell is open 8am–6pm in summer, 8.30am–4.30pm in winter; closed Thanksgiving, Christmas, and New Year's Day. Bullfrog Visitor Center on the Utah side is open 8am–5pm May–September only.
Charge Yes.
Handicapped Access Visitor centers and other public buildings.
Activities Backpacking, wildlife watching, interpretive programs, guided tours of Glen Canyon Dam, boating and houseboating, water-skiing, fishing, kayaking, and mountain biking.
Camping First-come, first-served. Reservations required at Bullfrog Marina during Memorial Day weekend.
Permits and Licenses Arizona and/or Utah fishing licenses.
Gateway Community Page.
Accommodations Hotel rooms are available in the park at the Wahweap and Bullfrog marinas; housekeeping units in trailers available at Bullfrog, Hite and Hall's Crossing marinas. Make reservations well in advance through Aramark, tel: 800-528-6154. Lodging also available in Page.
Food and Supplies Groceries and

supplies are available at Wahweap, Bullfrog, Hall's Crossing, Hite and Dangling Rope marinas; there are restaurants and stores in Page. The spectacular new Antelope Point Marina is within park boundaries on the Navajo Nation and has a large floating restaurant, tel: 928-645-5900, www.antelopepointlakepowell.com.
Weather Summer temperatures can exceed 100°F (38°C), with sudden, violent thunderstorms. Spring and fall are generally mild. Occasional snowfall in winter.
General Information Stringent Homeland Security measures are in place at Carl Hayden Visitor Center and Glen Canyon Dam. Be prepared to leave purses, backpacks, and other nonessential personal items in your car. Houseboat and motorboat reservations can be made by calling Aramark Lake Powell, tel: 800 528 6154. Rainbow Bridge National Monument with the world's largest natural bridge, 280ft (85 meters) high, may be reached by boat from Wahweap, Bullfrog, or Halls Crossing. Allow at least half a day. Just beyond Page is Antelope Canyon, a spectacular slot canyon on the Navajo Nation that is open to visitors.

Grand Canyon National Park

Address PO Box 129, Grand Canyon, AZ 86023-0129, tel: 928-638-7888, www.nps.gov/grca.
Access Grand Canyon Village and the South Rim visitor center are about 85 miles (137km) from Flagstaff, Arizona, via Highway 180/64. Although only 10 miles (16km) across the canyon, the North Rim is about 215 miles (346km) by road from Grand Canyon Village. Take Route 64 east to Cameron, Highway 89/Alt. 89 north to Jacob Lake, then Route 67 south to the North Rim. Visitors can also arrive by air at the Grand Canyon National Park Airport, just outside the park in Tusayan, or by rail from Williams, Arizona, on the Grand Canyon Railway. Once inside the park, a free shuttle bus system links Grand Canyon Village with South Rim attractions, including West Rim Drive, which is closed in summer.
Seasons and Hours The South Rim is open year-round; the visitor center is open daily 8am–5pm. (Note: Arizona does not observe Daylight Savings Time.) The North Rim open May–Oct.
Charge Yes.
Handicapped Access Canyon View Information Plaza and some shuttle buses. Contact park for free

Accessibility Guide.
Activities Scenic drive, backpacking, wildlife watching, river trips, mule packing, fishing.
Special Events *September*: Grand Canyon Music Festival.
Camping Campgrounds on North and South Rim usually fill by noon May–September; 7-day limit. Some sites can be reserved in advance by contacting 877-466-6777, www.recreation.gov. RV sites are available on South Rim year-round at Trailer Village, tel: 303-297-2757 for reservations.
Permits and Licenses Arizona fishing license. Inexpensive backcountry permits (required for overnight hikes only) can be obtained by mail from Backcountry Information Center, PO Box 129, Grand Canyon AZ, 86023, tel: 928-638-7875, fax: 928-638-2125. Reserve well in advance; popular trails tend to fill up early. The office is open to walk-in visitors 8am–5pm, closed noon–1pm. Note: Permits for private river trips are by lottery only and require planning many years ahead for a slot; casual visitors will not be able to do such a trip unless they make arrangements to join a private permit holder on an existing trip. One-day, 2–5-day, 3–18-day, 18–25-day river trips are available through commercial river running companies. List available from the park.
Gateway Communities Tusayan, Flagstaff, Williams, Cameron, and Jacob Lake.
Accommodations Hotels and lodges on the South Rim are managed by Xanterra Parks & Resorts, DBA Grand Canyon Lodges, Central Reservations, 6312 South Fiddlers Green Circle, Suite 600N, Greenwood Village, CO 80111, tel: 888-297-2757 or 303-297-2757 for advance reservations. The historic North Rim Grand Canyon

Forward Planning

Grand Canyon is heavily visited for most of the year, and you should plan ahead for lodging, backcountry permits, or mule trips. If you are planning a day visit in summer, get there early, as parking lots fill early. A free shuttle bus allows you to park and ride to see the main attractions at the South Rim. The North Rim is far less visited, but only open in summer. Write to the park in advance to request a Trip Planner (or Backcountry Trip Planner if you plan to backpack).

National Historic Sites and Historical Parks and Other National Monuments

Arizona

Casa Grande Ruins National Monument, 1100 Ruins Drive, Coolidge, AZ 85228-3200, tel: 520-723-3172, www.nps.gov/cagr. The monument preserves a massive four-story ruin, part of a 15th-century Hohokam town.

Coronado National Memorial, 4101 East Montezuma Canyon Road, Hereford, AZ 85615-9376, tel: 520-366-5515, www.nps.gov/coro. The first European exploration of the Southwest, by Francisco Vasquez de Coronado in 1540–2, is commemorated here.

Fort Bowie National Historic Site, 3203 South Old Fort Bowie Road, Bowie, AZ 85605-0158, tel: 520-847-2500, www.nps.gov/fobo. This 1,000-acre (405-hectare) park preserves the ruins of Fort Bowie, established in 1862 to protect settlers from Apache Indians.

Hubbell Trading Post National Historic Site, PO Box 150, Ganado, AZ 86505-0150, tel: 928-755-3475, www.nps.gov/hutr. A working trading post, established in 1878, on the Navajo reservation.

Montezuma Castle National Monument, PO Box 219, Camp Verde, AZ 86322-0219, tel: 928-567-3322, www.nps.gov/moca. A well-preserved five-story cliff dwelling built about 700 years ago by people of the Sinagua culture.

Navajo National Monument, HC 71, Box 3, Tonalea, AZ 86044-9704, tel: 928-672-2700, www.nps.gov/nava. Dramatic and well-preserved cliff dwellings built by the Kayenta branch of the Ancestral Pueblo culture in the mid-13th century.

Sunset Crater Volcano National Monument, 6400 North Highway 89, AZ 86004, tel: 928-526-0502, www.nps.gov/sucr. The monument features a 1,000ft (305-meter) cinder cone.

Tumacacori National Historical Park, PO Box 67, Tumacacori, AZ 85640-0067, tel: 520-398-2341, www.nps.gov/tuma. Ruins of Spanish missions established by Jesuits in the late 1600s.

Tuzigoot National Monument, PO Box 219, Camp Verde, AZ 86322, tel: 928-634-5564, www.nps.gov/tuzi. A large Sinagua pueblo in the Verde Valley inhabited from AD 1100–1450.

Walnut Canyon National Monument, 6400 North Highway 89, Flagstaff, AZ 86004, tel: 928-526-3367, www.nps.gov/waca. 13th-century Sinagua cliff dwellings around 900 years old.

Wupatki National Monument, 6400 North Highway 89, Flagstaff, AZ 86004, tel: 928-679-2365. Well-preserved red pueblo structures built by farming Sinagua about AD 1065.

New Mexico

Aztec Ruins National Monument, 84 County Road 2900, Aztec, NM 87410, tel: 505-334-6174, www.nps.gov/azru. Stabilized great house ruins and a reconstructed great kiva originally built in the early 1100s.

Bandelier National Monument, HCR 1, Box 1, Suite 15, Los Alamos, NM 87544-9701, tel: 505-672-3861, www.nps.gov/band. The remains of 12th- and 13th-century cave homes and pueblos built by immigrants from the Four Corners can be found in Frijoles and other canyons on the Pajarito Plateau.

Capulin Volcano National Monument, PO Box 40, Capulin, NM 88414-0040, tel: 505-278-2201, www.nps.gov/cavo. A symmetrical, 1,000ft (300-meter) cinder cone created by a volcanic eruption between 2,500 and 8,000 years ago.

El Malpais National Monument, 123 East Roosevelt Avenue, Grants, NM 87020, tel: 505-285-4641, www.nps.gov/elma. El Malpais ("The Badlands") is an area of lava flows, cinder and spatter cones, lava tubes and ice caves, as well as evidence of 12,000 years of human habitation.

El Morro National Monument, HC 61, Box 43, Ramah, NM 87321-9603, tel: 505-783-4226, www.nps.gov/elmo. The top of this 200ft (60-meter) -high sandstone formation with a permanent spring at its base was occupied by Ancestral Pueblo farmers from AD 1275–1350. The monolith bears Ancestral Pueblo petroglyphs as well as inscriptions made by Spanish and Anglo explorers.

Fort Union National Monument, PO Box 127, Watrous, NM 87753-0127, tel: 505-425-8025, www.nps.gov/foun. Ruins of the largest US Army fort in the Southwest built to protect travelers on the Santa Fe Trail.

Gila Cliff Dwellings National Monument, HC 68, Box 100, Silver City, NM 88061-0100, tel: 505-536-9461, www.nps.gov/gicl. Well-preserved cliff dwellings built by a late phase of the Mogollon culture in the 1200s.

Pecos National Historical Park, PO Box 418, Pecos, NM 87552-0418, tel: 505-757-6414, www.nps.gov/peco. The park preserves 10,000 years of human history.

Petroglyph National Monument, 6001 Unser Blvd NW, Albuquerque, NM 87120-2033, tel: 505-899-0205, www.nps.gov/petr. More than 15,000 prehistoric and historic rock carvings are protected on Albuquerque's West Mesa escarpment along the Rio Grande.

Salinas Pueblo Missions National Monument, Box 517, Mountainair, NM 87036-0517, tel: 505-847-2585, www.nps.gov/sapu. The park preserves the remains of three gateway pueblos built by Ancestral Puebloans on the southern frontier.

Texas

Alibates Flint Quarries National Monument, c/o Lake Meredith Recreation Area, PO Box 1460, Fritch, TX 79036-1460, tel: 806-857-3151, www.nps.gov/alfl. The monument preserves the site where Plains Village Indians, ancestors of the Caddo, Pawnee, and Wichita, quarried stone for tool making.

Fort Davis National Historic Site, PO Box 1379, 101 Lt Henry Flipper Drive, Fort Davis, TX 79734, tel: 432-426-3224, www.nps.gov/foda. A well-preserved fort established to protect pioneers in the mid- to late 1800s.

Lyndon B. Johnson National Historical Park, PO Box 329, Johnson City, TX 78636-0329, tel: 830-868-7128, www.nps.gov/lyjo. President Johnson's childhood homes, ranch, cemetery, and more.

San Antonio Missions National Historical Park, 2202 Roosevelt Avenue, San Antonio, TX 78210-4919, tel: 210-534-8833, www.nps.gov/saan. The park preserves five Spanish colonial missions by the San Antonio River, including the Alamo.

Utah

Golden Spike National Historic Site, PO Box 897, Brigham City, UT 84302-0897, tel: 435-471-2209. The Union Pacific and Central Pacific railroads met here in 1869, completing the first transcontinental railroad in the US.

Grand Staircase-Escalante National Monument, 190 East Center Street, Kanab, Utah 84741, tel: 435-644-4300, www.blm.gov/ut/st/en/fo/grand_staircase-escalante.html. This undeveloped national monument protects the natural and cultural history of the Escalante Canyons, Kaiparowits Plateau, and the Grand Staircase.

Accommodations

The price guide indicates approximate room/cabin rates:
$ = $110 or less
$$ = $110–250
$$$ = more than $250

Lodge (May–Nov) is the only lodging at the North Rim and offers frontier cabins and motel rooms. It is operated by Forever Resorts. Reserve well ahead at 877-FUN-4EVER, www.foreverlodging.com. Rustic Jacob Lake Inn (tel: 928-643-7232) and Kaibab Lodge (tel: 928-638-2389) offer the closest lodgings to the park on the North Rim. Other lodgings can be found in the Arizona Strip at Lees Ferry, Fredonia, and Kanab.
$–$$ *Bright Angel Lodge & Cabins.*
$$$ *El Tovar Hotel.*
$$ *Kachina Lodge.*
$–$$ *Maswik Lodge.*
$ *Phantom Ranch.*
$$ *Thunderbird Lodge.*
$$ *Yavapai Lodge.*
$$ *North Rim Grand Canyon Lodge*
Book far in advance, up to a year. Occasionally, rooms free up in Maswik and Yavapai lodge on the day. Check with the park. Lodgings are more easily available in Tusayan, Flagstaff, Cameron, and Williams, and to a limited degree at Jacob Lake on the North Rim and nearby Lees Ferry, Fredonia, and Kanab. For additional information, contact Grand Canyon Chamber of Commerce, PO Box 3007, Grand Canyon, AZ 86023, tel: 888-472-2696, www.grandcanyonchamber.com
Food and Supplies Restaurants in Grand Canyon Village. Groceries and supplies at markets and gift shops in both Grand Canyon Village and Desert View, also a small camper store on the North Rim, Lees Ferry, Jacob Lake Inn and Store, Fredonia, and Kanab.
Weather Conditions vary dramatically depending on location in the park. South Rim 50–85°F (10–29°C) in summer, 20–40°F (-7–4°C) in winter. North Rim 40–75°F (4–24°C) in summer, 15–40°F (9–4°C) in winter. Inner canyon 75–115°F (24–46°C) in summer, 35–60°F (2–16°C) in winter. For weather updates, tel: 928-638-7888 or log onto the website, which features audio weather reports daily.
General Information The inner canyon is subject to extreme heat conditions in summer. Hikers should carry adequate food supplies and drinking water, at least one gallon (4 liters) per person per day.

Organ Pipe Cactus National Monument

Address 10 Organ Pipe Drive, Ajo, AZ 85321-9626, tel: 520-387-6849, www.nps.gov/orpi
Access The park is located on Route 85 on the US–Mexican border about 140 miles (225km) west of Tucson and 135 miles (217km) southwest of Phoenix.
Seasons and Hours The monument is open year-round; the Kriss Eggle Visitor Center is open daily 8am–5pm; closed Thanksgiving and Christmas.
Charge Yes.
Handicapped Access Visitor center, a nature trail and some campsites.
Activities Scenic drive, backpacking, hiking, wildlife watching, interpretive programs.
Special Events *March:* Tohono O'odham Celebration – Native Americans demonstrate traditional arts and crafts.
Camping Two campgrounds, one large and one small, have first-come, first-served campsites.
Permits and Licenses Inexpensive backcountry permits required.
Gateway Communities Ajo, Why, and Lukeville, US, and Sonoyta, Mexico.
Accommodations None in the park. Lodging is available in Lukeville and Ajo. Contact Ajo Chamber of Commerce, 400 Taladro Street, Ajo, AZ, 85321, tel: 520-387-7742, www.ajochamber.com.
Food and Supplies Available in Lukeville, Why and Ajo, and Sonoyta, Mexico
Weather Summer temperatures exceed 100°F (38°C); thunderstorms are common August–September. Winter temperatures are mild and comfortable, usually 40–60°F (4–16°C).
General Information Scenic roads may be impassable during or after heavy rainfall. Do not attempt to cross flooded areas.
Carry adequate water in your car and on hikes (1 gallon/4 liters per person per day). Beware of the cactus and some dangerous wildlife: rattlesnakes, gila monsters (venomous lizards with an extremely strong bite) and scorpions are protected and should not be harmed. Keep clear of them and they will not trouble you.
Contact park headquarters for information about crossing the border into Mexico.
Note: Expect heavy Border Patrol activity here. Carry ID papers with you at all times.

Petrified Forest National Park

Address PO Box 2217, Petrified Forest National Park, AZ 86028-2217, tel: 928-524-6228, www.nps.gov/pefo
Access The park is located on I-40 about 26 miles (42km) east of Holbrook and 22 miles (35km) west of Chambers.
Seasons and Hours The park and visitor center are open daily 8am–5pm in winter, 7am–7pm summer. (Note: Arizona does not observe Daylight Savings Time.) Closed Christmas.
Charge Yes.
Handicapped Access Visitor center and museum.
Activities Scenic drive, backpacking, wildlife watching, interpretive programs.
Special Events *March:* Arizona Archeology and Heritage Awareness month.
June: Summer Solstice program (watch an ancient calendar at work at Puerco Pueblo) daily at 8am for 2-week period around June 21.
Camping No campgrounds in park.
Permits and Licenses Free backcountry permits required for overnight camping.
Gateway Communities Holbrook, Chambers, Gallup, and Winslow.
Accommodations Available in Holbrook, Chambers, Gallup, and Winslow. Contact Holbrook Chamber of Commerce, 100 East Arizona Street, Holbrook, AZ 86025, tel: 928-524-6558, www.4holbrook.com.
Food and Supplies Painted Desert Oasis and Cougar Cafe both have a cafe, gas station, and travel store. The Rainbow Forest Store has packaged goods and a soda fountain. Restaurants and supplies available in Holbrook, Chambers, Gallup, and Winslow.
Weather Summer days are hot (near 100°F/38°C) and sunny, with occasional thunderstorms. Winter temperatures can drop below freezing.
General Information Leave petrified wood and other objects where you find them. Removing any natural object or artifact from the park is a federal offense.

Don't Get Locked In

Petrified Forest National Park is locked at night and visitors must be in their cars and driving toward an exit at closing time.

Pipe Spring National Monument

Address HC 65, Box 5, Fredonia, AZ 86022, tel: 928-643-7105, www.nps. gov/pisp.

Access The monument is 14 miles (23km) west of Fredonia, Arizona, via Route 389, and 38 miles (61km) southeast of Hurricane, Utah, via Route 59.

Seasons and Hours The monument is open daily year-round. The visitor center is open daily 8am–5pm (winter), 7am–5pm (summer); closed Thanksgiving, Christmas, and New Year's Day. (Note: Arizona does not observe Daylight Savings Time.)

Charge Yes.

Handicapped Access Visitor center. Paved sidewalks to all the historic structures; interiors not wheelchair-accessible.

Activities Museum interpreting Kaibab Band of Paiute Indians and monument's Mormon history. Self-guided tours of fort, Ancestral Pueblo ruin and grounds. Winsor Castle tours led by costumed rangers on the hour and half-hour 9am–4pm in winter, 8am–4.30pm in summer. Living history demonstrations and talks in summer.

Special Events *March* Arizona Archeology and Heritage Awareness month activities.

Camping No campgrounds in park; the Kaibab Band of Paiute Indians runs a campground on adjoining reservation lands just north of the monument, and there is at-large camping available on surrounding BLM and US Forest Service lands in the Arizona Strip. Commercial campgrounds are available in Fredonia and Kanab.

Permits and Licenses No.

Gateway Communities Fredonia, Arizona, and Hurricane, Utah.

Accommodations No lodging in park. Accommodations are available in Kanab, Fredonia, Hurricane, and St George. Contact St George Area Convention and Visitors Bureau, 1835 Convention Center Drive, St George, UT 84790, tel: 800-869-6635, www. utahstgeorge.com.

Food and Supplies The Kaibab Band of Paiute Indians runs a gas/

Accommodations

The price guide indicates approximate room/cabin rates:
$ = $110 or less
$$ = $110–250
$$$ = more than $250

convenience store at the turn-off to the park. Additional food and supplies are available in Kanab, Fredonia, St George, and Hurricane. Contact Fredonia Chamber of Commerce, 25 North Main Street, Fredonia, AZ 86022, tel: 928-643-7241.

Weather Summer days are hot and sunny (80–100°F/27–38°C), with frequent afternoon thunderstorms. Winter temperatures dip below freezing, with occasional snow.

General Information Livestock wander around the grounds of the monument: they are not tame, so use caution and keep a safe distance. There are rattlesnakes and other desert wildlife in the area. To preserve the historic fort and its period furnishings, tour size is limited to 15 people. The Kaibab Band of Paiute Indian's tribal headquarters adjoins the monument, and the tribe co-manages the monument, offers guided tours of the reservation, a campground, and a convenience store.

Saguaro National Park

Address 3693 South Old Spanish Trail, Tucson, AZ 85730-5601, tel: 520-733-5153 (Rincon Mountain District Visitor Center), 520-733-5158 (Tucson Mountain District Visitor Center), www.nps.gov/sagu.

Access The Rincon Mountain District visitor center is on South Old Spanish Trail, about 2 miles (3km) east of Tucson. The Tucson Mountain District information center is on Kinney Road, to the west of Tucson.

Seasons and Hours Both park districts are open daily from sunrise to sunset. The visitor centers are open daily 9am–5pm; closed Christmas.

Charge Yes.

Handicapped Access Visitor centers, picnic areas, and some trails.

Activities Scenic drive, backpacking, hiking, wildlife watching, interpretive programs.

Camping Backcountry camping in six small campgrounds spread through Saguaro Wilderness Area (Rincon Mountain District) only.

Permits and Licenses Inexpensive backcountry permits required for wilderness overnight trips.

Gateway Community Tucson.

Accommodations None in the park. Lodging is abundant in Tucson. Contact Metropolitan Tucson Convention & Visitors Bureau, 100 South Church Avenue, Tucson, AZ 85701, tel: 888-2Tucson, www.visit tucson.org.

Food and Supplies None in the park. They are available in Tucson.

Weather Summer temperatures in excess of 110°F (43°C) are not uncommon; occasional thunderstorms. Winters are mild (60–70°F/16–21°C) but nights can dip below freezing.

General Information Both visitor centers have slide shows, museums, and cactus gardens. Backcountry users should carry adequate water (1 gallon/4 liters per person per day). Sunscreen and hats are highly recommended.

NEVADA

Great Basin National Park

Address 100 Great Basin National Park, Baker, NV 89311, tel: 775-234-7331 (info and Lehman Caves ticket sales), www.nps.gov/grba.

Access The park is about 67 miles (108km) southeast of Ely near the Nevada–Utah border, via Highways 93, 50/6, 487, and 488, and 5 miles (8km) west of Baker.

Seasons and Hours The park is open daily year-round. The visitor center is open daily 8am–5.30pm summer, 8am–4.30pm winter. The visitor center and Lehman Caves are closed Thanksgiving, Christmas, and New Year's Day. Sections of the park road and some trails may be closed by snow October–May.

Charge None. Fees only charged for campgrounds and guided cave tours.

Handicapped Access Visitor center, first part of Lehman Caves, and three of the four developed campgrounds.

Activities Camping, hiking, backpacking, cave tours, wildlife watching, horseback riding, pine nut gathering, boating, fishing, cross-country skiing, snowshoeing, stargazing, interpretive programs.

Permits and Licenses Caving permits required for non-guided tours of any cave in park; voluntary registration for backcountry camping; reservations required for group picnic area; Nevada fishing license.

Camping Four developed campgrounds, two primitive campgrounds. First-come, first-served. Reservations are required for Grey Cliffs Group Campground and can be made by calling 775-234-7331 ext. 213. Only Lower Lehman Campground is open year-round (no water in winter); other campgrounds open as snow levels permit. Water may be limited at certain times of year and the fee reduced.

Gateway Community Baker.

Going Underground

When visiting Carlsbad Caverns, you should make advance reservations for all guided cave tours (tel: 800-967-CAVE), but this is not necessary for the basic self-guided tours of the Natural Entrance and Big Room. However you tour the caves, you should wear shoes with rubber soles for good traction.

Accommodations None in the park. Limited motel accommodation in Baker. Nearest city: Ely, NV. Contact the White Pine County Chamber of Commerce, 636 Aultman Street, Ely, NV 89301, tel: 775-289-8877, www.whitepinechamber.com.

Food and Supplies Café and gift shop near the visitor center operates summer only. Restaurants, grocery store, and gas station in Baker.

Weather Summer temperatures usually 45–90°F (7–32°C), colder at higher elevations. Winters are cold, with heavy snow accumulation at higher elevations; temperatures usually 20–45°F (-7–7°C). Temperatures in the caves remain about 50°F (10°C) year-round.

General Information No public transport is available to the park. Gas stations and other services are few and far between in this very remote area. Keep your eye on the gas gauge and carry water. Consult with rangers and obtain a permit before entering any cave in the park. Thin air at high elevations can make hiking difficult.

Lake Mead National Recreation Area

Address 601 Nevada Way, Boulder City, NV 89005-2426, tel: 702-293-8990, www.nps.gov/lame.

Access The Alan Bible Visitor Center is 4 miles (6km) northeast of Boulder City, Nevada, via Highway 93, about 25 miles (40km) southeast of Las Vegas via Highway 95/93, and 76 miles (122km) from Kingman, Arizona, via Highway 93.

Seasons and Hours The recreation area is open daily year-round. The Allan Bible Visitor Center is open 8.30am–4.30pm in winter, 8.30am–5.30pm in summer; closed Thanksgiving, Christmas, and New Year's Day.

Charge Yes.

Handicapped Access Visitor center, fishing pier, and some campgrounds.

Activities Camping, backpacking, horseback riding, wildlife watching,

ABOVE: Lake Mead National Recreation Area.

boating, water-skiing, fishing, swimming, interpretive programs.

Permits and Licenses Arizona and/or Nevada fishing license.

Camping First-come, first-served.

Gateway Community Boulder City.

Accommodations Several moderately priced motels are located in the park. Contact Seven Crown Resorts, tel: 800-752-9669, www.sevencrown.com. Additional lodging is available in Boulder City, Bullhead City, Henderson, and Las Vegas. Contact Boulder City Chamber of Commerce, 465 Nevada Way, Boulder City, NV 89005, tel: 702-293-2034, www.boulder-city-chamber.com.

Food and Supplies Store at major sites in the park. Additional services available in Boulder City, Bullhead City, Henderson, and Las Vegas.

Weather Summer temperatures exceed 100°F (38°C). October–May are much more comfortable. Be prepared for sudden rainstorms and potential flash floods. The sunlight is intense. Bring sunscreen, sunglasses, and a hat.

General Information For houseboat and motorboat rentals, information and reservations, contact Seven Crown Resorts (tel: 800-752-9669, www.sevencrown.com) or Forever Resorts (tel: 800-255-5561, www.foreverresorts.com).

Note: Grand Canyon-Parashant National Monument, a vast new wilderness monument co-managed by the NPS and the BLM, adjoins Lake Mead and the Grand Canyon on its northwestern end, including the western Arizona Strip and the scenic Virgin River Gorge. It is very remote. Access is on dirt roads across the Arizona Strip, from near Pipe Spring National Monument, and requires the specially designed Arizona Strip Visitor Map and good desert backcountry skills. For more

information, contact the Interagency Information Center, 345 East Riverside Drive, St George, UT 84790, tel: 435-688-3200, www.nps.gov/para, or Pipe Spring National Monument.

NEW MEXICO

Carlsbad Caverns National Park

Address 3225 National Parks Highway, Carlsbad, NM 88220-5354, tel: 505-785-2232, www.nps.gov/cave.

Access The park entrance is 23 miles (37km) southwest of Carlsbad, NM, and 150 miles (240km) east of El Paso, TX, via Highway 180/62.

Seasons and Hours The park is open daily year-round, except Christmas. The visitor center is open daily 8am–5pm, 8am–7pm in summer.

Charge Yes.

Handicapped Access Visitor center, large section of Big Room cavern tour, a nature trail, and picnic sites.

Activities Self-guided and wild cave tours, camping, hiking, wildlife watching, many interpretive programs. Experienced cavers may arrange exploration of terrific backcountry caves by contacting the park superintendent for an application form at least a month ahead of their trip, tel: 505-785-2232; permits are issued on a first-come, first-served basis.

Special Events *August:* Bat aficionados gather for an early-morning Bat Flight Breakfast to watch thousands of bats return to their underground home.

Permits and Licenses Free backcountry camping permits required.

Camping Backcountry camping only.

Gateway Commununities Whites

City and Carlsbad.

Accommodations None in the park. Lodgings are available in Whites City, a commercial tourist haven near the park entrance, and Carlsbad. Contact the Carlsbad Chamber of Commerce, 302 South Canal, Carlsbad, NM 88220, tel: 505-887-6516, www.carlsbadchamber.com.

Food and Supplies Food and gift shop at the visitor center. Restaurants, groceries, and food available in Whites City and Carlsbad.

Weather Summer temperatures usually 60–95°F (16–35°C), winter temperatures 30–65°F (-1–18°C). Be prepared for high winds, sudden rainstorms and possible flash floods. Cave temperature is a steady 56°F (13°C) year-round.

General Information If you plan on hiking, carry sunscreen, sunglasses, a hat, and adequate water (1 gallon/4 liters per person per day).

Chaco Culture National Historical Park

Address PO Box 220, Nageezi, NM 87037, tel: 505-786-7014, www.nps.gov/chcu.

Access Chaco is in the San Juan Basin in northwestern New Mexico. Due to poor, unmaintained road conditions on the Navajo Nation, it is best accessed via Highway 550 (formerly Highway 44) from Albuquerque, about a 2.5-hour drive. To reach the park, turn off Highway 550 at CR 7900, 3 miles (5km) southeast of Nageezi and approximately 50 miles (80km) west of Cuba (at mile 112.5). The route includes 8 miles (12.8km) of paved road (CR 7900) and 13 (21km) miles of rough dirt road (CR 7950). The roads to Chaco are not recommended for RVs.

Seasons and Hours The park is open daily year-round. The sites and trails are open sunrise–sunset. The visitor center is open 8am–5pm, extended summer hours; closed Thanksgiving, Christmas, and New Year's Day. Note: The visitor center is undergoing major renovations in 2010. A temporary visitor center will be stationed in the adjoining parking lot staffed by rangers, offering information and interpretive programs.

Charge Yes.

Handicapped Access Two campsites and some trails, with assistance.

Activities Camping, hiking, limited biking, guided and self-guided tours, stargazing, archeology, archaeoastronomy and other interpretive programs.

Permits and Licenses Backcountry hiking permit.

Camping First-come, first-served. Get to the park early in summer: the small campground fills quickly and is the only place to stay in the park.

Gateway community: Bloomfield.

Accommodations None in the park. The closest accommodations are in Bloomfield, north of the San Juan River. Other more distant communities offering accommodations include Thoreau, Farmington, and Gallup. For more information, contact Bloomfield Chamber of Commerce, 224 West Broadway, Bloomfield, NM 87413, tel: 505-632-0880, www.bloomfieldnm.com.

Food and Supplies Limited food and supplies (weekdays) at Blanco and Nageezi Trading Posts. Additional services available in Bloomfield, Crownpoint, Thoreau, Gallup, and Farmington.

Weather Summer temperatures 50°–90°F (10–32°C) with daily thunderstorms from July to September cooling things down. Winter temperatures are extremely frigid, ranging 10–40°F (-12–4°C) with occasional snow. Weather is very changeable and localized at all times of year. The park is very exposed. Bring plenty of weather protection.

General Information The six main Ancestral Pueblo great house and great kiva ruins are along a 9-mile (14km) paved scenic loop that may be driven, hiked, or biked; other pueblos, rock art, and ancient road segments are located in the backcountry and on the cliffs and require a permit to visit. Disturbing or removing artifacts or other objects is strictly prohibited. There are no food supplies in the park; bring whatever you need and fill the gas tank before entering.

White Sands National Monument

Address PO Box 1086, Holloman Air Force Base, NM 88330-1086, tel: 505-679-2599, www.nps.gov/whsa.

Access The monument is on Highway 70 in southern New Mexico, 15 miles (24km) southwest of Alamogordo and 52 miles (84km) northeast of Las Cruces, NM.

Seasons and Hours The monument is open daily year-round except Christmas. The visitor center is open daily 9am–5pm, 8am–7pm in summer. Dunes Drive is open daily 7am–sunset, 7am–9pm in summer.

Charge Yes.

Handicapped Access Visitor center, picnic areas, Interdune Boardwalk.

Activities Hiking, guided and self-guided tours, including sunset ranger-led hikes and monthly moonlight bike rides, and other interpretive programs.

Permits and Licenses.

Camping No camping in the monument. Oliver Lee Memorial State Park, 24 southeast of the monument, south of Alamogordo, has a large, attractive campground. In the summer, there are cool US Forest Service campgrounds in the Sacramento Mountains.

Gateway Community Alamogordo.

Accommodations None in the park. Lodgings are available in Alamogordo. Contact Alamogordo Chamber of Commerce, 1301 North White Sands

BELOW: the wave-like dunes of White Sands National Park.

Accommodations

The price guide indicates approximate room/cabin rates:
$ = $110 or less
$$ = $110–250
$$$ = more than $250

Boulevard, Alamogordo, NM 88310, tel: 575-437-6120, www.alamogordo.com.
Food and Supplies Refreshment and snacks at visitor center gift shop. Additional services available in Alamogordo.
Weather Summer temperatures usually 60–100°F (16–38°C) with occasional thunderstorms. Winter temperatures 25–60°F (-4–16°C). Park is very exposed; bring weather protection.
General Information The 8-mile (13km) scenic drive from the visitor center to the heart of the dunes has numerous parking areas to allow visitors to stop and walk in the white sands. The Dunes Drive is sometimes closed for up to two hours due to missile testing on the adjacent White Sands Missile Range. The Big Dune Trail is a one-mile (1.5km) self-guided nature trail. The Alkali Flat Trail is a 4½-mile (7km) backcountry trail into the heart of the dunes.

TEXAS

Big Bend National Park

Address PO Box 129, Big Bend National Park, TX 79834-0129, tel: 432-477-2251, www.nps.gov/bibe.
Access Panther Junction Visitor Center is about 106 miles (171km) south of Alpine via Route 118 and about 137 miles (221km) south of Fort Stockton via Highway 385.
Seasons and Hours The park is open daily year-round. Panther Junction Visitor Center is open daily 8am–6pm; closed Christmas. The other visitor centers have variable seasons and hours.
Charge Yes.
Handicapped Access Visitor centers, some nature trails, Chisos Mountain Lodge, and some campgrounds.
Activities Scenic drive, camping, hiking, backpacking, wildlife watching, float trips, interpretive programs.
Special Events October (3rd Saturday): International Good Neighbor Day celebrates goodwill between the US and Mexico with food, music, dance, and crafts at Rio Grande Village.
Permits and Licenses Free backcountry camping permits required.
Camping Three campgrounds. Some campsites in the Rio Grande and Cottonwood campgrounds may be reserved up to six months ahead in peak season November 15–April 15

Large and Remote

It is important to appreciate just how big Big Bend is. A minimum of two days is required to see most of the park from the main roads. Hikers and explorers should allow a week. The park is also remote: remember you will be at least 100 miles (160km) from a bank, hospital, pharmacy, or supermarket.

by contacting 877-444-6777, www.recreation.gov. The rest are first-come, first-served sites. Primitive backcountry campsites are available in the Chisos Mountains and along backcountry roads. A four-wheel-drive vehicle and a backcountry permit are required.
Gateway Communities Terlingua, Marathon, and Alpine.
Accommodations In the park: **93** Chisos Mountains Lodge, Forever Resorts, Inc., tel: 877-386-4383 or 432-477-2291.
Additional (sometimes unique and quite luxurious) lodgings are available in Lajitas, Terlingua Ghost Town, Marathon, Alpine, and Marfa. For more information, visit www.visitbigbend.com.
Food and Supplies Limited food and supplies are available at Rio Grande Village, Chisos Basin, Persimmon Gap, and Panther Junction. There is a restaurant in the Chisos Basin. Additional visitor services in Alpine, Marfa, Study Butte, Lajitas, and Marathon.
Weather Temperatures vary depending on elevation. Summer temperatures 60–105°F (16–41°C), with frequent afternoon and evening rains July–October. Winter temperatures 30–65°F (-1–18°C) with little snow.
General Information The sun is intense, even in winter. Bring sunscreen, sunglasses, and a hat. Carry water in your car and on hikes (1 gallon/4 liters per person per day).

Guadalupe Mountains National Park

Address 400 Pine Canyon Road, Salt Flat, TX 79847, tel: 915-828-3251, www.nps.gov/gumo.
Access The park is 55 miles (89km) southwest of Carlsbad, New Mexico, via Highway 62/180, and 110 miles (177km) east of El Paso via Highway 62/180.
Seasons and Hours The park is open daily year-round. McKittrick Canyon

area is closed just before dusk. Visitor centers are open 8am–4.30pm, extended hours in summer; closed Christmas.
Charge Yes.
Handicapped Access Visitor centers, Pinery Trail, and select campgrounds.
Activities Scenic drive, camping, hiking, backpacking, wildlife watching, interpretive programs.
Permits and Licenses Free backcountry camping permits required.
Camping First-come, first-served campsites in Pine Spring Campground. Get there early in summer. Dog Canyon has primitive backcountry sites.
Gateway Community Carlsbad.
Accommodations None in the park. Lodging is available in Carlsbad, Whites City, and Van Horn. Contact Carlsbad Convention and Visitors Bureau, 302 South Canal, Carlsbad, NM 8820, tel: 575-651-6887, www.carlsbadchamber.com or Van Horn Convention & Visitors Bureau, PO Box 488, Van Horn, TX 79855, tel: 432-283-2682, www.vanhorntexas.org.
Food and Supplies There are no supplies in the park. Services are available in Carlsbad, Whites City, and Van Horn.
Weather Temperatures vary depending on elevation. Summer temperatures 60–95°F (16–35°C), cooler at higher elevations, with highs in excess of 100°F (30°C) and occasional thunderstorms; winter temperatures 25–65°F (-4–18°C) with occasional snowstorms. Be prepared for sudden changes of weather and high winds, especially spring and early summer.
General Information Bring everything you need during a visit: no concessions or supplies in the park. If you plan on hiking, carry sunscreen, sunglasses, a hat, and adequate water (1 gallon/4 liters per person per day). Be prepared for sudden weather changes.

UTAH

Arches National Park

Address PO Box 907, Moab, UT 84532-0907, tel: 435-719-2299, www.nps.gov/arch.
Access The visitor center is 5 miles (8km) northwest of Moab off Highway 191.
Seasons and Hours The park is open daily year-round. The visitor center is open daily 8am–4.30pm, 7.30am–

6.30pm April–October; closed Christmas.

Charge Yes.

Handicapped Access Visitor center, one campground and Delicate Arch Viewpoint and trail area.

Activities Scenic drive, camping, mountain biking, hiking, backpacking, wildlife watching, interpretive programs.

Permits and Licenses Free backcountry camping permits required.

Camping Pre-register at the visitor center between 7.30 and 8am, or at the entrance station after 8am. The Devils Garden Campground fills daily spring through fall, often by mid-morning; however, you may reserve campsites between March 1 and October 31 by contacting 877-444-6777, www.recreation.gov, no less than 4 days and no more than 6 months ahead of time. The Moab area has 44 campgrounds, including camping on BLM lands along the Scenic Colorado Riverway and adjoining parklands and in commercial campgrounds in Moab.

Gateway Community Moab.

Accommodations None in the park. Lodging is plentiful in nearby Moab. Contact Moab Area Travel Council, PO Box 550, Moab, UT 84532, tel: 800-635-6622 or 435-259-8825, www.discovermoab.com. For information, stop at the Multiagency Information Center (MIC) on Center Street in downtown Moab, open daily 8am–5pm.

Food and Supplies No food service or supplies in the park. Services are available in Moab.

Weather Summer temperatures usually 60–105°F (16–41°C) with sudden thunderstorms; winter temperatures 15–45°F (-9–7°C) with occasional snow.

General Information The basic road tour with stops at overlooks requires half a day. Off-road biking is prohibited. If you plan on hiking, carry sunscreen, sunglasses, a hat, and adequate water (1 gallon/4 liters per person per day). Note: Moab is busiest during Spring Break and the Jeep Jamboree in March/April as well as summertime.

Bryce Canyon National Park

Accommodations

The price guide indicates approximate room/cabin rates:

$ = $110 or less
$$ = $110–250
$$$ = more than $250

Address PO Box 640201, Bryce Canyon, UT 84764-0201, tel: 435-834-5322, www.nps.gov/brca.

Access The park is 80 miles (129km) east of Cedar City via Routes 14, 89. and 12, and 26 miles (42km) southeast of Panguitch via Routes 89 and 12.

Seasons and Hours Park open daily year-round. The visitor center is open 8am–4.30pm, 8am–8pm in summer; closed Thanksgiving and Christmas.

Charge Yes.

Handicapped Access Visitor center, some campgrounds and a section of Sunset–Sunrise Point Trail.

Activities Scenic drive, camping, mountain biking, hiking, backpacking, horseback riding, wildlife watching, interpretive programs, snowshoeing and cross-country skiing in winter.

Permits and Licenses Backcountry camping permits must be bought in person from visitor center.

Camping Two popular campgrounds – one open year-round. First come, first served. Reservations may be made for some sites from the first week in May to the last week in September through 877-444-6777, www.recreation.gov no less than 2 days and no more than 6 months ahead of time.

Gateway Community Tropic.

Accommodations In the park:

$$ *Bryce Canyon Lodge*. Historic lodge is open April 1 through October 31. Reserve well ahead of time through Forever Lodges, Forever Corporate Plaza, 7501 E. McCormick Parkway, Scottsdale, AZ 85258, tel: 877-386-4383 or 435-834-8700, www.foreverlodges.com.

Additional lodging is available at historic Rubys Inn, just outside the park boundary in Bryce Canyon City, tel: 866-866-6616, www.rubysinn.com. Also in Panguitch, Tropic, Cedar City, Escalante, and on highways leading to the park. Contact Garfield County Travel Council, 55 South Main, Panguitch, UT 84759, tel: 800-444-6689, www.brycecanyoncountry.com.

Food and Supplies There is a restaurant at Bryce Canyon Lodge, and a general store at Sunrise Point (open April–October). Additional services available in Panguitch, Tropic, Escalante, Cedar City, and on highways leading to the park.

Weather Summer temperatures usually 40–85°F (4–29°C) with sudden thunderstorms; winter temperatures 5–45°F (-15–7°C) with heavy snow at higher elevations.

General Information Hiking at this high elevation can affect many individuals. The flat Rim Trail is easy, but hiking out of the amphitheaters on

steep, rugged desert trails can be challenging. Be careful. If you plan on hiking, carry sunscreen, sunglasses, a hat, adequate water (1 gallon/4 liters per person per day), and high-energy snacks. Off-road biking prohibited. Parking space is limited and park roads can become congested. The new free shuttle bus service (daily from late May through September) has alleviated traffic problems. You can park outside the park and board the shuttle to the visitor center and scenic drive.

Canyonlands National Park

Address 2282 SW Resource Blvd, Moab, UT 84532-3298, tel: 435-719-2313, www.nps.gov/cany .

Access The Island in the Sky District is 32 miles (51km) from Moab via Highway 191 and Route 313. The Needles District is 80 miles (129km) from Moab via Highway 191 and Route 211. Both roads are paved. The remote Maze, west of the rivers via I-70 or Highway 95, is accessed via paved Highway 24 and a 46-mile (74km) rough dirt road.

Seasons and Hours The park is open daily year-round. Island in the Sky and Needles visitor centers are open 9am–4.30pm, extended hours March–October; Hans Flat Ranger Station in the Maze is open 8am–4.30pm. Closed Christmas and New Year's Day.

Charge Yes.

Handicapped Access Visitor centers, some campgrounds and some overlooks.

Activities Scenic drive, four-wheel driving/Jeeping, mountain biking, camping, hiking, float trips, river-running, backpacking, horseback riding, rock-climbing, wildlife watching, interpretive programs.

Permits and Licenses Backcountry camping permits required. For backcountry information, tel: (435) 259-4351.

Camping First-come, first-served.

Gateway Communities Moab, Monticello, Green River, Hanksville.

Accommodations None in the park. Lodging is available in Moab, Green River, Monticello, and Hanksville. Contact Moab Area Travel Council, PO Box 550, Moab, UT 84532, tel: 800-635-6622 or 435-259-8825, www.discovermoab.com. For information, stop at the Multiagency Information Center (MIC) on Center Street in downtown Moab, open daily 8am–5pm.

Food and Supplies There are no services in the park. Supplies are available in Moab, Green River, Hanksville, and Monticello.

Weather Summer temperatures usually 65–105°F (18–41°C) with sudden thunderstorms; winter temperatures usually 5–45°F (-15–7°C) with occasional snow.

General Information Each district has its own character, with different opportunities for exploration. The Island in the Sky, closest to Moab, offers 100-mile (161km) views from many overlooks, short hiking trails, and is the easiest to visit in a short time. The Needles, closer to Monticello, offers more of a backcountry experience, requiring some hiking or four-wheel driving/ Jeeping to see the area's attractions. The Maze, south of Green River, is entirely a backcountry area, which requires a good deal of hiking and/or four-wheel driving/Jeeping over rough desert terrain, and considerably more time to visit. The Green and Colorado rivers are managed as a fourth unit by the NPS, and include flat water above the Confluence and challenging white water through Cataract Canyon. River companies based in Moab offer 1-day and multiday trips into the park.

Capitol Reef National Park

Address HC 70 Box 15, Torrey, UT 84775-9602, tel: 435-425-3791, ext. 11, www.nps.gov/care.

Access The visitor center is 11 miles (18km) east of Torrey via Highway 24.

Seasons and Hours The park is open daily year-round. The visitor center is open 8am–4.30pm, 8am–6pm in summer; closed Christmas.

Charge Yes.

Handicapped Access Visitor centers (with assistance), a campground, and part of the Fremont River Trail.

Activities Scenic drive, camping, hiking, biking, backpacking, backroad driving, rock climbing, wildlife watching, interpretive programs.

Permits and Licenses Inexpensive backcountry camping permits required.

Camping One developed and two remote primitive campgrounds. First-come, first-served campsites. Free backcountry camping with permit.

Gateway Community Torrey.

Accommodations None in the park. Lodging is available in nearby Torrey, Bicknell, and Loa, and in Hanksville, Boulder, and Escalante. Contact Utah's Canyonlands Region, PO Box 550-R9, Moab, UT 84532, tel: 800-635-6622, www.canyonlands-utah.com.

Food and Supplies No services in the park. Food and supplies are available in Torrey, Bicknell, Loa, Boulder, Escalante, and Hanksville.

ABOVE: the colorful landscape of Canyonlands.

Weather Summer temperatures usually 60–95°F (16–35°C) with sudden thunderstorms causing flash floods; winter temperatures usually 15–45°F (-9–7°C) with occasional light snow. Spring and fall are the most moderate times to visit, but weather can change quickly.

General Information If you plan on hiking, carry sunscreen, sunglasses, a hat and adequate water (1 gallon/4 liters per person per day). Carry water in your car. Unpaved roads may be impassable during or after rainstorms. Contact the park for road and weather conditions. Driving back roads may require 4-wheel-drive vehicles. Off-road biking is prohibited. Gas stations are few and far between in this area; fill the gas tank before a long trip.

Cedar Breaks National Monument

Address 2390 West Highway 56, Suite 11, Cedar City, UT 84720-4151, tel: (435) 586-0707 (visitor center, May–Oct) or 435-586-9451 (park headquarters in Cedar City, offseason information), www.nps.gov/cebr.

Access The monument is about 23 miles (37km) from Cedar City via Highways 14 and 148.

Seasons and Hours The visitor center is open 8am–6pm, May 25 to October 13. All visitor facilities closed mid-October through late May due to heavy snow. The park road is open June–October, depending on weather and snow clearing.

Charge Yes.

Handicapped Access Visitor center, picnic area, select campgrounds, and overlooks.

Activities Scenic drive, camping, hiking, backpacking, wildlife watching, interpretive programs, snowshoeing, crosscountry skiing, snowmobiling.

Special Events Monthly star parties in the summer.

Permits and Licenses No.

Camping First-come, first-served.

Gateway Communities Cedar City, Brian Head, Parowan, and Panguitch.

Accommodations None in the park. Lodging is available in Cedar City, Parowan, Brian Head, Panguitch. Contact Iron County Visitor Center, 581 North Main Street, Cedar City, UT 84720, tel: 800-354-4849, www.scenic southernutah.com.

Food and Supplies No services in the park. The adjoining ski resort of Brian Head is closest. Cedar City, Duck Creek Village, Parowan, and Panguitch also have stores and restaurants. In winter, a yurt next to the Alpine Pond Trailhead is staffed on weekends by volunteers offering information and hot cocoa to skiers and snowshoers.

Weather Summer temperatures usually 40–70°F (4–21°C) with frequent thunderstorms July–August; winter temperatures usually 5–10°F (-15–4°C) with very deep snowfall.

General Information All visitor facilities and the scenic rim drive are over 10,000ft (3,000 meters) above sea level. If you plan on hiking, carry a warm jacket, even in summer, as well as sunscreen, sunglasses, and a hat. Contact the park for road and weather conditions. Off-road biking prohibited.

Natural Bridges National Monument

Address HC 60, Box 1, Lake Powell, UT 84533-0101, tel: 435-692-1234, www.nps.gov/nabr.

Access The monument is about 41 miles (66km) west of Blanding, UT, via Highways 95 and 275, and 33 miles (53km) north of Mexican Hat, UT, via Highways 261, 95, and 275.

Seasons and Hours The monument is open daily year-round. The visitor center is open daily 8am–5pm in winter, 8am–6pm in summer; closed Thanksgiving, Christmas, and New Year's Day. Some trails may be closed by snow in winter.

Charge Yes.

Handicapped Access Visitor center, several campgrounds, the three natural bridge overlooks.

Activities Scenic drive, camping, hiking, wildlife watching, interpretive programs.

Permits and Licenses No.

Camping First-come, first-served in a small, charming, inexpensive year-round campground (not cleared of snow in winter).

Gateway Communities Blanding and Mexican Hat.

A – Z

CALIFORNIA AND THE PACIFIC

THE SOUTHWEST

THE ROCKY MOUNTAINS

THE PACIFIC NORTHWEST

Accommodations None in the park. Lodging is available in Blanding, Mexican Hat, Bluff, Monticello. Contact San Juan County Travel Council, PO Box 490, Monticello, UT 84535, tel: 800-574-4386, www. southeastutah.com.

Food and Supplies There are no services in the park. Blanding, Mexican Hat, Bluff, and Monticello are the closest (note: historic Fry Canyon Lodge on Highway 95 is now closed).

Weather Summer temperatures usually 70–100°F (21–38°C) with sudden thunderstorms; winter temperatures usually 15–40°F (-9–4°C) with snowfall.

General Information The 9-mile (14km) Bridge View Drive is a one-way scenic route (plowed in winter) starting and ending near the visitor center. Overlooks for each of the three natural bridges and one Ancestral Pueblo cliff dwelling are reached by short trails from pullouts. An 8-mile (13km) loop trail links the three natural bridges and takes 6–8 hours to hike. It can be split into two shorter (3–4-hour) routes, each taking in two bridges.

Timpanogos Cave National Monument

Address RR 3, Box 200, American Fork, UT 84003-9803, tel: 801-756-5238 (visitor center in season), 801-756-5239 (park headquarters), www. nps.gov/tica.

Access Timpanogos Cave Monument is about 30 miles (48km) south of Salt Lake City via I-15 and Highway 92.

Seasons and Hours The cave and cave trail are open early May to November, weather permitting. During this time, the visitor center is open 7am–5.30pm (summer), 8am–5pm (fall) with cave tours all day.

Charge Fees are charged for the cave tour and for driving the Canyon Road.

Handicapped Access Visitor center; the cave is not wheelchair-accessible.

Activities Cave tour, hiking, wildlife watching, interpretive programs.

Permits and Licenses No.

Camping First-come, first-served in Uinta National Forest.

Accommodations None in the park. Lodging is available in Pleasant Grove, American Fork, Heber City, Provo, and Salt Lake City. Contact Utah Valley Convention and Visitors Bureau, 111 S. University Avenue, Provo, UT 84601, tel: 800-222-UTAH, www.utahvalley.org.

Food and Supplies No services in the park. Services are available in Provo, Salt Lake City, and surrounding area.

Weather Summer highs around 90°F

(32°C) with sudden thunderstorms; winter temperatures often dip below freezing with abundant snowfall. Cave temperature 43–47°F (6–8°C).

General Information The tour of the colorful limestone cavern takes about 3 hours, including a steep 1½-mile (2km) walk to the cave entrance. Cave tours fill early during busy summer season. Reservations can be made in advance by phoning park HQ.

Zion National Park

Address SR 9, Springdale, UT 84767-1099, tel: 435-772-3256 (24-hour recorded information), www.nps.gov/zion.

Access The Zion Canyon Visitor Center is 46 miles (74km) east of St George via I-15 and Highway 9. The Kolob Canyon Visitor Center is 18 miles (29km) south of Cedar City via Exit 40 from I-15. A free park shuttle system makes stops on a loop in the adjoining gateway community of Springdale and main attractions in Zion Canyon, using the park visitor center as the main hub. Zion Canyon is closed to private vehicles April 1 to October 31; visitors may only enter on foot, bicycle, or by shuttle bus. The only exception is Zion Lodge guests who must check in at the visitor center and can then drive to the lodge in Zion Canyon.

Seasons and Hours The park is open daily year-round. Both visitor centers are open 8am–5pm, though Zion Canyon has extended hours in spring, summer, and fall. Zion Canyon Visitor Center plaza is open 24 hours and has boards for park and regional trip planning.

Charge Yes.

Handicapped Access Visitor centers, Zion Lodge, three trails, Riverside Walk (with assistance), and some campsites at the South Campground.

Activities Scenic drive, camping, hiking, biking, backpacking, backroad driving, horseback riding, canyoneering, rock climbing, wildlife watching, interpretive programs.

Special Events *September:* The Southern Utah Folklife Festival is a celebration of the life of early Mormon pioneers using music, dancing, food, crafts, and storytelling.

Permits and Licenses Permits required for backcountry camping, canyoneering, rock climbing, and hiking through canyons. For backcountry information, tel: 435-772-0170 or visit the desk in the visitor center.

Camping Two developed campgrounds in Zion Canyon and a high-country primitive campground at

Lava Point offer first-come, first-served camping. Reservations are available at the Watchman Campground in Zion Canyon between March 6 and October 24, tel: 877-444-6777, http://recreation.gov, up to 6 months ahead of your trip.

Gateway Community Springdale.

Accommodations In the park: **$–$$** *Zion Lodge*, reservations through Xanterra, tel: 888-297-2757, www.zionlodge.com. Additional lodging is available in Springdale, Kanab, Hurricane, St George, Cedar City, and Mount Carmel Junction. Contact the Zion Canyon Visitors Bureau, PO Box 331, Springdale, UT 84767, tel: 888-518-7070, www.zionpark.com.

Food and Supplies Zion Lodge has a snack bar and dining room (dinner reservation recommended, tel: 435-772-3213). Additional food and supplies available in Springdale, Mt Carmel Junction, Kanab, Virgin, LaVerkin, Hurricane, St George, and Cedar City.

Weather Weather varies considerably depending on elevation. Summer temperatures usually 65–105°F (18–41°C) with sudden thunderstorms causing flash floods; winter temperatures usually 25–55°F (-4–13°C) with heavy snow at higher elevations. Spring and fall are the most moderate times to visit, but weather changes quickly in any season.

General Information If you plan on hiking, carry sunscreen, sunglasses, a hat, and adequate water (1 gallon/4 liters per person per day). Carry water in your car. Unpaved roads may be impassable during or after rainstorms. Contact the park for road and weather conditions. Off-road biking is prohibited. Stay alert on the trail; some areas have steep drop-offs; canyons, ravines ,and other low-lying areas may flood during or after rainstorms.

Getting Round Zion

In 2004, Zion National Park was the first national park to tackle noise and traffic congestion in the park by requiring visitors to use a mandatory free park shuttle system to access Zion Canyon from Easter to Halloween. A fleet of 21 shuttles with attractive picture windows runs on propane and makes 6 stops in Springdale and 9 stops in Zion National Park every 7 minutes. The shuttles have been an all-out hit, destressing visitors and restoring natural quiet to Zion Canyon.

T HE ROCKY MOUNTAINS

PRACTICAL INFORMATION ON THE ROCKY MOUNTAINS AND SURROUNDING AREAS

Accommodations

The price guide indicates approximate room/cabin rates:
$ = $110 or less
$$ = $110–250
$$$ = more than $250

COLORADO

Black Canyon of the Gunnison National Park

Address 102 Elk Creek, Gunnison, CO 81230-9304, tel: 970-641-2337, www.nps.gov/blca.
Access The monument is about 250 miles (400km) southwest of Denver; 15 miles (24km) northeast of Montrose, CO, via Highway 50 and Route 347.
Seasons and Hours The South Rim is open daily year-round, with limited access in winter; visitor center is open daily 8am–6pm, 8.30am–4pm in winter, closed Thanksgiving, Christmas, and New Year's Day. The North Rim is open daily year-round, but North Rim Road and the ranger station are closed in winter.
Charge Yes.
Handicapped Access Visitor centers, two campgrounds and three overlooks.
Activities Scenic drive, backpacking, camping, hiking, fishing, wildlife watching, interpretive programs.
Permits and Licenses Free backcountry permits; and Colorado fishing license.
Camping Two campgrounds offer first-come, first-served campsites. Reservations taken for South Rim

Campground loops A and B at least 3 days in advance.
Gateway Community Montrose.
Accommodations None in the park. Lodging is available in Montrose. Contact Montrose Visitors and Convention Bureau, tel: 800-873-0244, www.visitmontrose.net; or Gunnison Country Chamber of Commerce, tel: 970-641-1501, www.gunnison-co.com.
Food and Supplies Limited food service on South Rim (May–late September). Additional services available in Montrose.
Weather Summer temperatures range widely between 60°F and 100°F (16–38°C), winter temperatures between -10°F and 35°F (-23–2°C). Expect summer thunderstorms and heavy snowfall in winter. Weather can vary greatly between the canyon rim and canyon floor.
General Information The dark, sheer 2,000ft (610-meter) -high walls of this narrow canyon make it one of the most dramatic sights in the West. Steep, unmarked trails leading to the canyon floor are recommended for experienced, fit hikers only. Stay on the trails and behind guardrails.

Colorado National Monument

Address Fruita, CO 81521, tel: 970-858-3617, www.nps.gov/colm.
Access The monument is off I-70 near Grand Junction in western Colorado.
Seasons and Hours The monument is open daily year-round. The visitor center is open 8am–6pm summer, 9am–4pm winter, closed Christmas.
Charge Yes.
Handicapped Access Visitor center, one campground, three overlooks,

and Devils Kitchen picnic area.
Activities Scenic drive, backpacking, camping, hiking, horseback riding, wildlife watching, various interpretive programs.
Permits and Licenses Backcountry permits are recommended.
Camping One campground with first-come, first-served campsites.
Gateway Community Grand Junction.
Accommodations None in the park. Lodging is available in Grand Junction and Frulta. Contact Grand Junction Visitor & Convention Bureau, 740 Horizon Drive, Grand Junction, CO 81506, tel: 800-962-2547, www.visit grandjunction.com.
Food and Supplies None in the park. Services are available in Grand Junction and Fruita.
Weather Hot, dry summers with temperatures 60–100°F (16–38°C). Winter temperatures are usually 25–45°F (-4–7°C), with occasional dustings of snow.
General Information This 20,530-acre (8,310-hectare) park features a 23-mile (37km) scenic drive past small canyons and towering sandstone formations, and an excellent network of hiking trails.

Curecanti National Recreation Area

Address 102 Elk Creek, Gunnison, CO 81230-9304, tel: 970-641-2337, www.nps.gov/cure.
Access The recreation area is along the Gunnison River between Montrose and Gunnison, CO, 15 miles (24km) west of Gunnison via Highway 50.
Seasons and Hours Open daily year-round. Elk Creek Visitor Center open

daily, 8am–4pm (closed Mon, Tue, and federal holidays fall and winter), 8am–4.30pm (closed federal holidays spring), 8am–6pm (every day summer).

Charge Only at East Portal.

Handicapped Access Visitor center, nature trails, and select campgrounds.

Activities Backpacking, camping, hiking, boating, water-skiing, fishing, wildlife watching, interpretive programs.

Permits and Licenses Colorado fishing license.

Camping Various campgrounds have first-come, first-served sites, some may be reserved.

Accommodations None in the park. Lodging is available in Gunnison and Montrose. Contact Montrose Visitors and Convention Bureau, tel: 800-873-0244, www.visitmontrose.net; or Gunnison Country Chamber of Commerce, tel: 970-641-1501, www.gunnison-co.com.

Food and Supplies There are limited services at Elk Creek and Lake Fork marinas in summer. Additional services available in Gunnison and Montrose.

Weather Weather can vary greatly during the day. Summer temperatures usually 40–90°F (4–32°C), winter temperatures -20–35°F (-30–2°C). Expect thunderstorms and afternoon winds in summer and snowfall in winter.

General Information Three lakes created by dams on the Gunnison River are the centerpiece of this 42,114-acre (17,043-hectare) park, offering a variety of water sports and excellent backcountry hiking and birding. Boats can be reserved at Elk Creek Marina (tel: 970-641-0707).

Dinosaur National Monument

Address 4545 E. Highway 40, Dinosaur, CO 81610-9724, tel: 970-374-3000 (visitor center), 435-781-7700 (temporary visitor center number), www.nps.gov/dino.

Access The monument headquarters and visitor center is 1 mile (1.5km) east of Dinosaur, Colorado, just off Highway 40. The Dinosaur Quarry is 7 miles (11km) north of Jensen, Utah, on Utah State Highway 149. Note: The Dinosaur Quarry is presently closed for reconstruction of the visitor center. It is expected to reopen in fall 2011. In the interim, a temporary visitor center has been set up near Jensen, Utah, with information and ranger programs. Canyon Area Visitor Center, near Dinosaur, Colorado, remains open.

River Trips in Dinosaur

Several companies offer white-water rafting and boating trips on the Green and Yampa rivers within Dinosaur National Monument. Among those that offer one-day trips is **Adrift Adventures**, tel: 800-824-0150, www.adrift.com. The company is closed during the winter months.

Seasons and Hours The monument is open daily year-round. The two visitor centers are open 8.30am–4.30pm; Dinosaur Quarry Visitor Center is only closed Thanksgiving, Christmas, and New Year's Day, but Canyon Area Visitor Center is closed in winter.

Charge Yes.

Handicapped Access Lower floor of visitor center, one campground, one trail.

Activities Exhibits at dinosaur fossil quarry, backpacking, camping, hiking, float trips, boating, fishing, wildlife watching, interpretive programs.

Permits and Licenses Free backcountry camping/hiking permit from visitor centers. Colorado and/or Utah fishing licenses. River rafting permits by lottery after March each year. Call the River Office tel: 866-825-2995 for information.

Camping Six developed camp-grounds, three in each state, have first-come, first-served campsites.

Gateway Communities Dinosaur, Craig, Vernal.

Accommodations None in the park. Lodging is available in Dinosaur, Craig, and Vernal. Contact Craig Chamber of Commerce, 360 East Victory Way, Craig, CO 81625, tel: 800-864-4405, www.craig-chamber.com.

Food and Supplies No services in the park. Services are available in Dinosaur, Craig, and Vernal.

Weather Summer temperatures usually 60–90°F (16–32°C), winter temperatures 20–60°F (-7–16°C); snowfall is common.

General Information The Green and Yampa rivers have cut dramatic canyons and exposed an abundance of dinosaur fossils, many on display at the Dinosaur Quarry. Allow 1–2 hours to see the fossils, and at least another 1–2 hours for the Tour of the Tilted Rocks.

Great Sand Dunes National Park and National Preserve

Address 11500 Highway 150, Mosca, CO 81146-9798, tel: 719-378-6399,

www.nps.gov/grsa.

Access The monument is about 35 miles (56km) northeast of Alamosa via Route 160 and 150.

Seasons and Hours The monument is open daily year-round. The visitor center is open daily 9am–4.30pm, 9am–6pm in summer; closed Thanksgiving, Christmas, New Year's Day.

Charge Yes.

Handicapped Access Visitor center and three campgrounds.

Activities Backpacking, camping, hiking, wildlife watching, four-wheel-drive tours, interpretive programs.

Permits and Licenses Free backcountry permit.

Camping First-come, first-served.

Gateway Community Alamosa.

Accommodations None in the park. Lodging is available in Alamosa and Fort Garland. Contact Alamosa Convention and Visitors Bureau, 610 State Street, Alamosa, CO 81101, tel: 800-BLU-SKYS, www.alamosa.org.

Food and Supplies There are no services in the park. Services are available in Alamosa, Fort Garland, and at roadside stores outside of the park entrance.

Weather Summer temperatures usually 45–85°F (7–29°C), winter temperatures -10–35°F (-23–2°C) with occasional snow. Surface temperature of dunes in summer can make hiking inadvisable.

General Information At 700ft (213 meters), the tallest dunes in America are preserved in this 85,930-acre (34,800-hectare) park at the foot of the Sangre de Cristo Mountains in southern Colorado.

Mesa Verde National Park

Address PO Box 8, Mesa Verde, CO 81330-0008, tel: 970-529-4465, www.nps.gov/meve.

Access The park entrance is about 8 miles (13km) east of Cortez and 45 miles (72km) west of Durango via Highway 160.

Seasons and Hours The park is open daily year-round. Far View Visitor Center is open daily from mid-April through mid-October, 8am–5pm. Chapin Mesa Archeological Museum is open daily 8am–5pm, extended hours in summer. Ruins Road may be closed by snow in winter.

Charge Yes.

Handicapped Access Visitor center, museum, and some overlooks.

Activities Scenic drives, touring cliff dwellings, camping, hiking, interpretive programs.

Permits and Licenses Hiking

registration may be required depending on route; consult a ranger.
Camping First-come, first-served.
Gateway Community Cortez.
Accommodations
$$ *Far View Lodge*, open April 22 to October 21. To reserve, contact Aramark, PO Box 277, Mancos, CO 81328, tel: 800-449-2288, www.visit mesaverde.com.
Additional accommodation available in Cortez, Mancos, and Durango. Contact Cortez Chamber of Commerce, PO Box 968, Cortez, CO 81321, tel: 970-565-3414, www.cortez chamber.com.
Food and Supplies Food service and limited supplies are available in the park at Morefield, Far View, and Spruce Tree Terrace. Additional services in Mancos, Durango, and Cortez.
Weather Summer temperatures usually 50–95°F (10–35°C), winter temperatures 15–50°F (-9–10°C). Expect summer thunderstorms and heavy snowfall in winter.
General Information Tickets for scheduled ranger-led tours of the most important ruins are popular and must be purchased from the visitor center. Early-morning tours in summer avoid busier times later in the day. Allow plenty of time to drive between ruins. Visiting the ruins on foot may be strenuous. Trails may be uneven; steps and ladders must often be climbed. Most of the major cliff dwellings can be seen from overlooks To protect fragile archeological sites, hiking is restricted to six trails within the park. Disturbing or removing artifacts is strictly forbidden.

Rocky Mountain National Park

Address 1000 Highway 36, Estes Park, CO 80517-8397, tel: 970-586-1206, www.nps.gov/romo
Access The park is about 65 miles (105km) northwest of Denver via Highway 36 (south entrance), and 15 miles (24km) northeast of Granby via Highway 34 (north entrance).
Seasons and Hours The park is open year-round. Main visitor centers are open 8am–4.30pm, extended hours in summer; closed Christmas. Alpine

Accommodations

The price guide indicates approximate room/cabin rates:
$ = $110 or less
$$ = $110–250
$$$ = more than $250

Visitor Center, Moraine Park Museum, and Lily Lake Visitor Center are open summer only. Trail Ridge Road usually closed by snow from mid-October–mid-May.
Charge Yes.
Handicapped Access Visitor centers, museum and select trails and campgrounds.
Activities Scenic drives, camping, hiking, backpacking, fishing, horseback riding, cross-country skiing, snowshoeing, mountain climbing, rock climbing, wildlife watching, interpretive programs.
Permits and Licenses Backcountry camping permits required (free in winter, fee in summer, tel: 970-586-1242); Colorado fishing license.
Camping Five developed campgrounds. Campsites at Moraine Park, Aspenglen, and Glacier Basin campgrounds may be reserved in advance by contacting 877-444-6777, www.recreation.gov. Other sites available on a first-come, first-served basis.
Gateway Community Estes Park.
Accommodations None in the park. Lodging is available in Estes Park and Grand Lake. Contact Estes Park Chamber of Commerce, Estes Park, CO 80517, tel: 970-586-3543, www. estesparkresort.com, or Grand Lake Area Chamber of Commerce, tel: 800-531-1019, www.grandlakechamber.com.
Food and Supplies Services in the park are limited to a snack bar in the gift shop at Fall River Pass. Complete services are available in Estes Park and Grand Lake.
Weather Weather varies considerably depending on elevation. Summer temperatures 40–75°F (4–24°C), colder (often much colder) in the high country. Winter temperatures -5–30°F (-21°C to -1°C). Expect summer thunderstorms and heavy snowfall in

winter. Higher elevations are subject to freezing or near-freezing temperatures year-round.
General Information Free park shuttles run daily in summer on three routes in and around the park. Bear Lake and Moraine Park shuttles link trailheads and campgrounds. The Hiker Shuttle is an express shuttle between Estes Park and Beaver Meadows Visitor Center. And Estes Park runs a visitor center linking the town with the park. For rock and mountain climbing instruction and guide service, contact Colorado Mountain School, 341 Moraine Avenue, Estes Park, CO 80517, tel: 970-586-5758, www.totalclimbing.com.

IDAHO

Craters of the Moon National Monument and National Preserve

Address PO Box 29, Arco, ID 83213-0029, tel: 208-527-1300, www.nps.gov/crmo.
Access The park is 18 miles (29km) southwest of Arco, Idaho, via Highway 20/26.
Seasons and Hours Open daily year-round. The visitor center is open daily 8am–6pm in summer, 8am–4.30pm in spring, fall, and winter; closed Thanksgiving, Christmas, New Year's Day, and President's Day. Park road may be temporarily closed by snow November–April.
Charge Yes.
Handicapped Access Visitor center, nature trail at Devil's Orchard.
Activities Camping, hiking, wildlife watching, interpretive programs.
Permits and Licenses Free backcountry permit required.

BELOW: welcome to Dinosaur National Monument.

Camping First-come, first-served.
Gateway Communities Arco, Pocatello, and Idaho Falls.
Accommodations None in the park. Lodging is available in Arco, Pocatello, and Idaho Falls. Contact Idaho Division of Tourism Development, 700 West State Street, Boise, ID 83720, tel: 800-635-7820, www.visitid.org.
Food and Supplies Limited services are available in Arco. Additional food and supplies are available in Idaho Falls and Pocatello.
Weather Summer temperatures usually 35–80°F (2–27°C) with occasional highs above 90°F (32°C); winter temperatures 0–30°F (-18°C to -1°C) with extremes well below 0°F (-18°C) and heavy snow November–March.
General Information This 460,000-acre (188,000-hectare) park preserves a rugged landscape of lava flows, craters, caves, and volcanic cones. It also hosts a fascinating number of plants and animals adapted to live in the harsh volcanic and high desert environment.

MONTANA

Bighorn Canyon National Recreation Area

Address 5 Avenue B, PO Box 7458, Fort Smith, MT 59035-7458, tel: 406-666-2412, www.nps.gov/bica.
Access The recreation area is 43 miles (69km) south of Hardin, Montana, via Route 313, and 58 miles (93km) from Cody, Wyoming, via Routes 14A and 37.
Seasons and Hours The recreation area is open daily year-round. The Yellowtail Dam Visitor Center (Fort Smith, MT) is open 9am–5pm Memorial Day to Labor Day; the Cal S. Taggart Bighorn Canyon Visitor Center is open daily 8.30am–4.30pm, 8am–5.30pm in summer, closed Thanksgiving, Christmas, and New Year's Day.
Charge Yes.
Handicapped Access Visitor centers.
Activities Camping, hiking, backpacking, wildlife watching, boating, fishing, interpretive programs.
Permits and Licenses Backcountry camping permit; Wyoming and/or Montana fishing licenses.
Camping First-come, first-served.
Gateway Communities Fort Smith, Hardin, and Lovell.
Accommodations None in the park. Lodging is available in Hardin, Lovell,

ABOVE: the peaks of Glacier Park.

and Fort Smith. Contact Custer Country, Tourism Region, Box 904, Forsyth, MT 59327, tel: 800-346-1876, www.custercountry.com.
Food and Supplies Limited food and supplies are available in Fort Smith, Ok-A-Beh and Horseshoe Bend. Additional food and supplies available in Hardin and Lovell.
Weather Summer temperatures 45–85°F (7–29°C) with brief afternoon thunderstorms, winter temperatures -15–40°F (-26–4°C), with occasional snow.
General Information Bighorn Lake, formed by the Yellowtail Dam on the Bighorn River, extends 55 miles (89km) through spectacular Bighorn Canyon. The Crow Indian Reservation borders a large part of the area.

Glacier National Park

Address PO Box 128, West Glacier, MT 59936-0128, tel: 406-888-7800, www.nps.gov/glac.
Access The West Glacier entrance is 33 miles (53km) northeast of Kalispell via Highway 2. The St Mary entrance, on the east side of the park, is 31 miles (50km) northwest of Browning via Highway 89.
Seasons and Hours The park is open daily year-round. Sections of the Going-to-the-Sun Road are usually closed by snow mid-October–mid-June. Visitor centers are open 8.30am–4pm, summer only, except for Apgar Visitor Center, which is open weekends in winter.
Charge Yes.
Handicapped Access Apgar and St Mary visitor centers, one nature trail and select campgrounds.
Activities Camping, hiking, backpacking, horseback riding, wildlife watching, boating, fishing, cross-country skiing, snowshoeing, interpretive programs.

A Year of Glacier

For $35, a Glacier National Park Pass gives unlimited entry to the park for a year from the month of purchase. Inquire at any park entrance.

Permits and Licenses Free backcountry camping permits required.
Camping Fish Creek and St Mary campgrounds can be reserved in advance (tel: 800-365-CAMP); remaining campgrounds first-come, first-served.
Gateway Communities West Glacier, East Glacier, and St Mary.
Accommodations Lodging in the park is managed by Glacier Park, Inc., PO Box 2025, Columbia Falls, MT 59912, tel: 406-892-2525, www.glacierparkinc.com.
$$–$$$ *Glacier Park Lodge.*
$$ *Lake McDonald Lodge, Cabins, and Inn.*
$$–$$$ *Many Glacier Hotel.*
$$ *Rising Sun Motor Inn and Cabins.*
$–$$ *Swift Current Motor Inn and Cabins.*
$$ *The Village Inn at Agpar.*
$–$$ *Apgar Village Lodge*, Belton Chalets, Inc., PO Box 410, West Glacier, MT 59936, tel: 406-888-5484, www.westglacier.com.
$ *Granite Park Chalet*, Belton Chalets, Inc., PO Box 189, West Glacier, MT 59936, tel: 888-345-2649, www.graniteparkchalet.com.
$$ *Sperry Chalet*, PO Box 189, West Glacier, MT 59936, tel: 888-345-2649.
Additional lodging is available in East Glacier, St Mary, and West Glacier. Contact Glacier Country, 836 Holt Drive, Suite 320, PO Box 1035, Bigfork, MT 59911, tel: 800-338-5072, www.glaciermt.com.
Food and Supplies Food service and supplies are available in the park at Lake McDonald, Swiftcurrent, Apgar Village, and St Mary Lake; outside the park in East Glacier, West Glacier, and St Mary.
Weather Summer temperatures usually 40–75°F (4–24°C), colder at higher elevations. Winters are very cold with heavy snow, temperatures usually 0–35°F (-18–2°C). Be prepared for high winds, sudden weather changes and violent storms anytime.
General Information Never try to feed or approach wildlife. Glacier Park, Inc. (tel: 406-892-2525) offers a variety of guided bus tours. Glacier Park Boat Co. (tel: 406-257-2426)

A – Z

offers cruises on McDonald, Many Glaciers, Two Medicine, and St Mary lakes. Glacier Wilderness Guides & Montana Raft Co. (tel: 800-521-RAFT) offer a variety of escorted trips, from one-day hikes to eight-day combination backpacking/rafting expeditions.

For information about Waterton Lakes National Park, contact Waterton Park, AB, T0K 2M0, Canada, tel: 403-859-2252, www.pc.gc.ca/eng/pn-np/ab/waterton/index.aspx.

NORTH DAKOTA

Theodore Roosevelt National Park

Address PO Box 7, Medora, ND 58645 0007, tel: 701 623 4730 (South Unit Visitor Center), 701-842-2333 (North Unit Visitor Center), www.nps.gov/thro.

Access The south unit is near Medora, ND, 36 miles (58km) west of Dickinson via I-94. The north unit is near Watford City, ND, about 70 miles (113km) from Dickinson via I-94 and Highway 85, and about 60 miles (97km) south of Williston via Highway 85. A 20-mile (32km) dirt road runs from the south unit to the Elkhorn Ranch. Sections of park roads are closed by snow in winter.

Seasons and Hours The park is open daily year-round. Portions of the South Unit Scenic Loop Drive and North Unit Scenic Road may be closed in winter due to snow and ice. The visitor centers are open 8am–6pm Memorial Day through Labor Day, with more limited daily opening times in winter. The Painted Canyon Visitor Center is open April–November, 8.30am–4.30pm. Visitor centers are closed Thanksgiving, Christmas, and New Year's Day.

Charge Yes.

Handicapped Access Visitor centers, wayside exhibits, select campgrounds, Maltese Cross Cabin, and some nature trails.

Activities Scenic drive, camping, hiking, backpacking, horseback riding, float trips, wildlife watching, interpretive programs.

Accommodations

The price guide indicates approximate room/cabin rates:
$ = $110 or less
$$ = $110–250
$$$ = more than $250

Permits and Licenses Free backcountry camping permits required.

Camping First-come, first-served.

Gateway Community Medora.

Accommodations None in the park. Lodgings are available in Medora, Dickinson, and Williston. Contact Medora Chamber of Commerce, tel: 701-623-4910, www.medorandchamber.com.

Food and Supplies No services in the park. Services are available in Medora, Beach, Belfield, Dickinson, Watford City, and Williston.

Weather Summer temperatures usually 40–90°F (4–32°C), with occasional highs in excess of 100°F (38°C) and sudden rainstorms. Winter temperatures -10–30°F (-23°C to -1°C) with severe snowstorms. Be prepared for sudden changes in weather, storms, and windy conditions.

General Information Driving distance between the two units is 70 miles (113km). At least two days is recommended to visit both North and South units and walk some of the short nature trails. Fast-moving prairie storms may restrict travel on established trails and backcountry routes; check on closures at entrance stations and visitor centers. Never feed or approach wildlife.

SOUTH DAKOTA

Badlands National Park

Address 25216 Ben Reifel Road, PO Box 6, Interior, SD 57750-0006, tel: 605-433-5361, www.nps.gov/badl.

Access The park is about 60 miles (97km) east of Rapid City, and about 20 miles (32km) west of Kadoka via I-90. Take exit 131 (Cactus Flat) or exit 110 (Wall) and follow signs to Badlands National Park.

Seasons and Hours The park is open daily year-round. The Ben Reifel Visitor Center is open daily 7am–7pm in summer, 8am–5pm in winter; closed Thanksgiving, Christmas, and New Year's Day. White River Visitor Center is open June–August only. Roads may be closed by snow in winter.

Charge Yes.

Handicapped Access Visitor centers, some campgrounds and Fossil Exhibit Trail.

Activities Scenic drive, camping, hiking, backpacking, wildlife watching, interpretive programs.

Permits and Licenses No.

Camping First-come, first-served.

Gateway Community Wall and Interior.

Accommodations
$ *Cedar Pass Lodge* (open April to mid-October), 20681 South Dakota Highway 240, Interior, SD 57750, tel: 877-386-4383, http://foreverlodging.com/lodging.cfm?PropertyKey=67. Additional accommodations are available in Wall and Interior. Contact the Wall Badlands Area Chamber of Commerce, 501 Main Street, Wall, SD 57790, tel: 605-279-2665, www.wall-badlands.com.

Food and Supplies Cedar Pass Lodge has a restaurant open mid-April through mid-October. Additional services in Wall and Interior.

Weather Summer temperatures 50–90°F (10–32°C), with occasional highs in excess of 100°F (38°C) and sudden, severe rainstorms. Winter temperatures 0–40°F (-18–4°C) with occasional lows well below 0°F (-18°C) and blizzard conditions. Extremely high winds are common year-round.

General Information Be prepared for sudden changes in weather, high winds, and sudden hail, rain, or snowstorms. Hikers should carry adequate water – 1 gallon (4 liters) per day per person.

Jewel Cave National Monument

Address 11149 US Highway 16, Building B12, Custer, SD 57730. tel: 605-673-8300 (information and cave tour tickets), www.nps.gov/jeca.

Access The monument is 13 miles (21km) west of Custer via Highway 16.

Seasons and Hours The monument is open daily year-round. The visitor center is open May–September, 8am–7.30pm, October–April 8am–

Jewel Caving

Scenic Tours of Jewel Cave and the Discovery Talk are offered daily year-round; the historic Lantern Tour and the Spelunking Tour are available in the summer months only.

Tickets for the Jewel Cave Discovery Talk and Scenic Tour and the Lantern Tour are sold on a first-come, first-served basis (arrive early in the day to avoid a long wait). Reservations are required for the longer, more strenuous Spelunking Tour. Call or write to the park headquarters no more than a month in advance.

A – Z

CALIFORNIA AND THE PACIFIC

THE SOUTHWEST

THE ROCKY MOUNTAINS

THE PACIFIC NORTHWEST

Accommodations

The price guide indicates approximate room/cabin rates:
$ = $110 or less
$$ = $110–250
$$$ = more than $250

4.30pm; closed Thanksgiving, Christmas, and New Year's Day.
Charge A fee is charged for cave tours.
Handicapped Access Visitor center and one room of the cave.
Activities Cave tour, hiking, wildlife watching, interpretive programs.
Permits and Licenses No.
Camping No.
Gateway Communities Custer and Newcastle.
Accommodations None in the park. Lodging is available in Custer, SD, and Newcastle, WY. Contact the Rapid City Convention and Visitors Bureau, 444 Mount Rushmore Road North, Rapid City, SD 57701, tel: 800-487-3223, www.visitrapidcity.com; South Dakota Office of Tourism, 711 East Wells Avenue, Pierre, SD 57501, tel: 800-S-DAKOTA, www.travelsd.com.
Food and Supplies No services in the park. Services are available in Custer, SD, and Newcastle, WY.
Weather Summer temperatures 45–90°F (7–32°C). Winter temperatures 0–45°F (-18–7°C) with heavy snow. The cave is 47°F (8°C) year-round.
General Information Calcite "decorates" extensive limestone passages with sparkling, jewel-like crystals. The cave tour is offered on a first-come, first-served basis. You may have to wait for an opening during the busy summer season.

Mount Rushmore National Memorial

Address 13000 Highway 244, Building 31, Suite 1, Keystone, SD 57751-0268, tel: 605-574-2523, www.nps.gov/moru.
Access The memorial is 2 miles (3km) southwest of Keystone via Highway 244.
Seasons and Hours Lincoln Borglum Visitor Center and the Information Center are open daily 8am–10pm in summer, 8am–5pm in winter, with varying hours in spring and fall; closed Christmas.
Charge Yes.
Handicapped Access Information Center.
Activities Hiking, wildlife watching, interpretive programs, exhibits.

Special Events *March/April:* Easter Service.
July: Independence Day festivities.
August 10: Gutzon Borglum Day is commemorated with presentations and music.
Permits and Licenses No.
Camping No.
Gateway Community Keystone.
Accommodations None in the park. Lodging is available in Keystone, Hot Springs, Custer, and throughout the Black Hills. Contact the Rapid City Convention and Visitors Bureau, 444 Mount Rushmore Road North, Rapid City, SD 57701, tel: 800-487-3223, www.visitrapidcity.com; South Dakota Office of Tourism, 711 East Wells Avenue, Pierre, SD 57501, tel: 800-S-DAKOTA, www.travelsd.com.
Food and Supplies Food service is available in the park and surrounding towns.
Weather Summer daytime temperatures 45–90°F (7–32°C). Winter temperatures -10–45°F (-23–7°C) with heavy snow.
General Information The sculptor's studio is open May–September. The sculpture lighting ceremony is held every evening from Memorial Day through Labor Day in the amphitheater.

Wind Cave National Park

Address 26611 US Highway 385, Hot Springs, SD 57747, tel: 605-745-4600 (information and tickets for cave tours), www.nps.gov/wica.
Access The park is about 6 miles (10km) north of Hot Springs via Highway 385, and 26 miles (42km) southeast of Custer via Highway 16A and Route 87.
Seasons and Hours The park is open daily year-round. The visitor center is open daily 8am–7pm in summer;

restricted hours at other times of year. Cave tours offered daily, limited schedule in winter. Visitor center and cave are closed Thanksgiving, Christmas.
Charge For cave tour only.
Handicapped Access Visitor center, one campground and portion of cave tour (see rangers at visitor center). A special-needs tour is available by prior arrangement.
Activities Cave tours, caving, scenic drive, camping, hiking, backpacking, wildlife watching, interpretive programs.
Permits and Licenses Free backcountry camping permits required.
Camping First-come, first-served.
Gateway Community Hot Springs.
Accommodations There are no accommodations in the park. Lodging is available in Custer, Hot Springs, Keystone, and Rapid City. Contact the Rapid City Convention and Visitors Bureau, 444 Mount Rushmore Road North, Rapid City, SD 57701, tel: 800-487-3223, www.visitrapidcity.com; South Dakota Office of Tourism, 711 East Wells Avenue, Pierre, SD 57501, tel: 800-S-DAKOTA, www.travelsd.com.
Food and Supplies Cafeteria at visitor center May through October. Additional services in Custer, Hot Springs, Keystone, and Rapid City.
Weather Summer temperatures usually 50–90°F (10–32°C). Winter temperatures 0–50°F (-18–10°C) with light snow. The cave is 53°F (12°C) year-round.
General Information Standard cave tours are available on a first-come, first-served basis. Places on the terrific Wild Cave Tour and the spooky Candlelight Cave Tour should be reserved well in advance (tel: 605-745-4600).

BELOW: waiting for the fish to bite on Yellowstone River.

Never try to feed or approach the prairie wildlife. Bison may seem placid and slow-moving, but they can charge suddenly and at great speed if suddenly irritated.

WYOMING

Devils Tower National Monument

Address PO Box 10, Devils Tower, WY 82714-0010, tel: 307-467-5283, www.nps.gov/deto.
Access The monument is about 29 miles (47km) northwest of Sundance via Highway 14 and Route 24.
Seasons and Hours The monument is open daily year-round. The visitor center is open April–November, 9am–7pm in summer, 9am–5pm in spring and fall.
Charge Yes.
Handicapped Access Visitor center and select campgrounds.
Activities Camping, hiking, rock climbing, wildlife watching, interpretive programs.
Permits and Licenses Climbing permits required. Climbers must register before a climb and sign out afterward.
Camping First-come, first-served.
Gateway Community Sundance.
Accommodations None in the park. Lodging is available in Sundance, Moorcroft, and Spearfish. Contact Sundance Area Chamber of Commerce, PO Box 1004, Sundance, WY 82729, tel: 800-477-9340, www.sundancewyoming.com.
Food and Supplies No services in the park. Services are available in Sundance, Moorcroft, and Spearfish.
Weather Summer daytime temperatures 70–85°F (21–29°C). Winter temperatures -10–40°F (-23–4°C) with snowfall.
General Information The nation's first national monument protects an 865ft (264-meter) tower of volcanic rock, a favorite with rock climbers, surrounded by pine forests, deciduous woodlands, and prairie grasslands.

Touring the Park

For information on guided bus tours, cruises of Yellowstone Lake, snowcoach tours, boat rentals, and horseback riding, contact Xanterra Parks & Resorts, PO Box 165, Yellowstone National Park, WY 82190, tel: 866-GEYSERLAND, www.yellowstonenationalparklodges.com.

ABOVE: riding horseback.

Grand Teton National Park and John D. Rockefeller Memorial Parkway

Address PO Drawer 170, Moose, WY 83012-0170, tel: 307-739-3300, www.nps.gov/grte .
Access The Craig Thomas Discovery and Visitor Center is 12 miles (21km) north of Jackson via Highway 89/26/191. The Colter Bay Visitor Center and Indian Arts Museum is about 35 miles (56km) south of Grant Village in Yellowstone National Park.
Seasons and Hours The park is open daily year-round. The Craig Thomas Discovery and Visitor Center is open daily, 8am–7pm in summer, 8am–5pm winter, spring, and fall. Jenny Lake Visitor Center is open mid-May to September, 8am–7pm. Colter Bay Visitor Center and Indian Arts Museum is open early May to mid-October, 8am–7pm in summer, 8am–5pm in spring and fall. Some park roads may be closed by snow November–May.
Charge Yes.
Handicapped Access Visitor centers, Indian Arts Museum, selected campgrounds and some ranger-led activities.
Activities Scenic drive, camping, hiking, backpacking, fishing, float trips, boating, horseback riding, rock climbing, mountain climbing, cross-country skiing, snowshoeing, wildlife watching, interpretive programs.
Permits and Licenses Free backcountry camping permits required.
Camping First-come, first-served.
Gateway Community Moose.
Accommodations Three lodges in the park are managed by Grand Teton Lodge Company, PO Box 250, Moran, WY 83013, tel: 800-628-9988 (reservations), www.gtlc.com/index.aspx:
$–$$ *Colter Bay Village* (cabins)
$$$ *Jackson Lake Lodge*
$$$ *Jenny Lake Lodge*

$$ *Dornan's Spur Ranch Cabins*, PO Box 39, Moose WY 83012, tel: 307-733-2415, www.dornans.com/cabins.
$$ *Flagg Ranch Resort*, PO Box 187, Moran, WY 83013, tel: 800-443-2311, www.flaggranch.com.
$$$ *Signal Mountain Lodge*, Teton Park Road, PO Box 50, Moran, WY 83013, tel: 307-543-2831. Additional lodging is available in Jackson. Contact Wyoming Travel and Tourism, 520 Etchepare Circle, Cheyenne, WY 82007, tel: 800-225-5996, www.wyomingtourism.org.
Food and Supplies Restaurants and limited supplies are available in the park at Jackson Lake Lodge, Colter Bay Village, and Signal Mountain Lodge. Additional services available in Jackson.
Weather Weather varies considerably depending on elevation. Summer temperatures in lower elevations usually 35–80°F (2–27°C) with occasional highs above 90°F (32°C); winter temperatures 0–30°F (-18°C to -1°C) with extremes well below 0°F (-18°C) and heavy snow November–April. Temperatures are much colder at higher elevations, where snow remains well into summer. Expect a variety of weather conditions in any season.
General Information Park concessionaires offer horseback rides at Colter Bay and Jackson Lake Lodge. The Teton Range offers many opportunities for climbers and mountaineers. The Jenny Lake Ranger Station is the center for climbing information, routes, conditions, etc. Contact Grand Teton Lodge Co. (tel: 307-543-2811) for Jackson Lake cruises, float trips on the Snake River, boat rentals, and horseback riding.

Yellowstone National Park

Address PO Box 168, Yellowstone National Park, WY 82190-0168, tel: 307-344-7381, www.nps.gov/yell.
Access The Fishing Bridge Visitor Center is 80 miles (129km) west of Cody, WY, via Highway 20/16/14. The Grant Visitor Center is about 75 miles (121km) north of Jackson, WY, via 191/89. The Old Faithful Visitor Center is about 145 miles (233km) from Idaho Falls, ID, via Highway 20.

A – Z

CALIFORNIA AND THE PACIFIC

THE SOUTHWEST

THE ROCKY MOUNTAINS

THE PACIFIC NORTHWEST

The Albright Visitor Center is about 48 miles (77km) south of Livingston, MT, via Highway 89.

Seasons and Hours The park is open daily year-round. Many park roads may be closed by snow November–April. The Albright Visitor Center in Mammoth Hot Springs is open daily 8am–7pm in summer, restricted opening times other seasons.

Charge Yes.

Handicapped Access Visitor centers, some campgrounds.

Activities Scenic drive, camping, hiking, backpacking, fishing, boating, horseback riding, rock climbing, mountain climbing, cross-country skiing, snowshoeing, wildlife watching, interpretive programs.

Permits and Licenses Free backcountry camping permits needed.

Camping Some sites can be reserved in advance by contacting Yellowstone National Park Lodges, PO Box 165, Yellowstone National Park, WY 82190, tel: 307-344-7311.

Gateway Communities Jackson, Cody, and Livingston.

Accommodations Lodging in the park is operated by Xanterra Parks & Resorts, PO Box 165, Yellowstone National Park, WY 82190, tel: 866-GEYSERLAND or 307-344-7311, www.yellowstonenationalparklodges.com.

$$ *Canyon Lodge* (cabins).
$$ *Grant Village Motel.*
$$ *Lake Lodge & Cabins.*
$$ *Lake Yellowstone Hotel & Cabins.*
$ *Mammoth Hot Springs Hotel & Cabins.*
$$ *Old Faithful Inn.*
$$ *Old Faithful Lodge & Cabins.*
$$ *Old Faithful Snow Lodge & Cabins.*
$$ *Roosevelt Lodge & Cabins*

Additional lodging is available in Jackson, Cody and Livingston. Contact Wyoming Travel and Tourism, 520 Etchepare Circle, Cheyenne, WY 82007, tel: 800-225-5996, www.wyomingtourism.org or Travel Montana, 301 South Park, PO Box 200533, Helena, MT 59620, tel: 800-847-4868, www.visitmt.com.

Food and Supplies Restaurants and limited supplies available in the park at Lake, Canyon, Tower Fall, Mammoth Hot Springs, Grant Village, Old Faithful. Additional services available in Cody, Jackson, Livingston, Cooke City, West Yellowstone, and Gardiner.

Weather Temperatures are much cooler at higher elevations, where snow remains into summer. Expect a variety of weather conditions.

General Information Do not try to approach or feed wildlife.

Other National Monuments, Historic Sites, and Historical Parks

Colorado

Bent's Old Fort National Historic Site, 35110 Highway 194 East, La Junta, CO 81050-9523, tel: 719-383-5010, www.nps.gov/beol. A reconstruction of the fort that served as a major meeting place for fur traders, Native Americans, and pioneers on the Santa Fe Trail in the early 1800s.

Florissant Fossil Beds National Monument, PO Box 185, Florissant, CO 80816-0185, tel: 719-748-3253, www.nps.gov/flfo. The monument preserves an abundance of fossil insects, leaves, fish, and other creatures trapped by a volcanic eruption about 35 million years ago.

Hovenweep National Monument, McElmo Route, Cortez, CO 81321-8901, tel: 970-562-4282, www.nps.gov/hove. Many unusual canyon-top structures built and inhabited from AD 900–1300 by Ancestral Pueblo people of the Mesa Verde culture.

Idaho

Hagerman Fossil Beds National Monument, 221 North State Street, PO Box 570, Hagerman, ID 83332-0570, tel: 208-837-4793, www.nps.gov/hafo. An active paleontological site on the bluffs above the Snake River.

Nez Perce National Historical Park, 39063, Highway 95, Spalding, ID 83540-9715, tel: 208-843-2261, www.nps.gov/nepe. (Also in Montana, Oregon and Washington.) The park interprets the history and culture of the Nez Perce Indians.

Montana

Big Hole National Battlefield, PO Box 237, Wisdom, MT 59761-0237, tel: 406-689-3155, www.nps.gov/biho. The park interprets the clash between the Nez Perce Indians and the US Army in 1877 during the dramatic and tragic Nez Perce War.

Grant-Kohrs Ranch National Historic Site, 266 Warren Lane, Deer Lodge, MT 59722-0790, tel: 406-846-2070, www.nps.gov/krko. Once one of the largest ranches in the country, now a living museum of ranch life in the late 1800s and the early 1900s.

Little Bighorn Battlefield National Monument, PO Box 39, Crow Agency, MT 59022-0039, tel: 406-638-2621, www.nps.gov/libi. The site of "Custer's Last Stand," the fateful battle between the 7th US Cavalry and Lakota and Cheyenne warriors. Located on the Crow Reservation. Custer National Cemetery lies within the park.

Nebraska

Agate Fossil Beds National Monument, 301 River Road, Harrison, NE 69346-2734, tel: 308-436-9760, www.nps.gov/agfo. The monument preserves a wealth of ancient fossil mammals and more than 500 American Indian artifacts.

Homestead National Monument of America, 8523 West State Highway 4, Beatrice, NE 68310, tel: 402-223-3514, www.nps.gov/home. The monument preserves the land and structures of an early claim made under the Homestead Act of 1862 and interprets the life of American pioneers.

Scotts Bluff National Monument, PO Box 27, Gering, NE 69341-0027, tel: 308-436-4340, www.nps.gov/scbl. This 800ft (244-meter) landmark on the Oregon Trail features living-history demonstrations and wagon ruts left by westering pioneers.

North Dakota

Fort Union Trading Post National Historic Site, 15550 Highway 1804, Williston, ND 58801, tel: 701-572-9083, www.nps.gov/fous. This partially reconstructed fort was the center of fur trading on the upper Missouri River in the mid-1800s.

Knife River Indian Villages National Historic Site, PO Box 9, Stanton, ND 58571-0009, tel: 701-745-3300, www.nps.gov/knri. Preserves the site of Hidatsa and Mandan villages dating back to 1845 and earlier.

Wyoming

Fort Laramie National Historic Site, 965 Gray Rocks Road, Fort Laramie, WY 82212, tel: 307-837-2221, www.nps.gov/fola. The park preserves a military outpost established in 1849 to protect wagon trains heading west.

Fossil Butte National Monument, PO Box 592, Kemmerer, WY 83101-0592, tel: 307-877-4455, www.nps.gov/fobu. The monument preserves a great wealth of freshwater fish fossils; also turtles, birds, bats, and insect remains, in 55-million-year-old rocks.

THE PACIFIC NORTHWEST

PRACTICAL INFORMATION FOR ALASKA, OREGON, AND WASHINGTON

Accommodations

The price guide indicates approximate room/cabin rates:
$ = $110 or less
$$ = $110–250
$$$ = more than $250

ALASKA

Note: Remote wilderness lodges in Alaska are usually fly-in only, and are full service, all inclusive resorts. Due to the distances involved, with a few exceptions, rates are usually for a minimum of several days or a week.

Aniakchak National Monument and Preserve

Address PO Box 245, King Salmon, AK 99613, tel: 907-246-3305, www.nps.gov/ania.
Access There are no roads to Aniakchak. Charter flights are available from King Salmon, 290 miles (467km) southwest of Anchorage.
Seasons and Hours The monument is open daily year-round.
Charge No.
Handicapped Access No.
Activities Fishing, wilderness camping, float trips, wildlife watching.
Visitor Facilities None.
Camping Wilderness camping only.
Permits and Licenses Alaska fishing license.
Gateway Community King Salmon.
Accommodations None in the park; nearest lodging is in King Salmon. Get information at the multiagency King Salmon Visitor Center, PO Box 298,

King Salmon, AK 99613, tel: 907-246-4250.
Food and Supplies No services in the park; supplies are available in King Salmon.
Weather Temperatures usually -30–30°F (-34°C to -1°C) in winter, 40–70°F (4–21°C) in summer; violent wind, rain, and snowstorms in any season. Be prepared for prevailing weather conditions/volcanic activity.
General Information Visitors must be completely self-sufficient and experienced in wilderness travel. Insect repellent is recommended. Most travelers arrive between June and August. Contact park headquarters well in advance of your visit.

Bering Land Bridge National Preserve

Address PO Box 220, Nome, AK 99762-0220, tel: 907-443-2522, www.nps.gov/bela.**Access** There are no roads to Bering Land Bridge. Charter flights are available from Nome and Kotzebue.
Seasons and Hours The preserve is open daily year-round.
Charge No.
Handicapped Access No.
Activities Fishing, wilderness camping, coastal boating, float trips, wildlife watching, backcountry hiking.
Visitor Facilities None.
Camping Wilderness camping only.
Permits and Licenses Alaska fishing license.
Gateway Community None.
Accommodations None; nearest is in Nome and Kotzebue. Contact Nome Convention and Visitors Bureau, PO Box 240, Nome, AK 99762, tel: 907-443-6555,

www.visitnomealaska.com.
Food and Supplies No services in the park; supplies and restaurants are available in Nome and Kotzebue.
Weather Temperatures usually -30–30°F (-34°C to -1°C) in winter, 40–75°F (4–24°C) in summer; violent wind, rain, and snowstorms in any season. Be prepared for extreme conditions.
General Information Most travelers arrive between June and August. Contact park headquarters well in advance of visit. Visitors must be completely self-sufficient and experienced in wilderness travel. Insect repellent is recommended.

Cape Krusenstern National Monument

Address PO Box 1029, Kotzebue, AK 99752-1029, tel: 907-442-3890 (year-round information), 907-442-3760 (summertime information) www.nps.gov/cakr.
Access There are no roads to Cape Krusenstern. Charter flights and boats are available from Kotzebue.
Seasons and Hours The park is open daily year-round.
Charge No.
Handicapped Access No.
Activities Fishing, wildlife watching, backcountry hiking and camping.
Camping Wilderness camping only.
Permits and Licenses Alaska fishing license.
Gateway Communities Kotzebue and Nome.
Accommodations None in the park; nearest lodging is in Nome and Kotzebue. Contact Nome Convention and Visitors Bureau, PO Box 240, Nome, AK 99762, tel: 907-443-6555, www.visitnomealaska.com.

Food and Supplies No services in the park; food and supplies are available in Nome and Kotzebue.
Weather Temperatures usually -60–30°F (-51°C to -1°C) in (long) winter; 30–75°F (-1–24°C) in (short) summer; violent wind, rain, and snowstorms in any season. Be prepared for extreme conditions.
General Information Visitors must be completely self-sufficient and experienced in wilderness travel. Insect repellent is recommended. Most travelers arrive between June and August. Contact park headquarters well in advance of visit.

Denali National Park and Preserve

Address PO Box 9, Denali Park, AK 99755-0009, tel: 907-683-2294, www.nps.gov/dena.
Access Rail, bus (summer only), and charter air service available from Fairbanks and Anchorage. The park is 121 miles (195km) from Fairbanks and 237 miles (381km) from Anchorage by car via Alaska Highway 3.
Seasons and Hours The park is open daily year-round. Denali Visitor Center is open 8am–6pm, May–September, and Eilson Visitor Center is open 9am–7pm June–September; in winter, visitor center in Murie Science and Learning Center is open daily 9am–4pm.
Charge Yes.
Handicapped Access Visitor Center, Eielson Visitor Center, park headquarters, Denali Park Hotel, park auditorium, several campgrounds, post office, and shuttle bus.
Activities Fishing, camping, wildlife watching, hiking, float trips, mountain climbing, dogsledding, guided nature walks, cross-country skiing, bus tours.
Camping All of the park's tent and RV sites may be reserved in advance by calling 800-622-7275. Some campgrounds are open to private vehicles, others can be reached only by shuttle bus (see below).
Permits and Licenses Free backcountry permits are available on a first-come, first-served basis from the Visitor Center.
Gateway Communities Fairbanks and Anchorage.
Accommodations Lodging for Denali is operated by ARAMARK Denali Park Resorts, 241 West Ship Creek Avenue, Anchorage, AK 99501, tel: 800-276-7234, www.denaliparkresorts.com.
$$$ McKinley Chalet Resort
$$$ McKinley Village Lodge

Denali Shuttle

To see Denali, you must ride the park shuttle. Green shuttle buses run daily between late May and mid-September on four loops: Toklat River, Eielson Visitor Center, Wonder Lake, and Kantishna. Special buses are available for hikers and campers. It's important to plan ahead and reserve your seat online or tel: 800-622-7275; otherwise, you may wait 2–3 days for a seat to open up in summer. Other tour buses offer guided trips. Shuttles can be pricey, but free courtesy shuttles link major destinations and campgrounds.

$$$ Camp Denali and North Face Lodges, PO Box 67, Denali, AK 99755, tel: 907-683-2290, www.campdenali.com.
$$$ Denali River Cabins and Cedars Lodge Hotel, Mile 231.1 Parks Highway, Denali, AK 99755, tel: 800-230-7275, www.denalirivercabins.com.
Food and Supplies Restaurants and supplies are available at park entrance and along Highway 3 outside the park.
Weather Temperatures usually -40–30°F (-40°C to -1°C) in winter, 40–70°F (4–21°C) in summer; violent wind and storms in any season. Snow may close the park road from late September to mid-May.
General Information If you are driving, remember gas stations are few; fuel up at every opportunity. Backcountry travelers must be completely self-sufficient and experienced in wilderness travel. Insect repellent is strongly recommended.

Gates of the Arctic National Park and Preserve

Address PO Box 30, Bettles, AK 99726, tel: 907-692-5494 (Bettles Ranger Station and Visitor Center), www.nps.gov/gaar.
Access There are no roads to Gates of the Arctic, although the Dalton Highway comes within 5 miles (8km) of the park. Scheduled air taxis from Fairbanks serve Anaktuvuk Pass, Bettles, and Coldfoot. Contact Bettles Ranger Station for the list of licensed taxi operators.
Seasons and Hours The park is open daily year-round. Fairbanks Administrative Center, 4175 Geist Road, Fairbanks, AK 99709, tel: 907-457-5752, is open year-round Monday–Friday, 8am–4.30pm. Closed on holidays. Bettles Ranger

Station and Visitor Center is open 8am–5pm, daily mid-June to mid-September, Monday–Friday the remainder of the year. Arctic Interagency Visitor Center in Coldfoot is open daily 10am–10pm, Memorial Day through Labor Day.
Charge No.
Handicapped Access No.
Activities Fishing, wilderness camping, wildlife watching, mountain climbing, float trips.
Visitor Facilities There are no facilities in the park; ranger stations are located in Bettles, Coldfoot, and Anaktuvuk Pass.
Camping Wilderness camping only. There is a campground outside the park at Dalton Highway Milepost 180, 5 miles (8km) north of Coldfoot.
Permits and Licenses Alaska fishing license.
Gateway Community Fairbanks.
Accommodations There are several small rustic wilderness lodges:
$$$ Iniakuk Lake Wilderness Lodge, PO Box 80424, Fairbanks, AK 99708, tel: 877-479-6354, www.gofarnorth.com.
$$$ Peace of Selby Wilderness Lodge, PO Box 86, 90 Polar Road, Manley Hot Springs, AK 99756, tel: 907-672-3206, www.alaskawilderness.net. Limited accommodations are available outside the park in Coldfoot. Contact Fairbanks Convention and Visitors Bureau, 101 Dunkel Street, Fairbanks, AK 99701, tel: 800-327-5774 or 907-456-5774, www.explore fairbanks.com.
Food and Supplies No services in the park; limited supplies are available in Bettles. Bring all food from Fairbanks.
Weather Severe winter conditions and short summers; violent winds, rain and snowstorms in any season. Be prepared for extreme Arctic conditions.
General Information Visitors must be completely self-sufficient and experienced in wilderness travel. Insect repellent is recommended. Contact park headquarters well in advance of visit to plan your trip and to request a list of useful outfitters and guides.

Glacier Bay National Park and Preserve

Address PO Box 140, Gustavus, AK 99826-0140, tel: 907-697-2230, www.nps.gov/glba.
Access There are no roads to Glacier Bay. Scheduled flights are available year-round from Juneau to Gustavus. Mid-May through September, travel options include scheduled and charter air services, a passenger ferry,

Accommodations

The price guide indicates approximate room/cabin rates:
$ = $110 or less
$$ = $110–250
$$$ = more than $250

cruise ships, tour boats, and charter boats.
Seasons and Hours The park is open daily year-round. Visitor center is open only mid-May–mid-September.
Charge No.
Handicapped Access Visitor center, Glacier Bay Lodge, and Forest Loop Trail.
Activities Fishing, camping, whale watching, boat tours, wildlife watching, glaciers, mountain climbing, backpacking, boating, guided tours, interpretive programs, nature walks.
Camping First-come, first-served; 14-day limit.
Permits and Licences Alaska fishing license; camping and boating permits. For recreational permit information, tel: 907-697-2627.
Gateway Community Gustavus.
Accommodations $$–$$$ *Glacier Bay Lodge*, Aramark Glacier Bay Lodge and Tours, 241 West Ship Creek Avenue, Anchorage, AK 99501, tel: 866-761-6634, www. visitglacierbay.com. Open seasonally. A few basic accommodations are available outside the park in Gustavus. Contact Gustavus Visitors Association, PO Box 167, Gustavus, AK 99826, tel: 907-697-2454, www. gustavusak.com.
Food and Supplies A restaurant is located in Glacier Bay Lodge. Limited supplies in Gustavus. Campers should bring food and supplies from Juneau.
Weather Severe winter conditions and short summers; violent wind, rain, and snowstorms. Be prepared for wet, cold weather even in summer.
General Information Most travelers see the park by boat; tour boats leave daily in summer from Glacier Bay Lodge. Backpackers must be completely self-sufficient and experienced in wilderness travel. Insect repellent is highly recommended. Contact park headquarters well in advance of visit for reservations and information on guides and outfitters.

Katmai National Park and National Preserve

Address PO Box 7, King Salmon, AK 99613-0007, tel: 907-246-3305,
www.nps.gov/katm.
Access A 10-mile (16km) dirt road runs from King Salmon to Lake Camp just inside the park boundary. Flights connect Anchorage to King Salmon (290 miles/467km), where you can hike, boat, or hire a charter bush plane into the park.
Seasons and Hours The park is open daily year-round. Services are offered at Brooks Camp from early June to mid-September.
Charge No.
Handicapped Access Auditorium, campground restroom, Brooks Lodge.
Activities Fishing, camping, bear watching, mountain climbing, backpacking, boating, guided tours, nature walks, interpretive programs.
Camping Brooks Camp; reservations required (tel: 800-544-0551, www. katmailand.com).
Permits and Licenses Alaska fishing license; backcountry permits available at Brooks Camp Visitor Center and park headquarters.
Accommodations Katmailand manages rustic backcountry lodges and cabins including:
$$$ *Brooks Lodge, Grosvenor Lodge,* and *Kulik Lodge*, 4125 Aircraft Drive, Anchorage, AK 99502, tel: 800-544-0551, www.katmailand.com.
$$$ *Enchanted Lake Lodge*, PO Box 97, King Salmon, AK 99613, tel: 907-694-6447, www.enchantedlakelodge.com. Limited accommodations are also available in King Salmon. Contact the multiagency information center at King Salmon Visitor Center, PO Box 298, King Salmon, AK 99613, tel: 907-246-4250.
Food and Supplies Limited food and supplies are available in the park at Brooks and Grosvenor Lakes camp; outside the park at King Salmon.
Weather Severe winter conditions and short summers with highs around 65°F (18°C); violent wind, rain, and snowstorms. Be prepared for wet, cold weather even in summer.
General Information Backpackers must be self-sufficient and experienced in wilderness travel.

Kenai Fjords National Park

Address PO Box 1727, Seward, AK 99664-1727, tel: 907-422-0573, www.nps.gov/kefj.
Access Seward, about 6 miles (10km) from the park boundary, is 125 miles (201km) south of Anchorage via Alaska Highway 9. A single unpaved road enters the park as far as Exit Glacier, about 8½ miles (14km). The road may be closed by snow between mid-October and May. Train, bus,
plane, and ferry service to Seward from Anchorage.
Seasons and Hours The park is open daily year-round. Kenai Fjords Information Center is open 8.30am– 7pm daily in summer, 9am–5pm spring and summer; Exit Glacier Nature Center is open seasonally 9am–8pm, 9am–5pm spring and summer.
Charge No.
Handicapped Access Visitor center and paved trail at Exit Glacier.
Activities Fishing, camping, wildlife watching, mountain climbing, glaciers, backpacking, cross-country skiing, boating, guided tours, nature walks, interpretive programs.
Camping First-come, first-served.
Permits and Licenses Alaska fishing license.
Gateway Community Seward.
Accommodations Hotels and motels are available outside the park in Seward. Contact Seward Chamber of Commerce, PO Box 749, Seward, AK 99664, tel: 907-224-8051, www. sewardak.org.
Food and Supplies There is no food or supplies available in the park. Restaurants and supplies are available in Seward.
Weather Severe winter conditions and short, wet summers and falls (May is the driest month). Violent wind, rain, and snowstorms.
General Information Commercial guides provide camping, fishing, and kayaking services. Air charters fly over the coast for "flightseeing" and access to the fjords. Boat tours and charters available from Seward. Backpackers must be completely self-sufficient and experienced in wilderness travel.

Kobuk Valley National Park

Address PO Box 1029, Kotzebue, AK

Bear Facts

Prime bear viewing months in Katmai National Park are July and September. To avoid problems with bears, keep all food in bearproof containers, avoid perfumes, keep a clean camp, make noise in dense thickets, do not approach bears, stay calm, and do not run away from a bear. It's a good idea to make reservations for Brooks Camp Campground by contacting 877-444-6777, www.recreation.gov. The campground is protected by an electric fence and does not have individual campsites.

99752-1029, tel: 907-442-3890, 907-442-3760 (summer visitor information) www.nps.org/kova.
Access There are no roads to Kobuk Valley. Flights are available from Fairbanks to Kotzebue, where charter planes can be hired into the park.
Seasons and Hours The park is open daily year-round. Information center is open only in summer.
Charge No.
Handicapped Access No.
Activities Wilderness camping, wildlife watching, backpacking, float trips, fishing.
Camping Wilderness camping only.
Permits and Licenses Alaska fishing license.
Gateway Community Kotzebue
Accommodations Rustic accommodations are available in Kotzebue, Ambler, and Kiana. Contact Nome Convention and Visitors Bureau, PO Box 240, Nome, AK 99762, tel: 907-443-6624, www.nomealaska.org.
Food and Supplies No services in the park. Limited supplies can be purchased in Kotzebue.
Weather Short, cool, sunny summers; 24 hours of daylight for one month. Long, severe, extremely cold winters; about 1 hour of daylight by December 1. High winds throughout the year.
General Information Backpackers must be completely self-sufficient and experienced in wilderness travel. Insect repellent is recommended. Contact park headquarters well in advance of visit.

Lake Clark National Park and Preserve

Address 240 West 5th Avenue, Suite 236, Anchorage, AK 99501, tel: 907-644-3626, www.nps.gov/lacl.
Access There are no roads to Lake Clark. Charter flights are available from Anchorage, Kenai, Homer, and Iliamna.
Seasons and Hours The park is open daily year-round.
Charge No.
Handicapped Access No.
Activities Wilderness camping, wildlife watching, backpacking, float trips, fishing.
Visitor Facilities Aside from a visitor

Accommodations

The price guide indicates approximate room/cabin rates:
$ = $110 or less
$$ = $110–250
$$$ = more than $250

center at Port Alsworth (tel: 907-781-2218) on the shore of Lake Clark, there are no facilities in the park. Information is available at park headquarters in Anchorage.
Camping Wilderness camping only.
Permits and Licenses Alaska fishing license.
Gateway Community Port Alsworth and Anchorage.
Accommodations There are a few rustic lodges in the park:
$$$ *Koksetna Wilderness Lodge*, General Delivery, Port Alsworth, AK 99653, tel: 907-781-2227 (summer), 800-391-8651 (offseason), http://come.to/koksetnawildernesslodge.
$$–$$$ *Alaska's Lake Clark Inn*, 1 Lang Lane, General Delivery, Port Alsworth, AK 99653, tel: 907-781-2224, www.lakeclark.com.
$$$ *Silver Salmon Creek Lodge*, PO Box 3234, Soldotna, AK 99669, tel: 888-8-SALMON, 907-252-5504 (summer), www.silversalmoncreek.com.
For additional lodging, contact Anchorage Convention and Visitors Bureau, 524 West Fourth Avenue, Anchorage, AK 99501, tel: 907-276-4118, www.anchorage.net.
Food and Supplies Food and supplies should be brought into the park from Anchorage or Kenai.
Weather Severe winter conditions and short, mild summers: June–August temperatures 50–65°F (10–18°C); violent wind, rain, and snowstorms in any season. Be prepared for extreme conditions.
General Information Visitors must be completely self-sufficient and experienced in wilderness travel. Insect repellent is highly recommended. Contact park headquarters well in advance of visit. Backcountry patrol cabins, staffed on a limited basis, are located at Telaquana Lake, Twin Lakes, Crescent Lake, and Chinitna Bay.

Noatak National Preserve

Address PO Box 1029, Kotzebue, AK 99752-1029, tel: 907-442-3890 (year round), 907-442-3760 (summer visitor information), www.nps.gov/noat.
Access There are no roads to Noatak. Charter flights are available from Kotzebue.
Seasons and Hours The preserve is open daily year-round. Information is available at park headquarters in Kotzebue, open 8am–5pm during the week year-round. Innaigvik Education and Information Center at Kotzebue is open in summer only, call for hours.
Charge No.
Handicapped Access No.

Activities Wilderness camping, wildlife watching, backpacking, float trips, fishing.
Visitor Facilities Innaigvik Education and Information Center at Kotzebue is open in summer only.
Camping Wilderness camping only.
Permits and Licenses Alaska fishing license.
Gateway Community Kotzebue.
Accommodations Limited lodging is available in Kotzebue. Contact Nome Convention and Visitors Bureau, PO Box 240, Nome, AK 99762, tel: 907-443-6555, www.visitnomealaska.com.
Food and Supplies Food and supplies are not available. All supplies should be brought into the park.
Weather Severe winter conditions and short summers; violent wind, rain, and snowstorms in any season. Be prepared for extreme Arctic conditions.
General Information Visitors must be completely self-sufficient and experienced in wilderness travel. Insect repellent is recommended. Contact park headquarters well in advance of visit.

Wrangell-St Elias National Park and Preserve

Address PO Box 439, Copper Center, AK 99573, tel: 907-822-5234, www.nps.gov/wrst.
Access Two unpaved roads enter the park, one from Chitina in the central section of the park and the other from Slana in the northern section. The roads are usually passable in summer; they may be closed by snow September–mid-May. Regular passenger vehicles with high clearance can usually negotiate park roads in summer, but a four-wheel-drive vehicle may be necessary to tackle more difficult terrain and weather conditions. Charter flights can be hired in Tok, Gulkana, Valdez, McCarthy, Anchorage, and Fairbanks.
Seasons and Hours The park is open daily year-round. Park headquarters and the Wrangell-St Elias Visitor

Camping in Wrangell

Within Wrangell-St Elias, the Bureau of Land Management and the state of Alaska run campgrounds along the Richardson Highway. You may camp anywhere in the park, but be aware that there is a considerable amount of private land, particularly along the Nabesna and McCarthy road corridors.

Center in Copper Center is open daily 9am–7pm in summer; Monday–Friday 8am–4.30pm in winter; Kennecott Visitor Center is open Memorial Day to Labor Day 9am–5.30pm.
Charge No.
Handicapped Access Visitor center.
Activities Wilderness camping, wildlife watching, backpacking, float trips, fishing, mountain climbing, cross-country skiing.
Visitor Facilities Information is available at two visitor centers inside the park. Ranger stations are located outside park at Chitina (seasonal), Slana, and Yakutat; there's also an information station along McCarthy Road.
Camping There are private campgrounds on the Chitina-McCarthy Road. (See box, below left.)
Permits and Licenses Alaska fishing license.
Gateway Community Copper Center.
Accommodations Several private lodges and bed and breakfast establishments are located along the McCarthy and Nabesna roads and in the highway communities:
$$ Kennicott Glacier Lodge, PO Box 103940, Anchorage, AK 99510, tel: 907-258-2350, www.kennicottlodge.com.
$–$$ McCarthy Wilderness Bed & Breakfast, PO Box MXY, Glennallen, AK 99588, tel: 907-554-4433, www.mccarthy-kennicott.com/mccarthybb.
$$ Wolverine Lodge, HC 01, PO Box 1693, Glennallen, AK 99588, tel: 907-822-3988.
There are limited accommodations in and around Glennallen and Chitina. Contact Greater Copper Valley Chamber of Commerce, PO Box 469, Glennallen, AK 99588, tel: 907-822-5555, www.coppervalleychamber.com.
Food and Supplies Limited food and supplies are available in Slana, McCarthy, and Chitina. More extensive supplies are available in Glennallen and Tok.
Weather Summers are cloudy and cool, but clear, and hot days are not uncommon in July. August and September are cool and wet, but there are fewer mosquitoes about. Winters are long and cold, with temperatures sometimes dropping to -50°F (-46°C).
General Information This is a 13-million-acre (5.3-million-hectare) wilderness park with limited facilities for travelers. Visitors must be completely self-sufficient and experienced in wilderness travel. Insect repellent is highly recommended.

Yukon-Charley Rivers National Preserve

Address PO Box 167, Eagle, AK 99738-0167, tel: 907-547-2233, www.nps.gov/yuch.
Access There are no roads in the park. Enter by boat or plane from Circle or Eagle, accessible by road from Fairbanks and Tetlin Junction. Flights are available from Fairbanks to both Circle and Eagle.
Seasons and Hours The preserve is open daily year-round.
Charge No.
Handicapped Access No.
Activities Wilderness camping, wildlife watching, backpacking, float trips, fishing.
Visitor Facilities Information is available at the seasonal visitor center in Eagle, open daily Memorial Day to Labor Day, 8am–5pm.
Camping Eagle and Circle campgrounds; wilderness camping; no reservations required.
Permits and Licenses Alaska fishing license.
Gateway Community Eagle.
Accommodations None in the park. Lodging is available in Circle and Eagle. Contact Fairbanks Visitor Information Center, 550 First Avenue, Fairbanks, AK 99701, tel: 800-327-5774 or 907 456 5774, www.explore fairbanks.com.
Food and Supplies Limited food and supplies are available in Circle and Eagle.
Weather Severe winter conditions and short summers; violent wind and snowstorms in winter, rainstorms are common in summer. Local roads may be closed in winter.
General Information This 2½-million-acre (1-million-hectare) preserve along the Canadian border protects 115 miles (185km) of the Yukon River and the entire Charley River basin, considered by many to be the most spectacular river in Alaska. There are no facilities within the park. Visitors must be completely self-sufficient and experienced in wilderness travel. Insect repellent is highly recommended.

OREGON

Crater Lake National Park

Address PO Box 7, Crater Lake, OR 97604-0007, tel: 541-594-3000, www.nps.gov/crla .
Access The park is about 70 miles (113km) northeast of Medford via

Winter Walking

In winter, Crater Lake rangers lead popular snowshoe walks every Saturday and Sunday from Thanksgiving to the end of March. The walk starts at the Steel Visitor Center and lasts for a half-hour, including stops along the route where rangers explain how plants and animals survive the deep winter conditions. Snowshoes are provided free of charge. Group size is limited; call ahead and reserve your place.

Highway 62, 60 miles (97km) north of Klamath Falls and 143 miles (230km) southeast of Eugene via Routes 58, 97, and 138.
Seasons and Hours The park is open daily year-round. The north entrance and sections of park roads may be closed by snow October–June. Steel Visitor Center next to park headquarters is open daily 9am–5pm in summer, 10am–4pm in winter, closed Christmas. Rim Visitor Center is open in summer only, 9.30am–5pm.
Charge Yes.
Handicapped Access Visitor centers, Crater Lake Lodge, select campgrounds and most overlooks.
Activities Scenic drive, camping, hiking, backpacking, boat tours, wildlife watching, cross-country skiing, snowshoeing, interpretive programs.
Permits and Licenses Free backcountry camping permit.
Camping First-come, first-served (mid-June–mid-October only).
Gateway Communities Crater Lake and Mazama.
Accommodations Lodging in the park is operated by Xanterra Parks & Resorts, DBA Crater Lake Lodges, Crater Lake, OR 97604, tel: 888-774-2728:
$$ Crater Lake Lodge (mid-May–mid-October)
$$ Mazama Motor Inn (June–September)
Additional lodging is available in Diamond Lake, Prospect, Fort Klamath, Chiloquin, and Medford. Contact Klamath Chamber of Commerce, 205 Riverside Drive, Suite A, Klamath Falls, OR 97601, tel: 541-884-5193, www.klamath.org.
Food and Supplies Limited food service and supplies are available at Mazama Village and Rim Village. Additional services are available in Diamond Lake, Prospect, Fort Klamath, Union Creek, Chiloquin, and Medford.
Weather Summer temperatures

35–80°F (2–27°C). Winter temperatures 15–40°F (-9–4°C), with occasional lows well below 0°F (-18°C) and as much as 20ft (6 meters) of snow.
General Information Never try to feed or approach wildlife. Be prepared for cold weather in any season and snowy conditions October–April. Concessionaire-run boat trips to Wizard Island, led by a park naturalist, leave from Cleetwood Cove hourly from 10am to 4pm, typically between early July and mid-September.

Oregon Caves National Monument

Address 19000 Caves Highway, Cave Junction, OR 97523-9716, tel: 541-592-2100, www.nps.gov/orca.
Access The monument is 20 miles (32km) southeast of Cave Junction via Route 46 in the southwestern corner of Oregon.
Seasons and Hours The monument is open daily year-round; cave tours are offered late March–October. Oregon Caves Visitor Center (in Cave Junction) is open daily 9am–5pm. Illinois Valley Visitor Center is open daily (tel: 541-592-4076). Visitor center closed Thanksgiving and Christmas.
Charge A fee is charged for the cave tour.
Handicapped Access First room of cave only. Contact Park Service for assistance.
Activities Guided cave tours, hiking, wildlife watching, interpretive programs.
Permits and Licenses No.
Camping No.
Gateway Community Cave Junction.
Accommodations Lodging in the park is available in the historic lodge: **$–$$** *Chateau at the Oregon Caves* (May–Oct), PO Box 1824, 20000 Caves Highway, Cave Junction, OR 97523, tel: 877-245-9022, www.oregon caveschateau.com.
Additional lodging in Cave Junction. Contact Illinois Valley Chamber of Commerce, tel: 541-592-3326.
Food and Supplies Food service is available to guests at Oregon Caves Chateau May–October. Additional services are available in Cave Junction.
Weather Summer temperatures 35–80°F (2–27°C), with occasional highs above 90°F (32°C). Winter temperatures 15–40°F (-9–4°C) with snowfall. Cave temperature is 42°F (6°C) year-round.
General Information Acidic groundwater has carved the marble

bedrock into chambers and a variety of fascinating flowstone formations.

WASHINGTON

Lake Roosevelt National Recreation Area

Address 1008 Crest Drive, Coulee Dam, WA 99116-0037, tel: 509-633-9441 (park headquarters), 509-738-6366 (North District, Kettle Falls), www.nps.gov/laro.
Access The recreation area can be entered at various places along Franklin D. Roosevelt Lake, including Grand Coulee, Kettle Falls, and Fort Spokane.
Seasons and Hours The recreation area is open daily year-round. The Coulee Dam Visitor Arrival Center is open daily 9am–5pm, extended hours in summer; other visitor centers are open seasonally; closed Thanksgiving, Christmas, and New Year's Day.
Charge No.
Handicapped Access Visitor centers and some campgrounds.
Activities Camping, hiking, boating, swimming, water-skiing, fishing, wildlife watching, interpretive programs.
Permits and Licenses Washington fishing license.
Camping First-come, first-served.
Gateway Communities Grand Coulee, Kettle Falls, and Fort Spokane.
Accommodations None in the park. For lodging in the area, contact Grand Coulee Dam Area Chamber of Commerce, PO Box 760, Grand Coulee, WA 99133, tel: 800-COULEE2, www.grandcouleedam.org.
Food and Supplies Limited food and supplies are available in the park. Additional services available in Grand Coulee, Kettle Falls, Colville, Northport.
Weather Summer temperatures usually 50–100°F (10–38°C), cooler in the northern section of the lake. Winter is cold, with frequent fog and cloudiness, 5–40°F (-15–4°C).
General Information 130-mile (210km) -long Franklin D. Roosevelt Lake was created by Grand Coulee Dam. The recreation area offers a variety of water sports, hiking, and camping.

Mount Rainier National Park

Address 55210 238th Avenue East, Ashford, WA 98304, tel: 360-569-

2211, www.nps.gov/mora.
Access There are four entrances – Nisqually (southwest), Stevens Canyon (southeast), White River (northeast), and Carbon River (northwest) – and three visitor centers. The Nisqually entrance is the most popular entrypoint. It leads to Longmire Museum and Henry M. Jackson Memorial Visitor Center at Paradise, 74 miles (119km) southeast of Tacoma via Routes 7 and 706, 98 miles (158km) southeast of Seattle via I-5, Routes 7 and 706, and 87 miles (140km) west of Yakima via Routes 12, 123, and 706. Gray Line of Seattle offers a daily bus service between Seattle and Mount Rainier May–September.
Seasons and Hours After extensive parkwide flooding and damage in 2006, the park has reopened. It is open daily year-round, but some roads may be closed by snow November–June; call ahead before traveling. The new Henry M. Jackson Memorial Visitor Center at Paradise (tel: 360-569-6036) is open daily 10am–5pm year-round, extended hours in summer; Longmire Museum is open daily year-round 9am–4.30pm, extended hours in summer. Sunrise Visitor Center (tel: 360-663-2425), near the White River Entrance, and Ohanapecosh Visitor Center (tel: 360-569-6046), near the Stevens Canyon Entrance, are open in summer only.
Charge Yes.
Handicapped Access Visitor centers, Longmire Museum and some campgrounds; limited access to paved nature trails.
Activities Scenic drive, camping, hiking, biking, backpacking, rock climbing, mountain climbing, cross-country skiing, snowshoeing, wildlife watching, interpretive programs.
Permits and Licenses Free backcountry camping permits required. Note: All climbers who plan to climb above 10,000ft (3,000 meters) or traverse glaciers must buy an annual climbing pass. Passes are $30 per year and are available through the park's website, the visitor center and ranger stations and Paradise Climbing Information Center. Some 10,000 climbers attempt

Accommodations

The price guide indicates approximate room/cabin rates:
$ = $110 or less
$$ = $110–250
$$$ = more than $250

Other National Monuments, Memorials, Historic Sites, Historical Parks, and Reserves

Alaska

Klondike Gold Rush National Historical Park, PO Box 517, Skagway, AK 99840-0517, tel: 907-983-2921 (park headquarters), 907-983-9234 (summer), www.nps.gov/klgo. Historic buildings in Skagway and portions of the Chilkoot and White Pass Trail commemorate the gold rush of 1898. (See also Washington.)

Sitka National Historical Park, 103 Monastery Street, Sitka, AK 99835, tel: 907-747-6281 (park headquarters), 907-747-0110 (visitor center), www.nps.gov/sitk. Historic structures mark the site of the last major battle between Tlingit Indians and Russian colonists in 1804. Native art is exhibited and artists demonstrate their work.

Oregon

Fort Clatsop National Memorial, 92343 Fort Clatsop Road, Astoria, OR 97103, tel: 503-861-2471, www.nps.gov/lewi. This reconstructed fort is part of Lewis and Clark National Historical Park. Located at the mouth of the Columbia River, it occupies the

site of the Lewis and Clark expedition's 1805–06 winter encampment.

John Day Fossil Beds National Monument, 32651 Highway 19, Kimberly, OR 97848-9701, tel: 541-987-2333, www.nps.gov/joda. An abundance of plant and animal fossils from the Eocene to Pliocene epochs.

Washington

Ebey's Landing National Historical Reserve, PO Box 774, 162 Cemetery Road, Coupeville, WA 98239-0774, tel: 360-678-6084, www.nps.gov/ebla. Historic farms and the seaport community of Coupeville preserve a record of Puget Sound exploration and settlement from the 19th century to the present.

Fort Vancouver National Historic Site, 612 East Reserve St, Vancouver, WA 98661, tel: 360-816-6230, www.nps.gov/fova. The fort was the center of the Hudson's Bay Company's fur-trading network in the Northwest from 1825 to 1860.

Klondike Gold Rush National Historical Park Seattle Unit, 319

Second Avenue South, Seattle, WA 98104, tel: 206-220-4240, www.nps.gov/klse. Most prospectors left from here for the promising gold fields of Canada's Yukon Territory. The park has a visitor center in the Pioneer Square Historic District, which was the center of Gold Rush activity. (See also Alaska.)

San Juan Island National Historical Park, PO Box 429, Friday Harbor, WA 98250-0429, tel: 360 378-2240, www.nps.gov/sajh. The park commemorates the boundary dispute between the US and Britain on the San Juan Islands from 1853 to 1872, including the so-called Pig War of 1859.

Whitman Mission National Historic Site, 328 Whitman Mission Road, Box 247, Walla Walla, WA 99362-9699, tel: 509-522-6360 (park headquarters), 509-529-2761 (recorded visitor information available), www.nps.gov/whmi. This mission, established by Marcus and Narcissa Whitman in 1836, was an important site on the Oregon Trail. The Whitmans were killed during an Indian uprising in 1847.

Mount Rainier each year. Reservations for a campsite at base camp, Camp Muir, are, therefore, strongly suggested. A reservation form may be downloaded through the park website and faxed, after March 15, to the Wilderness Reservations Office, tel: 360 569 3131, or mailed to WRO at 55210 238th Avenue East, Ashford, WA 98304. More information at http://home.nps.gov/mora/planyourvisit/climbing.htm#CP_JUMP_149861.

Camping Three popular campgrounds. Reservations at Cougar Rock and Ohanapecosh campgrounds are vital between June 28 and Labor Day. Contact 877-444-6777, www.recreation.gov. Otherwise, first-come, first-served.

Gateway Communities Ashford, Enumclaw, Elbe, Packwood, and Mineral Lake.

Accommodations Lodging in the park is run by Mount Rainier Guest Services, 55106 Kernahan Road East, Ashford, WA 98304, tel: 360-569-2275, www.mtrainierguestservices.com. Note: Reserve well ahead; both lodges fill quickly:
$$ National Park Inn.
$–$$ Paradise Inn (mid-May–early October).
Additional lodging is available in Ashford, Packwood, and Elbe. Contact

Southwest Washington Convention and Visitors Bureau, 1501 East Evergreen Boulevard, Vancouver, WA 98661, tel: 877-224-4214, www.southwestwashington.com.

Food and Supplies Available in the park at Longmire, Sunrise, and Paradise. Additional services available in Ashford, Elbe, Packwood, Enumclaw.

Weather Weather varies wildly depending on elevation. Summer temperatures usually 40–80°F (4–27°C), cooler at higher elevations; winter temperatures usually 10–35°F (-12–2°C) with heavy snow. Weather can change quickly in any season.

General Information Summer is generally crowded; consider visiting in early fall. Hiking in high elevations can be extremely difficult, causing dizziness, nausea, and shortness of breath. Give yourself a few days to adjust. Crossing snowfields requires special skills and equipment, and you are urged to hire a professional guide to climb Mount Rainier. For mountain-climbing instruction and guide services, contact Rainier Mountaineering, PO Box Q, Ashford, WA 98304, tel: 888-892-5462, www.rmiguides.com. For cross-country skiing equipment, contact Longmire Ski Touring Center, tel: 360-569-2411.

North Cascades National Park Complex

Address 810 State Route 20, Sedro-Woolley, WA 98284-1239, tel: 360-854-7200 (park headquarters), 306-386-4495 (North Cascades Visitor Center), 360-854-7245 (Wilderness Information Center), www.nps.gov/noca.

Access The national park complex includes Lake Chelan and Ross Lake national recreation areas and is 50 miles (80km) east of Burlington and 70 miles (113km) west of Twisp via Route 20. Stehekin (in Lake Chelan National Recreation Area) can be reached via boat or floatplane from Chelan on Highway 97 or by foot from the south unit of North Cascades National Park. The only ramp for private boats on Ross Lake is at the end of an unpaved road from Hope, British Columbia.

Seasons and Hours The park is open daily year-round. Park headquarters in Sedro-Woolley is open year-round Mon–Fri 8.30am–4pm, closed Christmas. North Cascades Visitor Center in Newhalem is open daily 9am–6pm in summer, 9am–5pm spring and fall, closed in winter. Golden West Visitor Center at Stehekin open daily in summer

8.30am–5pm, very limited hours during the rest of the year; Wilderness Information Center in Marblemount open early May–mid-October, 7am–6pm in summer, restricted hours spring and fall. North Cascades Highway 20 between mile post 134 and 171 is usually closed by snow between mid-October and late April.

Charge No. Dock fee at Lake Chelan.

Handicapped Access Visitor centers, select campgrounds, some nature trails, and shuttle van (with wheelchair lift) from Stehekin to High Bridge.

Activities Scenic drive, camping, hiking, backpacking, rock climbing, mountain climbing, fishing, cross-country skiing, snowshoeing, wildlife watching, interpretive programs.

Permits and Licenses Free backcountry camping permits required and available through Wilderness Information Center or the nearest ranger station to the trailhead. Certain popular areas have quotas.

Camping Three campgrounds have first-come, first-served campsites. Group campsites and sites in Loop C of Newhalem Campground may be reserved by contacting 877-444-6777, www.recreation.gov.

Accommodations In the park:
$$ *Ross Lake Resort* (cabins), Rockport, WA 98283, tel: 206-386-4437.
$$ *Stehekin Landing Resort*, PO Box 457, Chelan, WA 98816, tel: 509-682-4494, www.stehekin.com.
$$–$$$ *Silver Bay Inn*, PO Box 68, Stehekin, WA 98852, tel: 800-555-7781, www.silverbayinn.com.
$$$ *Stehekin Valley Ranch*, PO Box 36, Stehekin, WA 98852, tel: 800-536-0745, www.stehekinvalleyranch.com.
Additional lodging is available in Concrete and Chelan. Contact Lake Chelan Chamber of Commerce, PO Box 216, Chelan, WA 98816, tel: 800-424-3526, www.lakechelan.com.

Food and Supplies Limited services available in the park at Newhalem and Stehekin. Additional services available in Marblemount, Concrete, and Chelan.

Weather Varies considerably depending on elevation. Summer temperatures in lower elevations usually 45–80°F (7–27°C); winter temperatures 25–45°F (-4–7°C) with heavy snow. Temperatures are much cooler at higher elevations, where as much as 20ft (6 meters) of snow can accumulate before melting in summer. Weather can change quickly in any season.

General Information Crossing snowfields requires special skills and equipment. Hiking in high elevations can be extremely difficult, causing dizziness. Give yourself a good few days to adjust.

Olympic National Park

Address 600 East Park Avenue, Port Angeles, WA 98362-6798, tel: 360-565-3000 (park headquarters), 360-565-3100 (Wilderness Information Center), www.nps.gov/olym.

Access The Port Angeles visitor center is about 140 miles (225km) northwest of Tacoma via Highways 5 and 101. The Hoh Rain Forest Visitor Center is about 100 miles (160km) north of Aberdeen via Highway 101 and Hoh Road.

Seasons and Hours The park is open daily year-round. Visitor centers and ranger stations are open year-round but hours vary; closed Christmas and New Year's Day. Some park roads may be closed by snow October–April.

Charge Yes.

Handicapped Access Visitor centers, some nature trails and campgrounds.

Activities Scenic drive, camping, hiking, backpacking, fishing, rock climbing, mountain climbing, cross-country skiing, snowshoeing, wildlife watching, interpretive programs.

Permits and Licenses Wilderness camping permits and campsite reservations are required and a use fee is charged. Strict quotas are in effect for popular wilderness destinations such as Mount Olympus, Ozette, and Lake Constance. Permits and reservations through the Wilderness Information Center or a staffed ranger station. Washington fishing license.

Camping There are 16 developed campgrounds with first-come, first-served campsites. The popular coastal campground of Kalaloch may be reserved in summer up to six months ahead of time by contacting 877-444-6777, www.recreation.gov. Altair, Deer Park, and South Beach campgrounds close in winter.

Accommodations Four lodges in the park are managed by Aramark and one is privately owned:
$$ *Kalaloch Lodge* (open year-round), 157151 Highway 101, Forks, WA 98331, tel: 866-525-2562, www.olympicnationalparks.com.
$$ *Lake Crescent Lodge* (late Apr–Oct), 416 Lake Crescent Road, Port Angeles, WA 98363, tel: 888-723-7127, www.olympicnationalparks.com.
$–$$ *Lake Quinault Lodge*, 345 South Shore Road, Quinault, WA 98575, 800-562-6672, www.olympicnationalparks.com.
$$ *Sol Duc Hot Springs Resort* (open March–October, weekends only in October), PO Box 2169, Port Angeles, WA 98362, tel: 866-476-5382, www.olympicnationalparks.com.
$$ *Log Cabin Resort*, 3183 East Beach Road, Port Angeles, WA 98363, tel: 360-928-3325, www.logcabinresort.net.
Additional lodging is available in Quinault, Port Angeles, Sequim, Port Townsend, Forks, Neah Bay on the Makah Indian Reservation, and La Push on the Quileute Indian Reservation. Contact North Olympic Peninsula Visitor and Convention Bureau, tel: 800-942-4042, www.olympicpeninsula.org.

Food and Supplies Restaurants and limited supplies are available in the park at Kalaloch, Sol Duc Hot Springs and Lake Crescent. Additional services available in Port Townsend, Sequim, Port Angeles, Forks, and Sappho campgrounds and other locations along Highway 101.

Weather Weather varies considerably depending on elevation. Summer temperatures in lower elevations usually 40–70°F (4–21°C); winter temperatures 20–45°F (-7–7°C). Temperatures are much cooler at higher elevations, where snow is heavy well into May. Most of Olympic's precipitation falls October–March. Expect heavy rain, wind, and fog in any season. For information call the 24-hr weather hotline on 360-565-3131.

General Information Only those with long climbing experience should attempt Mount Olympus. Crossing snowfields requires special skills and equipment. Hiking in high elevations can be extremely difficult, causing dizziness, nausea, and shortness of breath. Give yourself a good few days to adjust to the altitude. Obtain a tide table before hiking on the beach; incoming tides can trap unsuspecting hikers between headlands. Look out for floating logs, too. An unexpected wave can send them hurtling toward the beach, crushing anything that gets in the way. The ocean is very cold and currents are fierce; it is safer to swim in the lakes instead of the ocean.

Accommodations

The price guide indicates approximate room/cabin rates:
$ = $110 or less
$$ = $110–250
$$$ = more than $250

FURTHER READING

General

Beyond the Hundredth Meridian: John Wesley Powell and the Second Opening of the West, by Wallace Stegner. Penguin, 1992.
Coming into the Country, by John McPhee. Farrar, Straus & Giroux, 1991.
Desert Notes/River Notes, by Barry Holstun Lopez. New York: HarperCollins, 1990.
Desert Solitaire: A Season in the Wilderness, by Edward Abbey. New York: Ballentine Nature, 1990.
The Desert Year, by Joseph W. Krutch. Tucson: University of Arizona, 1985.
The Exploration of the Colorado River and Its Canyons, by John Wesley Powell, with Introduction by Wallace Stegner. New York: Penguin Classics, 2003.
A Fierce Green Fire: The American Environmental Movement, by Philip Shabecoff. Revised Edition. Washington, DC: Island Press, 2003.
My First Summer in the Sierra, by John Muir, Introduction by Galen Rowell. Boston: Mariner Books, 1998.
The National Parks: America's Best Idea, by Dayton Duncan and Ken Burns. New York: Knopf, 2009.
National Park: The American Experience, by Alfred Runte. Lincoln: University of Nebraska Press, 1979.
National Park Ranger: An American Icon, by Charles R. Farabee. Niwot, CO: Roberts Rinehart Publishers, 2003.
PrairyErth (A Deep Map): An Epic History of the Tallgrass Prairie Country, by William Least Heat-Moon. Boston: Mariner Books, 1999.
The Sense of Wonder, by Rachel Carson. New York: HarperCollins, 1998.
Silent Spring, by Rachel Carson, Afterword by E.O. Wilson. Boston: Houghton Mifflin, 2002.
An Unspoken Hunger: Stories from the Field, by Terry Tempest Williams. New York: Vintage Books, 1994.
Walden and Other Writings, by Henry David Thoreau. New York: Metrobooks, 2001.
Where the Bluebird Sings to the Lemonade Springs: Living and Writing in the West, by Wallace Stegner, Afterword by T.H. Watkins. New York: Modern Library, 2002.

Parks and Wildlife

The Complete Guide to the National Park Lodges, 5th Edition, by David L. Scott and Karen W. Scott. Globe Pequot, 2006.
The Complete Guidebook to Yosemite National Park, by Steven P. Medley. El Portal: Yosemite Association, 2008.
Grand Canyon: Today and All Its Yesterdays, by Joseph Wood Krutch. Tucson: University of Arizona, 1989.
In Denali, by Kim Heacox. Reno: University of Nevada Press, 1992.
Inside Death Valley, Fifth Edition, by Chuck Gebhardt. Tom Willis, 1995.
Introduction to Grand Canyon Geology, by Greer Price. Grand Canyon Association, 1999.
Lost in My Own Backyard: A Walk in Yellowstone National Park, by Tim Cahill. New York: Crown, 2004.
The National Audubon Society Guide to Photographing America's

National Parks, Digital Edition, by Tim Fitzharris. Firefly Books, 2009.
The National Parks of Utah, by Nicky Leach. Mariposa: Sierra Press, 2005.
The Parks of New Mexico, by Nicky Leach. Mariposa: Sierra Press, 2008.
Texas' Big Bend Country, by George Wuerthner. Two Bears Press, 1989.
Western Forests, by Stephen Whitney. New York: Alfred A. Knopf, 1985.
Wildflowers of the American West, by Rose Houk. San Francisco Chronicle Books, 1987.
Wind Cave: An Ancient World Beneath the Hills, by Arthur N. Palmer. Black Hills Parks and Forests Association, 1995.
Yellowstone and Grand Teton National Parks: A Traveler's Guide, by Steven Fuller and Jeremy Schmidt. Jackson Hole: Free Wheeling Travel Guides, 1991.

Other Insight Guides

The **Insight Guides** series cover every continent and include many titles devoted to the USA, from Alaska to Florida.
Insight Guide: Alaska goes from Anchorage to the Arctic Circle, highlighting what will please both casual visitors and intrepid hikers.
Insight Guide: California travels from Disneyland to Death Valley, taking in the hills of San Francisco and the streets of Los Angeles.
Insight Guide: Arizona and the Grand Canyon contains everything you'll need to enjoy the cities, the scenery, and the Native American tribes of Arizona, plus useful tips and stunning photographs of the great wonder that is the Grand Canyon.
Insight Guide: USA On The Road takes you on a journey from Route 66 to Highway 1, from the Atlantic coast to the Pacific Northwest.

ART AND PHOTO CREDITS

Alamy Images 6TL, 7CL, 50, 142, 143, 144B, 144T, 145, 213, 215BL, 215BR, 232, 287, 292, 293BL, 295, 338, 339
Alaska Tourism 340/341, 345, 349, 351BR, 352, 364, 397
@Michael 231BL
Arizona Tourism 134/135
Andreas F Bochert 234/235
Capitol Reef National Park 174BR, 178BR
Colorado Tourism 248/249, 301, 302, 303, 304B, 305, 389, 391
Christopher Connell 270
Corbis Images 22T, 23B, 23T, 26L, 27, 79, 330
Richie Diesterheft 207
Djfrantic on flickr 110T
Bill Eichenlaub 350L
Larry D Fellows/Arizona Tourism 204T
Flicka on Wikipedia 194
Fotolibra 60/61, 73, 129T
Michael Gabler on Wikipedia 266
Getty Images 333
Glacier Country Regional Tourism 280
Martyn Goddard/Apa 2/3, 4T, 10/11, 12/13, 14/15, 17B, 17T, 19, 32L, 32R, 33R, 34, 36L, 36R, 37, 38, 39, 48, 49, 51, 53, 54, 56, 62/63, 64, 65B, 71, 74B, 76, 77, 80, 81, 84B, 85L, 86/87, 94, 97, 98B, 100, 101, 102/103, 104, 105, 107, 108L, 108R, 110, 111L, 111R, 112, 354, 356, 358, 361, 363, 370, 371, 373, 374, 375
Dave Grimes 337
Raymond Guilford 206
Neil Hannan 344
Dave Harrison 336B
Lee Hilyer 231BR
iStockphoto.com 3B, 4B, 5T, 6BL, 6CR, 6T, 7B, 7C, 7CR, 7TL, 7TR, 8B, 8T, 9B, 9C, 16, 29, 31, 33L, 34, 41, 42L, 42R, 43, 44, 45, 46/47, 69B, 69T, 70, 74T, 78B, 78T, 84T, 85R, 89, 90, 91, 92, 93, 99, 116, 117, 118, 119, 121, 124, 125, 127BL, 127BR, 128, 129BL, 129BR, 131BL,131BR, 148, 149, 151, 152L, 152R, 153, 154B, 154T, 155L, 154R, 163, 168/169, 170,

171, 173B, 174BL, 175, 176, 177L, 177R, 178BL, 182/183, 184, 185, 188, 191, 195, 197, 198B, 200, 202, 205, 212, 216, 217, 218B, 218T, 228T, 229, 236, 238B, 238T, 245, 251T, 255, 259T, 261L, 261R, 262T, 264, 265, 268B, 268T, 269, 277, 278T, 282/283, 288T, 290R, 291B, 291T, 293BR, 294B, 294T, 299, 304T, 311B, 311T, 314, 318T, 322, 324T, 325R, 329, 334, 335, 336T, 342, 343, 346, 348, 350T, 350R
Ben Javelina 220L
Andrew Kalat 271
Kenny Karst 75
Frank Kovalchek 140, 141
Lietmotiv on Flickr 290L
Mary Evans Picture Library 20B, 20T, 21B, 21T, 22B, 26R
Moondigger on Wikipedia 203
National Park Service 24, 25, 28, 55, 57, 65T, 83, 95, 98T, 120, 122/123, 146/147, 156, 157, 159, 160, 160T, 162L, 162R, 173T, 174T, 178T, 179, 180, 181, 187, 189, 190B, 190T, 196, 198T, 199, 219, 239, 242T, 285, 286T, 315, 317, 347L, 347R, 351BL, 378
New Mexico Tourism 52, 220R, 227, 230, 233, 237, 240R, 244, 384
North Dakota Tourism 296L, 296R
North Dakota Tourism/Jason Lindsey 284
Richard Nowitz/Apa 1, 58/59, 113, 136, 137all, 139B, 139T, 164B, 164T, 165, 208/209, 210, 211, 214, 240L, 241, 242, 243, 367, 383
Olympic National Park 318
Pictures Colour Library 30, 88, 132, 133
Matt Power 298
Alex Proimos 387
Randy Roach 281
Ranger Mike on Flickr 324B, 325L
Chris Russininiello 353L
Donnie Sexton 40, 251B, 252/253, 254, 257, 258, 259L, 259R, 260, 263, 267, 272/273, 274, 275, 392, 394, 395
Ed Siasoco 222, 223

Davis Snyder 321, 323
South Dakota Tourism 9T, 286, 288B, 289
Wolfgang Staudt 192/193
Jon Sullivan 204
Corey Taratuta 6BR,
Theodore Rooseveldt National Park 297
Travel Montana 262, 278
Texas Tourism 224/225, 226
Tips Images 130
Kolin Toney 221
Topfoto 18B, 18T
Utah National Parks 201
Washington State Tourism 308/309, 311C, 312/313, 319, 320, 326/327, 328, 332, 367

PHOTO FEATURES

Pages 114–115:
iStockphoto.com 114BL, 114BR, 114/115T, 115BL; Martyn Goddard/Apa 115BR, 115TR

Pages 166–167:
Alamy Images 166BL, 166BR, 166/167T, 167BL, 167BR, 167TR; iStockphoto.com 167CL

Pages 246–247:
Alamy Images 246BL, 246CR, 247TR; iStockphoto.com 246BR, 246/247T, 247BL, 247C, 247CL, 247BR

Pages 306–307:
iStockphoto.com 306BL, 306BR, 307BR, 307TR, ; Alaska Tourism 306/307T; Martyn Goddard/Apa 307CL, National Parks Service 307BL

Map Production
Original cartography Berndtson & Berndtson, updated by Apa Cartography Department

Production: Linton Donaldson

INDEX

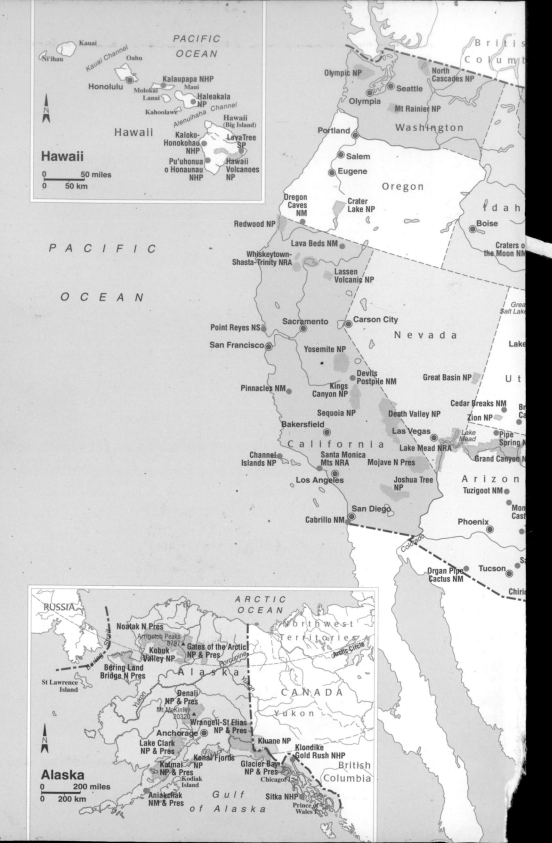

Hawaii

Kauai
Ni'ihau
Kauai Channel
Oahu
PACIFIC OCEAN
Honolulu
Molokai
Lanai
Maui
Kalaupapa NHP
Haleakala NP
Kahoolawe
Channel
Alenuihaha Channel
Hawaii (Big Island)
Lava Tree SP
Kaloko-Honokohau NHP
Pu'uhonua o Honaunau NHP
Hawaii Volcanoes NP

0   50 miles
0   50 km

PACIFIC OCEAN

Alaska

RUSSIA
ARCTIC OCEAN
Noatak N Pres
Arrigetch Peaks 8797
Gates of the Arctic NP & Pres
Kobuk Valley NP
Northwest Territories
Porcupine
Arctic Circle
Bering Land Bridge N Pres
Alaska
St Lawrence Island
Yukon
CANADA
Denali NP & Pres
Mt McKinley 20320
Wrangell-St Elias NP & Pres
Anchorage
Lake Clark NP & Pres
Kenai Fjords NP
Katmai NP & Pres
Kodiak Island
Glacier Bay NP & Pres
Chicago
Aniakchak NM & Pres
Gulf of Alaska
Sitka NHP
Prince of Wales I.
Kluane NP
Klondike Gold Rush NHP
Yukon
British Columbia

0   200 miles
0   200 km

Olympic NP
North Cascades NP
Seattle
Olympia
Mt Rainier NP
Washington
Portland
Salem
Eugene
Oregon
British Columbia
Idaho
Boise
Oregon Caves NM
Crater Lake NP
Redwood NP
Craters of the Moon NM
Lava Beds NM
Whiskeytown-Shasta-Trinity NRA
Lassen Volcanic NP
Great Salt Lake
Point Reyes NS
Sacramento
Carson City
Nevada
Lake
San Francisco
Yosemite NP
Devils Postpile NM
Great Basin NP
Utah
Pinnacles NM
Kings Canyon NP
Cedar Breaks NM
Sequoia NP
Death Valley NP
Zion NP
Bakersfield
Las Vegas
Lake Mead NRA
Lake Mead
Pipe Spring N
California
Channel Islands NP
Santa Monica Mts NRA
Mojave N Pres
Grand Canyon N
Los Angeles
Joshua Tree NP
Arizona
Tuzigoot NM
San Diego
Mon Cast
Cabrillo NM
Phoenix
Colorado
Organ Pipe Cactus NM
Tucson
Sa
Chiri